# THE WORLD OF RENÉ DUBOS

# THE
# WORLD OF
# RENÉ DUBOS

## A Collection from

## His Writings

Edited by GERARD PIEL and

Osborn Segerberg, Jr., for

**THE RENÉ DUBOS CENTER**

**HENRY HOLT AND COMPANY     NEW YORK**

Preface and Foreword copyright © 1990
by The René Dubos Center for Human Environments, Inc.
All rights reserved, including the right to reproduce
this book or portions thereof in any form.
Published by Henry Holt and Company, Inc.,
115 West 18th Street, New York, New York 10011.
Published in Canada by Fitzhenry & Whiteside Limited,
195 Allstate Parkway, Markham, Ontario L3R 4T8.

Library of Congress Cataloging-in-Publication Data
Dubos, René J. (René Jules), 1901–1982
[Selections. 1990]
The world of René Dubos : a collection from his writings / edited
by Gerard Piel and Osborn Segerberg, Jr. for The René Dubos Center.
—1st ed.
p. cm.
Includes bibliographical references.
ISBN 0-8050-1360-1
1. Microbiology. 2. Environmental protection. I. Piel, Gerard.
II. Segerberg, Osborn. III. René Dubos Center for Human
Environments. IV. Title.
QR6.D8325 1990
576—dc20 89-26927
CIP

Henry Holt books are available at special discounts
for bulk purchases for sales promotions, premiums,
fund-raising, or educational use. Special editions
or book excerpts can also be created to specification.

For details contact:
Special Sales Director
Henry Holt and Company, Inc.
115 West 18th Street
New York, New York 10011

FIRST EDITION

Designed by Kate Nichols

Printed in the United States of America
Recognizing the importance of preserving
the written word, Henry Holt and Company, Inc.,
by policy, prints all of its first editions
on acid-free paper. ∞

1 3 5 7 9 10 8 6 4 2

Notice of copyright for the individual pieces included
in this collection appears on the opening page
of each piece.

TO

*Mary Madeleine Dubos Alcay,*
*who follows, as did her*
*brother, the Benedictines' path of*
*divine creation*

Symbiotic relationships mean creative partnerships. The earth is to be seen neither as an ecosystem to be preserved unchanged, nor as a quarry to be exploited for selfish and short-range economic reasons, but as a garden to be cultivated for the development of its own potentialities of the human adventure. The goal of this relationship is not the maintenance of the status quo, but the emergence of new phenomena and new values.

—RENÉ DUBOS (1901–1982)
*Inscription at the entrance*
*to "The Land," Epcot Center,*
*Orlando, Florida*

# Contents

# CONTENTS

# CONTENTS

# Preface

Dubos's ideas have been taking hold and spreading
and becoming part of human consciousness—part
of what historians will like to term someday, looking back, the thought of this period in the evolution of culture. And this is no small achievement
for a man and a single mind.

—Lewis Thomas, 1987

WITH A SCIENTIST'S CLEAR EYE and a philosopher's long gaze,
René Dubos pursued his obsession with all of life. His early understanding of the need to study bacteria in the soil, where they live,
rather than in petri dishes in the laboratory, led to his teaching the
world the principles of finding and producing antibiotics. And the same
ecological view led to his seminal role in the first United Nations
Conference on the Human Environment held in Stockholm in 1972.

In the scientific community, René Dubos continues to be honored
for his ground-breaking work. In October 1989, the Rockefeller University paid him tribute in a symposium ("Launching the Antibiotic
Era—Personal Accounts of the Discovery and Use of the First Antibiotics") celebrating the fiftieth anniversary of his discovery of gramicidin, also known as tyrothricin. And a month later, in November,
*Science* reported: "Most people think that Alexander Fleming discovered the first clinically useful antibiotic, but that honor should really go
to René Dubos, science historians say."

Beyond the scientific community, Dubos's aphorisms have become
world famous: "Think globally, act locally," "Only one earth," "Optimism despite all," "Learn from success," "Will the future." These are
not only a call to arms for environmentalists, they are also an inspiration
to all to take heart—as Dubos himself did—in the knowledge that
"wherever human beings are concerned, trend is not destiny."

As the decade of the nineties dawns, people everywhere are renewing their concerns for the environment. In 1990, we celebrate the

twentieth anniversary of Earth Day; in 1992, the United Nations convenes its second world conference on the environment, this one to be held in Brazil. In all of these events, one can appreciate the groundwork laid by René Dubos. It is time, then, that we rediscovered his work and celebrated it as well. Time, too, to rediscover the man himself. Just who was René Dubos?

Although the "good doctor," as he was called by Rachel Carson, was not a medical doctor, his colleague at the Rockefeller University, Walsh McDermott, referred to him as "the conscience of modern medicine." Three of his over forty honorary degrees from six countries were MDs, but twenty were in fields other than science. Although he never set out to become a writer, he penned over twenty books (one of them winning a Pulitzer) and hundreds of scientific papers and essays, and was widely known for his column "The Despairing Optimist," which appeared in every issue of Phi Beta Kappa's *The American Scholar* for a decade. And though he never set out to lead a movement, he was widely acclaimed for his ideas, which he promulgated in his lectures as well as in his writings. "It is a celebration of life to listen to this wise and gifted man who is among the least parochial of researchers and the most scientifically trained of the humanists," said Donald Fredrickson, then director of the National Institutes of Health. "Among scientists, Professor Dubos is one of the few who truly merit the *ancien titre* Natural Philosopher." And *The New York Times*, noting his work on behalf of environmental quality and how it helped to change public policy, called him "the philosopher of the earth."

All of this is a matter of record. Still, as his colleague Rollin Hotchkiss has said: "More in danger of being lost than the record of his honors is the flavor and personality of this investigator and scholar—the attitude of wonderment and optimism about the integrated relationships of organic life. The sense of wonder, selfless and contagious. Leaning back, physically relaxed, usually with a broad smile, fingering (for forty years) the durable wisps of hair at the top of his balding head, René Dubos typically joyed in vicariously experiencing one or another phenomenon described to him."

That was the Dubos my husband, Bill, and I remember meeting for the first time in his office at the Rockefeller University. We were seeking his advice on the results of a UN-funded program developed by Total Education in the Total Environment, Inc. (TETE), a nonprofit organization Bill had founded in the mid-sixties. That first meeting was to become a turning point in our lives. A few years later, in 1975, in collaboration with TETE, René Dubos would found The René Dubos Forum (later renamed The René Dubos Center for Human Environments) in response to the need for a more humanistic approach to environmental problems. Over the past fifteen years, the Dubos Center has become an internationally acknowledged facilitator of constructive dialogue among policymakers and the concerned public as well as a disseminator of original primary resources for educational purposes.

"The only profound justification for being involved in the activities of the Center," René Dubos said on "Bill Moyers' Journal," "is that we are not only concerned with pollution, with problems of natural resources, with problems of making the world richer, but in some way or another, with making the environment—the natural environment—more compatible with human beings, and if my dreams come true, in creating a kind of symbiosis between the natural environment and human beings."

In 1988, then EPA administrator Lee Thomas said: "When I look back and think about my time at EPA, where we are today and what the environmental issues are, I think it's critically important that we remember the ideals of René Dubos and the center named in his honor, and use them to guide our thinking about what we need to deal with, both in this country and throughout the world."

In 1990, The René Dubos Center for Human Environments in cooperation with the United Nations Environment Program launched "A Decade of Environmental Literacy" and announced a comprehensive education program based on the socio-environmental philosophy formulated for the center by its founder. It is time, then, to reexamine that philosophy.

RENÉ DUBOS DIED on his eighty-first birthday, February 20, 1982. There was, it has been said, an appealing symmetry about the way he lived his life and even to his leaving of it. When he was certain that he was dying, he asked his wife to bring recordings of Gregorian plainsong and of church bells to the hospital room. He died listening to the ringing of church bells. As he had written in his last book, so it came to pass for him:

> We thus relate not only to our physical, biological and social surroundings but also to the cosmos as a whole even when we are not conscious of this relationship. . . . The response to the

ringing of bells, for example, is not so much to the sound waves themselves as to their symbolic overtones. Endlessly modified as sound spreads in all directions through space, the pealing bells symbolize for me that we are related to everything in the cosmos. They reach into the great beyond where they lap on the shore of the ultimate mystery which science may never be able to solve.

RUTH A. EBLEN
Executive Director
The René Dubos Center for
Human Environments
February 1990

# Acknowledgments

GERARD PIEL AND RENÉ DUBOS were longtime friends and, despite their age difference, shared many mutual interests. Savants with Old World charms and New World pursuits, they often found themselves sharing the same honors, scientific and literary awards, and affiliations with organizations concerned about the quality of life in our city, our Capitol, and our world: for example, U.S. Capitol Master Plan, Health Research Council of the City of New York, Gateway National Park, Jamaica Bay, New York Botanical Garden, The American Philosophical Society, The Harvey Society. Their paths crossed often as they willed our future.

Both Jean and René Dubos would be delighted and touched to know that Gerard Piel assumed the formidable task of editor, devoting many hours and weekends to the book when Jean's illness made continued work on it impossible. And they would be reassured to know that he made the final selections and difficult decisions necessary to complete the work.

And, if it had not been for Osborn Segerberg, Jr., this book might not have come to pass. Well versed in Dubosian philosophy, having produced several national television interviews featuring Dubos, he read, or reread, over twenty Dubos books, culling the most relevant passages while Jean researched the scientific papers, journals, and essays. And he also did much of the archival and library research required.

# ACKNOWLEDGMENTS

In addition, we would be remiss in not thanking Peggy Tsukahira, science editor and editor of Dubos's *Celebrations of Life*, for donating so much of her time to developing the original outline with Jean and getting the project off to a good start. Bob Lebeau, working as a research associate for the Dubos Center, did an exemplary job of organization and coordination for the editors. And Michael Casey, Sue Ellinger, and Karen Guglielmone devoted many hours to documenting and proofreading this work.

William R. Eblen
President

Ruth A. Eblen
Executive Director

The René Dubos Center for Human Environments, Inc.
100 East 85th Street
New York, New York 10028

# Foreword

RENÉ DUBOS WAS a public scientist. He is one of that small company of scientific celebrities known outside the reticent community of science for their penchant for the popularization of science or their readiness to engage in the public controversies that arise from the impact on society of its daughter technologies. Dubos is remembered for both penchant and readiness, which he manifested with great vigor and style. To better public understanding of the substance and significance of the work of science, he addressed no less than twenty books, from 1950 to the year of his death, 1982. All were critically esteemed; one earned the accolade of a Pulitzer Prize, most remain in print, and some are on their way back to press.

Even more immediately, Dubos is remembered as a premier spokesman for the environmental movement. In the eighth and last decade of his life he went on the hustings, writing articles, editorials, and op-ed pieces as well as books and speaking in every available forum. He made no small contribution to the success of the movement, which was marked by the establishment of environment-protection agencies in every industrial country and the creation of the United Nations Environment Program (UNEP) in 1973. He gave the movement its mainstream message and its best slogans as well. Those slogans shout from bumper stickers: Think globally, act locally! Trend is not destiny! Will the future!

Early in the campaign, Dubos found environmental activists as much in need of his message as the public. In recoil from technology, many were prone to antiscientific, antirational attitudinizing. They derailed public discussion with Chicken Little stories. Echoing the Romantic English poets of the age of Carboniferous Capitalism, they held out a natural order in which only man is vile. To keep the sky from falling, Dubos had to take time that he might have otherwise devoted to real environmental issues. It was at his insistence that the U.N. Stockholm conference that organized the UNEP in 1972 did so under the title of the Conference on the *Human* Environment. Humankind was at the center of the Dubos landscape, and not merely because that is where science and technology have put us. On the other hand, to technology-intoxicated futurologists, he had to insist that earth is a garden, not a spaceship.

René Dubos brought to the environmental movement the same habit of mind that underpinned his immensely consequential career as a scientist. Early in his life, as he explains in this book, he decided that nothing can be understood in isolation; everything must be studied in connection to everything else. That is, of course, a tall order. It is only now, seventy years after he made that resolve, that understanding from the many branches of the life sciences has begun to converge in the science of ecology.

His holistic habit of mind made Dubos impatient with the reductionist, piece-part analysis to which the disciplines of science constrain the investigator. He was torn between the experiment he could do and the question he wanted to answer. The habit and the tension served him well, for Dubos would always choose his experimental target in the context of his big question.

Thus it was that Dubos sought and in 1938 demonstrated the first antibiotic from a bacterium of the soil. He had begun his study of the web of life in soil science at an agricultural school in France. He handed off his "gramicidin" to medical scientists and had no interest in hunting the second antibiotic. Antibiotic activity was but an elementary, if useful and dramatic, demonstration of the dynamic balance of bacterial life in the soil: with antibiotics, soil bacteria keep one another's numbers in check.

Dubos was now himself recognized as a medical scientist. He had less interest, however, in fighting germs than in the question why bacteria, which at all times inhabit the human organism, only sometimes make people sick. He chose the ubiquitous tubercle bacillus for study. For other investigators, he solved the tricky problem of cultivating the bacillus in quantity for animal and other experiments. More important, he showed that the disappearance of tuberculosis in the industrial societies can be credited only in minor part to medicine and has to be attributed to the favorable material circumstances of the one-quarter to one-third of the human species that is industrialized. For his historical thesis he developed experimental-animal models. He demonstrated in mouse colonies the benefits of early sufficiency and the costs of early deprivation, emotional as well as physical, in the growth of infants, explaining well-documented observations of human experience. This work led Dubos to consider whether and how humankind can make itself at home on the only earth it will ever know, and it completed Dubos's metamorphosis to environmental scientist and publicist.

The reader of this book will have from René Dubos his own account of that metamorphosis. For this anthology is at the same time an autobiography. It presents his pivotal scientific papers, key chapters from his books, fugitive newspaper and magazine pieces, a sampling of his "Despairing Optimist" columns from the *American Scholar,* speech transcripts, and his famous Lichen Sermon at the Cathedral of St. John the Divine in New York City.

Dubos himself supplies an engaging outline and guide to the book in the oral autobiography that opens it. The voice of the raconteur, who talked with the same grace and pace that distinguish his writing, can almost be heard. His joie de vivre, which he defines as the sheer biological pleasure of being alive, is patent. In embracing America, his new-found land, this proud Frenchman makes the English language his own, the instrument of the precision and poetry of his intellection.

The demonstration of the first antibiotic came as a follow-on to Dubos's fulfillment, in 1929, of his first assignment in his first job as a newly minted Ph.D. He was hired by Oswald T. Avery at the Rockefeller Institute in New York City to help in the research that made the momentous discovery of the molecule of heredity, so well known today by the initials DNA (for deoxyribonucleic acid). As so often happens in the life of science, that research had an entirely different objective. Avery and his colleagues were trying to develop a therapy for pneumonia, then still a major cause of death and "the old man's friend." Their strategy turned on mobilization of the body's immune system and its reinforcement by antitoxins, after the model of the therapy for diphtheria that was current at that time.

For Avery, Dubos produced from a soil bacillus an enzyme to dissolve the tough capsule that encloses the pneumococcus and keeps the body's white cells from engulfing it. He had got his doctorate at Rutgers University in the study of soil bacilli that digest cellulose, the most abundant organic material of all. In solving Avery's problem out of his understanding that all living tissue thus goes through recycling in the soil (or in the ooze on the ocean floor), Dubos was the first to demonstrate another profound principle of life. Against accepted practice in laboratory culture of bacteria, he put his cultures on a starvation diet, feeding them only the pneumococcus capsule material. He thereby isolated the right bacillus. More important, he showed that his culture medium had induced the bacillus to manufacture the enzyme.

Dubos did not have the biochemistry necessary to explain his "adaptive enzyme." That work was to bring fame to three of his countrymen—Jacques Monod, François Jacob, and André Lwoff—two decades later. As Dubos tells the story (in Part II), he went on instead to find another soil bacillus that would produce an antibiotic lethal to the pneumococcus and its formidable cousins, the streptococcus and staphylococcus. While gramicidin had too many side effects for use in medicine, he had set in motion the work that accomplished Avery's original objective, a cure for pneumonia.

In his appointment soon afterward to a joint professorship at the Medical School and School of Public Health of Harvard University, Dubos had license to pursue his enlarging interests in the ecology of the human host and its infectious organisms. With his Harvard colleague Lawrence J. Henderson, he agreed that the germ theory had brought on "an era of atrophy in the thinking process of medicine." There was much to be learned about the variable susceptibility of the host and the mutable virulence of viruses and bacteria. He dealt with half of the problem in his *Bacterial Cell*. That comprehensive and lucidly comprehensible work is sampled in Part III. It continues to be consulted today, nearly a half century later, as a primary reference in bacteriology.

Returning to the Rockefeller Institute at the end of the Second World War, Dubos pursued the other side of the relationship. In the *White Plague*, his first book for lay readers, sampled in Part IV, he developed the role of economic inequity and social cruelty in establishing tuberculosis as the No. 1 killer in populations undergoing the Industrial Revolution during the nineteenth century. His mouse-colony demonstrations of this thesis attracted little notice from his colleagues, perhaps because the forces that exclude two-thirds, or more, of humankind from participation in the success of the Industrial Revolution lie so far beyond the reach of medicine. That exclusion must be lifted, he shows, if the population avalanche is to terminate during the twenty-first century in the last doubling of our numbers. The economic development of the nations of the poor stands paradoxically as the ultimate environmental conservation measure.

Dubos was thereupon moved to contemplate the role of science in the modern world and its limits in human affairs. As can be seen in Part V, he did not settle for the jejune means/ends dichotomy that usually terminates examination of the question. Dubos recognized the role of science in generating new dilemmas in human value. The latest development in science settles the last dilemma and poses the next. Poverty is no longer acceptable because it is no longer inevitable, being enforced by social relations, not material circumstance.

Dubos began now, in the late 1950s, to give more of his time to writing about social questions in the perspective of the life sciences. From soil ecology he turned to global ecology. His theology of the environment (see Part VI) was concerned as much with man's alienation from man, implicit in so much writing and preaching about "Nature," as with the alienation of industrial man from nature. The Dubos heresy—that human beings can improve on nature—has its ratification in landscapes all around the globe. The stewardship he urges is not only admirable but practical and soon to be compelled by the pressure of population on the finite bounty of earth. This was the half of the argument he supplied to balance the environmentalist outrage and despair of Barbara Ward in the writing of *Only One Earth,* the book that framed the agenda for the 1972 UN Conference on the Human Environment in Stockholm.

In the Dubos vision of the City of Man, which can be sampled in Part VII, suburbia has no place: the single-family detached dwelling cannot be sustained by that finite bounty. Worse, it is now being sustained at the expense of the urban slum. The Dutch, who live at closer quarters in greater harmony on their man-made land than any other people, can give us and did give Dubos courage to reckon with the next doubling of the world population. In the vertical city of Manhattan, he found the joint triumph of the beast and angel in man.

From this background of understanding and reflection came the hortatory speeches, lectures, and sermons with which Dubos informed and inspired the environmental movement. A selected few make up Part VIII. If he has to scold at times, it is only to persuade his listeners that their good impulses can make a difference. They can escape captivity in technological determinism, they can make the world they want by taking thought and then action on the part of the world that is within their reach.

In exercise of his faith in the rational process, Dubos established and presided at his own forum on the environment during the last years of his life. The forum each year chose a current controversy and brought together the contending parties. In keeping with his faith, they would often find consensus on the facts and sometimes on what to do about them. The René Dubos Center for Human Environments in New York City carries on this good work today.

As a public scientist, René Dubos ran some risk to his standing as a scientist. He had to stand down politely from the nomination to cult figure that some young environmental absolutists pressed upon him. A scientist works for the respect and esteem of peers inside the community of science. These are not only the reward but the essential ratification of his work. Celebration and adulation from outside are secondary to the primary ratification and reward and sometimes even subtract from it. That Dubos's standing as a scientist suffered not at all from his remarkable success as a public figure stands as testimony to the solidity and significance of his scientific work.

Such repute is not always proclaimed by the bestowal of the Nobel Prize, despite its awesome authority in making the reputation of scientists outside the community and much as the Swedish academies take care to consult the invisible colleges. Oswald Avery and his principal collaborators—Colin MacLeod and Maclyn McCarty—are missing from the Nobel roster. Sir Alexander Fleming, Ernst B. Chain, and Sir Howard W. Florey, to whose attention Dubos personally called his gramicidin, got the first Dubos prize, and Selman A. Waksman, in reward from his pupil Dubos, got the second. Monod, Jacob, and Lwoff got the Nobel Prize for showing how the gene for, say, the adaptive enzyme gets turned on and off. The Dubos solution for the cultivation of the tuberculosis bacillus may be compared to the work on the culture of the polio virus that got the prize for J. F. Enders, F. C. Robbins, and T. H. Weller.

This book is going to press on the fiftieth anniversary of the demonstration of gramicidin. It holds another legacy for which René Dubos will be remembered as long and as well.

Gerard Piel
October 30, 1989
New York City

# PART I

## Celebrations of Life

We may differ in our tastes and goals; we may even despise much of what we see around us, but most of us would join in Thoreau's clarion call in *Walden:* "I do not propose to write an Ode to Dejection, but to brag as lustily as Chanticleer in the morning, standing on his roof, if only to wake my neighbors up"— for a Celebration of Life.

# Each a Part of
# the Whole

IN SEPTEMBER 1978, A young French physician named Jean-Paul Escande persuaded René Dubos to join him in a tape-recorded conversation that ran on for several days. From the tape came a book, entitled *Chercher* in France and *Quest* in the United States, a title that Dubos said "fit the rambling, exploratory nature of our conversations." From the book comes this one-sided excerpt. It gives the reader at once an autobiography of René Dubos, his voice, and an overview of the wide-ranging interests that he developed at greater depth in the other pieces in this anthology.

First, however, let Jean-Paul Escande tell what inspired him to this enterprise:

> *1939. For the first time a systematic method is worked out for the discovery of antibiotics and for their production on a large scale. Gramicidin, also known as tyrothricin, is the first antibiotic to be developed rationally and produced industrially. The door has been unlocked. Penicillin and streptomycin are yet to be used. Who took this decisive step? René Dubos, a Frenchman born at the turn of the century at Saint-Brice, a village near Sarcelles, not far north of Paris.*

*Quest* (New York: Harcourt Brace Jovanovich, 1979), pp. xiii–xv, 4–15, 20–23, 36–39, 44–47, 58–63, 70–73, 76–77, 88–91, 96–107, 110–111, 116–117, 120–121, 128. Reprinted by permission of Editions Stock.

*1955. The effects of isoniazid, a powerful medication for tuberculosis, are being tested. One group of patients is being given this drug along with bed rest; the others continue to go about their daily activities. The two groups get well at the same rate. Conclusion: Tuberculosis patients need no longer spend endless months in bed. Where was this study carried out? In René Dubos's department.*

*1972. Pollution is making the industrialized world shudder, for that world is finally discovering that one day it may well smother in the waste it has been producing. Anxiously, world leaders called for the United Nations Conference on the Human Environment at Stockholm to examine the situation and plan a program of action. Who was selected to chair the distinguished group of international experts that provided the conceptual framework for that now historic meeting? René Dubos, who with the British economist Barbara Ward coauthored the report that became the landmark book* Only One Earth.

*1975. Where will we find energy sources? And how should we use the energy available? He founded a new organization called The René Dubos Forum (now known as The René Dubos Center for Human Environments) to help decision makers and the public formulate policies for the resolution of environmental problems and for the creation of new environmental values. He takes as the themes of the first two Forums "The Greening of Energy" and "Better Life Through Less Energy."*

*So what do you imagine René Dubos is like? Pedantic, pontificating, sententious? Quite wrong! Vindictive, grumpy, spouting maledictions and prophecies of doom? Even more wrong! A hermit, inaccessible, walled up in his ivory tower? No, wrong again!*

*René Dubos is very simply a splendid man with a rare blend of sincerity, knowledge, pensiveness, humor, and esteem for his fellow human beings, a man whose thirst for truth causes him to expand his horizons daily. For Dubos's whole life has never deviated an inch from his overall view of the world; he has managed to integrate into his thought all the realities that individually make up the fabric of our everyday life in its humblest aspects as well as in its most ambitious achievements. The result is the René Dubos of today: an American Frenchman, very tall, smiling, attentive, and accessible, who says marvelous and sim-*

*ple things, who demonstrates that there are no big or little problems but rather a chain of realities that you can master only by looking at the links that bind them.*

*This great scholar, to whom many of us surely owe our lives today, this sought-after man who has been asked to preach in the Cathedral Church of St. John the Divine in New York City, to preside over meetings of the most eminent scholars, and to teach students in the most sophisticated universities—this unusual man defies easy categorization. He is not only a very great biologist, a pioneer ecologist, and a specialist in the social sciences who is recognized the world over; he is also, very simply, a universal man.*

*Dubos is also a talented storyteller to whom one could listen for hours without ever tiring. His life takes on the contours of a Grimm fairy tale, with its shadowy corners and its brightly lighted areas. His is a very new and very original conception of life that leaves stereotypes, prefabricated ideas, and modish theories behind.*

*I was very lucky one day—I met René Dubos.*

I BEGAN my scientific training in Paris, at the College Chaptal, a public high school. My recollections of this period are indelible. I recall having read Hippolyte Taine's *La Fontaine et ses Fables.* He asserted that if La Fontaine had been born in the forests of Germany, the deserts of the Sudan, or a Mediterranean country, he wouldn't have written his fables in the same way. Indeed, Taine asserted, the form of the French countryside gave the fables their form. Strangely enough, I've never forgotten this. I reread Taine's book three or four years ago, and when all is said and done this point isn't as clearly stated as I remembered, but it's there all the same. So at a very young age I was already prepared to believe that things aren't easy to understand, and that if they are to be understood at all, they must be studied according to their relationships with other things rather than individually, in isolation.

Having graduated from the College Chaptal, I first studied at the Institut Agronomique in Paris, and then at the Ecole D'Agriculture Coloniale in hopes of going to Indochina. But as a boy I had suffered from severe rheumatic fever that left me with a serious heart lesion, so I wasn't permitted to go to Indochina. Bad luck must be good for something, for a few months afterward I was fortunate enough to get a job in

Rome at the International Institute of Agriculture, an organization administered by the League of Nations, now called the Food and Agriculture Organization (FAO). For two years I worked in Rome as an editor, preparing articles on the agricultural sciences.

One day, in the French magazine *Science et Industrie*, I by chance read an article by a Russian who was working at the Institut Pasteur at the time. His name was Sergei Winogradsky. Winogradsky, a microbiologist, had come to the Institut Pasteur after the Russian Revolution. He was already very famous. In fact, he'd been offered a post at a section of the Institut Pasteur located at Brie-Comte-Robert, not far from Paris. His article made a profound impression on me. He was studying microbes in the soil and asserted in this article that microbiologists were committing a fundamental error in studying microbes solely in the laboratory, in pure cultures, in artificial surroundings, since in nature microbes never live in pure cultures. Microbes whose natural habitat is the soil live there in association with other microbes, under completely unique conditions that, of course, are different from those in the laboratory. In addition, this article had broader implications. In a word, it meant that if you want to study life, you have to study it in its natural habitat and not proceed only as microbiologists do, by isolating microbes from their environment.

I was so impressed that I immediately decided to become a microbiologist and promptly took a course in microbiology at the University of Rome. Since I had no money, I did all sorts of jobs, especially working as a guide. I spoke Italian well and had learned English by dating English girls. I had absolutely no specific idea about what I was going to be, but for a long time I'd been yearning to travel. I wanted to go to the United States. By taste, by inclination. Perhaps also because I was a bit afraid of Parisian society. I really don't know. In any case, I really wanted to get away. Then fate stepped in: in Rome I met two people who later opened the first American doors for me.

The first of these two people was the American representative to the International Institute, Asher Hobson, a professor of agricultural economics at the University of Wisconsin at Madison. Each nation sent a delegation to Rome, presided over by an eminent figure. Almost all of them wore top hats to official dinners, but Hobson would appear for dinner without one. I used to meet him on the way to the office because we often arrived a bit earlier than the others. Our paths crossed a few times; he soon recognized me and greeted me with a casual wave, and I would reply with an equally casual gesture. That's how we became friends! Such a thing would have been impossible with the French representative. One day Hobson asked about my plans, and I replied that I wanted to go to the United States. "Well, why don't you?" "Because I don't have enough money yet!" Then he said very cordially, "Go to the States. If you have any problems, let me know and I will help you." And he added a remark that I'll never forget: "I know how to pick a winner."

That's America in a nutshell. Of all the young people there, I alone had dared wave casually to an official delegate, so he had concluded that I must have some originality. I was on my way to America.

In those days the crossing took eleven days. I was leaning on the rail of the steamship *Rochambeau*, watching the French coast recede into the distance. I wasn't homesick, but I really didn't know what I was going to do. I had just enough money for maybe three or four months. I was standing there, lost in thought, when I felt a tap on my shoulder. A strange man and woman. Well, not total strangers—I'd seen them somewhere before. But where? They knew exactly where. I'd been their guide in Rome. Now at this time anti-Semitism was really very strong in America, and this couple, Selman Waksman and his wife, had been totally snubbed by all the other American passengers. So I became very close to them and found out that he was a professor of microbiology at Rutgers University in New Brunswick, New Jersey, not far from New York City! Toward the end of the crossing, Professor Waksman said, "Why not come to New Brunswick? We have a good faculty." So shortly after I set foot in New York—about five o'clock the very next afternoon—I left for New Brunswick to register as a student, in microbiology. Of course, I looked for work right away, in order to earn some money. That was very easy at the time, and I did all sorts of things, even taught German. But above all I specialized in microbiology and completed my doctorate. So now I had a Ph.D.

To tell the rest of the story, I must add that after World War II, in 1952, Waksman won the Nobel Prize for his discovery of streptomycin and in this way confirmed that a good deed is never performed in vain. He had helped me, but I repaid him amply, since it was thanks to my earlier work with antibiotics—I'll talk about this later—that he was able to undertake his own work.

Now that I had my doctorate, I tried to get a research grant from the National Research Council. But I learned that I wasn't eligible, because I wasn't an American citizen. However, the secretary (a total stranger) who sent me this bad news added a brief P.S.: "Why not go see your

[ 7 ]

compatriot Dr. Alexis Carrel, at the Rockefeller Institute for Medical Research in New York City?"

I went to see Dr. Carrel. He received me cordially, told me that he couldn't help me, but nonetheless invited me to lunch in the dining room at the Rockefeller Institute. He seated me beside a professor, a very friendly man, who asked me what my doctoral thesis was about. I replied, "My dissertation is a study of the microbes in the soil that break down the cellulose of plants." And this professor answered, "That's similar to something we're trying to do in the lab here." He took me to his office. He was head of the department of infectious respiratory diseases and was especially interested in lobar pneumonia caused by a microbe, the pneumococcus. "We've shown," he told me, "that the pneumococcus is able to resist the white blood cells that would otherwise destroy it, because it's encapsulated in a substance—polysaccharide—that resembles cellulose. This capsule protects it. If only we could find some way to destroy the capsule!" Then, with the audacity of a twenty-six-year-old, I asserted, "I'm convinced that a microbe exists in nature that will attack those polysaccharides, because if such a microbe didn't exist, polysaccharides would cover the earth, which they don't. So something must exist somewhere that destroys them." And we left it at that.

Shortly afterward I got a job out West, but I was barely settled when I received a telegram. I'd been awarded a fellowship by the Rockefeller Institute to work with that very man, Professor Oswald T. Avery. It was the great turning point in my life.

Immediately, I returned to New York City and set to work. Two years later I discovered a microbe that broke down the polysaccharide of the pneumococcus. From this microbe I obtained a substance, an enzyme, and demonstrated that when this enzyme was injected into animals with advanced pneumococcal infections, the enzyme did indeed destroy the capsule surrounding the microbe, and so permitted the white blood cells to do away with the pneumococcus.

Then immediately afterward I made another discovery—from my point of view, the more important of the two. I discovered that the microbe that destroyed that capsule of the pneumococcus produced the destructive enzyme only when it had to—that is, when it had to use the polysaccharide. If, on the other hand, this microbe was grown in an ordinary culture medium, it grew very well but it didn't produce the enzyme.

This fact taught me a lot. It shows that we can develop latent qualities to the degree that we function. I'll give you a very simple example. All of us are born with muscles, but they develop well only if they are made to work. In the same way we're all born with mental capabilities, and these mental capabilities develop only to the degree that the brain functions. So ever since my earliest research, I've been convinced that while it's important to know the organism, it's equally important, in order to reveal its full potential, to know the conditions under which it develops and functions. In passing, I'd like to say that in my opinion the medicine of the future won't necessarily invent a mechanical substitute to replace a lost organ but will teach the individual to function without that organ.

But let's get back to the conflict between microbes. About 1935 I asked myself whether I could find some microbes in nature that would attack and kill other microbes besides the pneumococcus—the staphylococcus, for example. I began to search, and in a short time I did indeed find a microbe in the soil that would kill the staphylococcus. From cultures of this soil microbe I extracted substances, which I called tyrothricin and gramicidin, that accounted for the killing effect. They were the first antibiotics produced commercially. They were used topically rather extensively and were quite successful in veterinary medicine. Indeed, they were very effective against mastitis in cows, which is caused by a streptococcus.

At that point I read that a few years earlier Alexander Fleming had also found an antibiotic—penicillin—to combat the staphylococcus. But he had abandoned his work with it because he didn't know how to prepare penicillin in a stable form. In 1939 I told Fleming that he should resume his work on penicillin, and I also talked with Howard Florey, who, in collaboration with Ernst Chain, prepared a stable form of penicillin in the early 1940s with the resounding success that we all know about.

But even before many antibiotics were available, I realized that microbes would become resistant to them, and I issued a warning about the dangers resulting from this resistance. As early as 1942 I even gave a lecture in which I stated that one of the great problems of the future would be the resistance that microbes would develop to antibiotics.

In the meantime something much more important to me occurred in my personal life. At the time, 1939–1940, Europe was at war. My first wife was French, born at Limoges. In 1939, at the beginning of the war, she came down with tuberculosis. I asked myself, "Why did she get tuberculosis, when we live as well as we do?" So I dug into her past and discovered that she'd had tuberculosis when she was about six or seven and had gotten well by herself, as most people do. Then why did she have a relapse? I theorized that the disasters in her family resulting from the war had caused her very great anguish. I'm convinced that this anguish reactivated the tuberculosis that to all appearances had been cured. She died three years later.

In my grief I said to myself, "Infectious diseases obviously are caused by microbes, but countless people are infected and don't develop the disease. It only becomes manifest if the infection occurs in a weakened organism. And there are all sorts of factors in the natural environment that determine whether or not the disease will appear." Then I thought that it would be intellectually more interesting to observe the sick persons in their surroundings than to restrict myself to studying the microbial causes of disease. I changed the focus of my laboratory research and began to perfect methods by which we could demonstrate that an animal's susceptibility to an infection (first to the bacillus of tuberculosis, then to the staphylococcus) varied according to its environment. From then on I tried to recognize the factors in the environment that influence a person's resistance to infection. In fact my second wife, Jean, and I subsequently wrote a book showing how certain conditions in the surroundings were responsible for the great tuberculosis epidemics, especially during the nineteenth century.

During that century huge segments of the population moved from the country to the city for the first time. The new living conditions of these people were so different—even though they weren't always worse—that they posed enormous health problems, and tuberculosis become prevalent. It appeared everywhere and influenced literature, art, and music. This influence has a simple explanation: the behavior of the tuberculosis victims themselves. The benign form of tuberculosis causes a fever. This fever doesn't usually stun the individual but instead may stimulate him. Alexandre Dumas the elder, and his son as well, stated that being slightly feverish was stimulating and definitely good for you. Then there's Honoré de Balzac's extraordinary remark, which goes more or less like this: "Being a bit feverish for a week or a month may keep you from sleeping, but it lets you write a great deal more!" We've forgotten that a person didn't necessarily die of tuberculosis. Most people went through a long period of stimulation that was viewed as desirable. The pale complexion of the individual with tuberculosis became stylish; the romantic heroine was tubercular. But sometimes it turned out badly for the sick, as was the case with my first wife.

So I began to work on the influences in the surroundings that make one susceptible to tuberculosis. Soon I moved on to the influences in the surroundings that make one susceptible to other infections. Finally I realized that each civilization, each type of culture, has its own particular illnesses, and that the influence of the surroundings upon health is a widespread phenomenon. Ever since then I've continually asked myself to what degree illness results from infection or other assaults upon the individual by something in his surroundings— indeed, to what degree it results from his way of life in general. This has become an obsession with me. Then, instead of thinking solely about the effect of the surroundings upon disease, I became interested in the effect of the surroundings upon human development in general. I often give students the following example. If you visit a kibbutz in Israel, you'll see that in a single generation the Central European type has completely changed and that the tall young men and women of the kibbutzim are totally different from their parents.

General human development is what I'm interested in. I'm concerned about the environment, but always as related to the human being. And I've become convinced that people should give up the notion that human beings are so fragile as to constantly need all kinds of medication or therapy. Medicine must learn to recognize the potentials of human nature and also learn to cultivate them in our own environment.

This is a totally new kind of science, a science with great potentialities. It almost disagrees with established doctrine, even with the teachings of Claude Bernard, who held that the human body adapts to new conditions through the mechanism of homeostasis—that is, by returning to its exact state before the attack. As I see it, and my position can easily be proved, the body adapts, but often by changing.

If you look at the history of the biological sciences, without exception you'll find confirmation of this. You'll see that if one branch of the tree breaks, the tree doesn't heal by growing another branch but by reorganizing its entire structure. An animal that loses a leg as a result of some accident relearns to walk by changing anatomically. A person who becomes blind readapts without regaining his sight. Some thirty years ago a very brilliant young man was working in my laboratory. He became totally blind because of a severe case of diabetes. This young man, who had a will of steel, reorganized his life so that he could perceive many things in the world about him that we too could perceive if we cultivated our other senses. He could go into a restaurant and tell you what was happening there, simply by listening. But you'd have heard nothing.

Living the civilized lives that we do, we've lost our ability to live in nature and to perceive the world as the primitive people of the Stone Age did, for whom this was a necessity. After millennia of history and civilization, some Europeans decided during the eighteenth and nineteenth centuries to go live in the American wilderness more or less like primitive people. They were called *coureurs de bois*. Instead of remaining on the coast and farming, these Europeans chose a life of hunting and gathering that was the equivalent of Stone Age life. Whether they lived in Canada or in the Rocky Mountains or the Sierras, within a few years many of them had regained these forgotten powers—how to track down an animal, how to live in the wilderness, as Stone Age man did.

The lesson is obvious. We still have these powers within us and can call on them if conditions require it. In like manner, Cro-Magnon man bore within him all our intellectual capabilities. If he returned to earth today he might become an astrophysicist! We still have at our disposal powers we thought had permanently atrophied because of our civilized life.

It would be a promising research project to discover methods for activating all sorts of potentialities latent within us, temporarily lying fallow because of the way we live. We must understand that useful adaptation isn't merely homeostatic adaptation, which strives to return the subject to its previous state. Just the opposite: Useful adaptation is adaptation that helps us compensate for irreversible inadequacies, both physical and mental. Medicine today believes that individuals must conform to a norm and that medicine's only goal is to bring them to that norm. But I say that the important issue is understanding and promoting adaptation. On the one hand adaptation, of course, strives to repair damage, but on the other hand it strives to exploit the organism's reserve potentialities. A very famous Englishman who has written about physiology said that the big difference between the living organism and inert matter is that if you put on shoes, they will wear out. And if you walk with bare feet, your feet will develop thicker calluses. That's a very big difference. It's even a fundamental difference, and it's just what I'm talking about. We must learn how to develop thicker calluses from every point of view!

Now, when I first came into contact with the Rockefeller Institute, I knew absolutely nothing about medicine or medical microbiology, or even what a pneumococcus was. When Oswald Avery described the pneumococcus, with "its capsule of polysaccharide that prevents phagocytosis," he was using words I didn't even understand. At that moment, by the accident of my already established interests, I had an idea, and that's why I was given the opportunity to work it out.

From then on I began to look for places in nature where there were polysaccharides similar to those of the pneumococcus. And it so happened that I found some in a marshy region rather close to New York City. I took some soil from that region, put it into contact with the polysaccharide produced by the pneumococcus—and you know the rest!

Obviously, when I tell the story this way, it seems extremely harebrained and not far removed from the eccentric scientist. It was a matter of intuition. Jacques Monod, whom I knew very well and who, unlike me, was a marvelous logician, used to tell me with charming and benevolent scorn, "You and André Lwoff, you're both intuitives!" Yes, I'm intuitive. Research must start with phenomenology, and I certainly am a phenomenologist. I've had numerous successes in the laboratory, and I've really demonstrated new things, but I did it as a phenomenologist—that is, as a man who looks at the problem as a whole but doesn't analyze its innermost details. But Monod and François Jacob made their extraordinary discoveries as analysts and logicians. In fact, they used some of my work as a point of departure. As I've told you, I discovered that the microbe producing the enzyme that broke down the capsule around the pneumococcus produced that enzyme only when it needed to. Monod drew his inspiration from the system that I brought into focus, but he was concerned with understanding the inner mechanism.

As for me, I indeed suspected the genetic origin of all these phenomena. I'd written a very long chapter on the subject in one of my books, *The Bacterial Cell*, which was very influential. In it I gave examples of other microbes that put their genetic potentialities to work only when necessity prompted. One of these microbes produced a lactase—that is, an enzyme that destroyed lactose, a sugar. But before it would do so, it had to be subjected to conditions in which it had to use lactose. So I'd pointed out the phenomenology of the problem. I'd even tried to go deeper, but although I'd pointed to genetics, I lacked sufficient knowledge of genetics, sufficient knowledge of chemistry, and probably sufficient analytical capabilities. I'm almost certain that even if I'd persevered, I couldn't have solved the problem. But Monod and Jacob applied their astonishing analytical capacities.

I don't in any way want to create the impression that I underestimate the importance of the Cartesian scientific approach, which is an eighteenth-century attitude. Monod was an extraordinary Cartesian. We were friends, true friends, and he'd always say to me, "I wish I could have lived in the eighteenth century." So when he said of Lwoff and me, "You're intuitives," he certainly meant it, but I suppose that at the same time he valued intuitives and thought they were needed to state problems.

Louis Pasteur was also a great intuitive. When Professor Pasteur Vallery-Radot talked about his grandfather Pasteur, he would invariably say, "Pasteur was logical, Pasteur was supremely logical." Well, that's part truth and part fantasy! Pasteur wasn't one hundred percent logical. First of all, he was intuitive. Then, from the moment he was convinced that something should be a certain way, he became logical in his scientific work. But he always began—and he himself stated this with great precision—with extraordinarily intuitive insights.

I'd like to give you another example, that of a medical scientist who made essential discoveries that he was incapable of analyzing. During World War II, this Harvard physician was surprised to note that when a soldier was wounded, sometimes he didn't suffer at all at the moment of the injury, and sometimes not even for a long time afterward. This occurred when the soldier was certain that his wound would lead to a permanent discharge and that, as a result, the war had ended for him. In fact, the phenomenon proved to be far more general. When, in one way or another, an event occurred—even a painful event—and brought an agreeable change in a person's future, the person mobilized something within his body that prevented him from feeling pain. These facts were accepted as real, became part of medical thought, and were talked about a great deal, but for a long time they couldn't be explained scientifically.

Then, very recently, someone using scientific methods discovered that under certain circumstances the brain secretes substances that make pain go away, substances that some people thought resembled morphine in their action. This led to a research program to try to isolate these encephalins and endorphins—hormones produced by the brain—that have been recently discovered and that we now know affect many aspects of human behavior.

Even more recently, at the Neurological Institute of Montreal, it's been shown that the secretion of these endorphins increases when acupuncture is done under the proper conditions. It has also been demonstrated that acupuncture doesn't work if the patient has previously received a substance that prevents morphine from working. So we've suddenly moved from Chinese empirical knowledge, dating back two or three thousand years and ignorant of scientific medicine, to precise scientific formulation.

This is one more reason why we should pay attention to whatever phenomenology is available to us, thanks to which we can make progress. This phenomenology often depends upon the observations by individuals who know how to look at things and be surprised. And the explanation may not come for two thousand years!

We must distrust hasty conclusions based on incomplete observations. Take an example dealing with tuberculosis. We know the death rate for tuberculosis a century ago: roughly five hundred deaths a year for every one hundred thousand people.

But today the rate has fallen to two. In the end, what was responsible for this phenomenon? If you looked at the matter closely, you could defend various hypotheses. If you wanted to prove that discovering the guilty microbe caused the drop in the disease rate, you could show that after 1890 the death rate fell from five hundred to two hundred. If you wanted to prove that vaccination with BCG [bacillus Calmette-Guerin] was of prime importance, you could demonstrate that after BCG came into use, the death rate fell to forty. If you wanted to prove the role of specific antibiotics, you could demonstrate that after the discovery of streptomycin, the death rate dropped to five.

But the other truth is that the death rate for tuberculosis had begun to decline shortly after 1845—even though no therapeutic program had been developed—and that between 1845 and 1890 this decline was just as regular as after 1890. These data are very widely accepted today; social changes occurring during the nineteenth century made people less susceptible to tuberculosis, even when they came into contact with the bacillus. It's essential to know this, for until a few decades ago ninety percent of all people in Europe and America still showed positive tuberculin reactions and had therefore been infected; they had reacted by developing a very mild infection and a positive reaction to the skin tests without suffering any serious effects. It must be pointed out, however, that during the 1950s the introduction of isoniazid made it possible to speed up the decline in the death rate. But by this time tuberculosis was already killing far fewer people than in the past.

At this point the tuberculosis sanatoriums were closed, for isoniazid not only cured the patients, but also let them be treated while going about their daily tasks. It was no longer necessary to remain in bed for months on end. This was demonstrated in our department, using a very small group of patients—or rather, two groups. Some received isoniazid and stayed in bed; the others received the drug and continued to work. Well, the second group got well just as quickly and completely as the first one. So sanatorium treatment was no longer necessary.

About thirty years ago I wrote a biography of Pasteur that is still being read. When it was reprinted recently, I added a new introductory chapter but didn't change anything in the original text. This new chapter seemed indispensable once I had reread Pasteur's writings from an ecological perspective. Everyone summarizes Pasteur with a maxim: "The microbe causes the illness." Of course Pasteur said that. But no one's noticed how all his life he stressed the fact that besides the microbe, which is obviously important, there are all sorts of other factors involving both the climate and the patient himself, his past, his genetic structure (he didn't use the word "genetic" because it didn't exist yet), which are all essential to understanding the onset and course of the illness. At the end of his life Pasteur, whose initial work on infection had dealt with the diseases of silkworms, was even able to write: "If I were younger and had to resume my work on silkworms, I'd focus above all on the conditions under which they were raised: the worms could be made more resistant to illness if their living conditions were changed." And he even went so far as to write, "Moreover, I'm going to suggest to M. Duclos that he try to find substances that could be included in their diet to make the worms more resistant." Pasteur also wrote: "I'm convinced that when a wound becomes infected and festers, the course that the wound takes depends upon the patient's general condition and even his mental condition." All this can be found in Pasteur, and no one has paid any attention to it.

Pasteur even conducted picturesque experiments to show that all sorts of factors besides microbes set the stage for illness. I'll describe only one of them. Pasteur was a professor at the École des Beaux Arts in Paris, where he taught science as applied to the arts. Specifically, he taught the physiology of architecture, and to illustrate the importance of good room ventilation, he set up an astonishing experiment. He took a bird—a canary or a finch—and put it in a bell jar, in which the oxygen was not renewed and therefore gradually diminished. In order to survive, the bird adapted by decreasing its activity, by remaining almost immobile. The bird was taken out while still alive, then a new bird was put into the same glass container. Abruptly placed in an atmosphere low in oxygen, this bird didn't have time to adapt, so it immediately began to move about and promptly fell dead.

He wanted to demonstrate by this experiment that a person can unconsciously adapt to unfavorable conditions, as long as they come upon him gradually. In Pasteur's view, it was very dangerous to adapt to bad ventilation. So he told the students they must think about providing adequate ventilation and not wait until people begin to suffer. In short, Pasteur was a very modern man. He placed great importance on all those complex effects of the surroundings that we think of as our discoveries. And no one talks about these ideas. Pasteur was completely betrayed, I now realize, by everyone who wrote about him.

In this very connection, recently I made a "discovery" about René Descartes. People talk as if Descartes had been nothing but a logical reductionist. Well, last week—purely by chance, for I wasn't doing research on it—I ran across a book in New York, *Descartes par lui-même* (Descartes in his own words), part of a well-known French series. Here's what I found: Descartes wrote to Princess Elizabeth of Germany, telling her, "In truth, the most important thing for curing illnesses and maintaining health is good humor and joy."

The life of Edward Livingston Trudeau, who did so much for victims of tuberculosis, gives a perfect illustration of Descartes's thesis. Trudeau was a French-speaking American physician who was born in Louisiana and studied in New York City. He came down with tuberculosis just over a century ago. He thought that he was going to die, for his tuberculosis had reached such an advanced stage that he was sure he had no chance of pulling through. So he said to himself, "Well, I'm going to spend the few months I have left doing the things I like most. I'll go hunting in the Adirondacks." He went to those mountains, which aren't far from New York City, and hired a guide. There are big lakes in those mountains, and he'd set off in a boat with his guide and hunt. He spent each day that way, and instead of dying, he got better. Almost cured, he returned to New York, once again became immersed in the medical and social life of the city, and suffered a relapse. Again he was told that he was going to die. "If I have to die," he said, "I'll go off again." So he went back to the Adirondacks, resumed his hunting, and once again got better. This time he decided to set up a medical practice in the Adirondacks and also to create a small sanatorium (it wasn't called that at the time) to admit sick people from New York City, to see whether life in the Adirondacks would improve their tuberculosis. This was the first important sanatorium in the United States.

Trudeau became the great expert of his day on tuberculosis. He was the first person in America to employ Robert Koch's methods for cultivating the tuberculosis bacillus. He became a very important man, a personal friend of the chief organizer of the public health services. When he died a statue was erected and bore in French the maxim that he was so fond of using to describe that physician's powers: *"Guerir quelquefois, soulager souvent, consoler toujours!"*—to cure sometimes, help often, console always.

One might object that these words make no mention of prevention. And with good reason: in 1870 smallpox vaccination was the only technique of preventive medicine that existed. While there are grounds for skepticism about the progress of curative medicine, one certainly can't deny that preventive medicine has become quite effective during the intervening century, not only against infectious diseases but against malnutrition and work-related illnesses. This really constitutes an extraordinary chapter in medical history, a chapter based on close collaboration between the medical and the nonmedical worlds. Those great campaigns supporting preventive medicine at the turn of the century were at first chiefly organized by people who weren't physicians. The physicians who cooperated—and of course they did so at a very early date—were physicians with considerable social concern. As I see it, this is the most extraordinary example of close and absolutely essential collaboration between the medical and the nonmedical worlds. People can invent all the preventive methods they want, but if these methods aren't incorporated into a suitable social structure, there's no chance of their being effective. Not even vaccinations. So a whole world of preventive medicine exists that isn't sufficiently recognized and that did not exist in Trudeau's time.

Now, let's look first at *guerir quelquefois*, to cure sometimes. Today a lot of diseases still aren't curable. I've never made a list of them, but I suppose that truly dependable cures exist for very few diseases, in particular for some bacterial infections and a few diseases treated by surgery. The rest of the time the patient's condition is merely improved, or else he gets well all on his own. Cures are the result of concentrated scientific effort to understand the diseases in question. Curing infectious diseases by means of antibiotics became possible only when it had been demonstrated that such diseases were caused by microbes.

Next we come to *soulager souvent*, to help often. Exactly what does that mean? I believe you can't answer that question without asking what you mean by "illness." I've always noticed that people consider themselves to be ill when they can't do what they want to do, when they can't become what they want to become. People naturally like to know what's wrong with their body, but above all they're concerned about being able to do the things they want to do.

That brings to mind the example of Dr. Avery. He had a disease that could have been considered serious, Graves' disease. The laboratory was his whole life. He lived only a ten-minute walk from the laboratory and hardly ever went anywhere else. He used to come to the laboratory, do his work, go back home, sleep, then return to work. He scarcely ate, and he certainly could never have walked a mile without stopping. Yet he thought that his health was good, for he had everything he needed to keep functioning in the laboratory. That was his only barometer.

Well, he began to encounter serious difficulties in his laboratory. Nothing worked any more, and worse still, something happened that made all his work appear useless. Most of his effort had been focused on the production of serums and vaccines for pneumonia. But sulfa drugs appeared in 1937, and overnight his approach appeared useless, out of date. He felt that he'd wasted his entire life.

Then his Graves' disease erupted; he couldn't bear it any longer. He had to have an operation, and for two or three years he was a dispirited man; he thought it was the end.

Then he pulled himself together, we started on other projects completely different from his previous work on pneumonia, and this work went very well. He began to come out of his depression. He lived until he was seventy-five, happy and with no further worries about his thyroid. So he provides another illustration of how impossible it is to define what people call "health," how difficult it is to separate health from the person's total life.

That leaves Trudeau's maxim: *consoler toujours*. I've never really understood what Trudeau meant. Everyone, almost everyone, thinks that if a tragedy occurs, the patient himself or his family should be consoled. And perhaps that's all that Trudeau meant. Here I can't help thinking of the marvelous final sentence of Maupassant's story "Une Vie": "Life is never as good or as bad as one thinks." I may be attribut-

ing to physicians qualities that they don't always have, but for me this is
what Trudeau's *consoler* means: the physician uses his experience to
tell someone who's suffering, someone who's in difficulty, that everyone
experiences a certain amount of suffering, that everyone goes through
difficult moments, and that in the end most people pull through. It
involves more than merely expressing sympathy; it means giving en-
couragement by appealing to the patient's good sense, by evoking the
complexity of life: "Life is never as good or as bad as one thinks." So for
me, Trudeau's *consoler* goes beyond consoling the family because
someone has just died, or consoling an individual because he can't get
well. It means, if you will, teaching him how to become master of the
situation again.

The Industrial Revolution created very serious health problems.
There was, of course, malnutrition, but I believe that the worst problem resulted chiefly from the fact that masses of people, enormous
groups of peasants, were shifted to the cities and at first didn't know
how to live in this new urban context. After one or two generations,
these people generally learned to live in the city, even if they were still
poor.

In Sarcelles-Saint-Brice, where I was born so long ago, Saint-Brice
has remained what it was, a little village in the greenbelt surrounding
Paris, while Sarcelles became an enormous new city, the first of the
large housing developments built in France after World War II. At the
beginning, people in Sarcelles suffered from just about every complaint. Meanwhile everything remained normal in Saint-Brice, which
is separated from Sarcelles only by the railroad tracks. But the situation
in Sarcelles was alarming—to the point that a few years back people
were talking about "sarcellitis." Three years ago, when I was in Paris
lecturing to a medical society, I stated that there were enormous
powers of adaptation in both the human organism and the social organism, powers to adapt to all sorts of circumstances. And I said in passing,
"I'm willing to bet that 'sarcellitis' will disappear all on its own, because
people will learn to live in these huge developments." At the end of my
speech a woman rose and said, "Sir, I'm a physician in Sarcelles. What
you predicted for the future has already happened. 'Sarcellitis' has
essentially disappeared."

Sarcelles-Saint-Brice is in the Île de France region around Paris.
The charm of the Île de France is admired the world over. Before man
appeared there, this region was rather flat, rather ordinary, and covered with forests and marshes. Only during neolithic times did man

begin to cut down the forests, control the rivers, and create fields and pastures. People think that the landscapes created in this way are nature, but they're a "nature" that was entirely conceived by man.

This summarizes all of human life. Human beings have transformed the earth in order to satisfy certain needs acquired as they evolved during the Stone Age, when they lived on the savannas of Africa or Asia. The savannas have trees, shrubs, and rivers, but also vast open spaces and therefore great topographic diversity. Within this landscape man can see far into the distance, can keep an eye on the trails passing through it, and can also withdraw into a shelter if the need arises.

Now think of the Vezere region or the Dordogne Valley of France. The most striking example of this is the Cro-Magnon cave. If you stand at the mouth of the Cro-Magnon cave, you have a vast vista before you. It was easy for man to withdraw into his cave and look out into the distance to watch for passing animals. In addition, the forest is there close at hand. So I think there's something very important here, something vital from a physiological point of view. Man needs a shelter, water, and a distant and varied view. Moreover, think of paintings representing happy outdoor scenes. Such scenes always take place in a clearing. They always show a thicket or woods, a river, and a vast expanse. So wherever man is, in all the countries of the world where he's settled, in one way or another he tries to recreate the savanna.

The day when human beings stopped living solely by hunting and gathering and began to construct houses or shelters, to cultivate wheat or rice, and even more to build fires for warmth, they began to leave the natural life behind. We've retained our power to return to the "natural" life, as was shown by the people of European descent who settled in the Rocky Mountains during the nineteenth century and rapidly readapted to the life of the Stone Age. We still have the capacity to live naturally, but today we never live in a natural state, because what we call the Temperate Zone is a region that's theoretically incompatible with human physiology.

A few thousand years ago the region where we're sitting right now was covered with forests and marshes. And as soon as human beings, biologically adapted to live on the savannas of southern Africa, arrived, they began to create surroundings that were adapted to them. And so, because our prehistoric past taught us to use only plants that live in the sun, we've cut down the trees in order to plant things that live and grow in the sun. For almost without exception, all the plants we use are plants that would never grow under trees. One of the few plants that will grow even a bit under trees and that we use frequently is coffee, which requires shade. But certainly none of the plants consumed as our basic foods could grow under trees.

What we call going back to natural things means creating surroundings that resemble the savanna. It's an astonishing paradox. Wherever we go, we transform nature in order to adapt it to our needs, and then once we've transformed nature, we call it "natural." I saw an extraordinary example of this at the International Conference on the Human Environment held in Stockholm in 1972. At the end of the conference Olof Palme, the Swedish prime minister, invited five or six of us to visit him at his house in the country and talk about environmental problems. A very kind Swedish woman picked me up at my hotel in Stockholm and drove me the fifty miles to the prime minister's home. During this little trip she pointed at the landscape and said very sadly, "As you see, in Sweden we're in the process of destroying nature." By that she meant that a large number of the farms that weren't very fertile had been abandoned. Swedish farmers now earn far more money by working in the Volvo or Saab automobile plants than they would if they continued to work these farms with their poor soil. Well, as soon as one of these farms is abandoned, brush grows, then the forest reclaims the land. In the past, that entire part of Sweden was an unbroken forest. So I replied, "You say that nature is being ruined, but that's not so—on the contrary! At this very moment nature is reclaiming her rights." When I reached the prime minister's house, I told him this story and he replied, "I'm quite aware of this. We Swedes have become accustomed—and I'm glad—to seeing part of the Swedish countryside without trees, to seeing our lakes surrounded by fine meadows, cultivated fields, and pastures with cows. And we're horrified at the thought that once again there will be trees everywhere. The Swedes are haunted by the idea, so we've undertaken studies to see how we can most economically preserve the countryside cleared by the farmers. We could grant subsidies to farmers (for their work is no longer economically profitable), or else—and this might be more economical— every year, or twice a year, we could use big machines to cut everything down."

As agriculture becomes increasingly productive and as marginal farmland is abandoned, every society encounters serious difficulties in preserving the humanized countryside, which for us is a physiological need. I repeat: We need to see open landscapes. So in the forests around Paris, the area under the trees is kept cut down because people wouldn't go into the woods if the underbrush were allowed to grow. I'm convinced that a human being set down in the midst of an impenetrable woods would suffer. I'm not even certain he'd survive. We have a psychological need to see around us. This is why we must preserve the humanized countryside. No matter how we do it, we must preserve the countryside, for the temperate regions would no longer be livable for the human race if we let nature, true primitive nature, reassert its rights. I'm continually telling my ecologist friends, "We couldn't live in France, in the United States, in Sweden, or in England if we let nature revert to what it was before the advent of man." This is why the word "natural" seems to me a very difficult word to use. I don't really know what "natural" means; there are so very few things that are natural and hence better. If you tried to eat natural wheat, you couldn't digest it. It must be transformed by a bit of fermentation and by cooking, after which it's no longer "natural" but it is edible. Like it or not, from the moment we learned to transform things according to functions we developed a hundred thousand years ago, we drove the "natural" out. Today the "natural" is something that we've adapted to our needs.

This brings me to some very perplexing philosophical problems. We can't keep from being anthropocentric. It isn't possible for us to view or judge things otherwise. It isn't possible for the human race to survive on earth if (to use an expression that I coined and that's brought me a lot of criticism) it doesn't achieve the humanization of the earth. In France, England, Germany, or America, nature is the humanized earth.

The most powerful animals in the world never leave the restricted ecological zone to which they've adapted. Even monkeys—who know how to use a branch to catch termites and eat them—even monkeys, monkeys of every species, never leave the small ecological zone to which they've totally adapted. The other day my wife mentioned the extraordinary example of that charming Australian animal the koala, which can live only on a diet of the leaves of a single species of eucalyptus tree. Animals of whatever kind are specialized. They live only in the ecological surroundings to which they've adapted. But for the past ten thousand years, and perhaps before that, we have been transforming the land in order to adapt it to ourselves. And that, I believe, constitutes a fundamental difference setting the human race apart from all other species.

Even migratory animals are total prisoners. They always take the same paths, they return to exactly the same places, and if you move their dens or their stopping places just a short distance, they become totally lost. All this shows the extent to which I think the word "nature" is very dangerous, unless a person agrees that nature is something man has transformed.

There has been criticism from environmentalists that I neglect the tragic problems confronting us. So I'll not only list the major problems—the tragic problems that the world faces—but I'll also list them in order of importance and tell why I put them in that order.

I put pollution at the end of the list. Not because it's unimportant, but because throughout the world people have already become quite aware of the problem and have achieved quite a bit. Of course pollution is very important, but we've begun to take the necessary steps.

The first problem, nuclear war, is all too obvious. If a nuclear war should occur one day, it will just about destroy our civilization, and unfortunately I don't see that we've made any real political progress to prevent it.

The second great tragedy is the fact that our society is increasingly unable to provide people with a function that has a profound meaning for their lives. On the one hand this constitutes a condemnation of unemployment, but it also goes far beyond. When you see the enormous proportion of young people who can't begin to integrate themselves into active life as they had hoped to, or who'll never enter that life, you have to observe that both a desocialization and a dehumanization are likely to follow. And this, it seems to me, is truly the most tragic human problem confronting the industrialized nations.

Third on my list is the destruction of the tropical forests. Human beings are destroying these forests with phenomenal rapidity the whole world over! Here again no one is doing anything, no one knows what to do to prevent it. The tropical forests are located in poor countries, which of course are using them to obtain money by selling the produce of these forests to the capitalist nations. If we let things go on as they are, the disastrous climatic and ecological consequences will affect the entire world.

There are also the problems of overpopulation, environmental degradation, and depletion of natural resources. I put the problem of energy sources in sixth place. I'm not very worried about finding raw materials and energy. Our societies can learn to produce energy and find resources.

The real problem is the excessive use of energy. The René Dubos Center organizes symposia with a lot of eminent people from a great variety of backgrounds. The first symposium was a discussion of how much energy we can produce from vegetation, the so-called biomass. To discuss this question, we invited not only scientists but also engineers and businessmen, who asked, "How much energy can we obtain from the biomass? What will it cost?" We also had ecologists, who presented the dangers to the earth if we use this biomass too extensively. We even had humanists—some of whom, incidentally, turned out to be less humanistic than the scientists. And we reflected on what would happen to our conception of nature if we decided to create what might be called "energy plantations."

I didn't state the theme of the second symposium in question form. Instead, I made an assertion: "Live better with less energy." First of all we have to envisage the risks inherent in energy production. Whatever energy source is used—be it coal, nuclear power, the biomass, or solar energy—it can provoke atmospheric disturbances once a certain production level is exceeded. Thus, enormous and very poorly defined problems confront us. Even if we decided to use only solar energy, which has the reputation of being a "clean" energy, we'd have to concentrate its production in certain regions and therefore increase the amount of heat generated in those regions, which might cause all manner of trouble.

That's one aspect of the problem. Another aspect to be considered is the relationship between energy use and physical health. For example, we all know only too well the consequences of the excessive use of food. But the numerous ways in which energy is used excessively in over-developed countries pose a multitude of other problems. Today, when people play golf, they ride around in little carts. While this may sound humorous, I'm citing only one example among a hundred thousand that ultimately all have profound biological repercussions. Because we're in the process of creating a society in which energy is used excessively, we're preventing the existentialization of our physical potentials. The overconsumption of energy in our societies favors a trend to replace the direct experience of things with an indirect experience. We prefer to watch a tennis match on television rather than play tennis ourselves. We prefer to see springtime or fall in pictures rather than go out into the countryside in all kinds of weather. The greatest danger in television, as I see it, isn't that it turns children into criminals because they've watched violent films, but that it prevents them from acquiring a direct experience of life. They watch the world passively, instead of experiencing it actively. This is a major factor in the dangers inherent in the excessive use of energy. Of course I can't prove this statement. It's still a hypothesis, only a hypothesis. Even so, it's already based upon solid foundations!

Architecture is another facet of the same problem. If we permit ourselves to consume enormous amounts of energy to heat and to cool, then we don't have to adapt architecture to our natural surroundings. In the past, one of the chief reasons why architecture was interesting—especially the architecture of modest houses—was their extraordinary diversity. Houses weren't constructed of the same materials in the south as in the north, or in the snowy mountains as in the regions where snow never falls.

Energy also permits us to build the little houses of those new "towns," houses that have space, a lot of space, between them. On the one hand it's all very nice, but on the other hand it destroys both the social structure and the human relations indirectly created when we strolled along Main Street or in the public square.

The use of energy also has repercussions on the fertility of the soil. Energy permits us to make quantities of nitrogen fertilizers. As a result, the plants having the potential to use nitrogen from the atmosphere no longer do so if they are given large amounts of fertilizer. They no longer make the effort.

So by bringing in outside energy we prevent all kinds of adaptive phenomena: the adaptation of the body, the adaptation of the senses to perceive things, the adaptation of the land, the adaptation of plants to take nitrogen from the air. We introduce massive laziness. I repeat, I'd like all these problems to be studied in terms of their interrelationships, rather than one by one. Instead of saying, "Let's make energy and use the energy," we should think about the fact that when we use energy excessively, we stop doing a great number of things necessary to our well-being. Since I've no doubt that we'll manage to produce all the energy we need (all sorts of techniques exist that will enable us to do so), the major problem will be the pertinent use of energy.

For the conference on the environment held at Stockholm, Barbara Ward, a famous English economist, was asked to write a book that would serve as a working paper for the entire conference. She's an extremely brilliant economist. But when she finished the book, she wasn't satisfied. So I was asked to collaborate with her, and, together, we wrote *Only One Earth*. This English economist had lived in Africa for many years, but what she wrote applied to the earth in general. As for me, I discussed the rest. And everyone says that it's impossible to distinguish what she wrote from what I wrote. By a lucky bit of chance, our two writing styles fit together perfectly. Yet she and I made very different contributions. If you look at any one chapter, you'll see that some assertions are worldwide, but also that particular stress is placed on the fact that each of us belongs to his own country, possesses a certain culture and a certain approach toward life, and develops certain needs that differ from the needs of people from another country with a different culture. I'm the one who added those particular points to each chapter. They reveal one of my deepest concerns, and in synthesizing them I came up with a very simple formula. In fact, I used it as the title of a lecture I gave in New York City and of an article I wrote recently: "Think globally, act locally."

Students always want me to talk with them about the problems of pollution in a general way. And I reply each time, "If you haven't already made it a practice to clean up your campus and the gutters on your own street, don't try to deal with pollution as a worldwide problem."

But to get back to the developing nations, I want to say first that if a disaster occurs somewhere in the world, I definitely want an effort to be made to help the endangered populations. But I'm against a policy of systematic aid as it's conducted today. Sending American wheat to Lima, Peru, is nonsense. The rural Peruvians leave their land, come to Lima, and end up abandoning their farms. I think the result is disastrous. It seems to me that the problems of the developing countries should be handled differently for each nation. Let each of these countries find the needed formula. We can, of course, help each of them to find the formula that best fits its needs.

Let me return to a problem of enormous importance: the tropical forest. This is certainly a global problem, because if the tropical forests are destroyed, all sorts of climatic and other ecological consequences will affect the entire world, consequences that can be rather accurately predicted. In addition, we shall witness the destruction of species that may be necessary for the equilibrium of our planet. We must dare to tell the people who are destroying their forests, "Stop! The consequences may be too serious." But on the other hand, we Europeans and Americans are in a poor position to tell the Brazilians or the Malaysians, "Don't destroy your forests," for one or two thousand years ago in the case of the Europeans and three hundred years ago for the Americans, we destroyed our own forests for the sake of wealth. We must provide these people with technological aid—and we're in a position to do so—

that will help them reforest immediately, as they gradually exploit the forest. We're quite aware where the major problem concerning the tropical forest lies: as soon as the forest is cut down, the soil becomes totally worthless as a result of the climate and other factors, so that nothing will grow there any more. So I see this as a possible role for the world community. It should help the developing countries in the tropical zones to use their forests intelligently and help them to replant the tropical forest as it's being cut down. But I'm opposed to the disastrous approach that simply says, "We'll help the sub-Saharan countries by sending them food or any other foreign-made item," without seeing that this really is no solution at all, since once we stop helping them they'll be just as impoverished as they were before and even more so. In fact, we've already stopped sending them things! So we must help the sub-Saharan peoples to organize their production methods and their grazing methods, so that a viable system can be established there.

But that's very difficult, because our societies present themselves as models and also because these developing countries are captivated by the mirage of the modern world and want to construct extremely sophisticated hospitals before they even set up elementary sanitation systems or else want to construct atomic reactors or computers before they know how to use the tools adapted to their country. So both sides encounter extraordinary difficulties.

The solution involves a revision of our concept of things, and I summarize what should be done by repeating, "We must think globally but act locally." This formula, I repeat, is applicable not only to developing countries but to the United States and other industrialized nations. I find it ludicrous to go to a large American university, where the students want to talk about a whole bunch of issues involving worldwide pollution, and then go out into the street where pollution is right before my eyes.

When I retired nine years ago, I was asked to teach in two universities. One was part of the New York State system, the other was part of the New York City system. I seemed to be a big success. But I was a "big success" in a way I found extremely dangerous. The students saw me, at the end of my life, working on very general problems and making observations about every discipline, be it social, medical, or scientific. Immediately they wanted to do the same thing, to come to grips from the start with problems on a worldwide scale, without being willing to work before thinking. Yet I'd tell them every day, "I want to stress that for forty years I was the most disciplined microbiologist possible, and not until I realized that I'd mastered that discipline could I permit myself to look at it from the outside." But they simply wouldn't accept my explanation. I believe that from then on I began to feel that I was a bad influence on them. Because my courses were going too well, I gave up teaching and from then on gave no more courses of that sort. This attitude may seem a marked contradiction to everything that I've been saying, but on the contrary it's right in line with my thoughts. When you believe that, above all, the most indispensable thing is to view problems in terms of their interrelationships rather than in terms of the elements they're made up of, it means that you must first be very familiar with these elements. If not, you're just jabbering. I know that if I'd continued to teach, my influence would have been a bad one—no, a dangerous one. Young men—more than young women, by the way—were attending lectures about any broad subject without having first mastered with any precision even a bit of that subject.

I believe, and I've often said so, that social transformations never occur through the initiative of existing governments. Not the government in Washington, not those in the European capitals, nor anywhere else. They always occur within a community, within a group that's independent from the existing administrative units. This pattern results in astonishing outbursts, because this sort of independent initiative develops under the influence of a few very strong personalities and also through the intermediary power formed by the press and television—the mass media, to use today's term. The vigor and rapidity with which these decisions and changes can occur, without government intervention, is truly phenomenal. I'll give you an example that's almost a caricature, yet perfectly true.

Three years ago two Harvard professors announced that they had scientific reasons to believe that the fluorocarbons used in numerous spray cans were destroying the ozone layer found in the upper atmosphere, which is indispensable to life on earth. I believe that this so-called destruction of the ozone layer has not yet been proved, but their statement was immediately taken up by the press and television, and the reverberations were astonishing. At that point people began to assert that ultraviolet rays were going to increase on the earth's surface, with all the dramatic consequences imaginable. Well, believe it or not, in less than two years the purchase of spray cans using fluorocarbons decreased by half, and a dozen firms had marketed other spray cans to replace those said to be so dangerous!

Another example concerns the war in Vietnam. In the space of three or four years—independently of government decisions, of course—the nation refused to participate in the war, and this phenomenon took on extraordinary dimensions. This shows, in my opinion, that in very complex societies—and all our societies are complex—it's illusory to hope that change will come from the established government units.

About ten years ago the directors of a very large brewery, a huge company with considerable capital, asked me to advise them during some studies on the effects of breweries on the environment. They intended to and did construct a very large brewery where the ecological conditions were very special. I didn't work with them very long, but all the same I got to know them well enough to ask the company president one day, "Who gave you the environment religion?" He replied, "Oh, it's very simple. I have two children, sixteen and eighteen, and each of the members of my board of directors has children between sixteen and twenty. All day long our children would ask us, "What's the company doing for the environment?" This is a very typical example. As far as the environment is concerned, the ideas generated among young people have achieved changes in the policies of big businesses far more profound than government directives could ever have achieved. Government directives only come later! I believe that phenomena of this sort are gradually occurring in almost every field. At the moment we see religious groups—Protestant, Catholic, Jewish—and student groups and citizen groups of all sorts putting pressure not only on banks but also on large universities not to invest their money in South Africa. And now these organizations are telling them, "Not only should you stop investing, but you must pull your money out of South African businesses!" Of course an official government position exists, but public opinion is far more powerful. And I believe its power is gradually increasing.

I'd like to give you one final example in which I personally played a part. It happened at Jamaica Bay, Long Island, a large bay on the outskirts of New York City and adjacent to Kennedy Airport. To expand the airport, which was overcrowded, they planned to extend the runways out over Jamaica Bay. Technologically the plan was extremely easy to carry out. When the decision was announced, a great commotion broke out in New York City. Numerous groups—not just ecology groups but citizen groups as well—wanted to save Jamaica Bay. The governor of New York State therefore asked the Academy of Sciences to conduct an inquiry into the ecological consequences of extending the runways over the bay. At that point I made a public statement to the effect that the Academy of Sciences didn't have to spend two years on an inquiry, for people already knew how much the bird population would be upset, the climate modified, and so forth. This statement was immediately snatched up by one of the leading New York newspapers. This drew attention to my "speech," and then a group of people formed—I don't even know how it happened—and held a meeting at Jamaica Bay for all sorts of people. The organizers saw to it that one of the biggest television networks was present, and they asked me to speak. They managed to take my picture with my arms in the air, just as a large flock of birds was flying over one of my arms and a jet over the other. I seemed to be saying, "If you let jets come in, you'll have no more flocks of birds." The next morning my photo was on the front page of the *New York Times*. That's all I did, absolutely all. Well, the *New York Times* is naturally very influential, so the next morning the governor stated, "We don't need an inquiry by the Academy of Sciences after all, and no runways will be constructed over Jamaica Bay."

This completely true story is a good illustration of how spontaneous reform never comes from the established institutions. On the other hand, once public opinion has clearly and forcefully taken a position, everything becomes possible.

Liberty is something that can't exist per se, and here's why: No organism—be it an animal, a human being, or a society—no living organism exists solely as an entity. An animal or a human being also exists and above all exists to the degree that it forms a part of a whole. In like manner, the social group is a part of a larger whole. So existence necessarily implies constraints. Liberty, you see, means collectively accepting certain constraints. Which boils down to saying that you shouldn't look at something for itself alone: you should see it only in terms of the relationships that it forms with everything else. This is the precept that has guided me throughout my life, from childhood to this very day.

# Discovering America

THE SMALL NUMBER of Englishmen who founded the Virginia Company in 1607 and who landed on Plymouth Rock in 1620 have been followed by some forty-five million men, women, and children who came from all over the world to settle in the United States. I am one of these old-fashioned immigrants, one of the Europeans for whom the simple phrase "the New World" acted as a catalyst that made me cross the Atlantic because it conjured up a land of absolute freedom and unlimited possibilities. I was twenty-three years old when I first landed in New York in October 1924—half a century ago. I had then no plan for the future, no job in view, not even a student visa, just the hope for adventure—any kind of adventure.

Although my life has long been completely identified with the American scene, intellectually and emotionally, I feel compelled at the end of these fifty years of residence to stand back and look at my adopted country as if I were a stranger—which obviously means that I am still somewhat of a stranger. I am even tempted now and then to engage in the game so popular among travelers and new settlers of defining what is American about America. But I shall limit myself to a few remarks concerning the urge that brought millions of people, including me, to the New World, and also concerning the differences that I still detect between Europe and the United States. More accu-

"The Despairing Optimist" column, The American Scholar, vol. 43, no. 4 (1974), pp. 544–50.

rately, I shall take this half-century landmark as an excuse to speak about a few of my early American experiences.

I have often been asked, and ask myself even more often, why I left Europe with the definite intention of settling in the United States. While I cannot give a clear answer to this question, I know at least that my move was not motivated by the desire to escape from a hostile environment or from a difficult situation. I had received a fairly extensive and successful education in Paris and had worked happily for two years on the editorial staff of the International Institute of Agriculture in Rome. I loved the physical and human atmosphere of Western Europe and could have functioned in it successfully.

While growing up as a child in the French countryside, however, I had read with passion the *Aventures de Buffalo Bill*, which were then published as a weekly magazine; I could not imagine a more exciting life than roaming on horseback over the Great Plains and the Rocky Mountains. I was also a devotee of the stories about the American detectives Nick Carter and Nat Pinkerton; their feats in combating the criminal elements of American society had familiarized me with what I then imagined to be the downtown atmosphere of New York, Chicago, and San Francisco. Later, in Paris and in Rome, I assimilated anything that came my way concerning the technologic and economic possibilities of North America. Although I had no clear idea of what these possibilities were, I was nevertheless eager to take my chance at them.

As I now realize, this distorted and fanciful introduction to American life was not peculiar to me. I participated unconsciously in the collective utopian dream of countless Europeans who imagined America as a land of complete liberty and material abundance, where people had been freed once and for all from the social shackles and economic restraints of a despotic, tired, and depleted Europe. The New World had a more real existence in my reveries than on the map. When, in October 1924, I boarded the old steamship *Rochambeau*, which took me in ten days from Le Havre to New York, I was not escaping from the Old World or searching for a new social philosophy, but simply attempting to convert into reality my daydream about the New World.

In ways that I could not have foreseen, chance has helped me to fulfill some of the expectations that motivated me to cross the Atlantic, but in a much more diversified way than I had imagined. To my chagrin, however, my acquaintance with the Rocky Mountains has been gained from trips by train, automobile, and airplane, rather than from adventures on horseback. Although the greatest adventures of my

American life have been sedate and sedentary, some of my most pleasurable memories are of the countless trips that have taken me repeatedly to each of the fifty states and also over most of Canada.

In 1927, before moving from Rutgers University in New Jersey, where I had taken up graduate studies, to the Rockefeller Institute for Medical Research (now Rockefeller University), where I became a laboratory scientist, I had the chance to travel by train over most of North America, acting as interpreter for the International Congress of Soil Science organized to visit agricultural experiment stations and typical soil formations in the United States and Canada. My first overall view of the continent was therefore from a traditional Pullman car. Ever since that time, the immensity of the continent has been registered in my mind as a kind of moving picture orchestrated with the lonely call of the American trains clicking off the miles. In my mind, this call was not suited to crowded settlements—as is the call of the European trains—but to the solitudes of a wild continent.

The experience of this long railroad trip has helped me understand the peculiar satisfaction that many Americans find in being constantly on the move. There is, in fact, a biological basis to the appeal of migratory life. The Stone Age hunters followed the seasonal migrations of wild game, a practice that may be at the origin of the great dispersals of mankind during prehistory and history. The colonization of the whole of North America in less than three centuries constitutes the most recent example of massive movement of people. Since the "winning of the West" will probably be the last of the great dispersals of mankind that began in Africa, the concept of the open road may well turn out to be one of the most characteristic features of American history, and perhaps its most romantic aspect.

In 1930 I spent the summer vacation driving from New York to the Northwest Pacific coast. Crossing the continent on dusty or muddy log-crossed roads in an old car was then a strenuous enterprise, but one that helped me to recapture my childhood imaginings and give them substance. The Far West was then only half-tamed, and I had no difficulty recognizing Buffalo Bill's holy hunting grounds in Nebraska and Wyoming; I could also worship at his grave on Lookout Mountain in Colorado. Along the Snake River Valley in Idaho, the rows of poplar trees and the greenness of the irrigated farmland reminded me of the French countryside, but the friendly casualness of the human contacts in crude eating places and primitive overnight cabins made me experience a way of life different from anything I had known in Europe, and in most cases quite congenial to me. From the Snake River, I proceeded to the Columbia River and eventually had my first glimpse of the Pacific Ocean from a high elevation among the huge trees of an evergreen forest. This was the completion of my personal discovery of America, and I have wished ever since that fate had made me settle somewhere on the Northwest coast. The phrase "Oregon Trail" still has for me rich overtones of adventure and romance; it symbolizes experiences that go back to the great migration through which mankind colonized the whole globe.

Like other French people of my generation, I began developing a global view of the earth in the 1920s while reading books such as Paul Morand's *Rien que la terre* (Only the Earth). I am amused by the fact that half a century later, I coauthored with Barbara Ward a book with a similar title, *Only One Earth*, prepared for the United Nations Conference on the Human Environment, in Stockholm. While the two books are, of course, very different, they both have in common the theme that in some respects the earth can and should be understood as a global village. On the other hand, I also believe that we are now beginning to witness a revival of regionalism that will complement the global point of view.

While it is obvious that North America and Western Europe now share the same scientific technology and to a large extent the same economic and social problems, I still perceive in the United States a vibration and a mood that makes the New World a social entity very different from the Old World. As Mexico's diplomat and author Octavio Paz remarked, "The word American designates a man defined not by what he has done but what he wanted to do." The novelist Thomas Wolfe also expressed the view that America was to be known not so much for what it is as for what it could become: "The true fulfillment of our spirit, of our people, of our land is yet to come."

Despite what Peter Schrag writes in his recent book, *The End of the American Future*, I believe that the urge for adventure and an almost physiological need to initiate new projects are still powerful components of the American ethos. Moving constantly in the academic as well as the technological world, over the whole continent, I find everywhere immensely vigorous people far more interested in change than in stability, more concerned with processes than with products. This dynamic attitude creates a national spirit of place that transcends the still strong and growing regional loyalties.

The psychological attitude toward landscape is one of the aspects of the national spirit of place by which the New World differs from the Old World. A sense of nostalgia is commonly the basis of psychological needs for a certain type of environment. Most normal human beings yearn to experience the environmental qualities they associate with a golden age or at least with a past they revere. For many Europeans and Asians, this feeling of nostalgia is identified with antiquity and with the great historical periods, as revealed by the influence of classical styles in the design of buildings and parks, and even in the management of nature. Such historical influences are, of course, also detectable in American life, but environmental nostalgia in the United States turns especially to experiences derived from a more recent past.

The pre-colonial occupation of North America by Indians left few permanent structures; furthermore, it had little impact on the ways of life of the white settlers. Consequently, the environmental nostalgia of Americans, especially of those descended from the early settlers who cleared the land, rarely goes further back than the eighteenth and nineteenth centuries. The heroic age of America cannot be antiquity or other classical periods, as is the case for Europe or Asia, but the short period—a century ago—that saw the clearing of the primeval forest, the breaking of the prairie, the winning of the West. The memories of this adventurous and turbulent past probably explain the tendency in the United States to identify the word "nature" with wilderness, and the pervasive longing among many Americans for life in the wild.

In practice, the wilderness is now more a subject of conversation than of direct experience. There is little if any primeval forest or other forms of wilderness left east of the Rockies, and not much on the Pacific coast. Except for earnest campers and forest rangers, few are the Americans who really come in direct contact with untamed nature. But their nostalgia for wilderness expresses itself in the way they manage nature. The people of France and Italy emphasize formal design in their private gardens and in public landscape architecture. English people cultivate a picturesque seminatural atmosphere. In contrast, North Americans commonly prefer their nature to be rather wild; they maintain the rough and the unpruned even in their most humanized landscapes.

Qualitative differences between the Old World and the New World may have been produced even with regard to systems of transportation by the rapid spread of immigrants from the Atlantic to the Pacific coast. In Europe travel means chiefly going from a particular place to another, either to visit a scenic area or, more commonly, to see a famous building. In contrast, moving for the sake of moving became very early a widespread behavioral pattern in America. This trait probably has its origin in the fact that instead of settling more or less permanently on the land they had cleared, as was the case for the Old World peasantry, a large percentage of American people continued to move in search of better lands or places of business. From Walt Whitman's "The Open Road" to Jack Kerouac's *On the Road* a century later, American literature has constantly given glamour to human restlessness—whether motivated by the desire to escape from sedentary life or by the search for new experiences.

The cultural conditioning for mobility certainly influenced the history and development of American railroads and highways. Much was being written in Europe a few decades ago about certain famous trains such as the Orient Express, the Trans-Siberian, the Flying Scotsman, and the Blue Train, but the stories concerning them emphasized the romantic adventures of political intrigues taking place in the compartments rather than what could be seen of the countryside from the train windows. In contrast, the various American railroad companies operating between the Middle West and the Pacific coast used to compete by advertising the scenic wonders along their routes. In our times, several of the most famous American highways seem to be designed not so much for convenience and speed of transportation as for making available to the traveler the most spectacular aspects of the landscape. The hobo riding the rails is a picturesque and typically American symbol of the desire to be on the move, regardless of the destination.

In America, travel is, thus, often an end in itself, a value for its own sake. But being constantly on the move, taking to the open road, has become more and more commonly a social form of escape. In *On the Road*, Kerouac expressed the beatnik's horror of taking roots anywhere for fear of having to accept the constraints of society. The line "Where are we going, man? I don't know but we gotta go" speaks to all those who wish to escape—and who does not want to escape from social constraints at certain moments of his life? This longing for motion is far different from the desire to travel as a tourist for the sake of experiencing a pleasant or new sensation. It is different also from the urge that motivated 45 million people, including me, to migrate to the United States because they believed they were coming to the land of abundance and freedom.

In our times, boredom or economic reasons certainly motivate in part the enormous mobility of the American population, but this is not the whole story. As President Franklin Roosevelt told the conservative Daughters of the American Revolution, "Remember, remember always, that all of us, and you and I especially, are descended from immigrants and revolutionists." People of action and people with a purpose were probably at the origin of the American passion for travel, and for many of their descendants mobility is still associated with a sense of purpose and an eagerness for action.

Benjamin Franklin also was taking an activist view toward social and geographical mobility when in 1784 he published, both in French and English from his private printing press in Paris, a pamphlet entitled *Information to Those Who Would Remove to America*. In America, according to him, even poor people can "buy land sufficient to establish themselves," and artisans are always eager to receive apprentices and even to pay them while giving them training. "In America," Franklin told the Europeans with pride, "people do not inquire concerning a stranger, 'What is he?' but 'What can he do?' "

Speaking from my own experience as an old-fashioned immigrant, I believe that what Franklin wrote two centuries ago is still largely true today.

# Joie de Vivre vs. Happiness

YEARS AGO I jotted down a remark that G. B. Shaw is asserted to have made concerning the healthy and prosperous, yet disenchanted, young adults whom he saw in England during the second quarter of the twentieth century: "They've got enough food, sexual freedom, and indoor toilets. Why the deuce aren't they happy?" This remark amused me as a succinct expression of the obvious truth that there is more to happiness than material satisfaction. It interested me because I have often wondered what the signers of the Declaration of Independence had in mind when they listed the pursuit of happiness among the citizen's inalienable rights.

I have also found it puzzling that the expression "joie de vivre" has been adopted into English and other languages, as if the French had copyrighted the pleasures of life. There may be a point in using the words "sputnik" and "bulldozer" in all main languages to acknowledge that the Russians were the first to orbit an object around the earth and the Americans the first to use powerful earth-moving equipment on a large scale, but joie de vivre has been a universal human experience since the beginning of time.

"The Despairing Optimist" column, *The American Scholar*, vol. 46, no. 4 (1977), pp. 424–30.

My curiosity about the expressions "happiness" and "joie de vivre" has been recently intensified by their frequent use in discussions concerning the quality of life—an ill-defined concept that is now assumed to provide a philosophical basis for the development of the industrial world and in particular for the formulation of environmental policies.

The French again are style setters in the way they have used language to associate environmental problems with the quality of life. Whereas all countries have distinct technical departments and administrative agencies to deal with pollution, crowding, natural resources, and other aspects of the total environment, all these concerns were, until recently, represented in France at the highest level of government by a full-fledged Ministère de la Qualité de la Vie—as if the quality of life could be achieved by governmental edict.

In North America, the medical professions seem eager to take the responsibility that the French government had vested in a cabinet ministry. They have recently organized several symposia called "Medicine and the Quality of Life," apparently with the thought that physicians have professional qualifications, not only for the maintenance of health and the management of disease, but for advising on circumstances conducive to happiness as well. They are also attempting to express, in dollars and cents, the effects of the various medical interventions on the quality of life, so as to incorporate this value into formal cost-effectiveness analyses of medical practice. The assumption by physicians that they can put a price on the quality of life and advise on its achievement hardly seems justified in view of the fact that the rates of suicide, alcoholism, drug addiction, and other social difficulties are higher among them than among comparable professional groups.

Whether one is concerned with the environment or with medical care, joie de vivre and happiness are certainly two of the values that contribute to the quality of life, but what these values are cannot be readily discovered from dictionaries or encyclopedias. Since definitions are not likely to be of help in such subtle concepts, I shall take the matter into my own hands and explicate what the expressions "joie de vivre" and "pursuit of happiness" mean to me, and how I shall use them here in discussing what determines the quality of life. In so doing I behave, of course, like Humpty-Dumpty affirming in *Alice Through the Looking-Glass*, "When I use a word . . . it means just what I choose it to mean—neither more, nor less." My justification for being arbitrary in this matter of meaning is that the vagueness of the expressions "joie de vivre" and "happiness," as commonly used, goes hand in hand with our uncertainty about the elements involved in the quality of life.

I have not found the expression "joie de vivre" in any of the few standard French dictionaries at my disposal, even though its meaning is far from self-evident. The *American Heritage Dictionary* translates it as "carefree enjoyment of life," a definition that certainly does not go far enough and is almost misleading. For example, it does not do justice to the subject of the novel that Émile Zola wrote under the title *La Joie de vivre*, and for which he had written an elaborate explanation.

The novel is the story of rather mediocre provincial people, victims of the usual sufferings and participants in a few tragic events. One of the striking passages occurs when a maid commits suicide for trivial reasons and her master, on hearing the news, exclaims, *"Faut-il être bête pour se tuer"* (You have to be really stupid to kill yourself). This remark is crucial to the story because the master is an old man, completely paralyzed and helpless, and one might assume that his own life was hardly worth living. Zola clearly wants to convey the message that it is stupid to destroy one's own life, whatever its conditions, because, in his words, "La joie de vivre est . . . l'immense desir de vivre qui soutient l'humanité *malgre ses larmes et sa souffrance, malgre l'angoisse de la mort"* (italics mine). The immense desire to live does indeed persist in mankind, despite tears, sufferings, and thought of death. This persistence accounts for the fact that, paradoxical as it may sound, joie de vivre is compatible with Unamuno's tragic sense of life—the awareness that all moments of life, even the most joyous, are clouded by the knowledge that death is inevitable.

Few are the human beings who do not regard life as a good thing in itself, whatever its miseries and despite the fact that it must end. Attempts at suicide are rare; many of them are carried out with the hope that they will fail, and indeed are a call for help. The one fundamental experience is to feel life pulsating in one's own body, almost irrespective of what one does with this unique attribute.

This is apparently what Albert Schweitzer tried to convey by the expression that has been translated into English as "reverence for life" and into French as *"respect de la vie."* According to a recent biography of Schweitzer by James Brabazon, neither the English nor the French translation does justice to the original German text, *"Ehrfurcht vor dem Leben,"* which has semimystical overtones of fear before an overwhelming force—of awe before the immensity and power of life. Repeatedly, Schweitzer emphasized that the most elemental perception is not the *cogito* of Descartes, but the very awareness of existence. In his words: "The most immediate fact of man's consciousness is the assertion 'I am life which wills to live, in the midst of other life which also wills to live.' " For him, reverence for life did not mean protecting every living form under all conditions, but rather apprehending the force and continuity of life, as it permeates the vastness of nature.

The sheer ecstasy of existence is, of course, most obvious in the simple well-being that results when life flows through the body in harmonious relationship to the rest of creation. Joie de vivre is, then, a purely biological experience, enchantingly manifested in the playfulness of a kitten, a puppy, a lamb, or a foal during the early spring, and in the relaxed attitude of a cat stretched in the sun or near the heat of a fireplace. Movements like running and climbing are as essential a part of development in young primates as they are in human children; strenuous physical exercise is joie de vivre expressing itself through the motions of the body and the delights of exploring the external world.

The essential factors of biological joie de vivre exist in every human being because they are inscribed in our genetic code. In fact, this aspect of life has probably not changed significantly since the Stone Age. Sophisticated as we may be, we still derive some of our most elementary and also most profound satisfactions from the events of everyday life—when we eat, drink, play, and love; when we participate in the life of our social groups, either as actors or spectators; when we enjoy the spectacles of nature or simply engage in daydreaming. Today, as in the distant past, young people hunger for emotional and sexual experiences; aged people relish comfort and quietness; people of all ages are sustained by awareness of their biological existence.

One can recognize carefree joie de vivre in its almost pure biological form among human populations living under primitive circumstances, even among the most underprivileged classes of industrial societies—wherever people relax in the sun, play with their children, enjoy the company of their friends, or participate in communal activities.

The purely biological enjoyment of life can, in addition, evolve into a more subtle experience of universal fellowship with all other human beings and even with other forms of life. It derives from the subconscious feeling that humankind is an entity in which the living are bound to the dead and also to the unborn—a sympathy that may even extend to the rest of creation.

Ever since the Stone Age, and in all parts of the world, human beings have expressed their awareness of solidarity with other forms of life through ceremonies and festivals that integrate the social group by incarnating experiences and aspirations shared by all members of the group. Rites are not anthropological oddities; they are events that symbolize the past of the community and the vision it has of the future, as well as the way it relates to the forces of the cosmos. The effects of tribal rites are reinforced by the conventions of everyday life. In this regard the most useful members of the social group are not necessarily those who increase its knowledge or productivity but rather those who facilitate its biological and communal existence by a reassuring and optimistic attitude that generates the collective joie de vivre.

Joie de vivre involves the organism as a whole, and perhaps the body even more than the mind; it persists throughout life, though at different levels, since it is fundamentally the perception of biological existence. There are other aspects of the quality of life, however, that involve social and personal values and therefore transcend biological criteria. The word "happiness," vague as it is, seems to denote better than any other word the nonbiological values of the quality of life, those that are conditioned by a person's responses to the environment. When considered in this light, happiness is inevitably transient—an expression of the interplay between the person and the environment, both of which are forever changing.

Admittedly, happiness is commonly assumed to be a gift from heaven, almost a passive state of bliss, but this assumption does not fit the facts. In reality, happiness is not a gift; it has to be won. Instead of being a passive state, it depends on acts of will and commonly involves struggle against hostile circumstances. This is why the signers of the Declaration of Independence wisely referred not to happiness itself but only to the inalienable right that each citizen has to pursue happiness in his own way.

Etymologically, the word happiness has the same root as happening, and it therefore implies being involved in some enterprise. Furthermore, its first two definitions in the *Unabridged Oxford Dictionary* refer to success in that enterprise:

1. Good fortune or luck in a *particular affair; success* and *prosperity.*

2. The state of pleasurable content of mind, which results from success or *the attainment of what is considered good.*

The italics in these definitions are mine. I have introduced them to emphasize that happiness, far from being a passive state of bliss, is the result of reaching a particular goal or completing a worthwhile task.

When considered in this light, happiness is conditioned not so much by biological determinants as by highly subjective social and personal values. It may involve painful choices that are not based on biological necessity and may indeed have dangerous biological consequences.

The choices that lead to happiness are rarely made in an attempt to find happiness. In fact, the wise men of Buddhism, Judaism, and Christianity, and many philosophers in all ages, have taught that we cannot find happiness by seeking it. We can hope to find it only by becoming involved in some enterprise that has a value of its own, independent of its effects on our own individual life. What, then, are the enterprises from which we can hope to derive happiness as a by-product? There are as many answers to this question as there are views concerning the quality of life, and these answers differ from social group to social group, from person to person. For example, the quality of life does not mean the same thing to a European peasant operating a small family farm, a Texas rancher engaged in large-scale agribusiness, a performing artist hungering for the applause of his public, a monk worshiping God in the silence of a monastery.

The more evolved the social structure in which they live, the more human beings are likely to be concerned with the future instead of deriving their satisfaction from the world around them. Paradoxically, the future we imagine is often more important for us than the present conditions we experience. For this reason daydreaming may be one of the states most likely to bring happiness.

The dreams of a particular person or society are often more significant than reality in deciding choices and courses of action. At a given time in its historical development, a society may be so eager for economic growth that it will hardly notice murky skies and polluted rivers. The pageantry of nature, the song of birds, the fragrance of flowers will be less important for its happiness than the hope of a prosperous future. This state of mind was prevalent in the United States and in Japan during the periods of industrial expansion in these two countries, and it is the official attitude today in many developing countries that are eager to raise their economic level. For the immense majority of people everywhere, environmental quality becomes a conscious determinant of happiness only after the dream of economic security has been fulfilled and the hope for greater prosperity is no longer imperative.

Happiness thus refers primarily to what the society and the person want to do and to become—almost regardless of biological considerations, of comfort, and of physical well-being. Prosperity is the goal for some people, fame for others, and complete independence for still others, as it was for Dostoevsky. "Man only exists for the purpose of proving to himself that he is a man and not an organ stop," he wrote. "He will prove it even if it means physical suffering, even if it means turning his back on civilization." For certain artists and scholars, giving expression to their genius is the only worthwhile goal. "Work is more important than life!" Katherine Mansfield confided to her journal as she was dying of tuberculosis. "I want to be all that I am capable of becoming, so that I may be . . . a child of the sun." Being a child of the sun means different things to different people. For some it means capturing the atmosphere of a sunset in a poem or converting a sunrise into splashes of paint on a canvas; for others it means developing reflectors to generate solar energy; and for still others it means returning to a Polynesian way of life.

Some people are so intensely concerned with what they do that they regard symptoms of illness as a contribution to their happiness if these symptoms are associated with greater creativity. "Six weeks with fever is an eternity," Honoré de Balzac wrote. "Hours are then like days . . . and the nights are not lost." When Jean-Paul Sartre was told that he was endangering his health by dosing himself with amphetamines to accelerate his work, he answered, "What is the use of health? . . . I am happier writing a long book which is well structured and which I consider important than I am in remaining in good health." Happiness can thus be found in the sacrifice of one's biological existence on the altar of ideals that are conceived in the soul rather than experienced in the flesh.

The quality of life is such a personal value that it cannot be institutionalized. However, society and medicine can contribute to it by providing conditions for good health and good environments— conditions that are obviously favorable to joie de vivre and to the pursuit of happiness. Social and medical experts can often give useful advice about the expected effects of certain attitudes and courses of action, but they cannot formulate rigid criteria for health and environmental quality because opinions about the good life are not uniform and are forever changing.

In the design of human settlements, for example, it is fairly easy to formulate criteria for sanitation, comfort, and efficiency, but it is impossible to create environments that satisfy the tastes of all social groups. Some of the so-called "new cities" of Great Britain are quite successful from many points of view, but the young people living in them get bored simply because their daily life does not offer them sufficient challenge. In Harlow, for instance, many of them commute to London in order to participate in solving the social problems of the slums. Thus an environment must not only be good in its physical characteristics; it must also offer people a diversity of possible ways of living and possible areas of social involvement.

What we mean by good health also changes from time to time and from place to place. Obesity was a respected symbol of bourgeois success a century ago but is no longer fashionable. People of all ages now make desperate attempts to control their weight, partly for reasons of health and aesthetics, but partly also because slimness is socially desirable. Another example: The criteria of physical and mental health are different for a young Jewish woman who aspires to success as a fashion model in Paris or New York and for another woman of the same age who elects to live in a pioneering kibbutz in the Negev desert. For most people, in fact, health does not mean so much the absence of disease as the ability to conduct life according to personal choices and social conventions.

This behavioral view of health helps to define one way in which medicine can contribute to the quality of life. Inevitably, all forms of organic and mental disease interfere with people's ability to play a desired role and to reach desired goals—an interference that amounts to a loss of freedom. They go to a healer—that is, any member of the health profession—in the hope of recovering this lost freedom. Even when the disease cannot be cured, the healer can often help the patient to function in a fairly normal way, either by drugs and other forms of medical technology or by advice based on a knowledge of human nature. Bear in mind that "to heal" does not necessarily imply "to cure." It can mean simply helping a patient to achieve a way of life compatible with his own aspirations, even though his disease continues.

This caring (as against curing) aspect of medicine can enhance joie de vivre—the biological satisfaction derived from the mere fact of existence, irrespective of what one does with one's life. It can also help in the pursuit of happiness—living in accordance with individual values that usually transcend biological criteria. It can therefore contribute to the quality of life, which includes both joie de vivre and the pursuit of happiness.

# A Celebration
# of Life

AS I LIE HERE in a hospital bed in my eighty-first year, I am more convinced than ever that life can be celebrated and enjoyed under the most trying and humble of circumstances.

I know that I have enjoyed most periods of my life and I am under the impression that I have always loved the world. I first became aware of this biological joie de vivre at the time of partial recovery from a severe disease contracted between ages seven and eight that has conditioned the rest of my life.

I must have been a vigorous and lively boy, since I was able to engage in bicycle races with other boys of my and neighboring villages. I once won the race but returned home in a state of extreme perspiration. Within a few days I developed a severe sore throat, which was followed by extremely severe rheumatic fever. This resulted in a heart lesion (in the aortic valve), which is still obvious now and has always prevented me from engaging in strenuous games or even running. I now realize that my sore throat was certainly caused by a hemolytic streptococcus infection which was then extremely frequent and commonly led to heart disease. I had to stay in bed almost motionless, suffering from the acute joint pains caused by rheumatic fever, but as much as the pains I now remember the loving care of my mother, who

*United Magazine*, April 1982.

attended to my needs during any time she could spare from her responsibilities in the butcher shop.

After being kept indoors for several months, I was allowed, on a beautiful sunny day, to take a short walk in the village—accompanying my mother, who went to buy milk from a farm not far from our house. This walk was one of the most important events of my life.

The stretch of street from our house to the farm was at best ordinary and dull, but on a sunny day and after I had been indoors so long, it appeared to me as an enchanted world. The few people we saw, probably fewer than ten, seemed to me a crowd and made me feel that contact with human beings other than my family was an immensely exciting experience. I then fell deeply in love with the world of things and of people and have remained in love with it even though I have always been handicapped by the heart lesion associated with this early experience of joie de vivre. From then until now, I have known that simply being alive is the greatest blessing we can enjoy.

The disarray and disenchantment so common in the technological societies of our times reveal the extent to which many of us fail to take advantage of this innate ability to appreciate the simple wonders of life. Abundance of goods, physical comfort, and control of disease are clearly not sufficient to bring about individual happiness and harmonious social relationships.

Everywhere in the countries shaped by Western civilization, the amenities of existence are threatened by environmental degradation and existential nausea. The mounting roster of material and psychological problems creates the impression that humankind has lost control of its affairs. The deteriorating conditions in our cities, our adversarial relationship with nature, the futile occupations that waste our days are—unnecessarily and unconsciously—determined more by technological imperatives than by our choice of desirable human goals.

To rediscover our innate celebration of life, the first obstacle to be overcome is the widespread belief that things are now going from bad to worse and that little can be done to reverse the trend. Countless expressions that reinforce this defeatist mood can be found in the writings of economists, sociologists, and environmentalists.

Certainly great tragedies do exist in the world today. Paradoxically, however, much contemporary gloom comes not from actual tragic situations but from the prospect of social and technological difficulties that have not yet occurred and may never materialize. We are collectively worried because we accept the highly inaccurate predictions that if demographic and technological growth continues at the present rate, the earth will soon be overpopulated and its resources depleted; food shortages will be catastrophic; pollution will alter the climate, poison the environment, rot our lungs, and dim our vision. I believe, as do many others, that industrial civilization will eventually collapse if we do not change our ways—but what a big *if* this is.

Human beings inevitably alter the course of events and make mockery of any attempt to predict the future from an extrapolation of existing trends. In human affairs, the logical future, determined by past and present conditions, is less important than the willed future, which is largely brought about by deliberate choices made by the human free will. Our societies have a good chance of remaining prosperous because they are learning to anticipate, long in advance, the shortages and dangers they might experience in the future if they do not take technologically sound preventive measures.

A key to overcoming the passivity born of pessimism is to remember that the really important problems of our times are not technical. They originate in our thoughts, our uncertainties, or our poor judgment concerning parascientific values. Unclear values allow us to accept the possibility of nuclear war for reasons of national prestige when every sensible person knows that the inevitable result of nuclear warfare would not only be immense suffering for human beings and immeasurable damage to every living and inanimate thing on earth, but also the virtual collapse of Western civilization.

Poor value judgment also leads us to ignore an already existing tragedy, the greatest pollutant of our peacetime world—youth unemployment. Because they are not given the opportunity to function in normal society by being meaningfully employed, young people are organizing themselves into social groups of their own. Their struggle for their inalienable rights will inevitably lead to disastrous social conflict.

Yet there is no reason to wallow in despair. The success of several public and privately financed youth conservation programs leaves no doubt that even delinquent youngsters can be reintegrated into normal society by being given the opportunity to do meaningful work. So, too, the fledgling peace movements here, in Europe, and in Japan are reminders that we can choose the world we live in by changing even these enormous threats to our existence . . . one step at a time.

How? By thinking globally but acting locally. This is the motto of the Center for Human Environments in New York, which bears my name. We have begun documenting stories of how single individuals have started movements that successfully changed the social and biological environments around them. Lakes, rivers, mine-adjacent land once given up for "dead" have been rejuvenated, as have the communities that flank them.

The Industrial Revolution placed a premium on the kind of intelligence, knowledge, and skills best suited to the invention of manufactured articles, as well as to their production and distribution on a large scale. In contrast, a really humanistic society will have to emphasize skills that facilitate better human relationships and a more creative interplay between nature, technology, and humankind. Such a society would prize joie de vivre and happiness over the achievements of power and the acquisition of wealth.

Happiness is contagious. For this reason its expression is a social service and almost a duty. The Buddhists have a saying about this commendable virtue: "Only happy people can make a happy world." Since optimism and cheerful spirits are indispensable to the mental health of technological societies, the most useful people may turn out to be those who, through empathy and happiness, have the gift of spreading a spirit of good will.

We are still on the way, renewing and enriching ourselves by moving on to new places and experiences. Wherever human beings are involved, social adaptations make it certain that trend is not destiny.

Life starts anew, for all of us, with each sunrise.

# PART II
# From Soil Ecology: The Antibiotics

Far from being hypnotized with the idea that micro-organisms are the only factors of importance in medicine, Pasteur knew that humans as well as animals, in health or in disease, must always be considered as a whole and in relation to their environment.

# The Capsule of the
# Pneumococcus

WHEN I ARRIVED at the Rockefeller Institute, my first impression was that the atmosphere of the laboratory of Oswald T. Avery was so peaceful that I had some doubt that there was much eagerness among the workers in the laboratory. I believe it took me at least one or two months to realize the manner in which Dr. Avery conducted his department. Dr. Avery never asked anyone to do anything. In fact, he almost urged people not to do too much. Of all the persons I have known in science, he certainly was the man who most was concerned with thoughts, long thoughts and meditations, before doing experiments, instead of the usual manner of rushing in and doing as much laboratory work as possible.

So that in practice, when Dr. Avery returned from vacation, hours and hours were spent for weeks doing nothing but talk. And in fact, it was chiefly Dr. Avery himself who did the talking. He would have each and every one of us in his office to review, in the form of conversation— not in the form of a systematic review, in the form of conversation—the problems that he had dealt with the year before and the problems he had thought about during his vacation, which he always spent on Deer Isle in Maine.

It is very difficult for me to remember what he talked about that

*Bulletin of the History of Medicine*, vol. 50, no. 4 (1976), pp. 459–77, transcript of an interview with René Dubos.

year, because everything was so new to me. All the occupations, preoccupations of the laboratory at the Rockefeller Institute were so completely different from that with which I was familiar that everything
seemed strange, and I can't remember now which thoughts stood out as
the most interesting or the most influential. However, it's certain that
my attention immediately was focused on some practical problems of
cultivation of the pneumococcus in the laboratory. Suffice it to say, the
pneumococcus, which was then the center of Dr. Avery's interest, or
the interests of his department, was very difficult to cultivate in ordinary culture media. Many of our experimental difficulties were due to
the fact that the culture media sent to us from the preparation room
often failed to give the growth that we expected. Very soon, through
conversation with other people in the laboratory and with Dr. Avery
himself, I became aware of that very simple technical difficulty—
growing the microorganism with which we were supposed to work.

In addition, Dr. Avery talked to me at great length of the work that
had been done the two or three years prior to my arrival by Dr. James
Neill, who had spent much time dealing with oxidation and reduction
processes in pneumococci.

It is important to remember that all the phases of Dr. Avery's
department activity that had to do with the pure methodological aspects of bacteriology were so new to me that I could not very well adjust
to them in operational terms. I had to learn the very words that were
being used, because essentially they were meaningless to me. However, Dr. Avery's conversations on Dr. Neill's work on the oxidation and
reduction processes dealt with an aspect of bacteriology with which I
was familiar, not only from the training I had received at Rutgers, but
more especially from my reading in the English *Biochemical Journal*,
where this area of biochemistry—namely, oxidation and reduction—
was being widely discussed. It was one of the most active fields of
biochemistry at that time.

Because the question of improving culture media was a very practical one that I could appreciate, and because Dr. Avery and Dr. Neill
talked about oxidation and reduction processes, I decided to undertake
the study of culture media as my first project. In fact, I probably never
made a formal decision. I just started doing experiments in this field,
because at that time those were the only experiments I knew how to do.
I could not experiment with immunochemical problems, because they
were too far removed from my experience.

The starting point of my experiment was this: It had been shown by Drs. Avery and Neill, some years before, that in culture media pneumococci gave rise to the production of hydrogen peroxide. Their findings further suggested that hydrogen peroxide, in certain cases, was toxic to the very pneumococci that produced it. So, for no better reason than that, I decided to set up some experiments removing oxygen from the medium to test the effect on the growth and viability of pneumococci. During these years, there was at the Johns Hopkins Medical School an investigator named William Mansfield Clark, who had gained great fame in the United States through a series of papers on oxidation and reduction processes, including the biochemical phenomena carried out by bacteria. Mansfield Clark had in particular introduced, as a technique, the measurement of oxidation and reduction potentials by observing the reduction of certain dyes that changed color from the oxidized to the reduced form.

There was available at that time a large series of dyes whose oxidation and reduction characteristics were known. These dyes had been made available to laboratory workers through the LaMotte Chemical Company, a very small company, which apparently must have been working in close cooperation with Clark, because I believe it disappeared as soon as interest in that line of work began to subside.

In any case, after reading Mansfield Clark's papers, I obtained from the LaMotte Company all the dyes that Mansfield Clark had studied, and I added them to the culture media that were then being used for the cultivation of pneumococci. I then observed what happened to these dyes when oxygen was removed from the culture medium. By the way, the advantage to all these techniques was that they were very simple once you had dyes made available to you by a commercial firm.

While carrying out these operations, I became aware of the fact that the ordinary culture media had the power to reduce the dyes when oxygen was removed from the environment. I carried out a number of experiments, which in retrospect were extremely crude but yet provided me with a fundamental piece of information—namely, that all culture media that were capable of growing pneumococci were also media that had a strong affinity for oxygen, since by themselves they were capable of reducing the dye when oxygen was eliminated from the medium. From this observation, through steps that I cannot remember now, I tested what the effect would be of the removal of oxygen on the growth of pneumococci, and to my great surprise found something which I believe I was the first one to find—namely, that pneumococci grew much more readily when oxygen was removed from the medium than they did when oxygen was bubbled through the medium.

In practice, that led me to the recognition that the factors determining the initiation of growth, the ability of the micro-organism to start multiplying in a culture medium, were different from those that determine the amount—the total amount—of growth that could be obtained in a certain medium. I came to realize that there was a dissociation between factors responsible for the initial multiplication of the organism (the ability of the organism to divide and therefore to multiply) and the factors that permitted the accumulation, within a given medium, of a very large number of cells. This is a point of view that has some importance, because I applied it much later to the cultivation of tubercle bacilli.

My attempts at growing pneumococci, and in particular attempts at initiating growth of a very small number of cells, led me to recognize that many of the ingredients used in the preparation of the culture media had in fact a toxic effect on pneumococci. Without having large practical or theoretical importance, this awareness led me to carry out purification of the peptones—commercial peptones—that were then being used, and to devise peptones of slightly better and different characteristics, which are still used in practice today.

But more important than these practical results was the fact that I became quite convinced that the phenomena controlling the multiplication of pneumococci were also applicable to all kinds of cells. I don't think that this point of view is yet quite generally appreciated, and I certainly have made little use of it myself. Most bacteriologists are likely to speak of a medium as a good medium, or a bad medium, or an indifferent medium, for the growth of a certain bacterial species. In reality, there are several independent characteristics of a medium that must be kept in mind. There are media that are very good for permitting a cell to start growing, but not satisfactory for obtaining large numbers of cells of the species under consideration. On the other hand, there are media that are not suited to the initial multiplication of a cell but which, if that cell can overcome the resistance offered by the medium, are quite satisfactory for obtaining very large yields of that particular cell. So if I were to use crude words to summarize a very complex situation, the circumstances, the environment, favorable to allow the beginning of the activity of a cell are not necessarily those that are best for permitting that cell to attain its maximum development.

This early phase of my work at the Rockefeller Institute gave me a chance to do a great deal of reading in biochemistry and establishing contacts with other workers in the field of biochemical metabolic activities of living cells. I obviously did not have a good enough training in chemistry to carry these studies very far from the technical point of view, but I had read so extensively in it that I was capable of discussing biochemical problems with other people, of incorporating them in my thinking. Soon enough, I realized that this was not my field, and I more or less abandoned it, although I came back to it later under certain circumstances when it became useful for my bacteriological work.

All this, I suppose, took me some eight months. During that time I was naturally in contact with other workers in Dr. Avery's department. By and large, these people had more medical interests; they were concerned with the behavior of the bacteria *in vivo*, or the reaction of the animal body, or the human body, to the presence of the bacteria. In other words, the center of interest in Dr. Avery's department was certainly immunology, immunochemistry, mechanisms of infection, problems of pathogenesis. And through conversation with the workers in Dr. Avery's department, and especially through an immense amount of reading, I soon became a fairly sophisticated immunologist and overcame my initial fear of the subject, fear that was due to lack of knowledge.

It must not be forgotten that the reason Dr. Avery had brought me to the institute was precisely to deal with one of these immunochemical problems. It is very likely that in the course of his endless conversations with all of us, he repeatedly brought back the problem to my attention, so that some time after eight months, I began orienting my interests toward immunochemical studies. And this brought me to deal with the very problem for which Dr. Avery had brought me to the institute.

Now the problem consisted in this: Dr. Avery and his associates had demonstrated that the virulence of pneumococci depended on the existence around them of a capsule made up of a complex polysaccharide. Dr. Avery had shown that this polysaccharide prevented the white blood cells from engulfing the pneumococci and destroying them. It was known, as a matter of fact, that there existed some forms of pneumococci that had lost this capsule and then rapidly became prey to the phagocytes and were destroyed by them.

What Dr. Avery had in mind was the possibility of finding a reagent, and if possible a fairly specific reagent, like an enzyme, that would be capable of removing, destroying, the capsule surrounding the pneumococci. Fortunately, the work of his department had led, during the preceding years, to the separation from the pneumococci of that capsular substance so that that polysaccharide was available in relatively large amounts and in a pure form in the laboratory. That amount consisted of several grams of purified polysaccharide of the various pneumococcus type strains.

This particular work had been begun in Dr. Avery's department, and carried almost to completion, by Dr. Michael Heidelberger, who had left the Rockefeller Institute and was then at the Presbyterian Hospital, where he eventually became professor of immunology. The work had also been continued by Walther Goebel, who was an immunochemist and was still associated with Dr. Avery and remained in the department as long as I did.

The important thing is that the capsular polysaccharide of pneumococcus was readily available in purified form. Equally important was the fact that there were exquisite, sensitive, and specific immunological techniques that permitted us to detect the presence or the absence of that polysaccharide, the technique depending on the fact that the polysaccharide reacted specifically in very high dilution with the serum of animals immunized against the pneumococcus. All these techniques had been worked out in previous years in Dr. Avery's department.

So in reality, the most important part of my retraining, from that point of view, was to become aware of the existence of this serological reaction for the detection of the capsular polysaccharide and of making use of it for searching for micro-organisms that could be capable of decomposing the polysaccharide. In fact, what I did was to start with the assumption that the polysaccharide of pneumococcus did not accumulate in nature. It disappeared. If it did not decompose, there would actually be mountains of it left, whereas it exists only where the pneumococcus grows—that's in the tissues of man—and then is eliminated in the urine and eventually disappears.

There did not seem to exist, in the tissues of man or animal, any enzyme that would decompose the polysaccharide. I made the assumption, pretty obvious now, I believe, that there did exist in nature bacteria or fungi or other micro-organisms that attacked the polysaccharide. The problem was merely one of finding where in nature there were bacteria or fungi capable of attacking the polysaccharide. The thought came to me that the polysaccharide produced by the pneumococcus probably was not unlike other polysaccharides existing in the soil under conditions where organic matter is deposited and has to be decomposed.

I began to select samples of soil and of sewage in the hope that one of these might contain some bacterium or some fungus capable of attacking the polysaccharide.

I then devised a culture medium, and that was really my personal contribution, in which the only source of carbon was the pneumococcus polysaccharide. Anything that could multiply in that culture medium had therefore to be something that attacked the polysaccharide, since that was the only source of carbon in the medium.

In practice what I did was to make a very dilute solution—one to a hundred thousand—of the capsular polysaccharide of pneumococcus (Type III), inoculate it with samples of soil or sewage, then place these mixtures under all sorts of conditions of oxygen, acidity or alkalinity, any environmental conditions that I could introduce as a variable. It was, in other words, really a kind of organized empiricism à la Edison. It was introducing all the possible variables that I could think of into a system where there was only one source of energy, one source of food— the polysaccharide capsule of pneumococcus.

Now, you will remember that I had a very exquisite way to test for the disappearance of that polysaccharide—namely, the ability of the polysaccharide to react with the serum of animals, rabbits or horses, that had been vaccinated against that pneumococcus. This was a highly specific reaction and a very rapid one that permitted me to trace in a few minutes whether the polysaccharide was still present or had been decomposed. Through this kind of organized empiricism I soon observed that in certain of the tubes the polysaccharide disappeared, and therefore I could readily assume that the polysaccharide had been decomposed by some bacterium or fungus.

The first positive series that I obtained was from a tube that had been inoculated with a sample of cranberry soil from New Jersey where a great deal of organic matter was undergoing decomposition. Now, having found a culture in which the polysaccharide was being decomposed, I devised other synthetic culture media still containing only the polysaccharide as a source of carbon, and I made many transfers into this medium, eliminating thereby anything that was not living either on the polysaccharide itself or on the breakdown products of that polysaccharide.

I finally obtained a culture in which the polysaccharide was decomposed even though I had heated the culture to 80 degrees Centigrade. Now, 80 degrees Centigrade is a temperature that will kill most of the bacteria or fungi—in fact, it will allow the multiplication only of those bacteria that produce those heat-resistant forms called spores. I finally had a crude mixture in which all the living things were resistant to heat and capable of decomposing the capsular polysaccharide. This limited the range so much that in practice there were only very few bacterial species to select in the mixture, and that made selection of them rather easy. Moreover, I even rendered selection more specific by having a specific culture medium, by refusing to use, at any time, any of the ordinary peptone media that all bacteriologists use, always insisting that my medium be so selective that very few kinds of bacteria could grow on it.

By the way, may I say that this is where I believe a person like Dr. Avery, or any of my colleagues in the field of medical bacteriology, could not have achieved what I achieved. In retrospect, I see that it was my earlier training—my earlier experience—with the development of media for culture of the pneumococcus that came to be useful. At that time I realized a good medium for my purpose was not one that gave a heavy growth, but rather a selective medium. So even though Dr. Avery urged me to enrich my media with peptones and sugars and with all the things that bacteriologists use, I steadfastly refused and selected a medium in which could grow only bacteria capable of attacking the polysaccharide of pneumococcus or of living on the split products of that polysaccharide.

Within an incredibly short time—the whole experiment didn't take me more than three or four months, as I remember—I obtained a pure culture that was capable of attacking the capsular polysaccharide of pneumococcus.

That was, I well remember, sometime in May 1929. I'm almost sure that I isolated the bacterium that decomposes the polysaccharide in the month of May. Now, Dr. Avery went on his vacation in late June. This certainly meant that he had little expectancy that this work would proceed very far during the summer. Otherwise he would have stayed.

After I had learned to grow the bacterium that decomposed the polysaccharide, I immediately tried to separate a soluble enzyme—the digestive juice, so to speak—through which the bacterium carries out the decomposition of the substances that it attacks. Here again, I was served with good luck. I decided that even though I obtained a very poor growth of the bacillus, I would grow it only on the capsular

FROM SOIL ECOLOGY: THE ANTIBIOTICS

polysaccharide. Since the amount of food was very small, the bacterium
went into the spore state, the protoplasm itself breaking down. I found
that when I filtered through a bacteriological filter, I could obtain a
solution that now was capable of decomposing the polysaccharide, even
though no bacteria multiplied in it. In other words, I had the enzyme.

Here again, I believe that my success was due to the fact that all the
time I used a very weak solution of the polysaccharide, which permitted me to detect its decomposition with the serological tests. In any
case, I did get an active solution that could decompose the polysaccharide.

At that time I did by myself animal protection tests; this was my first
venture in the field of animal experiments. It consisted simply in
infecting a mouse with the smallest possible dose of pneumococcus
Type III, which I knew would kill this mouse, and then immediately
afterward injecting into the mouse that filtrate, or enzyme, that I had
obtained, which was capable of decomposing the capsular polysaccharide of pneumococcus. Within about three or four weeks, I convinced myself that that filtrate was capable of protecting a mouse
against infection with Type III pneumococcus. I repeated the experiment several times on mice to be convinced of the phenomenon. These
experiments ran through July and August. By the month of August, I
had obtained a filtrate that, if injected into a mouse, would protect the
mouse against bacterial infection. That was a great achievement, since
nobody had ever been able to protect a mouse against infection except
with the classical technique of immunology by an antiserum.

After I had convinced myself of the validity of these experiments, I
wrote to Dr. Avery. He immediately returned from his vacation, and we
performed animal protection experiments under all sorts of conditions.
I must say these later experiments were far more carefully done. We
used a larger number of animals, calibrating the activity of the filtrate,
seeing against how many fatal doses of pneumococcus one could protect
a mouse, how late one could administer the enzyme, and even studying
the mechanism of the effect of the enzyme. By staining the blood of the
mouse, or its peritoneal exudate, one could see that the pneumococci
were attacked in such a manner that the capsule surrounding them was
being decomposed and then, when the capsule had been decomposed,
that the phagocytes would immediately engulf the pneumococci,
whereas these same phagocytes could not attack the pneumococci
when they were surrounded by their capsules. The experiment provided at the same time the most beautiful demonstration of the assump-

tion that the capsule protected pneumococci from destruction by phagocytes. It was the first demonstration that one could achieve a protective effect against infection by a substance, an enzyme, which attacked a well-defined component of a bacterium.

Dr. Avery and I completed these tests during the month of September. However, I must say that Dr. Avery's part and participation in the experiments was merely that of gilding the lily, because all the essential phenomena had been demonstrated by the time he came back from vacation. Nevertheless, when all the new tests were completed, Dr. Avery sent a paper describing them to *Science*, which we signed together, Avery and Dubos (see page 65). That paper produced a great sensation.

I think it's absolutely clear that I have an immense and abiding admiration for Dr. Avery. Yet I was grieved that he came back from vacation and put his name first to the paper, whereas I had considered that all the work was mine. It disturbed me very much because everybody was convinced that I had just been a pair of hands in Dr. Avery's laboratory and that everything had been Dr. Avery's work. The director of the hospital, Dr. Cole, for example, was convinced that all the work was Dr. Avery's. I resented that very much and was very upset. The endless letters of admiration for the achievement that Dr. Avery received from all over the world and showed me were, to say the very least, somewhat painful to me. It took me approximately three years to obtain a clearer view of this situation.

It's plainly obvious to me now that in reality the most difficult part of the experiment had not been in doing things but in imagining that one could affect the pathogenesis of pneumococcus infection by attacking a specific component of the bacterium. That idea was obviously not mine but Dr. Avery's. While I did introduce a certain originality in doing the experiment (by refusing to adopt the techniques that everybody wanted me to use), it's perfectly clear that the most original part of the work, the more difficult task of conceptualizing the problem, had been done before I came to the Rockefeller Institute.

This brings me to the last phase of my work with the capsular polysaccharide enzyme. In subsequent years we tested the effect of this enzyme on pneumococcus infection in rabbits, rats, and monkeys, and in every test our original findings were abundantly confirmed. These experiments did not introduce any new concepts, however. It was just doing the obvious things in immunology or immunochemistry. Fortunately some other aspects of the work developed that were entirely my own, and that perhaps have a greater interest than the possibility of attacking an infection by a substance directed against a specific component of a bacillus. I discovered that the bacterium that decomposed the capsular polysaccharide of pneumococcus grew very poorly on that capsular polysaccharide, whereas it grew very, very abundantly in the enrichment media that bacteriologists usually use, such as sugar, peptones, or proteins. At first it appeared that to produce the enzyme the only thing to do was to grow the bacteria in one of those media in which it grew abundantly. I soon discovered, however, that whereas the bacterium grew abundantly and rapidly in peptone solution, or in the presence of sugar, it did not under these conditions produce the specific enzyme. On the other hand, if the bacterium was grown in a struggling manner in the medium containing the capsular polysaccharide, it produced that enzyme. This phenomenon has since been duplicated many times by other workers. It brought me face to face with one of the most interesting biological set of facts I have ever seen—namely, that cells have multiple potentialities, and that these potentialities usually become manifest only when the cell is placed in an environment where it is compelled to use them. I am convinced that it is one of the most important biological laws that I have ever been in contact with, and I take a great deal of pride in the fact that I discovered it without anyone's help or advice.

Interestingly enough, just as I made my discovery a Finnish scientific worker, H. Karström, published a paper describing a similar phenomenon. Felicitously, he introduced a very good word for those enzymes that were produced by the organism only under circumstances when the organism had to make use of them, or needed them for survival. He called these "adaptive enzymes" as against, and in contrast to, "constitutive enzymes," which were the enzymes always produced by the organism. Clearly, the enzyme I had discovered was an "adaptive enzyme."

I think it's not without interest for the history of science that the fact that this Finnish worker (who, by the way, did a magnificent piece of work; it was his doctor's thesis), by introducing those two terms, "adaptive enzyme" and "constitutive enzyme," gained most of the credit for that discovery. The words were so good, so meaningful, that everybody associated the phenomenon with him. And in truth he discovered and well demonstrated it.

There were, in addition, other reasons why my discovery, although made and published a little earlier than that of the Finnish worker, was not recognized generally. I think that in part the lack of recognition was due to the fact that my papers were published in the *Journal of Experimental Medicine*, which is a journal that goes in the main to medical workers, so that that aspect of my work was known only through its application to medicine, not through its larger biological significance. His paper, on the other hand, was published in a biological journal concerned with general biological problems.

I do not want to imply, however, that I wasn't given any credit for my discovery, because soon after my work appeared, Marjorie Stephenson, of England, who was certainly one of the most respected biological workers in the world, devoted a rather long chapter in her book *Bacterial Metabolism* to my discovery of the multiple potentialities of cells that under normal circumstances remain hidden and only become apparent when the necessity arises for their manifestation. The fact, however, remains that the notion of adaptive versus constitutive enzyme is usually associated with Karström.

I was so delighted with my discovery that I immediately tried to develop it further, and I published two or three papers bearing on the mechanism of this phenomenon, showing that the cell produces the adaptive enzyme only when it produces new protoplasm as a response to the presence of that substance in the environment. Even though I struggled with the problem for three or four years, however, I couldn't carry it very much further. Now I realize that I couldn't have carried it further, because today many much better equipped scientific workers than I have been blocked by the same difficulties that I stumbled on. These difficulties rest on the fact that the solution of the problem bearing on the mechanism of the adaptive enzyme production involves two fields of knowledge that to date are still in the most primitive state. These are an understanding of protein synthesis (since enzymes are proteins) and an understanding of genetics (since the manufacture of an enzyme is controlled by the genetic makeup of the cell).

While I regret my failure, I have no reason to be ashamed of it, because not much has been added to this field since my early efforts, and what has been done has confirmed my early observations. Today the problem has been taken up again by Dr. A. M. Pappenheimer and Dr. Jacques Monod, both of whom are very well trained in chemistry and genetics. Perhaps a breakthrough in this problem will occur through their efforts.

## THE SPECIFIC ACTION OF A BACTERIAL ENZYME ON PNEUMOCOCCI OF TYPE III

A SYSTEMATIC search for enzymes capable of hydrolyzing the polysaccharides found in the capsular material of pneumococci of the various types has been carried on in this laboratory for several years. A number of enzymes from animal and plant sources, known to be active in the hydrolysis of simpler carbohydrates, were tested, but none of them were found capable of attacking the polysaccharides of pneumococcus origin. In addition, cultures of various moulds, yeasts, soil actinomycetes and bacteria, many of which were known to decompose cellulose, were tested without success. Recently, however, a bacillus has been isolated from the organic matter of soil taken from the cranberry bogs of New Jersey, which is able to split the specific capsular polysaccharide of pneumococci of Type III. The micro-organism is a pleomorphic, Gram negative bacillus, motile and spore-bearing. A detailed description of the special technique employed in its isolation and cultivation, together with a more complete account of its biological characters, will be given in a subsequent publication.

From cultures of this bacillus it has been possible to extract a soluble principle which, in the absence of the living cell, decomposes this specific carbohydrate. The decomposition of the specific polysaccharide is indicated by the appearance of reducing sugars in the hydrolyzed mixtures and by the simultaneous disappearance of serological specificity. The rate of reaction and the total amount of specific substrate decomposed appear to bear a quantitative relationship to the concentration of the active principle.

The active substance present in the sterile bacterial extracts is heat labile, being destroyed by exposure to a temperature of 60° to 65° C. It is extraordinarily specific in its action against the polysaccharide of pneumococci of Type III, since the capsular carbohydrates of the specific types of Friedländer's bacillus, and even those of pneumococci of Types I and II, are unaffected. The fact that the reacting substance is a product of living cells, that it is specific and heat labile and that its action seems to conform to the laws of enzymatic reactions strongly supports the view that the active principle is of the nature of a specific enzyme.

The addition of an active extract to media does not inhibit growth or cause lysis of pneumococci; however, organisms of Type III, when grown under these conditions, are not agglutinable in immune serum of the homologous type. That the *function* of elaborating the type-specific substance is not destroyed, however, is shown by the fact that pneumococci so treated continue to produce the capsular polysaccharide when transferred to a medium devoid of the active hydrolyzing agent. These two facts, namely, the decomposition of the specific carbohydrate removed from the pneumococcus cells and the hydrolysis of the specific capsular substance as rapidly as it is formed in growing cultures are evidence that the active principle is directed against this single, specific component rather than against the cell as a whole.

Previous studies on infection with pneumococci have led to the view that the invasiveness of these organisms is conditioned, in part at least, by the presence of the cell capsule. Since, early in the present work, the experimental evidence pointed to the fact that only the capsular material of the cell is vulnerable to the attack of this enzyme, it was tempting to determine whether the course of pneumococcus infection in a susceptible animal might not be favorably influenced by the injection into the animal of this specific enzyme. This possibility seemed more likely, since it was found that the activity of the enzyme *in vitro* is not inhibited or retarded by the presence of fresh animal serum. Repeated experiments with various preparations of sterile extracts containing the specific enzyme have demonstrated that the active principle has a distinct and specific protective action in mice experimentally infected with pneumococci of Type III. The protection afforded is type-specific, being effective only against pneumococci of this particular type. The protective value of the enzyme is destroyed by heating the bacterial extracts at 70° C. for 10 minutes. The capacity of any given preparation to protect animals against infection bears a definite relationship to its power to decompose the specific polysaccharide *in vitro*.

In addition to its protective action, the active principle has been found to exert a specific prophylactic and curative effect on experimental Type III pneumococcus infection in mice.

OSWALD T. AVERY
RENE DUBOS
HOSPITAL OF THE ROCKEFELLER INSTITUTE
FOR MEDICAL RESEARCH, NEW YORK

*This is the paper announcing the discovery of the enzyme that dissolves the polysaccharide capsule of Pneumococcus III. From Science, vol. 72, no. 1858 (Aug. 8, 1930), pp. 151–52. Courtesy of The New York Academy of Medicine Library.*

# The Biology of the
# First Antibiotics

ON AUGUST 3, 1857, Pasteur presented before the Scientific Society of Lille the first of his studies on the microbial theory of fermentation, *"Memoire sur la fermentation appelée lactique."* On this occasion, he expressed his belief that for each type of fermentation, one could find a specific ferment, characterized not only by its morphology and resistance to inhibitory substances, but also by its specific behavior as a chemical agent.

On December 21 of the same year, Pasteur announced at the end of his memoir on alcoholic fermentation that he had observed a new "mode of fermentation" that attacked the *d*-form of tartaric acid, but which was inactive against the *l*-form. Experimental details concerning this observation were presented on March 29, 1858; again in 1860 Pasteur reported that a mold, *Penicillium glaucum*, exhibited the same specific behavior toward tartaric acid, attacking the *d*-form and not the *l*-form. He pointed out that this selective fermentation afforded an easy technique for the separation of the *l*-tartaric acid from the racemic mixture, and that the method would probably be applicable to the separation of other isomers. He also emphasized that since "the character of dissymmetry of organic compounds can modify the chemical

New York Academy of Medicine, *The Harvey Lectures*, vol. 35 (1939–40), pp. 223–42. Copyright © 1939 by New York Academy of Medicine. Reprinted by permission.

reactions of physiological order," the phenomenon of specificity that he had observed was probably of great biological significance.

The very beginnings of experimental microbiology thus demonstrated the specific character of the biochemical reactions induced by micro-organisms, and suggested to biochemists and physiologists new techniques and new problems. It is hardly necessary to state that bacterial physiology has repeatedly confirmed Pasteur's views on the part played by microbial life in the economy of natural processes. If organic matter does not accumulate in nature, it is because countless species of micro-organisms hydrolyze it, oxidize it, and eventually break it down to carbon dioxide, ammonia, water, and mineral salts. We know, furthermore, that under natural conditions, each one of these microbial species is adapted to the performance of a limited, well-defined biochemical task. One may illustrate this statement by recalling the discovery of bacteria whose sole source of energy is the oxidation of ammonia to nitrites, of others that oxidize nitrites to nitrates, of still others that convert elementary sulfur to sulfuric acid, and so on. Several species of bacteria that readily decompose cellulose fail to attack cellobiose or glucose; there are micro-organisms that oxidize hydrogen, methane, petroleum, phenol, formol, and so forth. In fact, it can be stated that one can find in nature—in soil or water, for instance—micro-organisms capable of performing almost every possible type of biochemical reaction, many of which are not known to take place in the animal or the plant kingdoms. In many cases, the catalysts responsible for these reactions have been extracted from the microbial cells and have been found to exhibit a remarkable specificity. Because of their cellular origin, these catalysts are able to operate under physiological conditions (pH, temperature, etc.) and this property, together with their specificity, renders them ideal reagents for the analysis of biological problems.

It is apparent, therefore, that given enough time, patience, and skill, the bacteriologist can discover in nature microbial reagents adapted to the study of a great variety of biological problems. The few examples that will be considered in the following discussion have been investigated at the Hospital of the Rockefeller Institute; they have been selected because, in each case, new bacterial species were isolated from soil and active catalysis prepared from cultures of these organisms, in an attempt to discover reagents useful in the study of clinical problems under investigation in our hospital. It is perhaps justifiable, therefore, to emphasize that the facts here reported are not chance findings but are illustrations of a method that has a distinguished past in bacteriological chemistry and deserves the consideration of physiologists and biochemists. . . .

*The decomposition of the capsular polysaccharides of pneumococcus by bacterial enzymes.* Virulent pneumococci differ from the avirulent variants of the same bacterial species by the presence of a capsule surrounding the cell. Encapsulated pneumococci can be divided into a number of different serological types, and the type specificity is associated with differences in the chemical composition of the capsular material. The capsular substances of several types of pneumococci have been obtained in a reasonable state of purity, and all of them belong to the class of polysaccharides.

On the basis of immunological evidence, it appears, therefore, that the capsular polysaccharides of the different types of pneumococcus are of paramount importance in determining the serological specificity and conditioning the virulence of these organisms. It was felt that the evidence for this view would become even more convincing if one could obtain specific reagents—enzymes, for instance—that, by decomposing the capsular polysaccharides, would render the encapsulated pneumococci inagglutinable in the homologous antisera, and at the same time alter their virulence.

As far as is known, the capsular polysaccharides of pneumococci are not decomposed by enzymes of animal or plant origin, nor are they attacked by common species of bacteria, actinomycetes, or molds. It was possible, however, to isolate from soil a new bacterial species, a sporulating bacillus, which hydrolyzes the specific polysaccharide of Type III pneumococcus. A soluble enzyme, capable of catalyzing the same reaction, was separated from cultures of this soil bacillus grown under well-defined experimental conditions.

The enzyme depolymerizes the Type III capsular polysaccharide to the aldobionic acid stage. As a result of enzymatic hydrolysis, the capsular substance loses the ability to react *in vitro* with the specific antiserum obtained by immunizing experimental animals with the Type III capsular antigen.

It can be demonstrated by staining reactions that the addition of active enzyme to a suspension of living encapsulated Type III pneumococci causes the disappearance of the capsule; the specific agglutinability of the bacterial cells in the Type III antiserum is at the same time greatly impaired. It is important to mention, however, that the enzyme does not kill the bacterial cells; in fact, Type III pneumococci grow readily in media containing the enzyme, but they are deprived of their capsules. When the encapsulated cells are now transferred to a new medium not containing the enzyme, the capsule again reappears and restores to the pneumococci their full virulence and their agglutinability in Type III antiserum. It is clear, therefore, that the action of the enzyme is directed against the preformed capsular polysaccharide but does not affect the metabolism of the bacterial cell.

Enzymes capable of attacking the capsular polysaccharides of other pneumococcus types have now been obtained from different strains of soil bacteria. Several of these enzymes exhibit a remarkable specificity, and can differentiate between polysaccharides that give cross reactions in immune antisera; for instance, the polysaccharide of gum acacia, which reacts in Type III pneumococcus antiserum, is not affected by the enzyme that hydrolyzes the Type III polysaccharide. Even more striking is the difference between the enzymes attacking the polysaccharides of Type III and Type VIII pneumococcus. Both these substances are composed of glucose and glueuronic acid in different ratios, and because of this chemical relationship, they exhibit a certain amount of cross reaction in immune sera. On the contrary, the bacterial enzymes developed against each one of the polysaccharides fail to attack the other; in other words, the enzymes are even more specific than are the antibodies obtained by immunization of experimental animals.

Not only are the bacterial polysaccharides capable of hydrolyzing the capsular substances *in vitro*, but they exhibit the same activity *in vivo*. In fact, they can protect experimental animals against infection with virulent pneumococci. In view of the specificity that the enzymes exhibit *in vitro*, it was to be expected that the protection induced would also exhibit a specificity determined by the chemical nature of the capsular polysaccharide of the particular type of pneumococcus used for infection. In fact, experiments have shown that the enzyme that decomposes the Type III capsular substance can protect mice against infection with 1 million fatal doses of pneumococci of this type but is entirely ineffective against pneumococci of other types. The same polysaccharidase exhibits also a curative effect on the dermal infection of rabbits, as well as on the experimental pneumonia in monkeys of the *M. cynomologos* species, produced with Type III pneumococci.

The mechanism of the protection so induced is revealed by a microscopic study of the peritoneal exudate of mice during the course of infection with Type III pneumococci. The progress of events can be seen in photomicrographs that illustrate the differences in cellular reactions of treated and untreated mice two and four hours after injection of 1 million fatal doses of pneumococci. Two hours after infection, the peritoneal exudate of the untreated mouse showed numerous encapsulated cocci free in the fluid. In contrast to this, the pneumococci in the enzyme-treated animal at this time were devoid of capsules, and only naked bacteria were visible, many of which were already engulfed by leucocytes. At the end of four hours, the number of encapsulated pneumococci had increased in the peritoneum of the untreated mouse; in the treated mouse only an occasional decapsulated organism was seen outside the leucocytes, whereas many could be seen within the phagocytic cells. It is obvious, therefore, that the protective action of the enzyme lies in its capacity to decompose the capsular substance of the infectious agent.

In summary, three different tests have been employed to demonstrate the action of the polysaccharides: (a) decomposition of the purified capsular polysaccharides, with attendant loss of their specific precipitability in homologous antiserum; (b) destruction of the pneumococcus capsule, both *in vitro* and *in vivo*; (c) protection of experimental animals against infection with virulent pneumococci. All these reactions are type-specific. They confirm beyond doubt that the pneumococcus capsules consist of the specific polysaccharides and that the latter substances determine the serological specificity of pneumococci and condition their virulence. The polysaccharidases are neither bacteriolytic nor bactericidal; it is by destroying the protective capsules of the virulent pneumococci that they render the bacteria susceptible to the phagocytic action of the cells of the host and determine the recovery of the animal.

It is clear that two properties of the enzymes have made possible their application to the study of pneumococcus infections: (a) their specificity, and (b) the fact that they can function under physiological conditions. Microbial enzymes have also been used with advantage in studying the chemical nature of bacterial antigens, and there are many other biological problems the analysis of which would be greatly facilitated if enzymes specific for certain substrates were available. The addition of the test substrates to soil or sewage, for instance, will reveal in all cases the existence of micro-organisms capable of decomposing them. By isolating these microorganisms in pure culture from the natural sources, and growing them under appropriate conditions, it should often be possible to prepare enzymes adapted for use as specific physiological reagents.

*A selective bactericidal principle extracted from cultures of a sporulating bacillus.* The preceding discussion has considered the isolation from natural sources of micro-organisms capable of decomposing well-defined organic compounds (polysaccharides, etc.). It appeared possible that there also exist micro-organisms capable of attacking not only soluble, isolated substances but also the intact living cells of other unrelated microbial species. Specifically, an attempt was made to recover from soil micro-organisms that could attack the living cells of the pathogenic Gram-positive cocci. To achieve this end, suspensions of living pneumococci, streptococci, and staphylococci were added to a soil mixture, which was maintained at neutral reaction under aerobic conditions, in the hope that there would develop in the soil preparation a microbial flora antagonistic to the Gram-positive cocci. In fact, it was possible to isolate from the soil preparation an aerobic sporulating bacillus that can multiply at the expense of the living cells of Gram-positive bacteria. Cultures of this soil bacillus have yielded a soluble principle that kills the susceptible bacterial species.

The bactericidal principle of the soil bacillus can be obtained in a protein-free form that is soluble in alcohol and acetone but insoluble in water and ether. From the alcohol-soluble fraction there have been obtained as crystalline compounds three well-defined chemical entities, all of which exhibit bactericidal action *in vitro*; they have been called graminic acid, gramidinic acid, and gramicidin, with respective molecular weights of 900, 1,000, and 1,400. Although the complete structure of these substances is as yet unknown, it can be stated at this time that all of them consist largely of amino acids probably combined as polypeptides. Gramicidin, which has been the most carefully studied, contains two to three tryptophane residues per molecule; a large percentage of the other amino acids appears to be present in the *d* (so-called unnatural) form; gramicidin also contains an aliphatic fatty acid but contains neither free acid nor basic group. As stated above, the three crystalline substances exhibit a marked bactericidal effect *in vitro*. For instance, 0.005 mg of gramicidin is sufficient to kill $10^9$ pneumococci or virulent streptococci within two hours at 37 degrees Centigrade. Staphylococci, diphtheria bacilli, aerobic sporulating bacilli—in fact, all Gram-positive organisms so far tested—are also readily killed under the same conditions, although the amount of bactericidal substance required varies from one bacterial strain to another. On the contrary, none of the Gram-negative bacilli have been found to be susceptible, even to much larger amounts of the substance. Meningococci and gonococci are much more susceptible than the Gram-negative bacilli but more resistant than pneumococci or streptococci; this fact may be of some interest, since bacteriologists have often considered the Gram-negative cocci as intermediary between the Gram-negative bacilli and the Gram-positive organisms.

In spite of the great activity that they exhibit *in vitro*, both graminic acid and gramidinic acid appear ineffective *in vivo*. On the contrary, one single dose of 0.001 to 0.002 mg of gramicidin, injected into the abdominal cavity, is sufficient to protect mice against 10,000 fatal doses of pneumococci or streptococci. Larger amounts of the material, injected on three consecutive days, will also protect mice against larger infective doses or cure them of a well-established infection. The bactericidal substance has proved equally effective against infection with the five different types of pneumococci and the fourteen different types of hemolytic streptococci (groups A and C) that have been tested. It is permissible to hope, therefore, that it will also prove effective against all virulent strains of these bacterial species irrespective of type specificity. In fact, preliminary experiments have recently demonstrated that it does also protect mice against certain strains of staphylococci. On the contrary, as could be expected from the *in vitro* experiments, no protection could be obtained against infection of mice with *Klebsiella pneumoniae* (Type B), a Gram-negative bacillus.

Gramicidin is very insoluble in aqueous media; this insolubility may account for the fact that the substance is ineffective against pneumococcus peritonitis in mice when administered by any route (intravenous, intramuscular, subcutaneous) other than the intra-abdominal. Very recently, it has been possible to obtain from autolyzed cultures of the sporulating soil bacillus a form of the bactericidal substance that is readily soluble in water at neutral reaction. Not only does the new preparation cure mice of pneumococcus and streptococcus peritonitis when administered intra-abdominally, but it is also effective by the subcutaneous and intravenous route. Although much remains to be learned about this soluble fraction, it is evident that in some respects it is more effective *in vivo* than in the crystalline substance, which has been described under the name of gramicidin.

The findings just reported have revealed the existence and to some extent the chemical nature of a new type of bactericidal agent, which, although extremely active against many different species of Gram-positive micro-organisms, fails to attack the Gram-negative bacilli. It can be said, therefore, that this new bactericidal principle exhibits a specificity of a peculiar order, one that is correlated with the staining characteristics of the bacterial cells. Since the staining properties are necessarily conditioned by chemical and physical characters of a cellular structure, it is perhaps permissible to state that the specificity of the bactericidal agent is related to some structural difference between the Gram-positive and the Gram-negative cells. An analysis of the mechanism of the bactericidal action may therefore reveal important facts concerning cellular structure; this knowledge, in turn, may indicate what type of chemical structure can be expected to exhibit affinity for the cellular structure of the different bacterial species and may suggest new avenues of approach to the problem of antisepsis. It is also of obvious importance to establish the chemical differences between graminic acid and gramicidin that determine that only the latter is active *in vivo* whereas both are equally active *in vitro*. This knowledge will give us a clue to the factors that allow an antiseptic to remain active in the presence of animal tissues and thus render it a therapeutic agent.

Finally, it is permissible to hope that one will also discover in nature micro-organisms antagonistic to other types of pathogens and that the active substances by means of which they exert their antagonistic effect will be isolated. These agents may not themselves be effective in the animal body. An understanding of their chemical structure and of the mechanism of their action should, however, give the bacteriologist and the chemist useful information and new compounds for the development of chemotherapy on a rational basis.

*The adaptive production of enzymes by bacteria.* It is apparent that the biologist will discover in the microbial world a great variety of useful reagents. On the other hand, it is also true that microbial life has revealed a number of physiological processes of general biological significance. For instance, cultural conditions greatly affect the enzymatic constitution of the microbial cell. In some cases in particular, the production of a given enzyme is stimulated when the substrate which it attacks is a component of the culture medium. The bacillus that hydrolyzes the capsular polysaccharide of Type III pneumococcus does not form the specific enzyme when cultivated in ordinary peptone media (in which growth is very abundant), whereas the polysaccharidase is readily produced when the same organism is compelled to use the specific polysaccharide in the course of its growth. Karström (see pages 63–64) designated as "adaptive" those enzymes that are produced as a specific response to the presence of the homologous substrate in the culture medium. He differentiated them from the "constitutive" enzymes, which are always formed by the cells of a given species irrespective of the cultural conditions.

Adaptive enzymes exhibit a great specificity with reference to the substrates they attack, a property that suggests their use in the analysis of biological problems. It is of practical importance, therefore, to develop satisfactory techniques for their production. One may wonder also whether the readiness with which micro-organisms selectively change their enzymatic constitution in response to changes in the environment may not be of importance in determining the pathology of infectious diseases. Is it not possible that a pathogenic agent growing in living animal tissues may differ in important respects from the same agent grown in laboratory media? In other words, the pathogenic agent may produce during the infectious process a number of substances that do not appear during growth in the standard laboratory media and are the result of the reaction between the parasite and the tissues of the infected host. These products might account for some of the obscure reactions of infection.

In any case, the very mechanism of production of adaptive enzymes by micro-organisms challenges the bacterial physiologist; nothing is known of this mechanism. It seems established that the change in enzymatic constitution that results in "adaptation" does not necessarily require the production of new cells. Although production of adaptive enzymes has been described to occur in the absence of cellular division, all evidence available indicates that this formation always involves the synthesis of new protoplasm. It is possible that the synthetic process is, so to speak, oriented or guided by the chemical structure of the substrate, which thus determines the specificity of the enzyme evoked. And it is a common fact, as already pointed out, that adaptive enzymes exhibit a remarkable specificity toward the substrates that stimulate their production.

The phenomenon of adaptive production of enzymes offers great practical possibilities to the bacteriologist. Even more important, perhaps, it brings him back into the main channels of biological thought, to the biological problem "par excellence," the problem of adaptation. The study of the mechanism whereby micro-organisms produce those enzymes that appear as an adaptive response to the presence of the homologous substrates in the culture medium bids fair to throw light on some of the reactions involved in specific adaptation.

## 10395 P

## Bactericidal Effect of an Extract of a Soil Bacillus on Gram Positive Cocci.

RENÉ J. DUBOS.

*From the Hospital of the Rockefeller Institute for Medical Research, New York City.*

An unidentified spore-bearing bacillus, capable of causing the lysis of living gram-positive cocci, has been isolated from a soil sample to which suspensions of these cocci had been added over a long period of time. Autolysates of cultures of the soil saphrophyte have yielded a soluble factor which lyses living staphylococci, pneumococci (R and S forms, irrespective of type-derivation), hemolytic, green and indifferent streptococci (all types so far tested). The active principle is not volatile, does not dialyze through collodion membranes, and is heat-labile. It is very stable at alkaline reactions, is rapidly inactivated at more acid than 5.5, even at temperature. When the 0°C principle duced itated yme that hyd capsular te, charide of pneumococcus. As described in earlier stu this polysaccharidase does not in any way affect the viability of pneumococci; by decomposing the capsular substance, however, it renders the bacterial cells susceptible to destruction by phagocytosis.[1,2] The polysaccharidase does not attack the specific polysaccharides of other types of pneumococci, and consequently it protects only against infection with Type III organisms. On the contrary, the bacterial extract considered in the present paper inhibits the growth of all gram-positive cocci so far tested and exerts on them a bactericidal effect *in vitro;* its protective action *in vivo* has already been established against several different types of pneumococci and hemolytic streptococci. It is worth emphasizing again, however, that the extract does not affect the viability or inhibit the growth of gram-negative bacilli.

---

[1] Dubos, R. J., and Avery, O. T., *J. Exp. Med.*, 1931, **54**, 51.

[2] Avery, O. T., and Dubos, R. J., *J. Exp. Med.*, 1931, **54**, 73.

*This is the formal publication of the Dubos work that inaugurated the antibiotic era in medicine. Proceedings, of the Society for Experimental Biology and Medicine, vol. 40, no. 21, pp. 311–12. Courtesy of The New York Academy of Medicine Library.*

# Antibiotics and
# Infectious Disease

THE STARTLING RESULTS that have been obtained by the use of drugs in the prophylaxis and therapy of certain parasitic and bacterial infections have been heralded by many as the dawn of a new era in the control of infectious diseases. Although we can indeed confidently expect that the near future will see greater advances in the discovery and application of new chemotherapeutic agents, it must be emphasized that drug therapy constitutes only one facet of the complex problem of infection, and that its spectacular achievements and popular appeal should not lead to the neglect of the other aspects of the problem. The great strides that have been made toward the control of diseases caused by certain filterable viruses—such as agents of smallpox or yellow fever, bacteria like typhoid and diphtheria bacilli, animal parasites like hookworms and schistosomes—were the result of painstaking analysis of the epidemiology of these infections, of enlightened public health practices, and of the skillful application of immunity reactions. Chemotherapy had no part in these important achievements. There is no reason to doubt that in the future, as in the past, the control of infectious diseases will have to be based on a clear understanding of their natural history and of the many factors that determine the outcome of the host-parasite relationship. In the following discussion

*Proceedings of the American Philosophical Society*, vol. 88, no. 3 (1944), pp. 208–13. Copyright 1944 by American Philosophical Society. Reprinted by permission.

an attempt will be made to recognize some of the channels along which the study of the infectious process is at present engaged or could profitably be directed.

The discovery of the etiological agent of an infection is only one of the many steps in understanding the origin of a disease and in its description. The infectious process is the expression of a many-sided relationship between the pathogen and the host, and the complete analysis of this relationship requires a thorough study of its two components. It is for reasons of convenience only that we shall begin our discussion with a consideration of the parasitic agent.

Bacteria, and probably other micro-organisms, exhibit an extraordinary plasticity and can exhibit profound variations of their biological properties. Thus, a given parasite can exist in different states of virulence, and it is only when it is present in its most virulent form that it can give rise to disease and epidemics. Virulence, in fact, is an extremely complex property. In order to cause disease, the parasite must be able to reach the susceptible host; it must overcome the multiple defense barriers of humoral and cellular nature by means of which the body can rid itself of the many foreign substances that reach it; it must be able to multiply in the host and also do damage to it. Each one of these properties is an independent attribute of the micro-organism that can vary independently of the others, and no parasite can establish an epidemic state unless it possesses all these attributes at the same time. It will be sufficient to illustrate the complexity of the problem to consider some of the attributes that are required to render virulent the hemolytic streptococci of group A.

All streptococci isolated from pathological material are characterized by the possession of certain cellular constituents that can be demonstrated *in vitro* by the use of immunological reactions. Loss of these cellular constituents results in complete loss of virulence both for man and for animals, but, on the other hand, their presence is not sufficient to endow streptococci with maximal pathogenicity. In order to be fully virulent, these organisms must possess other subtle properties that have not yet been identified with any known *in vitro* reaction; furthermore, these unknown properties are apparently lost under all sorts of conditions, and particularly when the organisms are cultivated in artificial media. Although the nature of these elusive attributes of virulence is not known, it is possible to define and characterize some of them in terms of their manifestations *in vivo*. Thus, a certain strain of streptococcus can be highly invasive and cause a generalized bacteremia; it may produce a powerful erythrogenic toxin and cause intense scarlatina; one or more of its cellular constituents and products may produce severe febrile reaction and collapse of the host. Such highly pathogenic strains, however, may have only a low degree of communicability, or conversely, highly communicable organisms may produce little evidence of disease. All these factors vary independently of one another. To be capable of causing a severe epidemic, a given strain must possess several or all of the properties that have been considered, and probably others as yet unidentified.

The analysis of the factors of virulence is not only a problem of academic interest. It contributes to a better understanding of the cause and nature of the disease and, consequently, to its more intelligent management. From the more special point of view with which we are now concerned, moreover, an understanding of the factors of virulence provides some essential information for the description and prediction of epidemics and of their course. Thus, although strains of streptococci or of meningococci are constantly present in men grouped in military establishments, the presence of those pathogens is not necessarily sufficient to give rise to epidemics. The latter result from transformations in the micro-organisms that enable it to spread rapidly from one individual to another, from one station to another. What has been said of bacteria undoubtedly applies to filterable viruses. Much remains to be learned, for instance, of the circumstances under which influenza becomes epidemic.

There are, of course, many other factors that condition the establishment of an epidemic state. Among these can be mentioned variations in the general resistance and in the immunity state of the population, changes in the numbers and distribution of the vectors of the parasite, and so forth. Each one of these factors deserves the closest scrutiny, and it is only for lack of time that they will not be considered here.

As more knowledge becomes available of the many factors that condition the epidemic pattern of an infection, it will be easier to detect any qualitative and quantitative changes not only in the numbers of infectious agents present in the population but also in those properties of these agents that are concerned with virulence. This indeed is not an idle dream. There are already functioning organizations, national and even international in scope, that follow the occurrence of diseases like plague, cholera, influenza, and so on in different parts of the world. Unfortunately, enough accurate knowledge is not yet available to recognize in most pathogenic agents these changes that are significant for the development of epidemics. In order to illustrate the nature of the problem, however, a specific example will be presented, which, although it does not bear a direct relationship to the property of virulence, will serve to underline the importance of variability in micro-organisms.

It is known that bacteria susceptible to the sulfonamides can become resistant to these drugs when cultivated in media containing them. In fact, the development of drug-fastness has been recognized *in vivo* not only in experimental animals but also in human beings under treatment. There exists the possibility, therefore, that as a result of the widespread use of sulfonamides in therapy and especially for prophylaxis, there may develop in the population strains of pathogenic agents that have become resistant to these drugs. Although we have presented only a hypothetical possibility and although there is as yet no evidence of any real danger, the problem should not be ignored, and it is to be hoped that laboratories throughout the land will find it possible to maintain a permanent survey in order to follow the shift in susceptibility of the different pathogenic agents to the drugs in common use.

The understanding of the natural history of an infection and its epidemic pattern always suggests measures for its prevention and control. This has been the story of many of the enteric disorders, and it explains why, on the whole, these infections have been so effectively dealt with in well-policed countries. It is certain, however, that preventive and public health measures are not equally applicable to all types of infectious diseases and that all these measures break down under the stress of emergency situations—as, for instance, in times of war and other disasters. Whether preventive chemotherapy will ever become an advisable and effective practice is still a matter of conjecture. There is no doubt, on the other hand, that immunization can in many cases become an effective supplement to public health measures, as has been proved in the case of typhoid fever. It appears worthwhile, therefore, to consider briefly the trends in the development of immunization procedures.

Ever since the introduction of smallpox vaccination by Edward Jenner and the use of attenuated bacterial cultures by Pasteur, attempts have been made to produce a state of immunity in animals and in man by the injection of living attenuated avirulent germs. Vaccination against smallpox, yellow fever, plague, and brucellosis are outstanding practical achievements of this method. There are, however, obvious objections to the use of a living vaccine, since danger exists that attenuated cultures can regain their virulence under predictable conditions. Most bacteriologists, therefore, have preferred to use vaccines killed by heat or antiseptics, as is done in the case of antityphoid vaccination. Furthermore, the use of killed organisms permits preparation of the vaccines from cultures of the highest possible virulence, and there is a widespread belief that the more virulent the culture used in the preparation of the vaccine, the more effective it is as an immunizing agent.

The theory that cultures of the highest possible virulence are essential to the production of high levels of immunity is based on considerations—not all of them entirely valid—that cannot be presented at this time. In any case, it is a fact that in experimental animals, immunization with killed cultures of virulent pathogens can, under the proper conditions, elicit a high degree of immunity against the type of organism from which the vaccine was prepared. It must be emphasized, however, that this immunity exhibits an extraordinary specificity, since it does not protect against related organisms of another immunological type. Thus, mice immunized with a vaccine prepared from a certain type of pneumococci, streptococci, or dysentery bacilli are resistant to infection with bacteria of the same type but are still susceptible to infection with pneumococci, streptococci, or dysentery bacilli of another type.

Type-specific immunity has lent itself to the preparation of effective therapeutic sera. For the latter to be used successfully, however, it is necessary that the specific type of the organism responsible for the disease be established by adequate tests, in order to permit the selection of the proper serum. The preventive immunization of whole populations presents an entirely different problem. Under practical field conditions, pneumococci, streptococci, dysentery bacilli, and so forth exist in a large number of types, many if not most of which are capable of causing disease; there is, furthermore, no way of predicting the relative prevalence of the different types in any outbreak. Since it is a practical impossibility to establish an effective level of immunity against all different pathogenic types, there is reason to believe that immunization of threatened populations with type-specific vaccines is an impossible goal. It is not unlikely that the practical success of antityphoid vaccination may be due in part to the fact that in spite of minor differences, the strains of typhoid bacilli isolated from different outbreaks all possess essentially the same immunological constitution.

There exists, fortunately, a kind of immunity that transcends the limit of type specificity and is effective against all the strains of one given bacterial species. Thus it is possible to immunize experimental animals against pneumococcus infections under such conditions that the immune response is directed against a component of the bacterial cell that is common to all pneumococcus types. Similarly, one could probably find in all bacterial groups analogous cellular components, different from the type-specific antigens and capable of giving rise to non–type-specific protective immunity. Indeed, the effective immunity that follows the injection of attenuated nonvirulent filterable viruses or bacteria may well be due to the nonspecific protective antigens we are discussing, which persist in the micro-organism even after the factors essential to virulence have been lost. It must be acknowledged that the level of immunity achieved by nonspecific immunization is usually lower than that resulting from the injection of type-specific vaccines. Since, on the other hand, the attention of investigators has been focused almost exclusively on the latter substances, it remains possible that intensive investigations directed in the proper channels will lead to the development of improved methods of nonspecific group immunization.

Whatever the organism selected as immunizing agent, adequate techniques have to be devised to prepare from it an effective and safe vaccine. The methods that have been used heretofore are extremely primitive in their principle and consist in killing the pathogen with heat or antiseptics. The fact that in so many cases an effective state of immunity can be established by the use of killed bacteria or even killed filterable viruses indicates that the immune process is not directed against some mysterious living property of the bacterium or virus but rather against some chemical constituent of its structure. In fact, it has been possible in a few cases to identify the particular bacterial constituents concerned in the reaction, and it is important to emphasize in this respect that of the many various substances that constitute a microbial cell, only one or a very few are capable of eliciting the production of protective antibodies. Thus it is certain that a very large percentage of the total material injected in antityphoid vaccination has no value whatsoever in establishing the immune state and contributes only unfavorable reactions. The separation from the parasite of these singular cellular components that gives rise to protective immunity presents, therefore, great theoretical and practical interest. It is very likely that the use of purified antigenic preparations would tend to limit the untoward reactions that result from the injection of vaccines and would also permit a more accurate standardization of immunization procedures.

The preparation of purified antigens of bacterial origin suggests theoretical possibilities that haunt the dreams of the immunochemist. Since the immune process is directed against a well-defined chemical group, it is not beyond hope that the immunizing preparations of the future will consist of artificial materials designed to reproduce the immunological specificity of the pathogens we would like to control. Many steps must, of course, be taken before this aim is achieved. It is first necessary to recognize in the parasitic cell that particular substance concerned with the immunity reaction. This substance must then be isolated in pure form and its active radical identified before any attempt can be made to reproduce it by synthetic means. There is no prospect of any practical result in this direction in the immediate future, but the formulation of this goal serves to illustrate the view that, in the final analysis, the immune reaction is not directed against the infectious agent as a whole but rather against some of the specific chemical groups essential to pathogenic behavior.

It is interesting that three of the most important steps in the growth of chemotherapy are the results of accidental unrelated observations, a fact that makes it difficult to read in the history of this science any logical predictable trend for its future. Quinine was introduced as a specific for malaria long before anything was known of the parasitic etiology of the disease; furthermore, the mechanism of action of the drug is as obscure today as it was when cinchona bark was first introduced in therapy. The sulfonamides were originally used in the treatment of disease in the form of a red dye, protonsil, which has been since found to be inactive against bacteria. Fortunately, protonsil is broken down in the animal body to sulfanilamide, the substance that we now know to be responsible for the chemotherapeutic activity of the dye. Much progress has been made during the past decade toward an understanding of the mode of action of sulfonamides, but the next great achievement of chemotherapy—namely, the discovery of penicillin— came from an entirely unrelated accidental observation. A mold growing as a contaminant in the laboratory was found to inhibit the growth of certain microbial species and to release into the medium a soluble substance, penicillin, which exhibits its now so familiar chemotherapeutic virtues. Nothing is known to date of the mode of action of penicillin.

There is one basic fact that must be kept in mind in any attempt to formulate a rational approach to the problem of chemotherapy. Although we know of so few drugs that retain their antibacterial activity *in vivo*, bacteriologists have at their disposal a great variety of substances that exert a powerful effect *in vitro*. These antiseptics can be produced by the methods of synthetic chemistry or by a number of microbial agents, molds, actinomycetes, or bacteria. It is clear, therefore, that the difficulty is not in finding more and more antimicrobial substances but in defining that property or combination of properties that permits an antiseptic to retain its activity in the presence of animal tissues—to behave, in other words, as a chemotherapeutic agent. Although the facts known at the present time are too few to permit a statement in general terms, it is certain that the most effective chemotherapeutic agents do not behave as gross protoplasmic poisons that destroy the metabolic activity of all living cells but rather as selective inhibitors of some specific steps concerned in the nutrition, synthesis, or cell division of the parasites.

It is beyond the scope of the present discussion to consider the avenues of approach that are most likely to lead to the discovery of drugs useful in the treatment of infection. One may suggest, however, that the search for new chemotherapeutic agents should not be limited to the mere production by the methods of organic chemistry or from natural sources of more and more bactericidal substances, but that efforts should be made to determine what properties of a substance permit it to retain its antibacterial activity *in vivo* without causing irreversible damage to the host. Progress in this direction will depend in part on an increased knowledge of the steps of microbial metabolism for which there can be developed specific inhibitors exhibiting selective affinity for the parasite.

There is no apparent reason why the mere presence in the tissues or body fluids of any reasonable number of parasites of microscopic dimensions should exert any harmful effect on the host that harbors them. No mechanical theory of the pathogenic action of bacteria or filterable viruses is compatible with our knowledge of the way in which the tissues deal with the particles that have gained access to them. In the final analysis, the harmful effects of most infectious agents are chemical in origin. It is through a disturbance of the normal physiological process of the host that pathogenic organisms cause those symptomatic and pathological manifestations that characterize each individual infectious disease. In some cases it is possible that the parasite interferes with the normal physiology of the host by competing

with the latter for some factor essential to vital processes or by producing simple metabolic products that alter the course of the biochemical
events of normal metabolism. These possibilities have been so little
explored that they can be stated only in the most general terms. In most
cases, however, it has been established that pathogenic bacteria produce a variety of substances—the bacterial toxins—that are endowed
with great pharmacological activity and which are undoubtedly responsible for many of the clinical and pathological manifestations of each
infectious agent. It would be of the greatest interest, consequently, to
understand how toxins exert their physiological and pathological disturbances, since only then shall we gain an insight into the intimate
mechanism of infectious diseases.

Unfortunately, our ignorance of these problems is truly appalling.
Toxin action has been analyzed and described only in terms of the
secondary phenomena resulting in pathological and clinical manifestations. Much is known, for example, of the symptomatology and pathology of the toxemia caused by diphtheria, tetanus, and botulinus toxins,
but we know nothing of the primary biochemical or physiological
lesions for which these toxins are responsible, whether they act by
destroying tissues or cellular structures or by inhibiting essential metabolic functions. Knowledge of the initial reaction that takes place between the toxin and its susceptible substrate in the body would permit
a more accurate definition of the specific physiological functions that
are altered during the infectious process. This knowledge would contribute to the understanding of disease and would in the long run lead
to the development of specific therapeutic measures effective against
toxemia.

Our complete ignorance of the physiological basis of infectious
diseases is due in part to the fact that since the beginning of the
microbiological era, the study of infection has been almost exclusively
limited to the immunological aspects of the host-parasite relationship.
It is obvious, however, that not only the severity and the character of
the disease but even its very occurrence depend as much on the
reaction of the host as they do on the presence of the infectious agent.
Familial susceptibility to tuberculosis, to rheumatic fever, or whatever
is a well-recognized phenomenon, which has been confirmed experimentally by the breeding of selected lines of animals either highly
susceptible or highly resistant to a given infectious agent.

It is also known that obvious nutritional deficiencies can modify the
susceptibility to infection, and there is reason to fear, for example, that

an increase in the morbidity and mortality of tuberculosis will follow in the wake of the war in Europe. On the whole, however, very little is known of the relation of nutrition to resistance. Nor do we have any significant information concerning the effect of hormonal regulation on the course and outcome of the infectious process. The nature of the anatomical and physiological characters of the host that condition its response to the parasite is one of the most neglected and most important aspects of the problem of infection.

Because of the lack of the most elementary information, it is not possible to predict whether an understanding of the physiological factors of host resistance could ever be translated into terms of practical therapy. One could hardly doubt, however, that this knowledge would help and guide the physician in the understanding and treatment of the patient. Thus it is the present-day practice, based on a general statistical experience, to advise any individual showing evidence of incipient minimal tuberculosis to follow a severe routine of absolute bed rest. It is well known, on the other hand, that the course and outcome of tuberculosis varies greatly from one individual to another, and there is no doubt that the management of the individual patient would be greatly influenced if it were possible to predict the course of this disease under a given set of conditions. In other words, the whole policy of sanatorium treatment could be restated in more rational terms if it were possible to predict by adequate tests the expected response of a given individual to the tuberculosis infection.

The course of any science is often conditioned more by the availability of easy experimental methods than by the relative importance of the potential lines of investigation. There were developed early in the microbiological era a number of techniques based on serological and immunochemical reactions that are so rapid in their performance and have yielded such important and useful information that they have directed the study of infectious diseases along somewhat narrow channels. It is likely that by returning to the main channels of the biological and biochemical philosophy, the student of infection will achieve a more complete picture of the many reactions by which the host responds to the specific stimuli exerted by the parasite, and will thereby devise novel methods for the control of infectious diseases.

# Louis Pasteur:
# An Inadvertent
# Ecologist

TO VIEW Louis Pasteur's professional achievements gives one the impression that he led an enchanted life. His contributions to science, technology, and medicine were prodigious and continued without interruption from his early twenties to his mid-sixties. His skill in public debates and his flair for dramatic demonstrations enabled him to triumph over his opponents. His discoveries had practical applications that immediately contributed to the health and wealth of humankind. His worldwide fame made him a legendary character during his lifetime; he was, and remains, the white knight of science.

While writing Pasteur's biography a quarter of a century ago, I could readily document the fact that his extraordinary successes had been achieved at the cost of immense labor and against tremendous odds—including the stroke that paralyzed him on the left side at the age of forty-six. However, I felt I could also read between the lines of his public statements the frequent expressions of a melancholy mood, an intellectual and emotional regret at having sacrificed great theoretical problems to the pursuit of practical applications. Writing as if he had not been complete master of his own life, Pasteur stated time and time again that he had been "enchained" by the inescapable logic of his discoveries; he had thus been compelled to move from the study of crystals to fermentation, then to the then still debated hypothesis of the spontaneous generation of life, on to infection and vaccination.

One can indeed recognize a majestic ordering in Pasteur's scientific career. Yet the logic that governed the succession of his achievements was not as inescapable as he stated. At almost any point in the evolution of his scientific career, he could have followed, just as logically, other lines of work that would have led him to discoveries in fields other than fermentation and vaccination. Some of his actual remarks indicate that he was aware of the potentialities he had left undeveloped.

Early in his scientific life he predicted, for example, that a day would come "when microbes will be utilized in certain industrial operations on account of their ability to attack organic matter." Today, in fact, microbial processes are used on an enormous scale to produce organic acids, solvents, vitamins, enzymes, and drugs. In 1877, he observed that the anthrax bacillus loses its virulence when placed in contact with certain soil microbes, and he suggested that saprophytic organisms might be used to combat infectious agents. This was, of course, a vision of antibiotic therapy, more than sixty years before its actual beginning. Such lines of investigation, and others that he suggested, were within Pasteur's technical possibilities, and he could have followed them if he had had time. He had good reasons indeed to ask himself whether "the road not taken" might not have been the better road.

Many other aspects of his early scientific work continued to occupy his mind throughout his life and frequently surfaced in the form of casual remarks, suggestions for new lines of experiments, and prophetic views on the direction science should take.

The effect of environmental factors on the characteristics and activities of living things was a particular theme that he did not develop in his experimental work but that continually emerged in his writings. Here again one of his statements betrays regret at his not having followed his early hunches. He had entered the field of pathology almost by accident through his work on the diseases of silkworms. His first hypothesis had been that these diseases were nutritional and physiological in nature, but he eventually discovered that they could be controlled by protecting the worms against microbial contamination. However, despite the outstanding success of this control technique, he continued to believe that the resistance of the worms could be increased by measures that would improve their physiological state. In *Études sur la maladie des vers a soie*, he went as far as to state: "If I were to undertake new studies on the silkworm diseases, I would direct my effort to the environmental conditions that increase their vigor and resistance." The phrase clearly reveals an aspect of his thought that greatly intrigued him but that he did not have the time to convert into experimental work.

Even though Pasteur's name is identified with the "germ theory" of fermentation and disease—namely, the view that many types of chemical alterations and of pathological processes are caused by specific types of microbes—he was intensely interested in what he called the "terrain," a word he used to include the environmental factors that affect the course of fermentation and of disease. I now see more clearly than I did when writing Pasteur's biography that the magnitude of his theoretical and practical achievements derives in large part from the fact that his conceptual view of life was fundamentally ecological.

From the very beginning of his biological investigations, Pasteur became aware of the fact that the chemical activities of microbes are profoundly influenced by environmental factors. Furthermore, he developed very early a sweeping ecological concept of the role played by microbial life in the cycles of matter. During the 1860s, he wrote letters to important French officials to advocate support of microbiological sciences on the grounds that the whole economy of nature, and therefore man's welfare, depended on the beneficial activities of microorganisms. He boldly postulated that microbial life is responsible for the constant recycling of chemical substances under natural conditions—from complex organic matter to simple molecules and back into living substance. In a language that was more visionary than scientific, he asserted that each of the various microbial types plays a specialized part in the orderly succession of changes essential for the continuation of life on earth. Long before the word "ecology" had been introduced into the scientific literature, he thus achieved an intuitive understanding of the interplay between biological and chemical processes that brings about the finely orchestrated manifestations of life and of transformations of matter in natural phenomena.

Pasteur's ecological attitude can also be recognized in his repeated emphasis—to the point of obsession—on the fact that the morphology and chemical activities of any particular microbial species are conditioned by the physicochemical characteristics of the environment. He pointed out, for example, that molds can be filamentous or yeastlike in shape, depending on the oxygen tension of the medium in which they grow. He demonstrated also that the gaseous environment determines the relative proportions of alcohol, organic acids, carbon dioxide, and protoplasmic material produced by microbes from a particular substrate. Observations of this type give to the book in which he assembled his studies on beer (*Études sur la bière*, published in 1876) an importance that far transcends the practice of beer making. In that book he approached the problem of fermentation from an ecological point of view. By demonstrating that "fermentation is life without oxygen," he introduced the first sophisticated evidence of biochemical mechanisms in an ecological relationship.

The sophistication of his ecological attitude is perhaps best illustrated by his studies of butyric fermentation and of putrefaction. He noticed that the bacteria that produce butyric acid can function only in the absence of oxygen. When he preserved these microbes under the microscope, for example, he noticed that they were actively motile in the center of a drop of fermenting fluid but lost their motility at the margin of the drop where they were in direct contact with the air. He showed indeed that he could arrest butyric acid production simply by passing a current of air through the fermenting fluid. He established also that the evil-smelling decomposition (putrefaction) of meat or other products containing proteins was caused by microbes that functioned only when protected from the air.

The ecological attitude in Pasteur's laboratory certainly helped his associate Émile Duclaux, who eventually became director of the Pasteur Institute, to recognize that the enzymatic equipment of microbes can be modified at will by altering the composition of the culture medium. This was the first demonstration of a phenomenon that opened the way for discoveries on enzyme induction, and thus constitutes another fundamental link in the understanding of the ecological relation between environmental factors and biological characteristics.

Pasteur's recognition of the effects that environmental factors exert on metabolic activities is now incorporated into theoretical microbiology and technological applications. In contrast, his forceful statements concerning the importance of the terrain in infectious diseases have been overlooked, in part because he did not have time to support his intuitive views by systematic laboratory investigations, and perhaps even more because medical scientists continue to neglect this field, except with regard to the special approach that Pasteur himself had opened—immunological protection. Yet he had a sophisticated ecological concept of infectious processes, based on an awareness of the genetic and environmental parameters that condition evolutionary and phenotypic adaptations. This aspect of his biological philosophy can be illustrated with statements paraphrased from his writings.

Early in his work on disease, Pasteur recognized that it was a biological necessity for living things to be endowed with natural resistance to the agents of destruction ubiquitous in their environment. As he saw it, populations, of microbes or of men, usually achieve some sort of evolutionary adaptation to their environment that renders them better able to resist the causes of disease with which they often come into contact.

Furthermore, he took it for granted that the body in a state of normal physiological health exhibits a striking resistance to many types of microbial agents. As he pointed out, the body surfaces harbor various micro-organisms that can cause damage only when the body is weakened. In contrast, infection often fails to take hold even when antiseptic measures are neglected in the course of surgery. Indeed, human beings possess a remarkable ability to overcome foci of infection.

Pasteur's attitude regarding the importance of physiological wellbeing in resistance to infection had developed during his studies with silkworms. He had soon recognized profound differences in the pathogenesis of two diseases in these insects. In one, pébrine, the presence of the specific protozoan was a sufficient cause of the disease, provided the infective dose was large enough. In the other, flacherie, the resistance of the worms to infection was profoundly influenced by environmental factors. Among these, Pasteur considered that excessive heat and humidity, inadequate aeration, stormy weather, and poor food were inimical to the general physiological health of the insects. As he put it, the proliferation of micro-organisms in the intestinal tract of worms suffering from flacherie was more an effect than a cause of the disease. Here Pasteur was anticipating George Bernard Shaw's remark in the preface to *The Doctor's Dilemma* (1906): "The characteristic microbe of a disease might be a symptom instead of a cause."

Pasteur did not hesitate to extend these views to the most important human diseases. He accepted that resistance to tuberculosis was on the one hand an expression of hereditary endowment and on the other hand was influenced by the state of nutrition and by certain factors of the environment, including the climate.

In his words:

A child is not likely to die of tuberculosis if he is raised under good nutritional and climatic conditions. . . . Let me emphasize that there is a fundamental difference between the characteristics that define a disease—the disease per se so to speak—and the set of circumstances that increase susceptibility to it. . . . There may be more similarity than appears at first sight between the factors that favor pulmonary tuberculosis and those that are responsible for the spread of the flacherie disease among silkworms.

Again in his words:

All too often, the general condition of a person who has been wounded, his physiological misery, his poor mental state, are responsible for the fact that his body cannot offer an adequate resistance to the multiplication of microbes in the wound.

This point of view naturally led Pasteur to conclude that resistance to infection could probably be increased by improving the physiological state of the infected individual. He urged his collaborator Émile Duclaux to look for procedures that would increase the general resistance of silkworms. And he expressed the opinion that in man, also, successful therapy often depends on the ability of the physician to restore the physiological conditions favorable to natural resistance.

Although Pasteur thus had a clear view of the influence that the physiological state and environmental factors exert on resistance to infection, he did not carry out any significant experimental work in this area. He probably felt that in the state of scientific knowledge of his time, the more urgent task was to determine the specific causes of infection and to search for specific methods of protection. It is indeed certain that biological sciences in general and microbiological sciences in particular could not have gone far without the precise knowledge and the intellectual discipline provided by the concept of specificity. The time has come, however, when it would be profitable to follow more actively the other approaches that Pasteur visualized but did not follow—the physiological and ecological study of micro-organisms in natural systems and in pathological processes.

Pasteur's ecological philosophy had little influence on the practical policies he advocated for controlling the phenomena of fermentation and infection. When he discussed large theoretical problems in the light of ecological concepts, he professed that the activities of microbes are essential for the continuation of life on earth; he also suggested that microbes might safely coexist with animals and human beings if the infectious process took place under proper environmental and physiological conditions. In practice, however, he devoted most of his laboratory work to the development of practical techniques for the domestication or destruction of microbes. This dichotomy between conceptual theory and scientific practice can be partially explained by the climate of scientific and public opinion in the nineteenth century.

The germ theory was formulated at a time when many biologists and social philosophers believed that one of the fundamental laws of life is competition, a belief symbolized by phrases such as "nature red in tooth and claw" and "survival of the fittest." The ability of an organism to destroy or at least to master its enemies or competitors was then deemed an essential condition of biological success. In the light of this theory, microbes were to be destroyed, unless they could be used for some human purpose, as in desirable fermentations. Aggressive warfare against microbes was particularly the battle cry of medical microbiology and is still reflected in the language of this science. The microbe is said to be an "aggressor" that "invades" the tissues; the body "mobilizes" its defenses; the physician or the scientist is a disease "fighter" whose goal is to achieve the "conquest" of this or that infection.

As we have seen, Pasteur did not share the simple-minded view that killing and being killed are the only alternatives in biological relationships; indeed, he had perceived the ecological possibilities and advantages of peaceful coexistence. But he lived in a period when knowledge meant power used for the conquest of nature. It was during the nineteenth century that the findings of experimental science were for the first time converted into large-scale technological applications. Like his contemporaries, Pasteur identified progress with the use of science for achieving mastery over natural forces. As he was very much a man of his time, he focused most of his effort on the kind of scientific problems most likely to yield results of practical significance—for example, by helping in the "control" of fermentation and in the "conquest" of disease. For his public life, scientific progress meant the development of techniques such as sterilization, pasteurization, and vaccination, even though these practical lines of work prevented him from pursuing other questions that he considered of larger theoretical significance.

Scientists, like artists, unavoidably reflect the characteristics of the civilization and the time in which they live. In this sense, they are "enchained," as Pasteur complained he had been, by the inexorable logic of their time and their work. A few of the greater ones, however, have visions that appear to be without roots in their cultural past and that are not readily explained by direct environmental influences. These visionaries appear, indeed, almost as eruptive phenomena, seemingly unpredictable from their environment. Yet even they are not freaks in the natural sequence of cultural events. They constitute mentalities through which emerge and become manifest social undercurrents that remain hidden to less perceptive minds. Some of these visionaries succeed in converting their preoccupations—which are signs from the cultural subconscious—into messages and products of immediate value to their fellow men; they become the heroes of their societies. Others perceive the hopes and the tasks of the distant future but without providing definite answers or practical solutions; they give warnings of the questions and problems to come, but their anticipations are usually not understood by their contemporaries.

Pasteur, however, belongs in both classes. As a representative of nineteenth-century bourgeois civilization, he focused much of his scientific life on the practical problems of his time. But he was also a visionary who saw beyond the needs and concerns of his contemporaries; he formulated scientific and philosophical problems that were not yet ripe for solution.

His immense practical skill in converting theoretical knowledge into technological processes made him one of the most effective men of his century; he synthesized the known facts of biology and chemistry into original concepts of fermentation and disease and thus created a new science that dealt with the urgent needs of his social environment. The other side of his genius, although less obvious, is more original and perhaps more important in the long run. His emphasis on the essential role played by micro-organisms in the economy of nature, and on the interplay between living things and environment, made him perceive an area of science that is only now beginning to develop: He contributed to scientific philosophy by perceiving that all forms of life are integrated components of a global ecological system.

# PART III
# Living with Microbes

The real measure of health is not the Utopian absence of all disease but the ability to function effectively within a given environment. And since the environment keeps changing, good health is a process of continuous adaptation to the myriad microbes, irritants, pressures, and problems that daily challenge man.

# The Bacterial Cell

I have taken my drop of water from the immensity
of creation and I have taken it full of the elements
appropriated to the development of inferior beings. And I wait, I watch, I question it, begging it
to recommence for me the beautiful spectacle of
the first creation. But it is dumb, dumb since these
experiments were begun several years ago; it is
dumb because I have kept it for the only thing man
cannot produce, from the germs which float in the
air, from Life, for Life is a germ and a germ is Life.

—LOUIS PASTEUR

TO THE BIOLOGIST of the nineteenth century, bacteria appeared as
the most primitive expression of cellular organization, the very limit of
life. Speaking of what he considered "the smallest and at the same time
the simplest and lowest of all living forms," Ferdinand Cohen asserted:
"They form the boundary of life; beyond them, life does not exist, so far
at least as our microscopic expedients reach; and these are not small."
The minute dimensions of bacteria were considered by many to be
incompatible with any significant morphological differentiation; it encouraged the physical chemist to treat the bacterial cell as a simple
colloidal system and the biochemist to regard it as a "bag of enzymes."

This assured primitiveness of structure appeared to be confirmed
in biochemical terms when, at the end of the century, Sergei Winod-
gradsky (1887) announced that certain micro-organisms—those of the
autotrophic group—could synthesize their protoplasm from mineral
salts and carbon dioxide, utilizing for the reduction of the latter the
energy released by the oxidation of inorganic substances: ammonia,
nitrites, sulfur, and so on (van Niel, 1943). Could not this most primitive biochemical expression of life, the production of organic matter

purely for inorganic substances, be considered as the beginning of Life on earth?

Cytological studies were quick to dispel any illusions to the structural simplicity of bacteria. Differential staining reactions, study of spore germination and of sporulation, analysis of osmotic behavior, and even microdissection experiments revealed the existence of various kinds of intracellular bodies, organs of locomotion, plasma membranes, cell walls, capsules, and so forth that give to the morphology of each bacterial type a characteristic complexity. Enough knowledge had accumulated to justify in 1912 the publication of a monograph, *Die Zelle der Bakterien*, in which A. Meyer limited his discussion to the cytology of the bacterial cell. Evidence of the complexity of bacteria has continued to accumulate as new techniques have been introduced, such as an increase in the resolving power of microscopy, the use of staining reaction endowed with chemical specificity, and the analysis of cellular reorganization by indirect methods based on physiological behavior. Thus new structures have been revealed and the existence of others foreshadowed. At the cytochemical level, at least, the morphology of bacteria may not differ essentially from that of plant and animal life.

During the same time, the biochemist has come to recognize in microbial life the same metabolic reactions, the same metabolic channels and products, and the same biocatalysts that constitute the mechanism of organic life in the highest organisms. Even the autotrophic bacteria, those "primitive" beings capable of synthesizing life from the atmosphere and the rock, are shown to operate through the same elaborate mechanisms characteristic of the most evolved metabolic types. The autotrophic oxidation of sulfur by *Thiobacillus thiooxidans*, for instance, depends on an intimate linking between oxidation and phosphate turnover; the oxidative phase is accompanied by phosphate fixation and the reductive phase of carbon dioxide fixation by a release of phosphate. The same organism is fully equipped with the regular complement of water-soluble vitamins found in other organisms: thiamin, riboflavin, nicotinic and pathogenic acids, pyridoxin, and biotin. Not only do autotrophs utilize these multiple and complex biocatalysts, but they also have the ability to synthesize them from inorganic elements, a property that most plant and animal cells either never possessed or have lost. The high degree of biochemical organization required for the performance and the integration of these complex syntheses need not be emphasized; neither is it surprising that electron microscopy should reveal in the cells in which they take place a number of structures, often ill defined in their nature and functions, but expressing a morphological complexity that parallels biochemical complexity. The growth requirements of autotrophic bacteria are extremely simple indeed, but how complex their vital machinery, their performance, and their products!

If they are truly the first representatives of life on earth, they sprang, like Minerva, fully armed from the forehead of Jove.

Given the structural and chemical complexity of bacteria, their biological behavior reveals a pattern of organization very similar to that of plant or animal cells. Like the latter, they give rise to mutation-like phenomena at an approximate rate of 1 per $10^5$ to $10^6$ cellular divisions; their growth is governed by laws that recall those governing the growth of the multicellular organisms, since they exhibit in turn an embryonic, a mature, and a senescent form. In reality, it appears, therefore, that it is only their small size and the absence of recognized sexual reproduction that has given the illusion that bacteria are "simple" cells. Failure to recognize a multiplicity of structures underlying the multiplicity of functions should be regarded as an indication of the deficiency of our experimental techniques rather than as evidence of a simplicity of cellular organization.

Recognition of the complexity of bacteria—both structural and biochemical—explains why the early attempts to consider them as starting points for evolutionary systems were soon abandoned. On the other hand, the diversity of their structure and behavior seems to render impossible any definition that would include all the microbes commonly recognized as bacteria and would exclude at the same time those that clearly belong to the other well-defined divisions. One finds among bacteria organisms that show strong resemblances to certain of the blue-green algae, to the fungi, to the myxomycetes, or to the protozoa, and that can only be distinguished from these microorganisms by their much smaller size.

Some investigators have looked upon bacteria as a primitive homogeneous group from which higher types have arisen. It appears more likely, however, that these micro-organisms constitute a heterogeneous group of unrelated forms. Even among the Eubacteriales—the so-called true bacteria—one finds strange bedfellows, such as small Gram-negative autotrophic organisms, the Gram-positive proteolytic spore formers, and the acid-fast bacilli, which differ so profoundly from one another in metabolism, structure, and even mode of division as to have little in common except microscopic dimensions. One may indeed wonder whether the apparent unity of the group is not due to a narrow range of cellular size which determines, by a sort of convergent evolution, a number of physical and chemical characteristics. These in their turn have imposed certain experimental disciplines and techniques, which define the methods employed by bacteriologists rather than the biological material they study.

In the classification of higher plants and animals, systematists have relied almost exclusively on morphology, special attention being paid to the reproductive structures. In bacterial systematics, on the contrary, extensive use of physiological criteria has been made—a course imposed in part by the scarcity of morphological data. It is unlikely, however, that the distribution of metabolic characters can reveal the trends of physiological evolution, and for the present, any attempt to develop a phylogenetic system (family tree) will have to be based to a large extent on what morphological characters are available. Among these can be mentioned the nature of the cell wall, the presence and location of chromatin material, the functional structures (e.g., of locomotion), the method of cell division and the shape of the cell, the type of organization of cells into larger structures, and the nature and structure of reproductive or resting cells. It is possible that, eventually, serological reactions can be used to establish relationships between immunochemical specificities of homologous cellular constituents of different microbial species, and thus add an independent line of evidence to any phylogenetic system; unfortunately, only scattered data are available concerning these comparative serological reactions.

It is, however, always dangerous and often unjustified to attempt any reconstruction of the trends and direction of evolution in any group of living beings. In the case of bacteria, the problem is further complicated, not only by the paucity of morphological characters available for classification but furthermore by the great plasticity of this group of organisms. Not only can the cells of a single strain change their morphology depending on the composition of the medium in which they are growing, but even under the same environmental conditions, coccoid, bacillary, and even filamentous forms are the normal expression of growth according to the "phase" (mucoid, smooth, rough, etc.) in which the species under consideration happens to be. Important cellular components such as spores, flagella, capsules appear and disappear under conditions not always predictable, and there occur not only profound modifications of cellular and colonial morphology but at the same time startling changes in biological behavior. The ability to produce certain enzymes and to synthesize pigments, amino acids, growth factors, and so on can be reversibly gained and lost by a given culture, even though derived from a single cell. Even more extraordinary is the fact that the faculty of producing certain polysaccharides, heretofore thought to be specific for each pneumococcus type, can experimentally be transferred from one type to another. This newly acquired property is then retained as a permanently transmissible factor.

Finally, it should be emphasized that although most authors regard bacteria as primitive forms from which higher types have arisen, there are others who look upon them as having been derived from higher forms by a retrograde evolution—that is, by degradation or loss of certain characters. Thus it was recognized very early that the bacteria exhibit a close relationship to the blue-green algae, but it is not clear whether the algae evolved from the bacteria or whether the latter are products of retrograde evolution.

In fact, the view that bacteria, instead of being the most primitive organisms, have evolved from higher forms of life by loss of structure and function is repeatedly expressed in all fields of bacteriology. It is now suggested, for instance, that a long period of chemical synthesis of organic material preceded the emergence of life and that consequently the earliest living forms were heterotrophs. According to this reasoning, the autotrophic organisms, far from being original representations of life on earth, are the product of later adaptation to an environment in which organic materials had become scarce through the activity of heterotrophs. It has been stated that the Gram-negative intestinal bacilli, which exhibit such vigorous and varied fermentation reactions, "differ from one another by failure to ferment, or to ferment fully, one or more of a series of carbohydrates and other substances. In the case of the typhoid bacillus, which requires tryptophane for its initial growth upon isolation from pathological material, but can grow in its absence after repeated transfers in artificial media, this changed requirement is thought to be due to the temporary loss of ability to synthesize the amino acid as a result of parasitic life in the human body. In fact, loss of ability to synthesize amino acids or other growth factors is apparently a common occurrence and accounts in part for the specific growth requirements of individual microbial strains. Although the loss of morphological or antigenic constituents is often a reversible phenomenon, there are many cases where the variant strain appears to be stabilized in its "degraded" form. Thus flagellated or sporulated species may give rise to strains permanently devoid of flagella or spores. The multiplicity of salmonella types has been explained on the assumption that the simpler existing types were derived by loss variation from ancestors— probably related to *E. coli*—which were more complex both in fermentative power and antigenic structure. Even some of the filterable viruses, the macromolecules that appear today as the boundary between the living and the nonliving world, have been regarded as the ultimate phase of retrograde evolution of higher cells. According to this view, complete adaptation to the parasitic intracellular life had caused certain viruses to lose most of their vegetative faculties; while retaining the property of multiplication, they depend on the host cell for the performance of synthetic process.

Whatever the phylogeny of bacteria, it is certain that they constitute an extremely heterogeneous group of organisms and that their cells exhibit a great variability affecting not only their physiological activities but also their chemical composition and morphology. One may question, therefore, the value of any discussion dealing with the organization of the bacterial cell in general. It is true that individual studies of the various microbial species have revealed essential differences in the composition and properties of the respective cellular components. Progress in this line of work will undoubtedly contribute to the knowledge of phylogeny and will eventually permit generalizations and deductions concerning the characteristic cellular organization of each bacterial group. The present survey is more limited in its scope. It is concerned primarily with those aspects of the problem that directly or indirectly have a bearing on the phenomena of infection. What are the laws governing the extraordinary variability of the bacterial cell, according to which it adapts itself to the utilization of a new substrate, to the tolerance of an inimical environment, to the invasion of a new host? Are the heredity characters in microbic life transmitted through the same type of nuclear apparatus utilized in higher organisms or through other mechanisms as yet unrecognized and perhaps also present in other forms of life? What are the attributes that determine the property of virulence? Can they be identified with cellular structures capable of protecting the pathogen against the defense of the host, or with physiological properties resulting in invasive power? Are the protective agents that nature, and the physician, use in combating the infection directed against the microbe as a whole or rather against certain of its most vulnerable structures?

These questions, and many others of obvious interest to the student of infectious diseases, would find a readier answer if it were possible to visualize the structural components of the bacterial cell and to identify the nature of their reactions with the environment. The classical methods of cytology have contributed a great deal to this subject. By revealing the existence of spores, flagella, cell walls, and capsules, they have greatly aided in the understanding of many problems of epidemiology and immunity. Little by little, empirical staining reactions are gaining the dignity of cytochemical tests; with the help of monochromatic photography, especially in the ultraviolet range, they are giving chemical definition to morphological entities, allowing us to recognize possible nuclear structures among other cell granules. The electron microscope has greatly increased the resolving power of microscopy. Because of its lack of specificity, it has in most cases given to the bacteriologist only a confirmation of classical knowledge, but one can expect that it will in the near future render visible new cellular elements, especially if used in conjunction with specific reagents.

These cytological techniques aim at a direct visualization of the cell, but there are other indirect methods of study that, by an analysis of the response of the cell to the effect of certain reagents and procedures, suggest the existence—and often the chemical nature—of important cellular components. Much of this indirect approach consists in the study of the reaction of the cell to immune antibodies, antiseptics, and chemotherapeutic agents. It was Paul Ehrlich who first saw the possibility of describing these reactions in terms of cellular structures. He felt that, far from belonging to different disciplines, the laws of immunity and chemotherapy could be formulated in the same general terms. The living cell was assumed to possess a number of chemically reactive groups, called "receptors," with which dyes, bactericidal substances, and immune bodies reacted selectively. Ehrlich regarded these "receptors" as definite chemical entities, capable of entering into union with dyes, antiseptics, and antibodies. Characteristic staining reactions with immune bodies could all be explained by postulating the existence of a sufficient number of receptors in the bacterial cell. Unfortunately, neither Paul Ehrlich nor his immediate followers succeeded in identifying the chemical nature of these "receptors" or even in demonstrating their existence as well-defined entities. During the past three decades, however, immunochemists, and students of the theory of chemotherapy, have gone far toward recognizing the nature of some of the cellular components with which antibodies and antibacterial agents react selectively and in some cases separating them in purified state. Thus the "receptors" postulated by Ehrlich have now been given experimental reality and chemical definition.

Nor are antibodies and antiseptics the only reagents that can be used to recognize and identify the cellular "receptors." If it is found, for instance, that a given enzyme attacks the cells of a certain microbial species, causing some alteration of a characteristic cellular property, it can be surmised that the chemical substrate that is susceptible to this enzyme is present in the cell under consideration and that it plays some part in the function altered by the enzyme. If, furthermore, the enzyme or the antibody can react with the living cell, there is some likelihood that the cellular substrate that is susceptible to it is situated near the periphery of the cell, since the large molecular dimensions of antibodies and enzymes probably do not permit them to penetrate the plasma membrane. One can thus not only recognize the presence of certain specific components of the cell, but by bold, though admittedly dangerous, extrapolation, guess at the approximate position of these components in the architecture of the cell.

The parts of the cell situated at or near the surface are of special interest to the student of immunology, since they constitute the exposed, vulnerable structures of the parasites against which the antibacterial defense can be directed. The future will undoubtedly reveal other even more subtle physiological and biochemical techniques for the study of morphological problems. There is already some suggestion, for instance, that certain enzymatic functions are definitely associated with fairly well-defined situations—phosphatases being concentrated at the periphery of the cell, adenosine triphosphatase being closely related to myosin—and that the coupling of oxidations and reductions requires the morphological association of the enzymes involved.

The indirect approach to cytology, which we are considering, utilizes chemical and biological manifestations as indices and guides to the recognition and identification of morphological structures. Its shortcoming is that it depends entirely on the interpretation of results, and not on direct observation, to establish the place of these structures in cellular organization.

At the present stage, when the unknown components of the cell exceed the known in number, the indirect physiological approach may appear to be unreliable. It should be pointed out, however, that the history of science provides many examples of the fruitfulness of indirect methods—as witness, nuclear physics. The mode of experimentation and the reasoning involved in following this approach are parallel to those by which the vast body of structural knowledge has been built up in the accepted domain of organic chemistry. Thus the concept of hydroxyl group was arrived at from the study of reactions such as those that occur when two compounds of the same empirical composition— ethyl alcohol and dimethylether—are treated with metallic sodium or a halogen acid. The fact that, in these reactions, hydrogen can be released either in association with or independent of oxygen, depending on the compound and reagent used, revealed that one of the six hydrogen atoms occupies a unique position in the ethyl alcohol molecule, probably in association with the oxygen atom, whereas the oxygen atom in dimethyl ether is involved in linking the two methyl groups and does not exist as a hydroxyl group.

Even in the case of the tissues and cells of higher organisms, important discoveries concerning their cytology and morphology have depended on the use of an extremely indirect physiological approach. The existence of chromosomes and genes, for instance, was surmised from the analysis of the transmission of hereditary characters before they could be seen as definite morphological entities. Again, the recognition that the nervous impulse can be transmitted at different velocities revealed something of the significance of the diameters of the different fibers within the same nerve bundle. In the words of Claude Bernard, "anatomical localization is often revealed first through the analysis of the physiological process."

Many illustrations of this view could be found in the past, but instead of describing them, it may be sufficient to mention a situation that bids fair, in the near future, to illustrate again the power of the method. It is well known that the analysis of the immune reactions elicited by the injection of erythrocytes into experimental animals has revealed the existence in these cells of substances heretofore unrecognized, and one may confidently expect that the isolation of the specific polysaccharide of blood group A, for instance, will result in a knowledge of its role and place in the cells from which it is derived. Similarly, an understanding of the mechanism of hemolysis caused by specific anti-erythrocyte agents will help in describing the organization of the red cell. In brief, one may predict that immunological methods, as well as the study of the mode of action of enzymes and other reagents on different types of cells, will in the future become one of the techniques for the study of morphological, chemical, and physiological aspects of cytology.

Much of the morphology indirectly revealed by antibodies, enzymes, and cytotoxic substances lies beyond the microscopic range, and does, in fact, often reach the molecular level. It concerns the organization of those molecular groupings that, on account of their chemical activity, condition the behavior of the cell both as an independent functioning unit and in its relation to the environment. The ultimate understanding of the natural history of infectious diseases, and the rational development of methods for their control, depend on this knowledge. It is probable that without it epidemiology would have remained to a large extent a mere statistical statement of mysterious events; the pathology of infectious diseases a purely descriptive science; immunity and chemotherapy a set of empirical procedures.

# Tuberculosis

IN 1948, 45,000 persons died of tuberculosis in the United States. This death rate—30 per 100,000 population—is the lowest on record, and it is probable that the 1949 tuberculosis mortality will be even lower. The White Plague is no longer the most terrible affliction of civilization. Yet man is still far from the final conquest of this disease.

Tuberculosis remains the most important single cause of death in the age group fifteen to thirty-five. There are in the United States more than 500,000 individuals of all ages who suffer, in great or small degree, from active clinical forms of the disease. Indeed, it is a striking though not widely appreciated fact that very few city dwellers escape infection with tubercle bacilli at some time or other in their lifetimes. You as an individual may have remained unaware of your infection. But the widespread occurrence of the disease is well known to the pathologist, who often finds definite tuberculous lesions in the bodies of adults reaching the autopsy table after death from other causes, such as automobile accidents, suicide, or old age. The immunologist also knows that many people who have never noticed tuberculosis symptoms give a positive tuberculin test—that is, a strong skin reaction to the injection of the extract of tubercle bacilli known as tuberculin—which is evidence of past or present tuberculous infection. In the words of the

*Scientific American*, vol. 181, no. 10 (1949), pp. 31–40. Copyright © 1949 by Scientific American, Inc. Reprinted by permission.

old physician, "Everyone has, has had, or will have a little tuberculosis."

There was a time when the relation between the tubercle bacillus and man had a grimmer aspect. As John Bunyan put it, "The captain of all [the] men of death . . . was the Consumption." A hundred years ago, tuberculosis was in truth the captain of the men of death in the Western world. Its annual death rate was then of the order of 300 per 100,000 population—at least 10 times the present rate. This was true in Boston, New York, Philadelphia, and Charleston, as well as in London, Paris, and Berlin. Many of the most celebrated men and women of the nineteenth century died of tuberculosis or suffered from it: Friedrich Schiller, John Keats, Percy Bysshe Shelley, Anne, Charlotte, and Emily Brontë, Frédéric Chopin, Niccolò Paganini, Honoré de Balzac, Alfred de Musset, Elizabeth Browning, Henry David Thoreau, Ralph Waldo Emerson, Anton Chekhov, Marie Bashkirtsev, Robert Louis Stevenson, Cecil Rhodes. To these names should be added a long list of distinguished physicians, many of whom died of tuberculosis while engaged in the study of it. Indeed, so many of the famous children of the nineteenth century lived and died tuberculous that people thought there must be some tragic and mysterious relation between tuberculosis and genius. But tuberculosis affected with equal severity all intellectual and social strata and all age groups. It cast so heavy a shadow over society that it was darkly reflected in much of the literature of the Romantic age; it was, for instance, a central theme in *La Bohème* and *La Dame aux Camélias*. And then the White Plague began to wane. Sometime around the 1860s the tuberculosis mortality rate began to decrease in Europe and the United States. From a peak of approximately 400 per 100,000, it had come down to less than 200 at the beginning of the present century. Except for short, local flare-ups associated with influenza epidemics and the two world wars, it has continued steadily to decline.

When physicians became convinced that tuberculosis was a contagious disease caused by a specific bacillus, it appeared for a while that it would be a very simple problem to eradicate the disease. Let public health officials trace the human carriers of the infection and devise techniques to prevent the transmission of bacilli from one person to another; the chain of infection could thus be broken and tuberculosis would disappear from our midst. In fact, by applying this simple principle we have almost entirely eliminated tuberculosis from the cattle of the United States. For some thirty years, the Bureau of Animal Industry of the Department of Agriculture has carried out a very effective campaign for the detection (by the tuberculin test) and elimination (by slaughtering) of tuberculous cattle.

But the ruthless techniques used with cattle cannot be applied to human beings, even in the most regimented society. Too many of us would have to be slaughtered, and if all Americans infected with tubercle bacilli were to be segregated in sanatoria, few would be those allowed to remain outside the gates.

Although eradication of the tubercle bacillus from human societies is not in sight, fortunately in many places we now appear far better able than were our ancestors to accept the presence of the bacillus without too much inconvenience. The fact that tuberculosis mortality has decreased more than tenfold in the last century is a great achievement of which modern science is justly proud. But our pride is tempered by the realization that no one knows exactly how this achievement was brought about. Tuberculosis, like leprosy and scarlet fever, is being conquered in spite of the fact that we do not completely understand it.

The truth is that tuberculosis mortality began to decrease two decades before the tubercle bacillus was discovered; half a century before the wide adoption of such measures as early detection, segregation of patients in sanatoria, and treatment by bed rest, pneumothorax, and other forms of collapse therapy; almost a century before the first specific antitubercular drugs (streptomycin and para-amino salicylic acid) became available, and before vaccination was even considered in the Anglo-Saxon world. How, then, can one account for the downward trend that began around 1860? Many explanations have been suggested. A mere listing of a few of them will illustrate the complexity of the problem and the necessity for a many-sided approach to control of the infection.

Tuberculosis reached a very high peak in Europe and in the United States at the beginning of the Industrial Revolution, when vast numbers of human beings began to move from the rural areas to cities, where crowding, dirt, and poor nutrition prevailed. This state of insalubrious living probably contributed to increasing the prevalence and severity of infectious diseases. Around the middle of the nineteenth century, reformers and public-minded citizens started to preach the virtues of pure air, pure food, pure water, and less promiscuous spitting. Many hygienists claim that it was this sanitary awakening that turned the tide against tuberculosis. Others think that the chief factor was a steady increase in the abundance and variety of foodstuffs, resulting in better nourishment of the population.

Still others believe that the major factor was genetic. The human strains most susceptible to tuberculosis were practically wiped out by the scourge during the nineteenth century. As the victims often died too young to leave any progeny, there occurred a natural process of selection of those most resistant to the disease. Hence the present human stock has greater natural resistance.

All these reasons sound plausible, but there is as yet no technique available to establish their validity or the role played by the various factors in the natural history of tuberculosis. Of one fact, however, we can be almost certain: the bacillus itself has not changed much. It is still as virulent as it was in the days of the White Plague. This is indicated by countless experiments on animals, and in a more dramatic manner by recent epidemic outbreaks of tuberculosis in certain human populations. The galloping consumption of our grandparents, now rare among us, still has the power to ravage susceptible peoples. For example, it played havoc with the Polynesian islanders when the Europeans began to establish wide contact with them. In the 1914–18 war, it was more effective than German guns in destroying the Senegalese troops brought to the French front from Occidental Africa. Today it runs high among the American Indians on the reservations of Arizona and Canada. In the aftermaths of the two world wars of our century, epidemics reappeared in Europe wherever physiological misery became great. And in many countries of Latin America, in the tropical cities of India and China, and under the cold skies of Greenland, tuberculosis still reigns as the captain of the men of death.

It is clear, then, that the bacillus, although a necessary condition to clinical disease, is not in itself sufficient. The microbe needs a fertile soil. It produces clinical tuberculosis only when the individual's hereditary constitution, physiological disturbances, emotional upsets, overwork, and other excesses prepare the ground.

Thus there are two aspects of the disease to study: the conditions in the body that enable that bacillus to produce disease, and the bacillus itself. To understand the modern work on these problems, it is useful to review the history of tuberculosis research.

As everybody knows, the most advanced medical thinking of antiquity was codified in the writings of Hippocrates. Whether he was merely a legendary hero or a flesh-and-blood character, Hippocrates symbolizes the great Greek school of medicine that flourished on the Island of Cos during the fourth century B.C. This school was the first to teach that diseases were not visitations from capricious gods but the results of natural causes. Hippocrates was well acquainted with consumption. He described its symptoms and course with marvelous accuracy, noting furthermore that the disease appeared to be hereditary and was more common among individuals of a certain physical type and among those living in certain places. But nowhere do his writings mention the possibility that consumption might be caused by a living agent brought to the patient from the outside. The "germ" of tuberculosis, now glibly discussed by even the most uneducated layman, had no place in the medical philosophy of ancient Greece.

The Hippocratic view that consumption was an inborn disturbance of the body aggravated by environmental circumstances prevailed until the middle of the nineteenth century. During the long era from Hippocrates to Koch, physicians were much concerned with describing the various manifestations of the disease and the factors affecting its course and outcome, but few paid any heed to its contagiousness. In his *Phthisiologia*, published in 1689, the great English clinician Richard Morton listed "imprudent diet, overstudy, thick smoky air, and troublesome passions" among the most important causes of tuberculosis. It is not known which of these causes led him to fall victim to the disease—as his father had before him, and as his son did after him. Another student of the disease, William Stark, of Birmingham, also died of tuberculosis, in 1771, at the age of twenty-nine, after having been the first to state clearly that many varied afflictions were in reality different aspects of tuberculosis. In France, Gaspard Bayle (1774–1816) substantiated this view by showing that early and advanced pulmonary tuberculosis were two successive stages of the same disease. It was Bayle who first used the word "miliary" to describe small tuberculous lesions—because of their resemblance to millet grains. After having studied and performed post-mortem examinations on 900 tuberculous patients, Bayle, too, died tuberculous at the age of forty-two.

Most famous of all the students of tuberculosis who died of the disease was Bayle's close friend, the brilliant and fiery René Théophile Hyacinthe Laënnec (1781–1826). In 1802, he was appointed to teach morbid anatomy in the Paris School of Medicine to replace the celebrated M. F.X. Bichat, who had just died of tuberculosis at the age of thirty-one. Laënnec struggled with several acute attacks of the disease before he finally died of it at the age of forty-five. In the course of his short life this wasted, hollow-cheeked little man managed to contribute to medicine several fundamental discoveries, among them the invention of the stethoscope and its application to the diagnosis of pulmonary and cardiac diseases. By careful listening with the stethoscope, Laënnec gained an uncanny knowledge of the signs of pulmonary tuberculosis. He correlated these observations with the types of lesions found in autopsies on patients who died. In this way Laënnec established beyond doubt that many pathological conditions previously assumed to be unrelated in origin were in reality different forms of the same disease. All were characterized by the presence in the tissues of abnormal growths, which he called "tubercles," whence the disease eventually got its name. Yet Laënnec, despite his immense knowledge of the clinical and pathological aspects of the disease, failed to trace its origin to a parasitic agent and never was entirely convinced that it was contagious.

One of the first to insist that tuberculosis was infectious was the English epidemiologist William Budd, who stated in 1867: "The tuberculous matter itself is (or includes) the specific morbific matter of the disease, and constitutes the material by which phthisis is propagated from one person to another, and disseminated through society." At about the same time the French military surgeon Jean Antoine Villemin had also come to believe that tuberculosis was a contagious disease and that soldiers contracted it from their infected messmates. Moreover, he had shown in 1865 that it was possible to make rabbits tuberculous by injecting into them tubercle material from human beings or cows. But his observations and experiments remained largely unheeded by the medical world until Robert Koch (1843–1910) brought to their support the overwhelming evidence derived from the newly developed techniques of bacteriology.

Koch was thirty-nine when on March 24, 1882, he presented before the Physiological Society of Berlin a paper in which he demonstrated with an incredible wealth of convincing evidence that tubercles contained a peculiar small bacillus. This bacillus was very difficult to detect; it offered unusual resistance to staining by ordinary aniline dyes, and it multiplied so slowly that often weeks elapsed before its growth became evident even on the most favorable culture media. When pure cultures of the bacillus were injected into animals, they caused tubercles to form in the animals' tissues, and from these tubercles in turn bacilli could be recovered at will. The germ theory of disease was not entirely new when these discoveries were reported in 1882; Koch himself had established one of the first landmarks of the new science by cultivating the anthrax bacillus in 1876. But what gave particular glamour to his new achievement was the tremendous social importance of tuberculosis in the nineteenth century, and the technical difficulties involved in the detection and cultivation of its causative agent.

This paper of Koch's is regarded by many medical historians as the most spectacular pronouncement in the history of medical bacteriology, but Koch's discovery left unanswered most of the problems of clinical tuberculosis. As we have already seen, the presence of the bacillus is only one factor in the development and severity of tuberculosis. Good and abundant food and thorough rest from mental worries as well as from physical effort are regarded by every physician as the most effective weapons against the disease, although it is not at all clear how physiological well-being and mental rest can increase the ability of our tissues to cope with the bacterial invader. It is in this field of research that are to be found the most important problems of tuberculosis, but unfortunately physiological science has not yet begun to deal with them. At the most, it has helped in the improvement of certain surgical techniques and practices, such as therapeutic collapse of the lung. These measures, though helpful, obviously do not deal with the fundamental nature of the disease.

What about the other side of the problem, the bacillus itself?

The most important tool for the detection of tuberculosis is X-ray photography. Several other diseases, however, show abnormalities so similar to tuberculous lesions that convincing diagnosis must finally rest on the finding of tubercle bacilli. Thus the development of techniques for the identification of the bacilli is undoubtedly one of the most useful contributions of bacteriological science to the knowledge of tuberculosis. Besides these techniques, the tuberculin test also has diagnostic value, though it serves a somewhat different purpose. As we have noted, any individual who was once infected with tubercle bacilli exhibits an increased sensitivity, or allergy, to the toxic effect of tuberculin, an extract of these bacilli. In other words, allergy to tuberculin reveals a past contact with the organism, but it does not necessarily mean that the individual still has or has had the disease in an active form. So in practice the tuberculin test is used mainly as a convenient method for ascertaining the prevalence and distribution of tuberculous infections in a given community.

The knowledge that tuberculosis is a germ disease has of course stimulated a long and industrious search for drugs to treat it. The most spectacular fruits of this search have been streptomycin and para-amino acid (PAS). These substances help in controlling the disease by interfering with the multiplication of the bacilli in the tissues. Whatever their usefulness, however, it is unlikely that these drugs, or any that may follow them, will ever constitute the final solution to the problem of tuberculosis. The ultimate goal is not to treat the patient but rather to prevent the development of the disease.

A step in this direction, though a very short and uncertain one, is the vaccine known as BCG. BCG is a weak strain of tubercle bacillus that lacks the power to cause the progressive and fatal disease but retains the ability to elicit in the individual in whom it is injected a certain level of resistance against the more virulent strains. The initials BCG stand for bacillus of Calmette and Guérin, the names of the two French bacteriologists who isolated the strain more than thirty years ago and first advocated its use for vaccination of human beings and cattle. The BCG problem is so controversial and technically so complex that it would not be advisable to discuss it in detail in this article. Let us note in passing, however, that the strain BCG illustrates the fact that tubercle bacilli may undergo a type of hereditary variation that results in loss of virulence—a property we shall consider presently.

Although the germ theory has found so many applications, it has not thrown much light so far on the mechanism by which the tubercle bacillus produces disease. What weapons does it possess that enable it to become established in human tissues and to cause there the typical lesions of tuberculosis? This question has engaged the attention of our laboratory at the Rockefeller Institute for Medical Research during the past four years, and for that reason I shall deal with it in some detail as an example of the laboratory attack on the bacteriological aspects of the problem.

The tubercle bacilli belong to a large natural family of micro-organisms commonly designated as "acid-fast" because once they have been stained with certain aniline dyes, they are resistant to decolorization by acid treatment. These acid-fast bacilli are very widely distributed in nature; they are normally present in the human body, on objects such as rubber tubing, in certain foods such as butter, on many plants, and in soil and water. Yet of all these acid-fast micro-organisms, very few species can cause disease in animals or man. How do the disease-producing species differ from their innocuous relatives?

When we decided to attack this problem, a technical difficulty at once presented itself. Unlike most other micro-organisms, the tubercle bacilli are not readily wetted by water. Their surface repels water like a duck's back. Consequently, in any culture medium using a water solution populations of tubercle bacilli have a tendency to grow in the form of clumps, or thick "pellicles," consisting of millions or even billions of cells that adhere firmly to one another instead of becoming evenly dispersed throughout the medium. This peculiar mode of growth makes it difficult to prepare homogeneous bacterial suspensions and thus limits the possibility of doing quantitative work on samples of the culture. Moreover, the bacilli located in the center of the large clumps or pellicles are under physiological conditions far different from those prevailing at the periphery, where air and food are readily available. This results in marked variations in the bacterial population and increases the complexity of experimental work.

The answer to our problem came from chemical technology. Most people will probably remember a chemical experiment that was widely publicized in a commercial film some ten years ago. A duck was seen floating with ease in a tank of water. Then a small amount of a detergent, or wetting agent, was dropped into the tank, and the duck's feathers immediately began to lose their water repellency and became soaked. The last stage of the experiment showed the poor bird sinking helplessly despite its frantic efforts to remain afloat. What had happened was that the detergent permitted the water to penetrate the thin coating of oil beneath the duck's feathers which traps air and keeps the bird afloat. This released the air and destroyed the duck's buoyancy.

It was this sad experience of the duck that suggested a suitable technique for cultivating the tubercle bacillus. We found that esters of oleic acids and polyoxyethylene derivatives of sorbitan monooleate—when added to otherwise adequate culture media—are capable of rendering the surface of tubercle bacilli wettable by water. Thus it became possible to obtain homogeneous, well-dispersed bacterial populations instead of the large clumps of thick pellicles produced by the conventional cultivation techniques.

The solution of this technical difficulty greatly facilitated many bacteriological operations and permitted a more rapid investigation of our central problem: the mechanism of virulence. The term "virulence" itself is something of an abstraction; it merely means that a certain micro-organism can behave as a parasite for a certain animal or plant. In order to find some suggestion as to what the concrete physicochemical basis of this property might be, we undertook a comparative study of virulent and avirulent strains of tubercle bacilli, in the hope that we could thereby recognize some specific differences correlated with the ability to cause disease.

Fortunately, tubercle bacilli undergo variation as do all other living things, and they can mutate in such a manner that their progeny differ in some details from the original parent strain. Thus the virulent bacilli can give rise by mutation to forms that have lost the ability to induce disease; it is almost certain, for example, that the BCG strain originated from such a mutation.

It has long been known that the virulent and avirulent variants of tubercle bacilli do not behave in the same way toward the cells of animal tissues. Some twenty years ago the Russian cytologist Alexander Maximov, then working in Chicago, observed that the virulent bacilli exerted a destructive effect on animal cells growing in the test tube, whereas the avirulent bacilli failed to cause any obvious damage. Does this mean that the virulent forms liberate some peculiar substance that is toxic to the tissues? That would be a natural conclusion, for as everyone knows this is precisely what happens in certain common disorders. For example, in diphtheria and tetanus the damage is done by powerful toxins that are released into the body by the corresponding bacilli.

In the case of tuberculosis, we have a potentially poisonous substance—namely, tuberculin—to which, as already mentioned, human tissues become sensitive. Tuberculin is a protein fraction of the tubercle bacillus. But it was found that tuberculin is produced by the avirulent as well as the virulent bacilli, and both forms are capable of sensitizing the body to its toxic effect. Tuberculin, therefore, cannot be the primary cause of virulence, although it certainly plays an important part in the manifestations of the disease.

During the past two years there has come to light a type of subtle action of virulent tubercle bacilli that is not exhibited by the avirulent forms. Like most micro-organisms, tubercle bacilli—virulent as well as avirulent—are readily ingested by the devouring white blood cells known as phagocytes. Under normal conditions these phagocytes move about actively, especially when placed on certain types of surfaces such as plasma clots. Two years ago the Swiss bacteriologist Hubert Bloch began at the Rockefeller Institute a study of the behavior of phagocytes that had ingested tubercle bacilli. His experiments, later continued in Basel, and at the New York City Public Health Research Institute, where he is now working, showed that phagocytes that have engulfed avirulent bacilli continue to move about at the normal rate, whereas those that have taken up the virulent bacilli immediately become motionless. These observations, since confirmed and extended at the Rockefeller Institute by Samuel P. Martin and Cynthia H. Pierce, provide the first clue to a direct physiological inhibitory effect exerted by the virulent bacilli on normal cells.

Comparison of the virulent and avirulent bacilli has also revealed striking differences in their appearance. Much of the pioneer work in this field was done by William Steenken of the Trudeau Sanatorium Laboratory, of Saranac Lake. Like many other workers on tuberculosis, Steenken became interested in the disease because he himself had contracted it. Although untrained in bacteriology or other medical sciences, he began to take part in the activities of the Trudeau Sanatorium Laboratory as soon as he recovered his health, and he has continued ever since to observe new and curious facts concerning tubercle bacilli.

Steenken noticed that when the nonvirulent variants are allowed to multiply in ordinary liquid media, they tend to accumulate in the form of isolated floating islands, which coalesce slowly as growth proceeds. The virulent bacilli, on the contrary, tend to spread rapidly over the whole surface, covering it with a thin veil of growth. These observations have been much extended at the Rockefeller Institute by Gardner Middlebrook, another victim of the disease. He showed that the contrasting modes of growth are the expression of variant types of forces holding the bacilli together in the course of their multiplication. Under normal conditions, the avirulent mutants grow in the form of shapeless clumps, whereas the virulent bacilli adhere to each other sidewise, a fact that gives to their growth a highly characteristic oriented, serpentine pattern. Interestingly enough, this serpentine pattern of growth was strikingly visible in some of the very first microscopic pictures of the virulent bacillus, obtained by Koch in 1882. Maximov, the Russian investigator whose tissue-culture studies we have already mentioned, also noticed this difference in the appearance of the virulent and avirulent strains. Yet no one happened to attach any particular significance to it.

There is as yet no precise knowledge of the nature of the forces that cause the virulent bacilli to orient themselves in the direction of their long axis. It has been observed, however, that the bacilli tend to lose their characteristic orientation and to separate into individual cells when they are cultivated in a medium containing wetting agents. This suggests that the orientation of the virulent bacilli may be due to the fact that they possess a special water-repellent substance that is distributed over their surface in such a way that the bacilli can adhere to one another only in a certain peculiar pattern.

The virulent bacilli possess several other physicochemical characteristics not usually found in their completely avirulent counterparts. Thus we have recently observed that they have the ability to bind to themselves neutral red (as well as other basic dyes) in the form of its bright-red salt. This occurs even when the dye is added to the bacilli in extremely alkaline media, under which conditions the dye ordinarily would become yellow. And indeed it remains yellow and unbound when exposed to micro-organisms other than the virulent tubercle bacilli. This shows that the tubercle organisms possess some unusual structural characteristics that differentiate them from other living cells.

The dye bound to the virulent tubercle bacilli can readily be dislodged from them by minute concentrations of certain basic groups (ammonium ions and aliphatic amines). It is of particular interest that these same aliphatic amines, when used in concentrations adequate to prevent the binding of neutral red, can neutralize the power of the virulent bacilli to inhibit the movement of blood phagocytes that have engulfed them. Since amines are present in tissue and body fluids, here is a vague hint that substances normally produced by the body during metabolism may be able to counteract at least a part of the physiological effect exerted by the bacilli on the tissue cells. If this is true, it might open a new approach to the study of how human beings' susceptibility or resistance to infection is affected by their metabolic characteristics.

Little by little, other differences between the virulent bacilli and their variant, benign forms are being unveiled. Needless to say, it is possible, indeed likely, that many of these differences bear no relation to virulence. Nevertheless, it appears legitimate to hope that this comparative approach may lead to the identification of the peculiar structures of properties that permit the tubercle bacilli to establish themselves, multiply, and cause damage in the tissues of the body. There is intellectual satisfaction in thus elucidating the intimate mechanism through which a microscopic organism can behave as a parasite, causing disease and death. Beyond this lies the long-range hope that the investigation may help someday in formulating a more rational plan of attack against the "captain of all the men of death."

# The Gold-Headed Cane
# in the Laboratory

ALTHOUGH MOST of medical science is of very recent acquisition, the healing art has been practiced effectively for thousands of years without the benefit of laboratory knowledge. The skill of ancient physicians was largely empirical, but it permitted them nevertheless to formulate prognoses, relieve symptoms, and not uncommonly effect cures. It was an empiricism based on wisdom, experience, and knowledge of human nature.

The fashionable English physician of the late seventeenth century went on his sick calls dressed in a silk coat, breeches, and stockings, with buckled shoes, lace ruffles, and full-bottomed wig, and carrying a gold-headed cane. Typical of this class was John Radcliffe (1650–1714), physician to William and Mary and to Queen Anne. He amassed one of the great fortunes of medicine with which he endowed institutions of learning in London and in Oxford. Radcliffe was apparently a somewhat coarse, pompous, uncouth, and intemperate man with a sharp tongue, who attributed his success to the habit of "using all mankind ill." But even his personal enemies acknowledged him as a sagacious physician possessed of great power of observation, medical acumen, and knowl-

*National Institutes of Health Annual Lectures 1953*, Public Health Service Pub. #388, pp. 90–102.

edge of mankind. There was in his anteroom a bowl into which the departing patient could drop whatever gratuities he felt moved to leave. The fee was not stipulated, and many a purse of golden guineas was dropped therein by the grateful recipients of Radcliffe's sound advice.

When he retired from practice in 1713, Radcliffe presented his gold-headed cane to Richard Mead (1673–1754), the London physician whom he considered most worthy of inheriting his medical kingdom. At the end of his own life, Mead in turn passed the cane on to Anthony Askew (1722–72), who passed it on to William Pitcairn (1711–91), who passed it on to David Pitcairn (1749–1809), who passed it on to Matthew Baillie (1761–1823). Thus for 150 years, Radcliffe's gold-headed cane remained in the possession of some of the most successful practitioners of England. In Mathew Baillie, however, it found a master of a different mentality. Baillie was the nephew of the famous brothers, John and William Hunter, with whom he had studied normal and pathological anatomy and from whom he had acquired the belief that experimental science had become essential to the advance of medicine. Whereas the first four owners of Radcliffe's cane have left no written contribution to science, Baillie made a lasting name for himself as the author of a famous textbook on *Morbid Anatomy* and by observations in the pathology of tuberculosis.

With a few of his contemporaries, Baillie considered that science was rendering obsolete the assumed gravity and pompous airs of the fashionable physicians. Indeed, it was obvious that the clinical art had then come to represent a formal tradition, rather than an attitude based on living experience with disease. No longer regarding the gold-headed cane as a necessary appendage of the medical profession, Baillie discontinued carrying it on his sick calls. After his death, his wife found the cane in a corner of the consulting rooms and presented it in 1825 to the museum of the Royal Academy of Physicians. There it has remained ever since, among other relics of that learned body, a symbol of a phase of medicine without relevance to medical practice or science in the modern era. As the cane went to its final sanctuary, persons who were to change the course of medicine were beginning their lives: Florence Nightingale in 1820, Rudolf Virchow in 1821, Louis Pasteur in 1822, Joseph Lister in 1827.

It goes without saying that all over the world many physicians have continued after Baillie to exert with skill and success a type of care of the sick based more on intuition and art than on science. Indeed, many of the most brilliant practitioners of clinical medicine of the nineteenth century held that their art had nothing of importance to learn from the biological sciences. Some of them in particular achieved a place in history by the passion with which they opposed the germ theory of disease. The French clinician Pidoux, a representative of traditional medicine—always impeccably clad in a gold-buttoned coat—was one of those who took up the cudgels against Pasteur at the Paris Academy of Medicine. Where Pasteur saw disease as caused by specific kinds of microbes, Pidoux invoked the concept of diathesis, emphasizing that disease was determined by the particular constitution of the patient. He held the view that any disease could be caused by a multiplicity of external and internal causes and could not be regarded as due to one single specific agent. Necrotic processes could take place "along a number of roads each of which the physician should endeavor to close." Pidoux and his like spoke in broad clinical terms, basing their doctrines on the phenomena of disease as observed in human beings. But their vague arguments were no match for the precise experimentation by which Pasteur, Koch, and their followers defended the doctrine of specific causation of infectious disease. Experimental science triumphed over clinical experience, and within a decade the theory of specific etiology of disease was all but universally accepted, soon becoming the dominant force in medicine. Eventually, the doctrine of specificity was generalized to encompass the concept of specific "biochemical lesion," which is proving today as fruitful in the fields of metabolic, degenerative, and neoplastic diseases as the concept of specific microbial etiology has proved in dealing with the problem of infectious diseases. There is no doubt that the doctrine of specific etiology has constituted an instrument of unmatched power for the experimental study of pathological processes and has been responsible for most of the great advances, theoretical and practical, realized in medicine during the past century.

It is now apparent, however, that the concept of single etiology often fails to provide a complete explanation for the pathogenesis of diseases under natural conditions. In "complex infections," two or more microbial agents are required to reproduce the pathological picture—the participation of influenza virus and *Hemophilus influenzae suis* in swine influenza being the classic example. In the case of practically all infectious and metabolic disorders, physiological and environmental factors can readily be shown to be important determinants of the disease process.

. . .

IN GENERAL, the accounts of the controversies that heralded the germ theory of disease dismiss the views of those who objected to some of its extreme tenets as the voice of obscurantism and reaction in medicine. Yet there were shrewd thinkers among the physicians who were not convinced that micro-organisms alone could account for the causation of disease. They did not deny that micro-organisms were present in diseased tissue. They emphasized rather that disease was prevalent chiefly among individuals exposed to, and suffering from, the strains and stresses of life. In their opinion, micro-organisms could invade and cause disease only after the tissues had been weakened by some form of physiological misery.

It was not only the brilliant if somewhat superficial clinicians of the Radcliffe-Pidoux type who held this view. On their side of the controversy were many experienced and wise hygienists, epidemiologists, and pathologists. Rudolf Virchow was one of those who believed that micro-organisms are secondary invaders and that physiological disturbances are always the primary cause of disease. In 1847, while still a young man of twenty-six, he had served as a member of a medical commission sent by the Prussian government to investigate the widespread occurrence of epidemics in the industrial sections of Upper Silesia. There he noticed that fevers were particularly prevalent among those living under miserable circumstances, and he became convinced that poverty was the real breeder of disease. He pointed out, furthermore, that Negroes living in Europe were much more apt to contract tuberculosis than those who had stayed in their native lands or than whites of the same age working at the same trades and exposed to the same risks of infection. Did not this incriminate the physiological disturbance brought about by the change from the tropical to the northern climes as primary cause of the disease?

Although Virchow recognized the importance of Koch's discovery of the tubercle bacillus, he had good epidemiological reasons to remain unimpressed while presiding at the now famous meeting of the Berlin Physiological Society in 1882, where Koch first presented his report. Indeed, Virchow would have been even less impressed had he known, as we know today, that almost every adult individual in Europe at that time was infected with virulent tubercle bacilli and that Koch himself was certainly infected, as indicated by the violence of his reaction when he injected tuberculin into his own arm in 1891. Virchow could have argued that since the tubercle bacillus was a ubiquitous component of the environment, the factors that converted mere infection into overt symptoms and destructive pathological changes were the real determinative causes of tuberculosis.

The knowledge accumulated during the past seventy-five years has left unsolved many of the problems of the pathogenesis of tuberculosis. Tuberculin tests reveal that even in our communities a very large percentage of the adult population has been at some time infected with tubercle bacilli. Yet the morbidity and mortality of tuberculosis have decreased by tenfold to twentyfold during the past century. It is obvious, therefore, that while the tubercle bacillus is the specific etiological agent of *infection*, there are other factors that are responsible for converting infection into tuberculosis *disease*. In other words, the etiology of disease cannot be explained entirely in terms of the etiology of infection.

Would time permit, one could list many examples of infections caused by either protozoa, fungi, bacteria, rickettsia, or viruses that are ubiquitous in their distribution among human, animal, or plant communities but remain in a latent, essentially inactive state under ordinary "normal" circumstances. These latent infections express themselves in the form of disease only after some physiological or environmental factor has caused a primary disturbance that allows the microbial agent to manifest its potential pathogenicity. In fact, the nature of the pathological processes may to a large extent be independent of the specific microbial agent associated with it. Thus it has been frequently observed during recent years that the intensive use of chemotherapy in the treatment of subacute endocarditis caused by green streptococci, while successful in eliminating these organisms from the lesions and bloodstream, often results in their substitution by other microbial species. As a consequence, forms of endocarditis associated with staphylococci or even Gram-negative bacilli are not uncommon in patients treated with antistreptococcal drugs. Seventy-five years ago, this would have appeared to the opponents of the germ theory as just one more example of a situation where the fundamental disease is the organic lesion (on the heart valves) and the microbial agents merely opportunistic secondary invaders.

This point of view gains further support from experiments in man demonstrating that the presence in normal tissues of pathogenic agents even in colossal numbers may not always be sufficient to bring about the state of disease until other injurious agencies have prepared the ground for them. In 1893, Max von Pettenkofer and several of his students swallowed tumblersful of cholera vibrios directly isolated from fatal cases in the disastrous Hamburg outbreak. Although the vibrios could be recovered in huge numbers from the stools of the experimenters, the only pathological effect observed was a mild diarrhea. A few years later, Élie Metchnikoff repeated the experiment on himself and two other human beings with the same result. More recently, similar failures have been observed in attempting to produce bacillary dysentery or the common cold in human volunteers.

It is known that most, if not all, human beings can contract bacillary dysentery when first exposed to the disease under the proper field conditions, as shown by the fact that new bodies of troops transported to areas where dysentery is endemic rapidly fall prey to the disease. Yet despite all the available knowledge concerning dysentery bacilli, and despite the overwhelming evidence of the communicability of the disease, it has proved extremely difficult to establish experimentally in human beings or in animals an infection presenting the typical symptomatic and pathological characteristics of bacillary dysentery. A few years ago, human volunteers were made to ingest dysentery bacilli of the Flexner group recently isolated from patients and known to be virulent for mice. All precautions were taken to favor the establishment of the infection. It was first determined that the volunteers were not carriers of *Shigella* and had negative histories of diarrheal disease. They were given paregoric and sodium bicarbonate before and after receiving the infective dose, and water in order to dilute the gastric secretions and wash the material through the stomach quickly. Yet the administration of up to 95 billion bacilli failed to produce significant symptoms of dysentery in most volunteers, even though the bacilli could be recovered from their stools on several successive days. No greater success was achieved by introducing along with the bacilli a gelatin capsule containing 1 gram of feces collected from a patient with clinical dysentery and containing large numbers of living bacilli.

The occurrence of bacillary dysentery in monkeys presents epidemiological problems that are no less puzzling. Many monkeys suffer from dysentery caused by one of the *Shigella* types at the time they are received from dealers. They are then usually in a bad state of nutrition because of their unwillingness to eat the food provided during their shipment. In general, however, the dysentery disappears spontaneously when they have become accustomed to their new environment and diet. It is furthermore almost impossible to infect them experimentally unless they are first reduced to an extreme degree of malnutrition.

Few are the human beings who do not suffer from the common cold once or several times every year, and few are the epidemiologists and laymen who do not believe that the affliction spreads readily by contact and that certain environmental circumstances such as wet and cold weather, drafts, fatigue, and so on increase the susceptibility to it. Since people find it so difficult to avoid catching a cold although they are extremely reluctant to, one could expect that it would be easy for the experimenters to "give" the disease to human volunteers willing to submit themselves to all the conditions assumed to be favorable for its transmission. But this has not proved to be the case. It has been known for almost two decades that one can elicit mild symptoms of coryza in a certain percentage of human beings by administering to them filtrates of nasal washings and discharges from individuals in the early stages of the common cold. Thus the etiological agent appears to be a filterable virus. It has also been found in early experiments that human beings are less likely to develop symptoms when exposed to the infective dose in an environment conducive to physiological and mental well-being. Thus experimentation seems to confirm what had been suspected from observations in daily life—namely, that we are highly receptive to the common-cold agent under special circumstances. But these circumstances are difficult to define, as was the experience of the workers of the Common Cold Commission in England. In experiment after experiment, they introduced intranasally into human volunteers large volumes of presumably infective discharges freshly collected from patients in the acute phase of the disease, but only a small percentage of the would-be victims developed acute signs of cold, even if exposed to air drafts in wet socks for hours immediately after having the infective dose. Whatever the technique of infection used and whatever the environmental circumstances, the common cold so difficult to escape in ordinary life manifested itself to the experienced investigators who tried to conjure it only in a small percentage of their human volunteers. It appears, in other words, that the development of the overt cold in human beings is determined less by the quantitative degree of exposure to the virus than by ill-defined factors that make us susceptible to it.

It is somewhat entertaining to muse over the fact that although all textbooks of bacteriology and infectious disease present the Henle-

Koch postulates as the very bedrock that gives permanent basis and scientific dignity to the germ theory of disease, these postulates have hardly ever been satisfied in man. In reality, the faith that micro-organisms play the primary role in the causation of disease grew out of the forcefulness of Pasteur's and Koch's convictions, rather than out of the impeachability of the evidence they presented.

Lest this statement be considered as a facile and irresponsible exercise in "debunking," let us admit immediately the obvious fact that Pasteur, Koch, and their disciples and followers based their conviction on facts of absolute validity. But these facts were valid only for the very limited and well-described circumstances under which they were observed. It was no small part of Pasteur's and Koch's vision and genius that they selected for the demonstration of their thesis experimental situations in which it was not only necessary but also *sufficient* to bring the host and parasite together in order to reproduce the disease. Farm and laboratory animals *never* carry the anthrax bacillus, *all* guinea pigs are susceptible to tuberculosis, injection of rabies virus under the dura of dogs *always* gives rise to paralytic symptoms, and so forth. Thus, by the skillful selection of their experimental models, Pasteur and Koch could eliminate from their studies the factors other than the parasite that are necessary to demonstrate that infection can result in symptoms and pathological alterations. The techniques of experimentation they worked out were designed to test the pathogenic properties of parasites under reproducible conditions—ideally a highly susceptible animal placed in a simple, defined, and constant environment. Useful as this artificial system has been for the study of some of the properties of microparasites, it has led to the neglect—and indeed has often delayed the recognition—of the many other facts that are essential to the causation of disease under circumstances prevailing in the natural world—namely, the physiological characteristics of the host and the physicochemical as well as social environment.

WE HAVE USED so far examples taken from human pathology to illustrate the view that the causation of disease under natural conditions often involves the simultaneous operation of several independent etiological factors. In reality, however, this holds true as well for many varied types of pathological processes in all classes of living things.

In nature many bacterial species called "lysogenic" carry in an inactive form (prophage) one or several bacteriophages potentially capable of causing their lysis. Under ordinary conditions, the prophage is apparently reproduced with each bacterial division without causing any detectable disturbance in the cell. This equilibrium can be upset by a number of nonspecific procedures—for example, irradiation of the lysogenic culture—in such a manner that the prophage is converted into active bacteriophage, multiplies abundantly, and causes the destruction of its host cell. Thus the prophage behaves as a pathogen for the cell that carries it only when the latter is subjected to the proper kind of stimulus. One might say that the prophage renders the bacterium sensitive to the radiation, or that the radiation renders it susceptible to the phage, or that both agents are required for the causation of lysis. In fact, it has been shown that—in certain cases, at least—the activating effect of radiation can take place only in media of certain composition, thus rendering even more complex the etiological determination of lysis.

There are likewise many examples of plants that either live in harmony with fungi, bacteria, or viruses or are destroyed by them, depending on the nature of the physicochemical environment in which the association takes place. The root-nodule bacteria illustrate well this complex relationship. Under natural field conditions, leguminous plants establish with the nodule bacteria a spontaneous symbiosis, which is of great advantage to both partners. Invasion of the plant by the nodule bacteria is facilitated by the production in the root of a specific exudation at a certain stage in the germination of the plant. Modification of both bacteria and host tissues occurs after invasion, the root nodule constituting in reality a modified root adjusted to the requirements of the bacterial symbionts. Since excessive production of nodules would deprive the plant of its functional root system and thus terminate its existence, the association is regulated by inhibitors produced in the meristems of the root and nodules. But this regulating system itself is under the control of environmental factors, general invasion of the plant by the bacteria taking place if boron is omitted from the soil or culture medium. In this case, therefore, it takes both a nutritional deficiency of the plant (deficiency of boron) and the presence of the nodule bacteria to constitute the complete etiology of a change from symbiotic relationship to the state of disease.

As is well known, the agent responsible for mammary carcinoma among breeding female mice has all the characteristics of a virus. Although the Bittner virus occurs throughout the tissues of infected animals, it causes no obvious sign of disease and in particular no tumors until lactation has begun. Male mice do not develop breast cancer even if they carry or have ingested the virus, nor do female mice unless under the stimulus of continuous reproductive activity. Thus whereas the virus can remain latent in the animals that harbor it, the hormonal and other stimuli that accompany reproduction and lactation are necessary and sufficient to induce it to elicit pathological reactions. In other words, these physiological stimuli are, as much as the virus, etiological agents of the mammary tumors of mice.

All the pathological processes so far mentioned to illustrate the concept of multiple etiology involve the participation of microorganisms or of viruslike agents. But one could also find in other fields of pathology many examples where the causation of disease probably requires that several independent factors act together or in succession. Thus it is well recognized that conditions as varied as hemorrhagic shock, peptic ulcers, or degenerative diseases are multifactorial phenomena requiring for their genesis the simultaneous occurrence of several physicochemical and vascular disturbances conditioned by a variety of organic and psychogenic controls.

We shall briefly consider as a last example the problem of causation of the plant cancer known as crown gall, because the precise knowledge that has been gained of its physiological determinants and chemical basis illustrates in a striking manner the conceptual difficulties involved in the determination of etiology. It is possible to induce at will characteristic tumors (crown galls) by inoculating sunflower or certain other plants with pure cultures of *Agrobacterium tumefaciens*. Since no other foreign organism or substance is known to be capable of causing this pathological reaction, it seems fair to regard *A. tumefaciens* as the specific etiological agent. It has been established, however, that many of the secondary tumors developing on the same plant at sites removed from the initial infection are free of bacteria and yet can be transferred in series to new plants or propagated in tissue culture as self-reproducing structures. It is possible also to eliminate the bacterium from the tumor tissue by controlled heating, without affecting the power of autonomous growth of the latter. Thus, production of the cancer can be made independent of *A. tumefaciens*, which was at first its essential etiological agent.

It is known, furthermore, that extensive invasion of the plant by the bacterium may take place without resulting in tumor formation. Only plant cells that have been conditioned by certain stimuli associated with wound healing are rendered susceptible to transformation into tumor tissue by the bacterium. The physiological state of the host cells should therefore be considered also as an etiological determinant of crown gall.

Finally, it can be shown that whereas the normal plant tissue requires indoleacetic acid and the coconut-milk factor for growth in tissue culture, the self-reproducing tumor tissue can synthesize these essential growth factors (as well, perhaps, as others) and therefore does not need them. It is this biochemical characteristic that permits it to grow profusely and in a completely uncoordinated manner. Thus, at the present state of the analysis, the biochemical etiology of the disease appears to reside in an increased synthetic power, but on the other hand, it takes A. *tumefaciens* originally to induce the change.

Depending on the specialized interests of the investigator and the techniques that he chooses to use, the primary etiology of crown gall can be regarded as a specific bacterium, a transmissible cellular change dependent on a certain physiological state of the cell, or a biochemical disorder. The problem of etiology can be studied at different levels by the bacteriologist, the oncologist, the physiologist, or the biochemist. All points of view are justified, and discoveries at any one of the levels of investigation could add to the understanding of the mechanisms of the disease and probably lead to some technique of control.


IT IS OBVIOUS that the "normal" existence and performances of any living organism demand a state of subtle equilibrium between its different component parts, as well as between them and the factors—living and physicochemical—of the environment. Any change is likely to disturb the balance of forces upon which depends the maintenance of the normal state. "Disease," Virchow said, "is life under altered conditions."

The factor that disturbs the equilibrium may affect only one or a few individuals and give rise to isolated cases of clinical disease, or it may affect simultaneously many members of the community and then cause crowd diseases. To illustrate the wide spectrum of these complex interrelationships, one might mention the person who develops lobar pneumonia the week after attending a football game, not because he became at that time infected with pneumococci from the outside but rather because exposure to cold, or excitement, or excessive consumption of alcohol disorganized for a while the resistance of his tissues to the pneumococci that he normally carries. Or one might call attention to the fact that the most important problems of infection among internees in the German concentration camps during the war were not the acute dramatic epidemics but rather ordinary colds, bronchopneumonias, skin infections, pulmonary tuberculosis, and so forth—all conditions caused by organisms normally endemic in European communities. While life under normal circumstances usually permits a satisfactory *modus vivendi* with endemic pathogens, starvation and other forms of physiological misery soon cause infection to evolve into overt disease. It is of special interest in this regard that most internees rapidly recovered from these microbial diseases without the help of specific therapy, merely by being returned to their prewar normal environment.

The fact that the occurrence of peptic ulcers, arteriosclerosis and other vascular disorders, and even certain forms of cancer is markedly influenced by various social and economic factors is sufficient proof that here again, as for infectious diseases, it is necessary to broaden the concept of etiology if one is to achieve a comprehensive picture of pathogenesis. The logical evolution of this point of view is to lead back to the formula of medicine symbolized by the Hippocratic teachings. Any pathological process is the result of a multiplicity of diverse influences, and all its phases are influenced by everything that affects the organism as a whole.

It is because the physician must deal with situations involving so many independent variables that clinical medicine has remained an art even today—an art based on wisdom and skill derived from experience as much as on scientific knowledge and reasoning. The skill symbolized by the gold-headed cane was not mere charlatanism. It grew in no small part from the physician's awareness—though ill defined and often subconscious—of the many factors that play a part in the causation and manifestations of disease. Experience had taught him to manipulate many of the factors—physiological, psychological, and social—that affected the reactions of his patient.

But knowledge based on empirical experience either remains static or at best develops slowly. Progress demands systematic experimentation. Methodologically, there is danger in adopting too broad a biological and clinical point of view in the study of disease—the danger of substituting meaningless generalities and poor philosophy for the concreteness of exact knowledge. It is one of the most important contributions of the doctrine of specific etiology that it saved the science and practice of medicine from the morass of loose words and concepts. But insistence on concrete facts need not deter one from acknowledging that under natural conditions, the etiology of most diseases is multifactorial rather than specific. The laboratory worker can always circumvent the difficulty resulting from the multiplicity of etiological determinants by devising operations that permit him to study each of these separately and in various combinations.

By using a broadened concept of etiology, encompassing intrinsic and extrinsic determinants of disease, he will eventually develop a therapeutic science that will incorporate the human wisdom and empirical skill of the traditional medical art. "The variable composition of man's body hath made it an Instrument easy to distemper," Francis Bacon wrote. "The Office of Medicine is but to tune this curious Harp of man's body and to reduce it to Harmony."

# Tulipomania and Its Benevolent Virus

THE EXISTENCE of viruses was first recognized through their ability to cause disease in man, animals, or plants—a historical accident that has conditioned all subsequent research on the effects exerted by viral infections. A few years ago, when virologists met in New York to compare notes on a group of new viruses for which no role was known in nature, the expression "Viruses in Search of a Disease" emerged naturally among them to describe the topic of the meeting. It was obviously taken for granted by all the participants in the meeting that production of disease was the earmark of a true virus. Failing the discovery of a bona fide disease in an animal or plant, virologists try to satisfy their conviction that the *raison d'être* of a virus is to cause trouble by eliciting some sort of cytopathogenic effect in a tissue culture model—even, if need be, with a type of cell that the virus never has a chance to invade or even to encounter in nature. Not being a virologist, I can afford to take a more optimistic view of the problem and to entertain the fantasy that at least some viruses are now and then helpful rather than destructive to their hosts. I should like to consider with you the possibility that there are circumstances in which the

In M. Pollard, ed., *Perspectives in Virology* (New York: Harper & Row, 1958), pp. 291–99.

overall effects of viral infection are beneficial to the community and even to the infected host.

I shall build my discussion around the history of the tulipomania, a social disorder that reached its acute phase in the Netherlands and in Flanders during the early part of the seventeenth century. As some of you may not be familiar with this peculiar mania, allow me to tell you something of its origin.

The tulip has long been cultivated in Turkey but was unknown in Europe until the sixteenth century. It seems that the earliest European report of its existence came from Augier Ghislain de Busbecq, who was ambassador of Ferdinand I of Austria to the court of Suleiman the Magnificent. Busbecq saw fields of tulips in bloom for the first time while on a trip from Adrianople to Constantinople in January 1555, and he was so impressed by the flower that he immediately arranged to procure seeds and bulbs for several of his European friends. The following April Heinrich Herwart's garden in Augsburg was adorned with brilliant scarlet blooms. The tulip rapidly caught the fancy of Europeans. In Holland and in Flanders, its cultivation became almost a craze as well as a large matter of trade. Commercial growers and wealthy citizens competed for the production of new types of flowers characterized by attractive or unusual shapes, colors, or patterns of pigmentation. The production of a black tulip, for example, was a much desired achievement. The rivalries and tales to which it gave rise eventually found their way into Alexandre Dumas's novel, *La Tulipe Noire*.

Holland was at that time enjoying the most prosperous era of its history. An immense quantity of gold and silver was being introduced into the country by the Dutch buccaneers, who raided the Spanish and Portuguese ships homeward-bound with the precious metals from the West Indies. As a form of economic warfare against Spain, the Dutch government adopted a policy of "free" coinage, with the result that money was extremely abundant in the Netherlands. A general rise in local prices ensued, which encouraged speculation among the Dutch people. The tulip with its many varieties seemed to provide good speculative material; the fact that many bulbs could be produced from a single specimen led speculators to believe that unbounded wealth could be realized by propagating the more expensive flowers. After all, this was not sillier than other forms of gambling in a nonexistent commodity!

One of the earliest famous transactions was for one bulb of Semper

Augustus, a crimson-and-white "flamed" tulip that was bought for 13,000 florins in 1609. Interest in the flower continued to grow, and in Paris around 1630 it became the rage among fashionable ladies to wear tulip blooms as corsages. The tulipomania—this most attractive boom of history—finally reached its peak in Holland from 1634 to 1637.

During the tulipomania, the price of a single bulb of Semper Augustus went as high as 5,500 guilders. The following goods were exchanged for one bulb of Viceroy tulip: four tons of wheat, eight tons of rye, four fat oxen, eight fat pigs, twelve fat sheep, two hogsheads of wine, four barrels of beer, two barrels of butter, one thousand pounds of cheese, one bed with accessories, one full dress suit, and one silver goblet. History reports that profitable mills and inns were exchanged in Flanders for a single specimen and that a young woman became a very desirable bride when a famous bulb was made the single item of her dowry.

By 1637, the gambling had become so wild that the government of the Federated States of Holland and West Frisia undertook to discourage it by ordinances rendering more difficult the enforcing of time bargains in tulips. In 1648, moreover, the Dutch Republic discontinued "free" coinage when the Peace of Westphalia acknowledged its independence. This stopped the rise in prices and put an end to the acute febrile period of the tulipomania.

Some of the types of tulips that achieved greatest fame in history are well known from the handsome illustrations in Dutch, French, and English books of the seventeenth, eighteenth, and nineteenth centuries, as well as from paintings of the time. The Younger Brueghel ("Velvet" Brueghel) was one of the foremost tulip masters and has immortalized many types of flowers in a host of pictures. Other painters also have left portraits of tulips worthy of note—for example, that painted in 1619 by Ambrosius Bosschaert and now in the Rijksmuseum in Amsterdam. The Rembrandt and Zomerschoon tulips are among the famous ancient tulips that are still cultivated today.

In addition to elegance of form and beauty of color, many of the famous tulips were characterized by distinctive patterns of pigment. These variegated forms were first carefully observed by the botanist Charles de l'Ecluse of Arras, who cultivated tulips in his gardens in Vienna and in Flanders. Beginning in 1575, he described his findings in a series of accounts that were finally summarized in his book *Rariorum Plantarum Historia*, published in 1601. Charles de l'Ecluse's book, as well as many others published subsequently by Dutch, English, and

French gardenists, are illustrated by handsome pictures that leave no doubt that the highest prices during the tulipomania were obtained for variegated plants. Until very recently, indeed, nonvariegated flowers were rarely illustrated in books, because they were regarded as inferior and nondifferentiated forms. Only during the past few years and after the development of the handsome Darwins have nonvariegated flowers come to be preferred to the other because of their greater vigor and uniformity, especially for mass planting.

It was soon recognized that tulips raised from seeds do not produce variegated flowers at first. These plants (called breeders) have petals of uniform color—they are self-colored, as the expression goes—and their bulbs may continue to produce self-colored flowers for several years. Then, after an unpredictable period of time, there occurs a phenomenon referred to as "breaking," which results in variegation. From then on the bulbs of "broken" tulips continue to produce variegated flowers. According to van Slogteren and Ouboter (1941), Dutch growers knew as early as 1637 that breaking could be produced at will by grafting self-colored tulips with variegated ones; Blagrave, in England, described in 1675 detailed techniques for grafting halves of bulbs to this end. It was also believed that breaking could be hastened by planting bulbs in poor soil or even better by alternating cultivation in good and bad soil. But despite much practical knowledge, tulip breaking has remained an art, and the mystery attending the phenomenon probably contributed to the captivating charm of the plant.

In 1928, tulip breaking passed from horticultural lore into virus science when Cayley, in England, and McKay, in America, demonstrated that the change in the flowers was in reality the result of a viral infection of the mosaic type. Under natural conditions the virus is transmitted by aphids, but infection can also be achieved by experimental procedures, either by injection of plant juices or by grafting. Let it be mentioned in passing that the virus is widely distributed in wild lilies and in other plants; the tiger lily has been likened to Typhoid Mary in this regard. In consequence, a self-colored tulip has little chance of escaping infection in the field, even though it never comes into contact with the broken tulips. Breaking is likely to occur even when tulips are planted near apparently normal lilies, for healthy plants can carry the virus in a nonapparent form.

The viral infection can affect the color of the petals and also the leaves. Nor is breaking limited to tulip varieties containing anthocyanin pigments; it can also occur in clear whites or yellows, which show then

little or no change in color. The most striking manifestations of breaking, however, are changes in the distribution of anthocyanins in the
epidermis of the petals, which become splashed or striped with different colors. It is held by McWhorter (1938) that two antagonistic viruses
are involved in tulip breaking. According to this author, one virus
interferes with normal anthocyanin production and also causes a leaf
mottle, whereas the other interferes with the floral color and has no
effect on the leaves. Van Slogteren and Ouboter believe, however, that
one virus and differences in host response can account for the various
manifestations of breaking.

Breaking of tulips is, therefore, now considered as the result of
infection by a virus or by a combination of several viruses. In fact, the
seventeenth-century horticulturists and their followers had realized
that all was not well with some of their most attractive broken specimens. They had observed that broken tulips were likely to be less
vigorous than the self-colored plants and to produce fewer bulbs. In a
number of cases, indeed, death of broken tulips occurred after a few
generations. It is also true, on the other hand, that some broken tulips
have been in cultivation for more than 350 years—for example, the
Zomerschoon tulip has been known since 1620 and probably existed in
Turkey before being introduced into Europe. When propagated by
bulbs, a procedure that transmits the virus from generation to generation, these tulips continue indefinitely to produce broken blooms, but
they exhibit no evidence of any cumulative weakening effect caused by
the infection. It is almost ironic to call a condition that has contributed
to the spread of certain kinds of tulips all over the world, and has
enriched the lives of millions of people, a disease. In some respects,
broken tulips are like the frail-looking women who outlive their more
robust contemporaries and inherit their wealth.

Flower breaking caused by various types of viruses has now been
recognized in several plant species—the wallflower, the larkspur, the
pansy, the camellia. Specimens of these flowers that had been selected
as new varieties have turned out to derive their unusual and often
desirable characteristics from viral infections. Certain other ornamental effects are also known to result from interference with the chloro-
phyll of the leaves by viral infection. The pale, veined type of
honeysuckle is probably the most recently recognized example of this
type. Among the plants that became established as ornamental species
because of a mosaic-type viral infection, one of the best known is
*Abutilon striatum* var. *thompsonii* (also known in florist shops as flower-

ing maple). It is easy to grow abutilon from seed and thus obtain plants free of virus, with green leaves unmottled and unstreaked. But the public favors the infected plants, because their leaves exhibit interesting patterns of variegation. Thus abutilon owes much of its biological success (among human beings) to its accompanying virus. My colleague Dr. Francis Holmes informs me that all the specimens of the Wedgewood iris that he has observed are virus-infected. The iris—very popular in flower shops—is produced exclusively from bulbs and rarely exhibits any sign of infection except mottling of the leaves. Although flower breaking occurs in this species, it is unusual and not attractive.

Virologists regard the broken tulips and the ornamental abutilon as diseased plants, because they are virus infected—this despite the fact that infection does not affect the survival of the plants and has increased their world distribution. In contrast, botanists and general microbiologists regard many cases of bacterial and fungal infection as manifestations of symbiosis because of beneficial effects on the plant or animal hosts. The fixation of atmospheric nitrogen in legume plants by the nodule bacteria and the enhancement of seed germination in orchids and heather by fungus constitute familiar examples. Virologists will point out, of course, that the virus of tulip breaking often decreases the size and vigor of infected plants and occasionally causes the death of some. But the same probably holds true for many other types of biological associations known to have beneficial effects. Even the nodule bacteria of legumes can become invasive and kill their hosts under certain environmental conditions. As Noel Bernard pointed out long ago, symbiosis is always at the threshold of parasitism.

Many infections are known that protect the infected individual against infection with a more virulent strain. However, it is not easy to find in the literature examples of bona fide viral infection that virologists would accept as beneficial. One might regard certain viral infections that hasten the development of flowers of pome fruit trees, prolong the life of asters, or cause carrots to produce sterile seeds the first year as having ecological advantage for the infected plants under certain conditions. But no proof of such advantage has yet been obtained. The relation of some plant viruses to their insect vectors is also suggestive. Infected insects live as long and breed as freely as those not infected, even though the viruses multiply extensively in their bodies. Indeed, it has been claimed, but on the basis of inadequate evidence, that leafhoppers raised on celery or aster plants infected with aster yellows virus develop faster, live longer, and produce more young than those fed on healthy plants. Similarly, aphids fed on sugar beets infected with virus seem to be more fecund than those fed on healthy plants. It is possible, of course, that these beneficial effects are indirect and merely the expression of nutritional factors rather than of the presence of the virus in the tissues of the insect. But whatever their cause, their ultimate result may constitute an ecological advantage to the infected insect.

The rickettsia-like intracellular particles in insects and the chloroplasts in *Chlorella* might be registered as examples of useful infection, since they confer advantages and yet are not essential to survival of the insect or the plant—as shown by the fact that they can be eliminated by drug treatment. But endosymbionts are called plastids and not viruses by cytologists. It might be pointed out in passing that if endosymbionts with beneficial effects are called plastids by definition, then it becomes obviously pointless to search the literature for a useful virus.

Fortunately for my theme, there exist a few types of relationships between bacteria and bacteriophage for which objective evidence is available that the presence of the virus can be of advantage to the infected host under special circumstances. For instance, the diphtheria bacillus produced toxin only when infected with the proper kind of beta bacteriophage. Toxigenic strains no longer produce toxin when "cured" of their bacteriophage infection and produce it again after being reinfected. As the nontoxigenic bacilli are unable to proliferate in living tissues, it is apparent that the biological success of this bacterial species is enhanced by bacteriophage infection. The transduction by lambda phage of galactozymase to *E. coli*, type K12, also can be of some potential ecologic value, since the ability to produce the enzyme would be essential for multiplication in certain metabolic environments. Of greater practical influence is the transduction of somatic (O) antigens and probably of other virulence factors in Enterobacteriacea. It can hardly be doubted that the pathogenic behavior of these bacteria is profoundly affected by their ability to acquire new immunologic characteristics as a result of infection with the proper kind of bacteriophage.

It will be noted that in the examples of bacteria–bacteriophage relations just cited the biologic advantage accruing from infection could become manifest only under special environmental circumstances. This limitation probably accounts for the failure to recognize that other viruses may also exert beneficial effects on their host cells. In general, the techniques used by the virologist are designed to demonstrate pathogenic effects and almost by necessity, therefore, fail to detect beneficial relationships. The beneficial role of nodule bacteria in legumes was detected by growing these plants in soil or in media deficient in nitrogen. Legumes do not need the bacteria if soluble nitrogenous compounds are readily available, and moreover, they can be killed by the infection under certain circumstances.

Since beneficial relationships become manifest only in specialized ecological situations, the proof of their existence in viral infections will require the development of new techniques and new test conditions. It will be necessary, furthermore, to introduce broader criteria for evaluating the outcome of the virus-host relationships. One of the reasons why virologists do not accept that the variegation caused by viruses constitutes a characteristic with survival value is that they regard as valid only those criteria that are measurable by laboratory operations. Esthetic and emotional reaction certainly play a role as determinants of biological success, but they have not gained a place among scientific parameters because they cannot be readily measured. Nitrogen fixation can be measured, and for this reason infection of the sweet pea by nodule bacteria is regarded as symbiosis; if the effect of infection were merely to improve the fragrance or appearance of the flower, it would be regarded as disease.

It is true that human tastes change, but they do not always change for the better. Masses of healthy tulips all of the same color and size and arranged in rows like soldiers do not necessarily constitute a more desirable achievement than the virus-infected specimens lovingly portrayed by the seventeenth-century painters. Pink, or bronzed, the burly men and women in the health camps of political parties may not be the finest flowering of the human race.

It is probable that viral infections prevent the Zomerschoon tulip and the variegated abutilon from achieving their maximum potential size. But size is not a very significant criterion of success. By making the infected specimens of tulips and abutilon more interesting individuals, the viruses have given them a biological advantage that encouraged their spread. If we choose to call a process, which has carried these lovely plants all over the world and enriched thereby the life of men both literally and figuratively, a disease, then it follows that civilization certainly owes much to disease—for the most interesting and most creative individuals are not necessarily the healthiest members of the species.

# Microbiology in
# Fable and Art

WHEN MODERN SCIENTISTS tire of their austere textbooks and professional articles, they can, if they wish, seek relief and entertainment in the many strange tales found in the early annals of all fields of scientific endeavor. The astronomer can discover romance in the fanciful and poetical cosmogony of the ancients, the chemist in the weird imaginings of alchemy, the zoologist and botanist in the legendary creatures that enliven the lore of all people and give such festive and mysterious atmosphere to medieval books and tapestries. Furthermore, these quaint documents often yield facts of scientific value. The star that guided the wise men to Bethlehem, the prehistoric drawings of animals now extinct, the list of plants and flowers in the old herbals and in Shakespeare—all have found some place in the fabric of modern science.

Alone of biological sciences, microbiology appears at first sight to be without a remote and fanciful past. Its founder, Anton van Leeuwenhoek, was an acute, industrious, and factual—but unromantic—bourgeois. For a century after him, microbiologists continued to work earnestly on problems of description and classification. Then Pasteur and Koch taught them to harness their skill and energy to

American Society of Bateriologists, *Bacteriological Reviews*, no. 16 (1952) pp. 145–51.

the practical affairs of mankind in an effort to make their profession respected in the scientific community. The most diligent search discloses nothing but businesslike statements in the microbiological literature of Europe and America. It is true that a few years ago Dr. Paul Clark was bold enough to present, as his presidential address to the Society of American Bacteriologists, an essay entitled "Alice in Virusland," which he adorned with nonsense verses and delightful cartoons. But probably as a form of atonement, the society exacted a fine of one dollar on those of its members so frivolous as to wish to own a copy of this nontechnical document.

I shall not be as bold as Dr. Clark, nor do I have his skill as a versifier. I shall try, nevertheless, to show you that the lore of primitive civilizations, the poems, novels, drama, and arts of all times yield much material that microbiology can legitimately claim as belonging to its past. These traces of the prehistory of our science are often indistinct and can be detected only by trained eyes. Unlike stars, animals, and plants, micro-organisms cannot be seen by the unaided senses. And just as it is only through their effects that we become aware of them, similarly it is only by trying to recognize the influence of microbial life on the adventures of civilizations that we can hope to discover the early romance of microbiology.

Familiar examples immediately come to mind. The Bible is full of references to the effects of yeast in causing the grape to ferment or the dough to rise. And all of us know that the red spots occasionally seen on the wafers used for communion in the Christian churches were long regarded as the miraculous blood of Christ until the bacteriologist identified them as colonies of *Bacillus prodigiosus*. The soft glow of luminous bacteria and fungi growing on dead trees and leaf mold or on the decaying bodies of animals and human beings creates in the dark of the night an eerie atmosphere that has added mystery and terror to many events in the past.

The will-o'-the-wisp, perhaps better known as jack o'lantern, is also probably a microbial phenomenon. It plays a role in countless legends of Northern Europe, Ireland, French Brittany, and the South in this country. During much of the nineteenth century and until a few decades ago, the will-o'-the-wisp was a subject of lively discussion in learned scientific journals. Many trained observers have watched and measured these small balls of bluish fire hovering over marshy lands during warm nights, disappearing and suddenly reappearing a few feet away, like sylphids dancing lightly on the stagnant waters. In general, the accounts by modern scientists agree remarkably well with the description of storytellers recounting how mysterious and wicked lights lure the traveler astray and lead him to be lost in the swamps. Certainly the will-o'-the-wisp is not a mere product of imagination. But although it possesses physical reality, there is as yet no adequate account of its nature, and, to my knowledge, it has never been reproduced experimentally. All observers agree that will-o'-the-wisp appears only in waterlogged places during warm weather under conditions where organic matter can be presumed to decompose anaerobically. It is often associated with a faint smell of garlic, and its transient lights float a few inches above the surface of the ground or water. The known features of the phenomenon are compatible with the hypothesis that the will-o'-the-wisp results from the spontaneous ignition of phosphine in the presence of methane, since both gases can be produced simultaneously where organic matter decomposes in the absence of air. But I shall remember that hypotheses are themselves little more than will-o'-the-wisps that usually lead the scientist into disgrace. And instead of running the risk of letting myself be lured into the swamps of anaerobic fermentations, I shall return to the vaporous lands of history, where many things are so uncertain that hazy discourse is acceptable even to scientists.

Although the precise understanding of the relation of microorganisms to natural phenomena is a recent acquisition of science, the thought that minute invisible forms of life are responsible for many transformations of matter and for aspects of disease has certainly occurred many times in the course of ancient history. In Roman literature there is a suggestion of it in the sixth book of Lucretius' poem *De Rerum Natura:* "There are many seeds of things that support our life, and on the other hand, there must be many flying about that make for disease and death."

Even more explicit is the warning given by Varro in 50 B.C. to those about to select a place for a dwelling. Said he, "There exist in the air minute animals too small to be seen, but which can penetrate into the mouth and nose, and cause disease."

The germ theory of disease appeared again sixteen centuries later in the writings of one of the last great writers of the Latin language, the Veronese Fracastoro, who was a physician, better known as a poet. Fracastoro's interest in the disease that had spread like wildfire through Europe in the early part of the sixteenth century has come down to us chiefly through his great poem "Syphilis," published in 1530. Syphilis, as you will recall, is one of the chief characters of the poem, a young shepherd who had been stricken by the malady as a penalty for lack of respect to the gods. So immensely popular was the poem that the name of its hero has remained associated with the disease ever since. In addition to having introduced the word "syphilis," Fracastoro's poem also provides information concerning the severity and treatment of the disease during the sixteenth century. We learn, for example, that the shepherd went to worship at the altar of Mercury in an attempt to cure his malady, for the metal was even then known to have some value as a therapeutic agent. Fracastoro also begs his muse to assure immortality to the poem in order that subsequent generations be aware of the destructiveness of syphilis in its acute form. He had noticed that the disease was decreasing in severity but feared that it might someday recover its original virulence. So ancient is the recognition that epidemics fall and rise in an unpredictable manner!

Although diseases have long been recognized to exert an influence on history, it is chiefly their effects on large events that have been emphasized. Microbiologists cannot fail to recall how Hans Zinsser illustrated in his witty book *Rats, Lice and History* the part played by typhus in the great wars of the past. It is also held by many historians that malaria contributed to the downfall of the Greek, Roman, and Mayan empires by progressively sapping the energy of the affected populations. But wars and political events are not the only aspects of life affected by epidemics. Many microbial diseases have certainly played an immense historical role in modifying habits and emotions, literature and the arts, and indeed the very moods of civilizations. Thus leprosy has long held a strange sway on the minds of men. In the Bible, as you know, it is the object of very detailed instructions by Leviticus. The ritual devised by the Christian churches to deal with the leper during the Middle Ages betrays the horror inspired by the disease. In a dramatic ceremony, the leper was declared "dead to the world," being allowed to move among men only if he advertised his presence with a bell and with the word "unclean."

Plague also was a dreaded disease of the Middle Ages and Renaissance. As with leprosy, its prevalence and destructiveness are reflected in countless illustrations and paintings of the time. Let us note in passing that the depiction of rodents in all illustrations of plague makes it clear that the relation of these animals to the epidemics has long been recognized. Plague, the Black Death, had a profound influence on the history of Renaissance art through many indirect effects. Immediately after 1350, dire prophecies of new pestilences to come prompted the donation of huge sums of money for the creation and embellishment of churches, chapels, and monasteries. The immense death toll in Florence forced relaxation of the guild laws, which limited the immigration of artisans, physicians, and jurists into the city. Within a few years a class of nouveaux riches arose out of the reshuffle of wealth, and their unsophisticated tastes imposed more conservative formula of creation on the artists whom they commissioned.

The Black Death appears frequently in the literature of the Renaissance. You recall that Boccaccio's *Decameron* deals with ten young men and women of Florence who retired to a villa in the hills in an attempt to escape the epidemic that devastated the city in the year 1348 and how they spent leisurely days together entertaining themselves with the tales that have entertained the world ever since. Soon, however, Boccaccio himself became the victim of the dark state of mind that the Black Death engendered in his contemporaries. The pestilence was almost universally regarded as the manifestation of the wrath of an aroused God punishing mankind for its wickedness. The sense of guilt and resultant asceticism is reflected in Boccaccio's novel *Il Corbaccio*, published in 1354. In fact, the gloomy vision of the world that then pervaded most of Italy led the author of the carefree *Decameron* to turn bitterly against his own early work. It is also from the plague that Alessandro Manzoni derived four centuries later some of the most exciting situations that he introduced in *I Promessi Sposi*, the first novel of importance in the modern Italian language.

Throughout the nineteenth century in Europe and North America, it is easy to detect the influence of tuberculosis in diaries, letters, literature, the arts, and even in fashion. For example, the desire by young women and also by men to acquire the romantic and fashionable aspect of the tuberculous individual accounts in part for the widespread use of whitening powders. Even the symbols and images used in the literature of the time reflect the influence of the disease. Autumn and the falling of leaves come to represent the death of everything in nature, and the colors of the dying foliage were likened to the blood of the consumptive. In "Ode to the West Wind," Shelley described the falling leaves as "pale, and hectic red," like "Pestilence-stricken multitudes." Thoreau, observing the first spotted maple leaves "with a greenish center and a crimson border," was led to remark in his Journal, "Decay and disease are often beautiful, like . . . the hectic glow of consumption."

Although it is as agents of disease that micro-organisms have exerted their most obvious effects on civilization, other forms of microbial life have also influenced the emotions and beliefs of men, often in a more subtle but profound manner. "All are of the dust and return to dust again" had said Ecclesiastes, and Lucretius paraphrased the Bible many centuries later by proclaiming "Whatever earth contributes to feed the growth of others is restored to it . . . the universal mother is also the common grave." Thus the observed fact that all things that grow decay, and that new life grows out of the products of decay, gave birth to the concept that everything in nature is in a constant state of flux. Lucretius expressed his belief in this continuity of living matter through the symbol of the torch of life, passed from hand to hand as in an eternal race.

This resplendent vision was not born entirely *de novo* in the mind of the Roman poet. It had emerged in philosophy and poetry as a word structure from a deep substratum of ancient emotions and beliefs. Almost universally among primitive populations living in intimate contact with nature and its primeval forces, one can perceive the vague but overwhelming awareness that life possesses a continuity that transcends the existence of the individual organism—plant, animal, or human being. All religions and folklore have tried to symbolize and celebrate in their legends and festivals the reawakening of nature at the end of the winter. In ancient times, the pageantry of the rites of spring was not merely a display of gladness at seeing new foliage, flowers, birds, and young animals playing in the fields. It had a more profound and mystic inspiration, symbolizing as it did the resurrection of life through the fecundation of the earth. In Greece, the largest sacred monuments and the most elaborate celebrations were dedicated to Demeter, the goddess of the procreative power. She represented the fertilizing principle of nature in general and of the soil in particular. Every September there was held at Eleusis, in Attica, the great "mysteries" to commemorate the abduction by Pluto of Persephone, daughter of Zeus and Demeter, and her disappearance into the kingdom of the dead. And in the early spring another festival at Agrae near Athens celebrated the return of Persephone to the earth. It is clear the myth of Demeter and Persephone symbolizes the death of vegetation at the end of autumn followed by the resurrection of dead nature in the spring. It implied some form of belief in the continuity of life, a faith in immortality.

Similar myths with similar symbolism are found in all religions. Primitive man living in intimate contact with nature could not help experiencing the mysterious travail that goes on in the earth before it can again bear crops and flowers. He divined a multitude of living agencies, and before these could be identified by modern science, they were personalized and deified by popular beliefs. We, whose senses have been dulled by centuries of life in a man-made environment, can even now recapture in early spring the cosmic sense of participation in the rebirth of nature. We, too, feel the genial processes of nature actually at work, as if some spirit of life were really circulating beneath the leaf mold and in the sap of the trees. It is this intoxicating experience that is at the origin of the festivals of resurrection common to all religious faiths at the end of winter.

Indeed the rebirth in the spring means more than resurrection. It suggests some perpetual working, some continuous act of conception that assures the continuity of life. To most primitive people, decay does not appear as an end but merely as a phase in the transmission of the living principle. Thus, the concept that all life is part of some great whole and flows everlastingly from one form into another—and into humanity—is at the basis of many ancient philosophies and religions, and it has inspired some of our greatest poems.

This concept began to acquire scientific meaning during the seventeenth and eighteenth centuries, when it became understood that the minerals of the soil and the gases of the air are incorporated into living material during the growth of plants and pass from plants into the structure of animals. Furthermore, it was then realized that all organic matter eventually returns to the inorganic state before reentering the cycle of life. But while the conversion of matter from the inorganic to the organic state could be apprehended in general outline, the steps through which organic matter returns to the inorganic state were shrouded in mystery. As appears from a statement by Antoine Lavoisier, this problem haunted the natural philosophers of the pre-microbiological era. Said Lavoisier,

Plants extract from the air that surrounds them, from water and in general from the mineral kingdom, all the substances necessary to their organization. Animals feed either on plants or on other animals which themselves have fed on plants, so that the substances of which they are constituted originate, in final analysis, from air or from the mineral kingdom. Finally fermentation, putrefaction and combustion endlessly return to the atmosphere and to the mineral kingdom the principles which plants and animals had borrowed from them. What is the mechanism through which nature brings about this marvelous circulation of matter between the three kingdoms?

It was microbiology that provided the answer to this great riddle by revealing that many types of micro-organisms can precisely degrade complex organic molecules to the inorganic state and thus prepare them to become again available to plants. The practical applications of the new science of microbiology in medicine, agriculture, and industry were so great and immediate that they overshadowed completely the importance of the discovery of the microbial world for the understanding of the cycle of life. True enough, the philosophical import of the problem is discussed in Pasteur's early writings, and a vague awareness of it persists in the expressions "carbon cycle" and "nitrogen cycle," by which textbooks attempt to convey graphically the uninterrupted flow of matter from the inorganic to the living state through the agency of microbes. But few are the microbiologists who think in those terms today, and it is hardly ever emphasized that the events of microbial life have implications that transcend the understanding of the biochemical mechanisms involved in the transformation of matter. For the history of thought, it was a great step forward when microbiological science began to explain why decay is not death but merely a change of forms, as Lucretius and many before him had anticipated. Like plants and animals, microbes contribute some of the essential links in the endless chain that bends together the whole range of living forms. They, too, like runners in a race, hand on the lamp of life.

The pagans celebrating the fecundation of the earth in the rites of spring, the philosopher-poets of the Classical world pondering over the eternal flux of matter and life were motivated by preoccupations that still loom large in modern philosophy. The ancient myths are acquiring new significance as we begin to visualize the whole cycle of life. Wandering through the woods and fields on a warm humid day, we can decipher in part the message sent us through the pervasive odor of organic matter decomposing in the earth, the mysterious luminescence of bacteria and fungi in rotting wood. These microbial phenomena are more than the signs of biochemical reactions, they are the symbol of the creative power of life present always and everywhere in nature. To fully understand the symbol is beyond the reach of our time. But we have the right nevertheless to sublimate our small individual efforts by the faith that they will illuminate with the glorious light of reason obscure but venerable beliefs generated long ago by a mystic sense of wonder.

# PART IV

## Civilization and Human Biology

Each person is unique, unprecedented, and unrepeatable. . . . The species *Homo sapiens* can be described in the lifeless words of physics and chemistry, but not the person of flesh and bone. We recognize him by his voice, his facial expressions, and the way he walks—even more by his creative responses to surroundings and events.

# The Humanness of
# Prehistoric Man

IN A CAVE of eastern Oregon, near the village of Fort Rock, the American archaeologist L. S. Cressman and his students discovered in 1936 a cache of seventy-five sandals buried in volcanic pumice. Most of these are now on display in the archaeological museum of Oregon State University at Eugene. The sandals are woven from shredded sagebrush bark twisted into tight ropes thinner than an ordinary pencil, and they exhibit great uniformity in workmanship. They measure from 9 to 12 inches in length and would therefore fit a modern man. Yet archaeological evidence, recently confirmed by carbon-14 dating, proves that they were manufactured by Indians some 9,000 years ago.

Eastern Oregon is now a desert country, but during the Late Paleolithic period there was a large lake in the region where the sandals were discovered. The Indians who then lived around the lake had apparently developed a complex social organization, as is attested to by the storage of so many artifacts in a single cave. Human occupation of the area was probably interrupted by the volcanic eruption that deposited that layer of pumice over the floor of the Fort Rock cave. On first contact, the hot pumice charred the sandals somewhat, but after cool-

Reprinted with permission of Charles Scribner's Sons, an imprint of Macmillan Publishing Company, from *So Human an Animal*, pp. 31–47. Copyright © 1968 by René Dubos. Pulitzer Prize, 1969.

ing it acted as a protective layer preventing further deterioration from the inclemencies of the weather and attack by microbes and insects.

The detailed description of the sandals published by Dr. Cressman gives an idea of the workmanship of the Stone Age Indians:

Five pieces of rope laid lengthwise to the long axis of the foot served as warps and were fastened tightly together by twining weft strands. The toe ends of the warp strands, left untwisted, were forded back over the toes to form a protective pocket and, held slackly together, were fastened to the sides made by the looped weft strands. All were alike except a few which had cords running tightly and slightly diagonally across the sole. The purpose of this cord is unknown; if it had been serviceable as a non-skid device, it would probably have been more widely used. In some sandals pine needles had been added for padding.

Other types of sandals woven by Indians many thousand years ago have been discovered in several parts of the United States and can be seen in anthropological museums. They differ in workmanship and in style from region to region, indeed from one cave to another in the same region. Sandals found in Catlow Cave, Oregon, are not as well made as the ones from Fort Rock, even though the two sites are close to each other and were occupied by Indians during approximately the same period.

Sandals discovered in still other caves are made of tule, or more rarely of grass, instead of sagebrush bark. Irrespective of the material of which they are made, some are obviously designed for rough usage while others are more refined in style—some so elegant in design and workmanship that they would not seem out of place in a New York Fifth Avenue shop.

A few of the ancient Indian sandals are child-size and have rabbit fur woven into them as if for warmth and softness. Again quoting Dr. Cressman, an Oregon cave yielded

a pair of small sandals for a five- or six-year-old child, tied together by strings as we might tie a pair of sneakers. Nearby were two toy baskets, and a little farther off was a dart for a "dart and wheel" game. Because these objects lay close together, we are sure that they were the sandals and playthings of an Indian girl who had lived in that cave several thousand years ago. One day something happened; sandals and toys were left where they were last used, as we might leave shoes and toys on the living room floor.

The prehistoric sandals, large or small, crude or stylish, create a sense of kinship with the human beings who made and used them many thousands of years ago. The variety of workmanship and the design for various types of usage make it apparent, better than words ever could, that Stone Age human beings had mastered many skills and developed a complex familial and societal organization.

The humanness of prehistoric man is of direct relevance to our own lives, because we have inherited from him most of our physiological and mental characteristics and we share with him the same fundamental needs and urges. Many aspects of modern life are profoundly affected by the forces that shaped *Homo sapiens* and his life as far back as the Late Paleolithic or Old Stone Age, more than 100,000 years ago.

*Homo sapiens* does not differ from animals so much by his ability to learn as by the kinds of things he learns, in particular by the accumulation of his social experiences in the course of collective enterprises over thousands of generations. In other words, the human species is best characterized by its social history.

AS CONVENTIONALLY DEFINED, history begins with the period of the oldest written documents that have come down to us; these date from the Sumerian civilization, about 6,000 years ago. However, so many well-preserved artifacts providing precise information on human life have survived from the Stone Age that the preliterate period can also be included in the sociobiological history of mankind.

As far as is known, only man can control and use fire. This first technological achievement of mankind, which occurred perhaps a million years ago, is celebrated in the legend of Prometheus. The drama of the legend, and the role of hearth and altar in human traditions, suggest that man recognized very early that the mastery of fire has played a large role in his emergence from brutish life. For approximately 100,000 years, human life has been identified not only with the use of fire but also with shelter, clothing, tools, weapons, complex social structures, and the practice of some form of magic or worship. The fact that burial was practiced during the Stone Age, even by Neanderthals, suggests some form of ultimate concern.

The distribution of human skeletons and artifacts indicates that early people moved slowly north or south concomitantly with the retreats or advances of the Pleistocene ice sheets. Such migrations, extended over thousands of years, were probably at first largely unconscious. Since people in the Old Stone Age were primarily hunters, they did not follow the movements of the ice per se but rather the animals on which they depended for their livelihood. By the fourth ice age, however, large numbers of people seem to have remained in frigid Europe. Presumably their technological and social culture was then sufficiently advanced for them to develop the practices required for survival under difficult climatic conditions. It is possible also that large numbers of game animals persisted nearby. This was approximately 30,000 to 50,000 years ago; from that time on, human cultures rapidly became more complex, and human beings progressively achieved increasing control over their environment.

By the end of the Old Stone Age, the kit of human artifacts included needles, scrapers, knives, harpoons, spearheads, engraving tools, and a host of other objects. Certain flat stone containers apparently served to hold the burning fat or oil used to light the caves, probably during rituals and for painting. The famous statuettes of women, now referred to as Paleolithic Venuses, and the spectacular cave paintings and drawings of Europe attest not only to the artistic abilities of prehistoric man but also to the existence of elaborate beliefs and magical practices. In its magical forms, at least, religion seems to have emerged simultaneously with humanness.

Paleolithic weapons, tools, sculptures, drawings, and paintings, like the sandals of the Oregon Indians, differed in workmanship and style from one area to another. There were regional styles even then, and for all we know some of these may be reflected in human life even today. But despite local differences, the ways of life throughout the inhabited world probably had many characteristics in common and remained much the same as long as human beings continued to derive their livelihood chiefly from hunting. The situation changed when the ice made its final retreat from Europe, and when human populations became less nomadic. Civilization then entered the era generally referred to as the Mesolithic.

The domestication of the dog and the manufacture of bows and arrows are among the Mesolithic innovations. There is also some evidence that pottery manufacture was invented by Mesolithic people in northern Europe independently of its development in the Near East. However, of greatest importance for the future was the differentiation in ways of life that resulted from man's becoming progressively specialized in the utilization of the plant and animal resources peculiar to different regions. Some human groups adapted their life to grassland hunting; others to hunting and fishing in the deep forest; still others to shellfish collecting on the coast or to the exploitation of other marine resources. The tendency of Mesolithic life to achieve a close partnership with the local environment probably resulted in greater geographical stability of the populations, and in the progressive emergence of various human types. These changes prepared humanity for the Neolithic phase of civilization.

Neolithic life is identified with the manufacture of polished stone tools and weapons, the rapid development of the potter's art, and the domestication of plants and animals. Agricultural techniques not only increased food resources but made them more dependable; this resulted in a rapid increase in population and greater stability of human settlements.

In the Old World, the change from the hunting to the agricultural way of life apparently occurred independently in two separate areas, probably first in southwestern Asia, then in southeastern Asia. From its areas of origin, approximately 10,000 years ago, the Neolithic pattern of life diffused rapidly into Europe, Africa, and the rest of Asia, taking very different forms under the influence of local conditions and resources. Wheat, barley, and rye, cattle, horses, sheep, and goats soon became common in most of the human settlements identified with the cultures of southwestern Asia. Rice, sweet potatoes and other root crops, chickens, and pigs were more characteristic of life in southeastern Asia.

The greater abundance and dependability of food supplies, with the attendant stability of human settlements, set the stage for the rise of the great civilizations that are more or less identified with the Bronze Age. Men of the Near East learned to alloy copper and tin sometime around 5000 B.C.; they created large cities and a strong decentralized political structure; they developed specialized architecture, temples, pyramids, and many supportive arts. The early Sumerians of Mesopotamia were apparently the first to create a written language and to record the events of their life in a form that can be read today. With them, our knowledge of mankind passes from prehistory into classical history.

Cro-Magnon people became established over much of Europe some 30,000 years ago, long before the development of agriculture and village life. Although they lived chiefly as hunters, they seem to have been very similar to us both anatomically and mentally; their tools and weapons fit our hands; their cave art moves our souls; the care with which they buried their dead reveals that they shared with us some form of ultimate concern. Every trace of prehistoric humanity in the world provides further evidence for the view that the fundamental characteristics of *Homo sapiens* have not changed since the Stone Age.

Despite the constraints imposed by the unity and permanency of man's biological nature, the manifestations of human life have displayed a rich diversity that was already apparent during the Paleolithic Age and naturally increased during the Neolithic Age, and especially during the Bronze Age, when human populations became more stable. There are still in Africa, Asia, Oceania, and South America a few small tribes whose ways of life hardly differ from those of Stone Age man. They eke a meager living out of the natural resources of their surroundings; some, like the Australian Bushmen, do not practice even the most primitive form of agriculture. But all these tribes have extremely complex languages, traditions, social structures, and religious beliefs, in addition to possessing an extensive practical knowledge of their environment. Clearly culture—if this word is defined as everything learned by experience and transmitted from one generation to the next—can reach high levels without elaborate technology. Culture is the expression of man's responses to the physical and human environment. These responses take the form of behavioral patterns and emotional relationships as well as the development of utilitarian objects.

The interplay between man's nature and environmental forces is strikingly illustrated by the comparative histories of ancient Mesopotamia and Egypt. These two lands lie close to each other in the Near East and have therefore much in common. Of special importance for their early economic and social development were the facts that each is centered in a great river valley and each is blessed with a potentially fertile soil. In both areas, however, the agricultural land had to be created out of the wilderness by human toil and ingenuity. The annual floods provided both water and soil. But the land along the river was originally swamp and reedy jungle. To make it usable for crops was a stupendous task that required elaborate social organization. The swamps had to be drained by channels, the flood waters restrained by banks, the thickets cleared away, and the wild beasts brought under control. Furthermore, because of the peculiarities of the rainfall pattern in most of the Middle East, systematic irrigation was required before the agricultural potentialities of the land could be fully realized.

Both Mesopotamia and Egypt developed successful irrigation techniques and economic systems very early and thus were able to create great civilizations—the oldest in the annals of mankind. These two civilizations were in contact from the very beginning and advanced at about the same pace. However, despite the similarities of their origins and the extent of their contacts, Mesopotamia and Egyptian civilizations differed profoundly in spirit and in basic content. The prevailing orientation in Mesopotamia was cosmopolitan; in Egypt it was provincial. The Mesopotamians in their religious practices accorded much prominence to the sky, the sun, the moon, and the stars. The Egyptians, however, were more inclined to deify the animals in and along the Nile than the heavenly bodies. Students of the Middle East believe that these cultural differences can be accounted for in part by topographic considerations, in particular by the fact that the Nile Valley is narrow and confined on both sides by high cliffs, whereas Mesopotamia is much more open to the surrounding plains and consequently provided easier opportunities for communication with the outer world.

Prehistory and ancient history provide many other illustrations of the diversity and variability of human cultures. On the other hand, from what can be surmised of religious cults in Stone Age cultures, and from the discussions of political behavior by Plato and Aristotle, it is evident that the important characteristics of human societies have remained much the same for several thousand years. The manifestations of these characteristics have changed, but societies continue to serve the same essential needs and aspirations. While civilization obviously conditions what man becomes, it does not significantly affect his biological nature; Cro-Magnon man, if he were born and educated among us, could work in an IBM plant and might even become president of the company. Modern man can readily return to primitive life, and indeed he does to some extent whenever he needs to.

# Biological Freudianism

## Lasting Effects of
## Early Environmental Influences

The childhood shews the man
As morning shews the day.

—MILTON

AS COMMONLY USED, the phrase "early influences" denotes the conditioning of behavior by the experiences of very early life. Early experiences, however, do more than condition behavioral patterns; they also affect profoundly and lastingly many biological characteristics of the adult. I shall show that, in animals, events occurring during the very first days of life determine the initial growth rate, the maximum adult size, the efficiency in utilization of food, and the resistance to infection, malnutrition, and other stressful stimuli.

Early influences are, of course, at least important in human life as they are in animal life. In fact, the experiments to be reported here were designed to provide experimental models for the study of socio-medical problems first recognized in human populations.

During the past century, for example, there has been a constant trend toward earlier maturation of children. This phenomenon was first detected in the United States, then in other Westernized countries; it is now particularly striking in Japan. Evidence for earlier maturation is provided by the greater heights and weights of children at each year of age; by the faster growth rates during adolescence for both boys and girls; and by the earlier age of the first menstrual period. In England, for example, the menarchal age was fifteen and a half for the well-off townspeople in 1820, whereas it had fallen to thirteen in 1960.

Blackfan Memorial Lecture at The Children's Hospital Medical Center, Boston, 1966, first published in Pediatrics, vol. 38, no. 5 (November 1966), pp. 789–800.

Needless to say, the trend toward earlier maturation cannot be extrapolated far back in time. In fact there is evidence that the menarchal age was fourteen in Shakespeare's time, at least in the favored social classes. The beginning of the nineteenth century apparently corresponded to a low ebb in the rate of physical and sexual development, perhaps because of the poor health conditions that prevailed at the end of the Napoleonic Wars and during the early phases of the Industrial Revolution. What is certain, in any case, is that changes in the environment and in the ways of life during the past century have been associated with a marked increase in the growth rate of children throughout the Westernized world.

The fall in mortality caused by diarrhea, tuberculosis, and other respiratory diseases during the past century in the United States and in other prosperous countries provides a spectacular illustration of the direct relationship that exists between high living standards and increase in resistance. There is overwhelming evidence, furthermore, that the fall in mortality has been especially marked among the young age groups.

I shall not discuss the mechanisms of the fall in infant mortality but shall emphasize instead that the essential cause of the improvement was greater resistance to disease, rather than control of pathogens or more effective medical treatment. The increased resistance to disease was brought about by social advances.

The influence of social factors on growth and health has been particularly well documented in the countries of Central America. Very high infant mortality, slow rate of growth during childhood and adolescence, and physical and mental lethargy continuing throughout life are among the pathological manifestations common to all the deprived social groups of Central America. These disorders are not racially determined; they are found alike among the deprived Indians and among the populations of European origin who share their ways of life. In contrast, these disorders are rare among Indians and Latin people born and raised in social and economic environments similar to those now prevailing in the United States and in Europe.

While it is thus certain that physical and mental development, as well as physical and mental health, are profoundly influenced by social factors, the complexity of the interplay between man and his total environment has handicapped the epidemiological and clinical study of such sociomedical problems. My purpose in the present report is to show that it is possible to create laboratory models useful in the study of human population problems. I shall emphasize in particular some of the lasting biological effects of early environmental influences.

The development in our laboratory of models illustrating the effects of early influences was facilitated by the results of our earlier investigations with three mouse colonies that have the same genetic origin yet differ widely in several important biological characteristics.

The colony of so-called standard Swiss mice (SS) has been maintained at the Rockefeller Institute (now Rockefeller University) for more than fifty years. The CFW colony was originally derived from the SS colony but has been in commercial production outside New York. The NCS colony was developed at the Rockefeller Institute eight years ago out of nine animals obtained by Cesarean section from SS mice. Attempts have been made to maintain the NCS colony in a pathogen-free state at the Rockefeller University; a subcolony of it (NCS-D) has been continuously bred under semiprotected conditions in our own laboratories for the past eight years.

As reported elsewhere, the mice of the NCS colony, and especially of the NCS-D colony, differ profoundly from SS and CFW animals. The NCS mice are about 50 percent bigger than the SS at weaning time, reach a given weight thereafter as much as three weeks earlier, and complete their growth at close to the same larger size even on a diet that brings a one-third reduction in the adult size of the SS mouse.

In these experiments, all animals had been fed the same natural diet before mating as well as during gestation and lactation. Yet the young of the SS (or CFW) animals were smaller than those of the NCS animals at weaning time. The difference in size between these two groups persisted from then on, irrespective of the composition of the diet the animals received after weaning. The difference between the SS (or CFW) and NCS animals becomes even more striking when the diet is inadequate. The NCS mice continued to gain weight on a diet low in the amino acids lysine and threonine; in contrast, the SS animals failed to grow altogether, or at best remained abnormally small.

Earlier studies have revealed that the difference in efficiency of food utilization between NCS and SS (or CFW) mice is not genetically determined; rather, it is an expression of the different microbiota acquired by the animals during early life. The influence of the indigenous microbiota will not be discussed further at this time, because the effects of early influences have been more sharply defined in other types of experiments now to be described. The general principle of these experiments was to introduce a variable of short duration during early life and to observe the delayed consequences of this intervention in animals that were maintained thereafter under optimum conditions.

Despite the long inbreeding of the mouse colonies just described, and despite all efforts to standardize the breeding conditions, the litters exhibit marked differences in weaning weight, in growth rate, and in adult size. It was thought at first that these differences were due to the genetic constitution of the individual mice. For this reason, an effort was made to render the distribution of physical characteristics more uniform by pooling all the newborn animals and reallocating them randomly to foster mothers. The results of this pooling and random allocation, however, were very different from what had been expected. They showed that the growth characteristics of the newborn animals were highly uniform for each foster mother but differed markedly from one foster mother to the other. In other words, individual variability had its origin not in the genetic endowment of each animal but in the nursing effectiveness of the mother.

In one particular experiment, 240 mice born the same day were separated from their mothers two days after birth and pooled. They were then reallocated randomly to these mothers, each of the latter receiving eight young. All foster mothers accepted the eight young, which grew normally. The weaning weights of each particular foster group fell within a narrow range, while the groups fostered by different mothers differed measurably in weaning weight. Furthermore, the relative order of weights of individual animals remained the same after they had been separated from their foster mothers and fed thereafter the same diet in the same room.

In another experiment, the newborns were randomly allocated to foster mothers approximately 18 hours after birth. Measured by the growth of their nurslings, the nursing effectiveness of the foster mothers became apparent within a very few days and its effect on the relative weight rank of the newborns persisted thereafter.

The design of the two preceding experiments rules out that the groups of animals differed because of their genetic constitution, since they had been pooled and randomized; moreover, the differences among the groups did not have a prenatal origin, since the animals had been randomized after birth. All differences shown by these experiments must be traced, therefore, to the influence of the foster mothers during lactation. Quantity of milk, quality of milk, or other more subtle behavioral attributes of the foster mother account totally, or in part, for the differences in growth rates of the young. What is certain in any case is that the early experiences derived from the nursing mother had conditioned the development of the animals not only during lactation but also probably for long periods thereafter, and probably for their whole life span.

The general improvement in child nutrition certainly accounts in large part for the acceleration of physical growth and of sexual maturity that is occurring everywhere in affluent societies. There is much reason to believe that the very early nutritional influences are particularly important in this regard. The following experiments illustrate that, in animals, the nutritional state of the mother during lactation affects not only the initial rate of development of the young but also the final stature of the adult.

Pregnant NCS female mice were placed on various experimental diets just before delivery and were maintained on these diets throughout the lactation period. Their young were weaned at three weeks of age, and from then on all were fed the same mixed natural diet (commercial pellets D & G). In other words, the differences in nutritional regimen were limited to the mother and to the period of lactation.

The experimental regimen of the pregnant animals in one particular experiment consisted of a semisynthetic diet containing 20 percent wheat gluten (supplemented with cysteine) as sole source of protein. The diet was, therefore, low in lysine and threonine but was otherwise adequate with regard to all growth factors known to be essential for the adult mouse. The young of females fed this gluten diet were compared with those of females fed the complete natural diet (D & G pellets).

The young produced and nursed by mothers fed the gluten diet weighed less at weaning time than did those of mothers fed the complete diet. Furthermore, the difference between the two groups was maintained from then on, even though all animals were fed the same optimum diet and kept under exactly the same conditions from the time of weaning throughout the rest of their life span.

The difference, moreover, persisted to the fifty-sixth week of age; the weight differences between the two groups of animals are still present at the time of writing, more than twenty months after the beginning of the experiment. As mice rarely live much longer than two years, it is obvious that the mild nutritional deficiency experienced by the mother during lactation jeopardized the development of her young for their whole life span.

In these experiments the difference between the two groups of NCS mice was certainly caused by the low concentration of lysine and threonine in the diet of the mother during lactation, because the weight-depressing effect could be partly corrected by supplementing the gluten diet with a proper amount of these two amino acids. Even more interesting, perhaps, is the fact that a profound effect on weaning and adult weight can also be achieved by more subtle nutritional effects exerted on the mother during the lactation period.

In this set of experiments, nursing mothers were fed a diet (E) containing 15 percent casein, cystine, cornstarch, and all known essential growth factors. Diet E is nutritionally adequate, according to usual criteria, since it permits rapid growth of normal adult males or females. When females are fed E diet during lactation, however, the weights of their young are subnormal at weaning time. Moreover, these animals remain abnormally small thereafter, even though transferred permanently to an optimum diet after weaning.

The weight depression caused in the young by feeding E diet to the lactating mother can be prevented by adding "corn-steep liquor"— water-soluble extract of corn grain, widely used for penicillin production—to the diet during lactation. The weaning and adult weights of the young nursed by mothers on this diet were as high as those of animals nursed by mothers fed an optimum diet made of mixed natural foodstuffs. Unfortunately, it has not yet been possible to determine the nature of the active substance in the corn-steep liquor.

A few attempts have been made to determine whether there exists a period during which the nutritional deficiency of the lactating mother is most critical for the young. There was still some depression of growth when the E diet was first given to the mother on the fifth day after birth of her young, but there was no significant effect when the beginning of the regimen was delayed beyond that time. The first five days of life, therefore, constitute a critical period for the ultimate physical development of the mouse.

Clinical studies of human children indicate that infectious processes can retard development. The control of childhood infections has probably been one of the factors contributing to the acceleration of growth rates among children in the affluent countries.

As already mentioned, extensive experiments in our laboratory with three mouse colonies derived from the same genetic stock has provided experimental tools for demonstrating the effect of early minor infections on the initial rate and subsequent course of physical development. Thus newborn NCS mice were contaminated a single time two days after birth with intestinal homogenate of adult CFW mice or with material obtained by filtering this homogenate through a fine millipore filter. The animals thus contaminated weighed less than the controls at weaning time, and they remained smaller thereafter. In contrast, the growth rate was not depressed when the young mice were contaminated with material derived from NCS-D adult animals. This finding is of particular interest, since NCS-D animals have been raised under highly protected conditions in our own laboratories and were essentially free of mouse pathogens.

In many experiments, contamination of newborn NCS mice with CFW intestinal content did not cause any obvious sign of disease other than weight depression; even diarrhea was unusual. In other cases, however, paralysis of the hind legs was observed, and many of the animals so affected eventually died.

The microbial agents of the CFW intestinal content that are responsible for the weight depression of contaminated newborns have not yet been identified; it is probable that two different kinds of pathogens are involved. One of them, nonbacterial in nature, has been grown *in vitro* in tissue cultures of baby hamster kidney. When newborn NCS mice (two days old) were contaminated with a tissue culture of this agent, none of them developed paralysis, but all exhibited depression of growth. The depressing effect could be recognized as early as seven days after infection. The males were separated from the females after weaning (at three weeks of age). All contaminated males remained smaller than the control males, thereafter; the same was true for the females.

A high level of specific immunity commonly results from infections contracted during early life, or even *in utero*. In fact, the words "premunition, of infection immunity" were introduced by early immunologists to denote a state of resistance against malaria elicited by acquisition of the plasmodium shortly after birth. More recently, the phrase "bacterial interference" has been applied to the increase in resistance to staphylococcal infection that can be rapidly established in human babies by contaminating them shortly after birth with a nonvirulent strain of this microbial species. It has long been known, of course, that mice infected *in utero* with the lymphocytic choriomeningitis virus continue to harbor the agent thereafter; they are completely resistant to superinfection with this virus, even though their serum does not contain neutralizing antibody for it.

Experiments carried out in our laboratory have brought to light another striking example of antibacterial immunity resulting from intrauterine infection. It was found that while certain colonies of mice are extremely susceptible to pseudotuberculosis caused by *Corynebacterium kutscheri*, other colonies are highly resistant to this organism. As in the case of lymphocytic choriomeningitis, the resistance is related to the fact that all resistant mice are in reality latent carriers of *C. kutscheri*. The latent infection can be activated by administering large amounts of cortisone to the resistant animals. Under these conditions, the latent *C. kutscheri* infection becomes active, and the cortisone-treated animals die of pseudotuberculosis.

Thus a multiplicity of lasting effects can result from infections acquired during early life, even when the infectious agent is not highly pathogenic. The effects we have demonstrated include retardation of development during the lactating period, reduced stature during adulthood, and changes in the immunological state. The immunological effects deserve some further emphasis. While it is obvious that the heightened resistance to superinfection constitutes a lasting advantage, its value to the host is limited by its immunologically specific character. In any case, the advantage is often lost as a result of physiological stress, since, as is well known, many infectious agents become active in the course of such conditions. It is probable, in fact, that most of the endogenous infections that constitute such an important cause of disease in adult life have their primary origin in infections contracted during very early life.

In the experimental models considered so far, the environmental factors acted on the affected organism during the very early periods of its development. Needless to say, the organism continues to respond to the environment and to be thereby modified throughout its life. For example, the quantitative and qualitative aspects of food intake and utilization by the adult animal are directly and rapidly reflected in the level of resistance to disease.

Surprising as it may seem, there is very little precise knowledge concerning the relationship between nutritional state and resistance. In fact, the belief in such relationship has been established more by reiteration than by demonstration. Granted the paucity of knowledge, it is certain, nevertheless, that the younger the animal (or the human being), the more profound and varied are the effects of nutritional deficiency on resistance. Two different models will be mentioned here, each illustrating the effect of a particular type of dietary regimen on the resistance to stress of young adult mice.

We have shown elsewhere, for example, that mice still in the growing phase recover from the weight loss caused by bacterial endo-toxin only if supplied with large doses of a complete dietary amino acid mixture. Young animals do not recover from the weight loss caused by endotoxins when their diet is low in lysine and threonine. Bacterial endotoxins apparently increase catabolism, and new tissue synthesis is adequate only when the diet has the proper composition.

It has been found also that the ability of young mice to develop immunity to tuberculosis is dependent on the presence in the diet of unidentified materials that occur in certain natural foodstuffs. This dietary effect has been demonstrated by using as a vaccine either BCG or a small amount (0.02 mg) of mycobacteria killed with ethylene oxide.

These results indicate that the nutritional state at the time of first exposure to certain pathogens conditions the character of both the physiological and the immunological responses. Thus, nutrition during the early stages of life determines not only the extent of the damage caused by infectious processes but also the subsequent ability of the young organism to overcome the delayed effects of infection.

Needless to say, many types of early influences other than nutrition and infection can exert effects that persist throughout the life span. For example, temperature and humidity, housing conditions, and the de-gree of crowding are a few of the many environmental factors that modify lastingly the initial rate of growth, the ultimate size of the adult, resistance to various forms of stress, and, indeed, most physiological as well as mental characteristics. It would be desirable, of course, to understand the precise mechanisms responsible for the profound ef-fects exerted by such environmental forces. Useful working hypotheses could be formulated by considering hormonal activities, anatomical development, cellular metabolism, immunological processes, and other forms of tissue response, including those affecting mental attri-butes. My purpose, however, was not to discuss mechanisms but rather to illustrate that laboratory models can be devised for the study of the biomedical aspects of social situations.

I have tried to illustrate that the investigator can reproduce in the form of laboratory models most of the social conditions that have brought about the socioepidemiological phenomena mentioned at the beginning of this report—namely, the accelerated physiological devel-opment of children among Westernized people, the spontaneous changes in the pattern of disease that have occurred during the past century, and the physical and mental retardation of deprived people in certain parts of Central America. The study of such experimental models throws light on obscure sociomedical problems, and should help in the formulation of social programs for their control.

Consider for example one of the human tragedies in the highland villages of Guatemala. During the first few months of their lives, the Indian babies develop at a rate compatible with the values of the Iowa standard—at least its lower level. Around the fifth month of life, however, many of them become sick, and their growth rate falls dramatically. In fact, a very large percentage of them die at that time or shortly after from a great variety of pathological conditions. Pathogenic micro-organisms are so ubiquitous in the Guatemalan villages that virologists, bacteriologists, and parasitologists have no difficulty in isolating several different types of pathogens from the sick babies. There is no doubt, of course, that infection plays a large role in infantile morbidity and mortality. But our experimental models suggest that the nutritional state of the mother during the lactation period might be as important as the presence of pathogens, because it conditions the resistance of her baby to infection.

The laboratory models considered in the present report were devised to investigate some of the health problems of deprived populations. Other types of models would have to be developed for the problems of affluent populations. Still other models can be used to study various types of behavioral disturbances.

Whatever the peculiarities of the physical and social environment, many problems of adulthood and old age will be found to be the distant manifestations of environmental factors that were influential during the formative years of life. This relationship is well recognized, of course, with regard to emotional experiences and mental health. It can be demonstrated even more convincingly for early biological experiences and most aspects of physical health. In affluent as well as in deprived populations, the most compelling sociomedical problems have their origin in the lasting and often irreversible effects of early environmental influences.

From all points of view, the child is truly the father of the man, and for this reason we need to develop an experimental science that might be called biological Freudianism. Socially and individually the response of human beings to the conditions of the present is always conditioned by the biological remembrance of things past.

Many experiences of early life affect the biological characteristics of the adult in a lasting manner. This phenomenon has been illustrated by epidemiological observations in man and by several experimental models in mice.

It has been shown, for example, that when newborn animals are nursed by mothers fed diets that are slightly inadequate, their size remains subnormal throughout their life span, even though the young are fed an optimum diet after weaning. A similar depression of growth can be produced by subclinical infections shortly after birth.

Decrease in resistance to various forms of stress can be brought about in young animals by various types of nutritional and environmental disturbances so mild that their effects are not recognized when the animals are maintained under usual laboratory conditions.

These findings indicate the possibility of devising laboratory models for the analysis of many puzzling sociomedical problems.

# Tuberculosis and
# the Industrial
# Revolution

DURING THE NINETEENTH CENTURY each and every vice, large or small—in fact, almost any form of unconventional behavior—was regarded as a cause of tuberculosis, then called consumption. According to their personal prejudices, reformers and physicians traced the disease to immoderate love of food, spirits, or social life; to newfangled fashion, venery, or lack of exercise; to excessive use of tobacco or a passion for dancing. The *Boston Medical and Surgical Journal* published a note in 1851 called "Diary of a Tobacco Smoker and Chewer," said to be the veritable diary of the Reverend Solomon Spittle. The physician who performed the post-mortem examination had no doubt that Spittle's death was due to "phthisis, caused by inordinate use of tobacco." When waltzing became the rage in the early 1800s, the new dance was regarded by many as an "ally of consumption and death." And a few decades later, the polka gained the name of "Polka Morbus" for being performed with a vigor considered dangerous.

Discussing tuberculosis and heredity, S.A.K. Straham wrote in 1892,

This diathesis appears to be built up with equal certainty by impure air, drunkenness, and want among the poor, and by dissipation and enervating luxuries among the rich. From either set of causes it is capable of rapid development, and it is transmitted to the offspring with very great certainty. By injudicious marriages and persistent ignoring of the laws of health the necessarily fatal type is soon reached.

Since tuberculosis was then almost exclusively an urban disease, there was ground for the universal belief that susceptibility to it was increased by the artificialities of city life. In the United States in particular, it was easy to see the distemper advancing as the frontier life receded. "Phthisis . . . is scarcely known by those citizens of the United States who live in the first stage of civilized life and who have lately obtained the title of the first settlers," wrote Benjamin Rush in 1789. "It is less common in country places than in cities and increases in both." Tuberculosis was almost unknown among the early Ohio settlers. According to S. P. Hildreth:

> The invigorating effects of constant exercise, exposures to all kind of weather, a simple, but nourishing diet, and the enlivening faculties of the mind kept in continual play, forbade the approach of this scourge of indolence, and the refinements of modern fashions. Very few cases of it occurred until after the year 1808—and these did not average more than one death a year in a population of two thousand. Since the years 1815 and 1816 consumption has been gradually increasing, and at this time (in 1830) the average annual amounts of deaths is about two in a thousand inhabitants.

Identical views were held by F. H. Davis in 1848.

> In the early settlements of this country, New England and the N.E. States were as free from consumption as are now the much vaunted far-western States and territories. It was immediately consequent upon the change from an agricultural to a manufacturing population that the rapid increase in the death-rate from consumption is apparent in these States. Fifteen or twenty years ago Indiana, Illinois and the Lake region were the favorite resorts for consumptive patients. . . . Now we have a constantly increasing proportion of cases originating in this same region,

not evidently from any change that has taken place in the climatic conditions, but from the change in the occupation and hygienic surroundings of the people.

In 1857, H. Gibbons pointed out that the disease had become established in California as soon as the population had increased in the coastal cities.

A few years ago it was supposed that the climate of California was almost proof against Pulmonary disease. In 1850, if an individual happened to cough in church, all eyes were turned on him with curiosity and amazement. The native population, it was said, were entirely exempt from disorders of the lungs. But time has dispelled the delusions, and Pulmonary Consumption and the kindred affections, have become the great enemy of human life, as in the Atlantic States.

Only during recent decades has it become apparent that the spread of tuberculosis during the nineteenth century was the outcome of the social tragedies that followed in the wake of the industrial revolution, rather than the consequence of city life per se. The need for labor in the new factories brought about a huge and sudden shift of population from rural to industrial areas, an extraordinary migration of people, which gave to Émile Verhaeren's *Cités Tentaculaires* and to Oliver Goldsmith's *The Deserted Village* their dramatic atmosphere. In the mushrooming cities, migrants found the most dreadful working and living conditions. Long hours of exhausting toil were exacted of them in the suffocating atmosphere of coal mines, in the dark factories and the damp offices. Malnutrition prevailed in the shabby, filthy, and crowded tenements and the bleakness of life was relieved only by gin and vice.

One of the most tragic aspects of early industrialization was the growth of child labor, particularly in the textile mills. As appears from an account published in 1795, the situation was already very bad in England during the eighteenth century.

Children of very tender age are employed; many of them collected from the workhouses in London and Westminster and transported in crowds, as apprentices to masters resident many hundreds of miles distant, where they serve unknown, un-protected and forgotten by those to whose care nature or the laws had consigned them. These children are usually too long confined to work in close rooms, often during the whole night; the air they breathe from the oil employed in the machinery . . . is injurious; little reward is paid to their cleanliness and fre-quent changes from a warm and dense to a cold and thin atmo-sphere are predisposing causes to sickness and disability and particularly to the epidemic fever which so generally is to be met in these factories.

The working conditions for children were still as bad in 1838.

The profits of manufacturers were enormous; but this only whetted the appetite that it should have satisfied, and therefore the manufacturers had recourse to an expedient that seemed to secure to them those profits without any possibility of limit; they began the practice of what is termed night-working, that is, having tired one set of hands, by working them throughout the night; the day-set getting to beds that the night-set had just quitted, and in their turn again, the night-set getting into the beds that the day-set quitted in the morning. It is a common tradition in Lancashire, that the beds never get cold.

Many of the mills were "dirty; low roofed; ill-ventilated; ill-drained; no contrivance for carrying off dust and other effluvia; machinery boxed in; passages so narrow that they can hardly be defined; some of the flats so low that it is scarcely possible to stand upright in the center of the rooms."

Although these descriptions probably represent the darkest aspect of child labor, its abuses were sufficiently general to prompt inquiries. In 1843, the Children's Employment Commission of Trades and Manu-facturers published a report quoting examples of children at the age of five, and stating that general regular employment began between seven and eight. It described the victims as

stunted in growth, their aspect being pale, delicate and sickly, and they present altogether the appearance of a race which has suffered general physical deterioration. . . . The diseases most prevalent amongst them . . . are disordered states of the nutritive organs, curvature and distortion of the spine, deformity of the limbs, and distortion of the lungs, ending in atrophy and consumption.

But despite the report, child labor persisted uncontrolled for some twenty years longer.

Working conditions were equally bad everywhere in Europe and North America during the first half century of industrialization. In the mills of Massachusetts and Connecticut, young women from rural areas worked all day long in an atmosphere that was "stifling and almost intolerable to unaccustomed lungs." After the day's work, they retired to dormitories scarcely better ventilated than the mills. Four to six girls, and sometimes eight, slept in a room of moderate dimensions. The story is told of a manager who, attributing the morning "languor" of the operatives to a full stomach after breakfast, solved the problem by forbidding them to eat before work, and "succeeded in getting three thousand yards more of cloth a week for the same wagebill."

Within a few decades, millions of individuals raised on farms and in small towns were thus uprooted and exposed suddenly to the debilitating effect of inhumane employment. In the United States, many of them were Irish immigrants who constituted an almost virgin field for tuberculosis. Friedrich Engels described, in *The Condition of the Working Man in England*, the "pale, lank, narrow-chested, hollow-eyed ghosts," riddled with scrofula and rickets, who haunted the factories of Manchester and other manufacturing towns. Living in slums and fed on bread, porridge, and potatoes, with very rarely some cheese and even more rarely a small bit of bacon, they typified the proletariat bred by the early phase of the Industrial Revolution all over the world.

The hardships caused by industrialization were not limited to poor lodging, inadequate food, and physical exertion. Because man does not live by bread alone, standards of living cannot be defined merely in terms of crude economics. One of the worst evils of the Industrial Revolution was certainly to rob millions of human beings of the social and cultural values and of the emotional satisfactions that had made their lives bearable in the past. The most destitute villager in his native land had learned to adorn the dullness and drudgery of existence with bright ribbons and jolly tunes, and with the pageantry of his church.

[ 173 ]

But when he was uprooted into the anonymous gloom of the industrial cities, it was only with the help of gin that he could escape from squalor and despair. Several generations would be needed for his descendants to reach the state of relative harmony that man can achieve with almost any environment.

Most of the new recruits to industrial labor had known poverty in their former rural surroundings, but their life there had been relatively free from stresses and physiological hardships. More important, they had achieved some sort of physiological and psychological adaptation to their humble social status. When they moved into industrial areas in search of prosperity, adventure, and comfort, they found instead exploitation and other forms of poverty. And while under stress, before having adjusted themselves to their new ordeals, they came into contact with city dwellers among whom tuberculosis had long been prevalent. Intense crowding in workshops and in unsanitary living quarters provided all that was required for the rapid spread of infection, while physiological misery favored the development of destructive disease. It is probably this constellation of circumstances that brought about the great epidemic of tuberculosis of the nineteenth century.

The association of tuberculosis with rapid industrialization can be observed again in several parts of the world at the present time. Large-scale migrations from rural areas to the urban districts, disruption of ancestral habits and low standards of living—all these earmarks of the Industrial Revolution are now found in much of Latin America and Asia. Concomitantly, tuberculosis is manifesting itself with the fulminating course that was so frequent in Europe and the United States in the 1830s, and the annual death rates are reaching 200 to 500 per 100,000 in the newly industrialized areas.

Long and strenuous working days, malnutrition, and life amidst fumes, smoke, and dust seem sufficient reasons to explain the ravages of tuberculosis in the proletariat of the nineteenth century, but other causes must be found to account for the prevalence at the same time of fatal tuberculosis in the members of the more favored classes.

The mortuary registers for 1838 and 1839 in England reveal that the proportion of "consumptive cases" in "gentlemen, tradesmen and laborers" was 16, 28, and 30 percent, respectively. Thus, although tuberculosis affected the poor most severely, it was also a terrifying scourge in the well-to-do. The ever-recurring allusions to phthisis, chest disease, consumption, hectic fever, decline, through the diaries and other documents of the nineteenth century, bear witness to the fact that tuberculosis was ubiquitous, affecting young society women as well as their chambermaids and governesses; writers or musicians as well as unskilled laborers; physicians as well as patients. It was the cause of tragedy, not only in the ghastly suburbs of industrial cities but also in the small quiet towns, in the comfortable residential districts, and in the fashionable avenues of London, Paris, Rome, and New York. Exhausting physical labor was not demanded of the bourgeois and aristocratic classes; leisure and relaxation was their privilege. They were not displaced from their normal environment; their customs were not disturbed. But at all levels of society, there were certain aspects of life that must have been directly or indirectly the cause of much infectious illness and of tuberculosis in particular.

In her *Life of Charlotte Brontë*, Elizabeth Gaskell tells of the Brontë children being lectured, when they pleaded for more to eat, on the sin of caring for carnal things and of pampering greedy appetites. Life in a girls' school was described as follows in the medical journal *The Lancet* in 1839:

> The girls rose at six and did preparation until eight, when they breakfasted on porridge, bread and tea. At 8:30 preparation was resumed until school began at nine, lessons continuing without a break until one. For half an hour they were free to leave the classrooms, but were not allowed to go out of doors. Dinner, consisting of boiled or roast meat, or boiled fish, and potatoes, with perhaps a suet or rice pudding to follow, occupied half an hour, and was followed by another three hours of school. Tea and bread were served at five; at six, if it were fine, the girls took an hour's walk, otherwise they stayed indoors and read.

The picture presented by Charles Dickens in *Oliver Twist* shows that half-starvation of growing children was common practice of the time.

> The bowls never wanted washing. The boys polished them with their spoons till they shone again; and when they had performed this operation (which never took very long, the spoons being nearly as large as the bowls), they would sit staring at the copper, with such eager eyes, as if they could have devoured the very bricks of which it was composed; employing themselves

meanwhile, in sucking their fingers most assiduously, with a view of catching up any stray splashes of gruel that might have been cast thereon.

The lack of elementary sanitation was beyond our most ghastly imaginings. Up to recent times, a group of children gathered in a closed room around a consumptive elder was regarded as a picture of poetical charm. Promiscuous spitting long remained as readily accepted as in the days when Samuel Pepys wrote in his diary, "I was sitting behind in a dark place, a lady spit backward upon me by mistake, not seeing me, but after seeing her to be a very pretty lady, I was not troubled at it at all." The description of young schoolgirls drinking from a common cup appears as a matter of course in Charlotte Brontë's novels. These scenes betray an atmosphere of infection. Projected into the future, they take on the livid pallor of tuberculosis, and forecast young lives paralyzed or destroyed by disease.

The fact that tuberculosis was usually diagnosed only in its terminal phases also contributed much to its spread throughout the population, irrespective of social status. One often reads of the galloping consumption, so rare now under normal circumstances but so frequent a diagnosis in the nineteenth century. The case of Keats dying within one year after becoming sick, with both lungs completely destroyed, is often quoted to illustrate the virulence of his disease. But wherever information is available, it takes little ingenuity to recognize that the tuberculosis process had been going on for several years before diagnosis was made. Moreover, consumptive patients continued to live a life of normal activity almost to the end, not only spoiling any chance of arresting their own disease but seeding the germs of it all around them. Galloping consumption was probably more the result of medical ignorance than of high susceptibility to infection.

The intensity of contagion must have been enormous. Keats, Poe, Thoreau, and Trudeau nursing their dying brothers at home in small, closed rooms, without any precautionary measures; the Brontë children exposed for years to the chronic "bronchitis" of their father; the consumptive Virginia Poe giving singing parties only interrupted by profuse hemorrhages—these are typical examples of a behavior that was then commonplace. One reads of fashionable women in the last stages of consumption compelled by weakness to keep to their sick chambers through the day but dressing at night to participate in social life and dying upright in the midst of festivities. In one of her letters, Thoreau's sister mentions a certain Ann K. Ford who had come to live as a boarder in their house in 1846. Ann was obviously consumptive, coughed incessantly, and suffered two serious hemorrhages in January 1847. Yet she was cheerful, apparently unconscious of the seriousness of her situation, off visiting whenever she felt strong enough, enjoying in airtight rooms by hot stoves the company of her friends during the cold days of the New England winter. She died the following summer at the age of eighteen, having certainly contaminated many of her Concord neighbors and thus forged other links in the chain of contagion that was strangling New England.

In many places, this lack of any awareness of the process of infection continued until the twentieth century. As late as 1899, Sir William Osler reported seeing in south Baltimore a lad, one of five children, who had been ill with tuberculosis for months. The room was stuffy and hot, both windows shut. Some expectoration was visible on the floor.

> He had high fever, loss of appetite and was being fed on pan-opeptone and beef extracts. The room had a good exposure and I suggested to the young man to have the bed moved by the window, to be well covered up, and to rest in the sunshine during part of every day. The reply was that it would kill him and I could see by the mother's looks that she was of the same opinion. The doctor, too, I am afraid, regarded me as a fanatic.

It is probably this ubiquity of contagion that accounts for the prevalence of tuberculosis in the favored social groups during the Industrial Revolution. Physiological misery and crowding permitted the explosive spread of the disease among the labor classes, and from this huge focus the infection spread through society by means of countless unavoidable contacts. Interestingly enough, this had been recognized as early as 1769 in the report of a commission appointed by the Manchester Board of Health.

"Children and others who work in the large cotton factories are peculiarly disposed to be affected by the contagion of fever, and when such infection is received, it is rapidly propagated, not only amongst those who are crowded together in the same departments, but in families and neighborhoods to which they belong." However, the warning went unheeded. The passion for financial gains made acquisitive men blind to the fact that they were part of the same social body as the unfortunates who operated their machines. Tuberculosis was, in effect, the social disease of the nineteenth century, perhaps the first penalty that capitalist society had to pay for the ruthless exploitation of labor.

# Nutritional
# Ambiguities

MANY PEOPLE of the Western world, especially in the United States, are intensely worried about their nutritional state and the quality of their food. This worry, however, is not caused by malnutrition but by constantly reading and hearing about the dangers of bad diets and of food contaminated with additives and other chemicals. Any departure from what Westerners assume to be an ideal natural diet is publicized by the mass media, thus contributing to the prevalent social neuroses about the general state of the world.

The reality is that most people in the developed and even semi-developed parts of the world now have diets that are better balanced and freer of toxic contaminants than at almost any time in the past, except perhaps during the Old Stone Age. Since that time, food shortages occurred frequently, even in Europe. As recently as a century ago, vitamin and other deficiencies affected many people at the end of the winter, microbial spoilage of food was difficult to avoid, and contamination with toxic substances often caused acute disease and death. It took Upton Sinclair's hair-raising stories in *The Jungle*, published in 1906, to make Congress create the Food and Drug Administration, which, among other functions, oversees the safety and quality of foodstuffs.

I do not claim that our food and our nutritional state are now ideal,

*Natural History*, vol. 89, no. 7 (1980), pp. 14–21. Copyright © 1980 by American Museum of Natural History. Reprinted by permission.

but I believe that their most serious shortcomings do not stem from a deterioration of our dietary regimen. If some, and perhaps many, of us are in a state of malnutrition, it is because our dietary regimen is ill-adapted to modern conditions. It would be surprising if the nutritional regimens designed for the old ways of life were the right ones for the conditions prevailing in today's wheelborne, well-heated, air-conditioned societies. We know a great deal about the characteristics of the various kinds of food but very little about what would be the ideal food intake for a particular person in a particular physiological behavior or occupational situation.

Until recent times, nutritional science has dealt chiefly with such general problems as the chemical identification and synthesis of essential growth factors; the determination of the average requirements for each one of these factors, according to age, sex, and state of health; and the metabolic role and fate of each one of the foodstuffs in the body. Under normal conditions, this broad theoretical approach was based on the belief that within a given age group and sex, all human beings have essentially the same nutritional requirements. Initially, for example, the requirements for young male adults were determined by tests on healthy, vigorous American students at an Ivy League college. But many recent studies have revealed that every person has a nutritional-metabolic pattern that is characteristic—indeed, as unique as finger-prints. For this reason, a diet that is suitable for one person may be marginal, deficient, and even dangerous for another. Individual differences in nutritional requirements can be considerable. A recent study of nineteen healthy men found an almost fivefold difference in their daily requirements for calcium (from 220 to 1018 mg) and twofold to sevenfold differences in their needs for the various essential amino acids that maintain nitrogen balance. These differences are certainly due in part to genetic constitution, but experiments in animals and observations in human beings leave no doubt that the nutritional needs of an individual can undergo profound changes as a result of adaptation to a shortage or abundance of certain nutrients.

Some twenty years ago, a study was made in India of a large group of beggars who had long been on a diet deficient in calories, iron, calcium, phosphorus, vitamins A, B, C, and D, and proteins of animal origin. To their great surprise, the investigators found that only 4 percent of these beggars showed obvious signs of nutritional deficiency and that radiological examination showed most of them to have a normally calcified skeleton. In the women of this group, low nutritional intakes did not have a markedly deleterious effect on either pregnancy or lactation, and the growth rate of children was only slightly lower than normal. While these beggars probably used items of food that escaped the attention of the investigators, nevertheless chronic food shortage appears to have created in them some form of physiological adaptation to low nutritional intake.

The ability to survive and even to function well with an inadequate diet can probably be attributed in part to people in underprivileged countries learning to eat certain items—including insects—considered unacceptable in richer countries. Above and beyond these "social" adaptations, however, undernourished or malnourished people can also develop certain "biological" adaptations that supplement the food intake, such as the synthesis of vitamins and amino acids by intestinal microbes. Perhaps of greater importance are "metabolic" adaptations that enable the body to "gear down" its metabolic demands.

The existence of multiple forms of nutritional adaptation certainly accounts for the fact that people differ widely in their nutritional requirements, the result not only of genetic differences but also, and even more, of different cultural habits, ways of life, and behavioral patterns. These differences make a mockery of attempts to define precisely an optimum diet for the hypothetical average person.

Many people believe that they can function well only when provided with three square meals a day, and certain students of nutrition believe that this formula constitutes the surest way to a good nutritional state. But in fact, few are the societies in which the practice of three square meals a day is considered essential for health.

In the economically humble French environment from which I emerged, the substantial meal was eaten at noon, supper was a desultory affair, and as to breakfast, it consisted of bread with a cup of cocoa for children and coffee for adults. Never did a glass of orange juice or tomato juice reach my lips until I had settled in the United States. Yet here I am to tell the tale at the age of seventy-nine. My sister and brother, who are both in their late seventies and living in Paris, are still doing well on the same regimen, as are my French nephews and nieces. There are tribes in which people nibble constantly and others whose members partake of only one meal a day. At Harvard University, I knew a famous medical educator who ate only at dinnertime, when he could make the meal an elaborate social occasion.

In East Africa, the Kikuyu people are healthy and can develop a good physique on a vegetarian diet. In contrast, the Masai people, who live in the same region, derive practically all their nourishment from milk and from the blood of their cattle, which they bleed daily. Yet the Masai do as well as the Kikuyu without much intake of the plant fiber that is so much on our minds today.

I could go on and on with examples illustrating that social groups and individual people have successfully adapted themselves to very different dietary regimens. I find it more useful, however, to discuss at some length a more drastic phenomenon of nutritional adaptation— namely, adaptation to extremely low food intake throughout the life span.

During the 1940s, I participated in the research activities of the Institute of Nutrition for Central America and Panama, situated in Guatemala City. The average per capita food intake in the villages of Guatemala was then, and still is, extremely low and deficient in protein. Many children and young adults died of infection. But those who survived to adulthood, although of short stature and seemingly frail, were capable of far greater physical efforts than those expected of vigorous Europeans and North Americans—such as carrying heavy burdens on their backs over long distances up and down mountains. Physiological studies showed that they could maintain themselves in caloric and nitrogen balance on a diet that would have meant starvation for most Europeans and especially for North Americans. Furthermore, these skinny people, grossly undernourished according to our standards, commonly lived to a good old age.

Since Guatemalans raised in wealthier surroundings and fed a rich and abundant diet became as large as people of Europe and North America and exhibited the high nutritional requirements of these countries, we can assume that the anatomical and physiological characteristics of the adult village Guatemalans were not the consequence of genetic peculiarities but rather of adaptation to low food intake.

American nutritionists, under the auspices of the National Academy of Sciences, long ago worked out Recommended Daily Allowances for the various essential nutrients; they are cited today on every box of breakfast cereal. In particular, those nutritionists placed emphasis on the intake of proteins, deriving their values from the study of the requirements of vigorous young adults, chiefly college students. Almost unanimously, however, nutritionists of other countries have long considered the American Recommended Daily Allowances far too high. In the early 1970s, the commissions on nutrition of the World

Health Organization and of the Food and Agricultural Organization scaled down the protein requirements of a healthy person by some 30 percent—thereby eliminating, by administrative decision, the international "protein gap" that had been postulated in earlier decades.

Recent American research has been interpreted to mean that the redefined protein standards are in reality too low, because in one study a group of U.S. university students developed signs of deficiency two months after being fed the new recommended levels of protein. The explanation of this finding, however, is probably that some twenty years ago most American children were fed (and to a large extent most still are) diets much richer and more abundant than those given European children, let alone children of underdeveloped countries. The nutritional requirements of adults are probably largely determined by nutritional conditioning during the early years of life.

Average Americans, and now many Europeans, feel that they need a daily food intake containing more than 2,500 calories and 70 grams of protein, preferably meat protein. In contrast, whole populations of other ethnic groups seem well adapted to diets providing approximately 1,500 calories and 40 grams of protein, or even less, and often with hardly any meat. This was the case in Japan before the war and is still the case of most Guatemalan villagers. Moreover, the immense majority of people in all ethnic groups could almost certainly adapt successfully to either one of these two extreme types of dietary regimen or to any in between. We need to learn much more about the effects of nutritional conditioning, especially during early childhood, because several of these effects might be essentially irreversible and could therefore affect the person during the whole life span.

The most obvious long-range effects have to be on health. Good evidence exists, for example, that babies pressed to take more food become habituated to an abundant diet and tend to become obese, with all the health risks associated with obesity during adulthood and old age. The postwar generation of richly fed Japanese, both men and women, now tend to have the same disease patterns that are prevalent in North America and Europe, where cardiovascular diseases and various forms of cancer have become the leading causes of death. In all prosperous societies, people are becoming increasingly concerned about the harmful components of their diets—cholesterol, saturated fatty acids, processed foods, contaminants such as pesticides, and various forms of additives. They would worry even more if they realized that almost any article of food—even the most natural food—is toxic if taken in excess. For example, potatoes contain solanine, a substance that would create toxic effects if ten times the usual amount were eaten at one sitting; cereal grains contain phytic acid, which interferes with the absorption of calcium and iron; and certain plants of the cabbage family produce goiter. Even vitamins can be a cause of disease, as in the case of hypervitaminoses A and D.

While proving that many particular food items—artificial or natural—are dangerous if taken in large amounts is fairly easy, establishing the dangers of the typical rich American diet is much more difficult. A very recent study sponsored by the American Society for Clinical Nutrition examined a number of suspected relationships between diet and disease but found only three that could be statistically confirmed: between sucrose and dental caries; between alcohol and cirrhosis of the liver; between salt and hypertension. Convincing evidence could not be obtained that high intakes of cholesterol and fatty acids increase the chance of dying from cardiovascular disease.

Lack of statistical proof does not, of course, rule out that high blood levels of cholesterol and fatty acids can be involved in disease causation. The great differences of response among the people examined make it difficult to establish statistically valid correlations. As mentioned earlier, these differences may have their origin not only in genetic constitution but also in behavioral patterns. One example will suffice to illustrate how a seemingly trivial aspect of behavior can influence the digestion of lipids and, consequently, their possible effects on disease. After a meal, ingested lipids travel in the bloodstream for a short time in the form of microscopic particles called chylomicrons. These particles are rapidly digested under normal conditions, but they persist much longer in a person under stress, even when the stress is as mild as having to give an anatomy lecture to medical students. If lipids do contribute to the formation of vascular lesions, adaptation to certain stresses may thus decrease their ability to cause cardiovascular disease.

Nutritional science therefore involves much more than knowing the requirements for essential growth factors and the toxic effects of food additives. A time may come when a particular patient's need for a particular food will be evaluated not only by measuring growth rates but also by determining the food's effect on specialized functions, such as the ability to develop scar tissue; produce new cells in the liver, spleen, and bone marrow; and generate the proper kind of response to detoxify poisons or drugs. There is now some evidence that the nutritional state can affect even behavioral responses, as shown by the brain's production of at least two neurotransmitters: serotonin, which depends on the tryptophane level in the bloodstream, and acetylcholine, which depends on the choline level. Neither tryptophane nor choline can be manufactured by the body; they must be supplied in the diet.

We have an immense amount of detailed knowledge about foodstuffs but know very little about their effects on the body and even less about their effects on behavior and on the social aspects of life. Developing a large body size is obviously an advantage for certain activities but probably not for others. Voltaire was a midget compared with Washington but outlived him by seventeen years and was at least as influential on the course of history. The small prewar Japanese could not play basketball with Americans; nevertheless, they were excellent soldiers and proved immensely successful in the technological and economic world of the postwar period. The new generation of richly fed Japanese is much taller than the preceding one but we do not know that its members will live longer or be happier. A good, abundant nutritional regimen will keep us alive, make us grow to a certain size, and protect us from deficiency diseases, but beyond that, we really do not know much about its effects on our bodies, our society, and the future of civilization.

To illustrate our ignorance, and also the possibility of adapting successfully to extremely different dietary regimens, I shall mention the nutritional habits of two famous physicians whom I knew well during my early years at the Rockefeller Institute for Medical Research. One was Henry William Welch, the architect of medical and public health sciences in the United States. The other was Oswald T. Avery, who is famous for his studies on infectious diseases and for having first demonstrated that DNA is the carrier of hereditary characteristics. Welch and Avery were approximately the same height, had received similar college and medical educations, spent most of their lives in academic medicine, remained bachelors, smoked a great deal, took practically no physical exercise, and never tired of talking. But they differed completely in nutritional behavior.

Welch had a Gargantuan appetite, with a preference for rich, well-seasoned foods. He was inordinately fond of sweets and prone to end his meal with several helpings of ice cream—in a period when this meant real cream. He loved wine and hard liquor and seemed proud that his most violent form of exercise was taking off his shoes at night and putting them on in the morning. He early became obese, loved fun and the carnival aspects of life, and remained intellectually active to the end of his life. He died of cancer in his eighty-fifth year.

Avery ate sparingly. Two slices of toast, a few leaves of lettuce, and several cups of coffee seemed to be his ideal meal. We used to say that he could be in nutritional balance only by fixing atmospheric nitrogen. He never weighed more than ninety pounds during the thirty years I knew him, yet he was constantly active, either in laboratory work or participating in discussions. He suffered from mild hyperthyroidism, and his disease took a more active form during a period of disappointments in his research program. After surgery and a few months' rest, he came back to the laboratory and resumed his activities. He died of cancer in his seventy-ninth year.

As far as I know, no nutritional studies have been carried out on either Welch or Avery. One can take it for granted that genetic differences between them played a role in their contrasting attitudes toward food intake and responses to it, but one can also assume that their nutritional habits and their metabolism were profoundly influenced by other aspects of their ways of life and probably by their early experiences. It takes more than a knowledge of foodstuffs to create a science of human nutrition.

# The Weather,
# the Potato Blight,
# and the Destiny
# of the Irish

IN THE EPILOGUE to *War and Peace*, Tolstoy attempted to justify the structure of his novel by contrasting the techniques used by the historian and by the artist in reporting political and social events. The historian works under the illusion, Tolstoy claimed, that he can deal with his material in a scientific manner and provide rational accounts of past situations. He pretends that his knowledge of background, circumstances, and participants permits him to explain the outcome of historical happenings. In reality, however, he selects and emphasizes only those determinant factors that conform to his prejudiced views of history. The artist has no such illusion. He does not pretend to act like a scientist, and yet he presents of historical events a picture that is truer to reality. Instead of explaining history, he evokes its complexity and subtleties by describing the atmosphere in which events took place and the emotional reaction of each individual participant.

In *War and Peace*, Tolstoy labored the thesis that military commanders—Napoleon included—are passive instruments who register and exploit situations but do not determine their course. Wars, like all human affairs, are so complex in their determinism that they can hardly be accounted for by the ordinary processes of reason. Social forces, economic factors, personal ambitions, or political doctrines are not the real causative agents of history, and the feats or words of military heroes, statesmen, or philosophers influence its course even less. Men usually find themselves in circumstances they cannot comprehend and over which they have no control. Since the real causes of phenomena, wrote Tolstoy, are hidden beyond the reach of the human mind, historians can at most describe the behavior of individual and certain limited interrelationships, but they must abandon the futile search for the specific causality of human events.

Tolstoy wrote *War and Peace* between 1863 and 1869, and his skepticism with regard to historical causality was a reaction against scientific materialism. Ironically enough, however, his novel became immensely popular precisely at the time when the doctrine of specific causality was achieving its most spectacular successes and gaining almost universal acceptance in medicine. Nevertheless, Tolstoy had been somewhat of a scientific prophet. The difficulties encountered in determining the factors that brought Napoleon's retreat from Russia in 1812 have their counterpart in the failure to account for most of the phenomena bearing on health and happiness in terms of simple and direct cause-effect relationships. In fact, Tolstoy's view that historical events cannot be attributed to single causes applies to most situations in the world of nature. The story of the roundabout way in which a microscopic fungus probably native to Central America destroyed the potato crop in Ireland and exerted thereby a dramatic influence on the destiny of the Irish people illustrates the complexity of the interplay between the external environment and the affairs of man.

As far as is known, the potato originated in the Andes, where it still grows wild, yielding tubers so small as to be hardly fit for human use. In its native habitat, the plant is infected with the parasitic fungus *Phytophthora infestans* but suffers little, if at all, from its presence. Through evolutionary adaptation, the fungus and the wild potato have obviously achieved a state of ecological equilibrium that permits the survival of both. Eventually, the potato was improved for human consumption, and it became one of the most important sources of food in the Western world after the eighteenth century. While the fungus phytophthora has followed the potato wherever the plant has been taken, the relationship between the two has changed, the improved varieties of potatoes selected for large yields being much more susceptible to infection than are the wild varieties. Fortunately, it is possible by proper techniques of farming to arrange that most of the potato crop escapes destruction by the parasite. Now and then, however, the weather conditions upset the best farming practices, the fungus multiplies more rapidly and abundantly than usual, and it kills the plant.

The potato blight broke out on a disastrous scale in Europe, particularly in Ireland, around 1845. For two years in succession the blight not only killed the foliage but rotted the tubers in the ground and in storage. Because the impact of the disaster was so varied and so great, it is worth recording in some detail the constellation of circumstances under which it occurred and the scientific debates to which it gave rise.

Weather had been very unpleasant shortly before the blight broke out. For several weeks the atmosphere had been one of continued gloom, with a succession of chilling rains and fog, the sun scarcely ever visible, the temperature several degrees below the average for the previous nineteen years. The botanist John Lindley held the theory that bad weather had caused the potato plants to become saturated with water. They had grown rapidly during the good weather, then had absorbed moisture with avidity when the fog and the rain came. As the absence of sunshine had checked transpiration, wrote Dr. Lindley, the plants had been unable to get rid of their excess of water and in consequence had contracted a kind of dropsy. Putrefaction was the result of this physiological disease. The Reverend Miles Berkeley, a naturalist with much knowledge of the habits of fungi, held a different theory and connected the potato disease with the prevalence of a species of mold on the affected tissues. To this Lindley replied that Berkeley was attaching too much importance to a little growth of mold on the diseased potato plants. He added that

as soon as living matter lost its force, as soon as diminishing vitality took the place of the customary vigour, all sorts of parasites would acquire power and contend for its destruction. It was so with all plants, and all animals, even man himself. First came feebleness, next incipient decay, then sprang up myriads of creatures whose life could only be maintained by the decomposing bodies of their neighbours. Cold and wet, acting upon the potato when it was enervated by excessive and sudden growth, would cause a rapid diminution of vitality; portions would die and decay, and so prepare the field in which moldiness could establish itself.

Thus the professional plant pathologist, represented by Lindley, believed that the fungus could become established on the potato plant only after the latter had been debilitated by unhealthy conditions, whereas Berkeley saw the fungus as the primary cause of the disease, with fog and rain as circumstances that favored its spread and growth. In this manner the controversies that were to bring Pasteur in conflict with the official world of the French Academy of Medicine in the 1880s were rehearsed three decades earlier in the pages of the English *Gardener's Chronicle.*

It must be emphasized that the destruction of the crop in 1845 was not the result of a new infection by *Phytophthora infestans.* The fungus had been present on the potato plant since its introduction from Central America, but it took unusual weather conditions to render the plant highly susceptible to infection. Although the fungus persisted in Ireland after the Great Blight, it was only during occasional years that the weather was propitious for its proliferation, so that potato culture recovered progressively.

The two years of the blight, however, had been sufficient to ruin the economy of Ireland. Following the introduction of the potato during the eighteenth century, the Irish population had much increased, as is always the case when a new source of food becomes available. From 3.5 million around 1700, it had reached approximately 8 million in 1840. The potato blight caused an acute food shortage, with the result that a million people died of outright starvation. Furthermore, many of those who escaped death became more susceptible to a variety of infectious diseases. Thus began a great epidemic of tuberculosis, which after a century is only now beginning to abate. Also, lack of food and economic misery forced a large percentage of the Irish population to emigrate, particularly to America. Even today the population of Ireland is only half what it was before the potato famine.

In America the Irish immigrants found work in the mushrooming industries of the Atlantic seaboard. But they found also crowded and unhealthful living conditions. Coming from rural environments, they suddenly experienced the worst aspects of slum existence. The profound upheaval in their way of life made them ready victims to all sorts of infection. The sudden and dramatic increase of tuberculosis mortality in the Philadelphia, New York, and Boston areas around 1850 can be traced in large part to the Irish immigrants who settled in these cities at that time.

Thus all sorts of accidents played their part in linking tuberculosis—the Great White Plague of the nineteenth century—to a fungus living on the wild potato in Central America. The change in ecological relationship between fungus and potato that occurred when the latter was removed from its native habitat and was "improved" for human consumption; the disturbance in the internal physiology of the potato caused at a critical time by unusual weather conditions; the biological and cultural urges that brought about the rapid increase in the Irish population during the first part of the nineteenth century—all these forces and many social factors that can be spared discussion here played an essential part in transforming Pat the Irish pigtender into a New York City cop. If ever a writer succeeds in making a popular story of the potato blight, he may conclude, as Tolstoy did for Napoleon's invasion of Russia, that its determinism is beyond human analytical power. In fact, it is perhaps just an illusion of science to believe that the vagaries of the relations between the potato and a microscopic fungus, inadequate farming practices, and the weather conditions in the 1840s were the real factors that led the adventurous spirit of man to establish on the American continent the wit of the Irish, their Catholic faith, and their political genius.

# The Population
# Avalanche

THE MOST COMPELLING EVIDENCE of the ability of the human race to become adapted to a wide range of environmental conditions is that mankind has progressively spread over the entire globe. The most obvious and immediate danger arising from this adaptability is that the world population is now growing so fast that it might soon reach a level incompatible, first, with the maintenance of the human qualities of life, and then with the very survival of the human species. Thus the world population problem illustrates the indirect long-range dangers of adaptability.

It is not for the sake of originality that I shall use here the word "avalanche" instead of the more orthodox "explosion" to refer to the present increase in the world population. My reason is that the word "avalanche" conveys more accurately the important truth that this increase is not a sudden event, as the world explosion would suggest, but rather corresponds to a continuous process that has to reach a certain momentum before it becomes dangerous. Public alarm is justifiable, because the increase is now occurring simultaneously all over the world and because its rate seems to be accelerating.

The total human population was probably on the order of 10 million

From *Man Adapting* (New Haven: Yale University Press, 1980), pp. 280–318. Reprinted by permission of Yale University Press.

at the end of the Neolithic period; it had increased to approximately 300 million by the beginning of the Christian era and had reached 500 million around 1650. Then the rate of growth began to accelerate, bringing the world population to 2,500 million in 1950 and to over 3,000 million in 1961. As far as can be judged, the yearly rate of increase, which was about 0.3 percent between 1650 and 1780 and 0.9 percent between 1900 and 1950, is now 1.8 percent. At present, the world population is increasing by more than 100,000 persons a day, close to 50 million a year! It will reach about 4 billion by 1975 and 6 to 7 billion by 2000 if the present rate of growth continues. In brief, it took hundreds of thousands of years for *Homo sapiens* to achieve a population of 3 billion, but his numbers might be doubled in the next forty years!

The population will have to stop growing within the foreseeable future, simply for lack of space on earth, even assuming that science could find satisfactory substitutes to overcome the shortages of natural resources. The upper limit of the world population has been set at between 10 billion, a level that might be reached within a century, and 50 billion, according to estimates made by experts who have great faith in the power of technology to provide new sources of subsistence for man.

The really important question, however, is not so much the maximum population level that can be reached and maintained as the manner in which the rate of increase can be slowed down and ideally brought to zero. Will the break come from the operation of natural growth-limiting factors, such as those that maintain so many animal populations at stable levels in equilibrium with their environment? From a biological catastrophe similar in kind to the population crashes that occur repeatedly among lemmings and other rodents? From a technological accident, such as nuclear warfare or wholesale poisoning by environmental pollution? Or from concerted human action based on a reasonable assessment of what the upper population level should be in order that human life retain the qualities that give man his unique place in création?

As is well known, several programs are now under way in many parts of the world to bring the population avalanche under some form of rational control. But whereas there is general agreement on the dangers of unchecked population growth, there is great diversity of opinion on many other aspects of the problem. Surprisingly enough, however, both the lay public and many students of demographic problems have accepted as a matter of course a number of assumptions for which there is in reality no factual evidence.

It is usually taken for granted that (a) the most immediate and gravest consequence of continued population increase will be shortages of food; (b) that recent advances in medicine and public health have been responsible for the accelerated rate of population growth in our times; (c) that the one effective approach to population control consists in the development of new, convenient, and inexpensive contraceptive techniques, and in the education of the public in their use. All these statements are based on unproven assumptions and are certainly erroneous in part at least. It is therefore likely that control programs based on them will meet with failure. An attempt will be made in the following pages to identify the biological as well as the technological and social forces that play a role in determining population size, both in animals and in man.

After being so long discredited, the Reverend Thomas Malthus's famous essay is once more regaining prominence. True enough, Malthus's dire predictions concerning the hopelessness of the race between means of subsistence and population growth have been shown wrong by the events of the past century in the Western world, but their fundamental premise is nevertheless inevitably correct. Food production has so far grown faster than population size in the countries of Western civilization, and there is evidence that this trend may hold today, although to a smaller degree, even in the underprivileged parts of the world. But it is obvious that a critical state will be reached *eventually* unless the population stops growing. Malthus was not a poor prophet; he was an unlucky one. The immediate misfortunes that he foretold failed to materialize, not so much because his biological reasoning was wrong as because social events that he could not have foreseen occurred shortly after his time.

Throughout the nineteenth century, the Industrial Revolution in Europe created new sources of wealth and, especially, of power, thus making possible the rapid exploitation of many unsuspected resources. The lands of the New World, which were then almost empty, were rapidly brought under cultivation; railways, steamships, and other means of transportation facilitated the transfer of the enormous amounts of food and raw materials produced in the virgin lands of America, Asia, and Africa to the growing countries of the Old World. Thus the period immediately after the writing of Malthus's essay was characterized by a new social and economic situation that he had not foreseen. However, this situation cannot possibly recur. There are few empty hospitable lands left in the world, and the supply of natural resources is necessarily limited. More important, perhaps, is the fact that while science can invent new sources of power, it cannot create new space. Unless population growth soon levels off, Malthus's predictions will come to pass, even in the wealthy countries of the Western world.

Granted the general validity of these statements, the complexity of social factors makes it difficult to formulate an optimum population level on the basis of natural resources. For a hunting and gathering economy, the maximum population density is one person per square mile. For a purely agricultural economy it can exceed 1,000 per square mile when all available land is exploited, as it is in Java or Egypt; but then the standard of living is low. For an industrial economy, the figure falls to a lower level, a few hundred or less, because so much of the land is used for purposes other than food production, especially for the manufacture and transportation of commodities identified with a high standard of living. At present, the population density is around 50 for the United States, as well for the state of Minnesota in particular. This happens to be the density for the world as a whole.

Japan, China, the Philippines, India, Ceylon, and Puerto Rico have only from 0.2 to 0.5 acres of arable land per capita and are considered much overpopulated. In the United States, by contrast, there are 3 acres per capita, and in Canada, 6 acres. These differences suggest a clear relation between population density and prosperity. However, their significance for the problem of overpopulation is questionable in view of the fact that Holland, Belgium, Switzerland, the United Kingdom, and West Germany are just as land-poor as are the countries of Southeast Asia; like the latter, these European countries possess only 0.2 to 0.5 acres of arable land per capita and should therefore be considered overpopulated, yet they are prosperous. Clearly, then, population density per se is not the dominant factor in determining the level of prosperity and civilization that a country can achieve and maintain. In terms of average population density, Europe is more crowded than Asia (85 people per square kilometer as against 60).

While it is unlikely that food shortages will constitute the most alarming consequences of population increase in the future, it must be acknowledged that population changes have been often linked to the food supply in the past. According to the Chinese census, the population of China, which was under 64 million in 1578, climbed to 108 million by 1661 and to 144 million by 1741. This extremely rapid growth seems to have resulted from the introduction into China of three kinds of crops easily grown and giving very large yields: corn around 1550, the sweet potato around 1590, and peanuts a little later.

Interestingly enough, the most spectacular population spurt in Europe occurred at about the same time as in China, and seems to have been due in part to the introduction of the white potato from the Andes. Following this event, the population of Ireland increased from 3,200,000 in 1754 to 8,175,000 in 1846, not counting some 1,750,000 who emigrated during this period, and despite great poverty. A similar situation, on a smaller scale, was created by the introduction of the bean among the Pueblo Indians in the Rio Grande valley.

Thus, increased availability of food has often brought a rapid increase in population. The change resulted in some cases from the generalized acceptance of new crops, such as corn, potatoes, or beans; in other cases from the importation of animal and plant foodstuffs produced elsewhere, as occurred in Europe shortly after the beginning of the Industrial Revolution. The population of England and Wales trebled between 1700 and 1850, even though mortality rates did not decrease significantly, if at all. This phenomenon was certainly in large part an indirect result of industrialization; export of industrial goods financed the import of food from other lands.

The effects of food shortages on human populations are more varied and more complex. Hunger certainly reduces the desire or the ability to reproduce. Prisoners starved in concentration camps have reported that one of the earliest effects of undernutrition was a loss of sexual desire. The acute famine that prevailed in the Netherlands during the late phase of the Second World War was followed one year later by a marked decline in the number of births. These examples, however, correspond to extreme situations, in which people accustomed to a high level of nutrition and comfort were suddenly exposed to acute physiological misery. In contrast, food shortages do not, unfortunately, result in decreased birth rates in the underprivileged parts of the world. The poorest families are extremely ill fed, yet they commonly have the largest number of children.

The overall birth rate in South Asia and Latin America has not been reduced by either a chronic state of malnutrition or by the periodic famines of the past centuries. At least two very different factors can be invoked to account for the paradoxical fact that the populations least favored with regard to food supply are the ones with the highest birth rates. One factor is that the human body can achieve some sort of physiological adaptation to low food intake. It is not justified, therefore, to equate the physiological state of normally overfed Dutchmen suddenly placed on a famine regimen at the end of the war with that of Asiatics or Latin Americans for whom malnutrition is such a common and constant state that survival implies the ability to make physiological and emotional adjustments to food shortages.

The other factor, at least as important, is that human behavior is governed by mental states that usually take precedence over physiological and biochemical mechanisms. Despite lack of comfort and even of food, and irrespective of sexual appetite, the desire for children is one of the most fundamental urges of human beings, perhaps even greater in the poor than in the prosperous countries. Under the social and economic circumstances that control human behavior in most of the underprivileged parts of the world today, and for that matter prevailed almost everywhere in the past, children constitute the easiest and most rewarding source of emotional satisfaction, as well as a kind of insurance against the future. Only in prosperous countries have other incentives weakened this fundamental human urge.

While malnutrition does not reduce birth rates in the underprivileged parts of the world, there is no doubt that it shortens the life span. Indeed, a very large percentage of malnourished children die in infancy, carried away by infectious diseases to which their susceptibility is increased by their poor nutritional state. During the past two decades, however, the percentage of children who survive into adulthood has increased, thanks to modern techniques of public health and medicine. Insecticides, vaccines, antimicrobial drugs, nutritional supplementation have all contributed to the lowering of death rates, especially in the early years of life.

From the point of view of population growth, the most important contribution of medical science is that several types of infectious diseases can be controlled in part, and infant mortality thereby much reduced, by techniques so simple and inexpensive that they could be applied almost anywhere. This does not mean, however, that modern medicine and public health have been the most important causes of the population avalanche. The world population would probably be just about as large as it is now even if no medical or public health procedures had been brought into play.

It will be recalled that the growth of the European population began to accelerate markedly around 1750, long before modern medicine could have exerted any impact—indeed, before the beginning of the sanitary revolution. In China also the population rose from approximately 150 million around 1750 to 300 million around 1850, and to 600 million around 1950. This spectacular increase, corresponding to a geometrical progression, occurred despite recurrent periods of famine, pestilence, war, and social disturbance. Yet there was no sanitary revolution or modern medicine in China during these two centuries!

All over the world and throughout historical times, the long-range population trends have always proved to be independent of epidemics, wars, famines, and other catastrophes. The widespread and fantastically destructive epidemics of plague that ravaged Western Europe during the Justinian era, and again during the Middle Ages, did, of course, sharply reduce population size for a while, but this effect was soon obliterated. The influence of the notorious London plague in 1665 was no longer perceptible fifteen or twenty years later. In fact, the periods that followed the epidemics of plague from the fourteenth to the seventeenth centuries were among the most vigorous in European history! The famines and epidemics that have periodically laid waste China, India, and Egypt during historical times have not made these countries less densely populated. The four years of the First World War, and the pandemic of influenza that followed it, caused at least 20 million deaths, but it took only a few months to make up this number again! Interestingly enough, concern with overpopulation became acute immediately after the end of the Second World War, before DDT and antimicrobial drugs could have exerted any significant impact on world health.

The paradoxical truth is that the phenomenal increase in world population during the past fifty years has coincided with great epidemics, two world wars, several minor ones, and deep disruptions of social and economic life everywhere. Furthermore, as is well known, the most destitute and disease-ridden populations of the world are precisely the ones that are increasing the fastest. This is particularly the case for many rural areas in which the state of health is hardly affected by physicians, drugs, or sanitation. In fact, the shape of the curve depicting the growth of the world population makes it clear that the acceleration far antedates the introduction of vaccines, insecticides, and drugs. In many countries of tropical Africa, for example, the mean increase of the population was about 1.5 percent per annum for the period 1950 to 1960, even though malaria eradication had then barely begun in these areas.

It is therefore unjustified and dangerous to oversimplify and falsify the world population problem by picturing the malariologists and other medical groups as irresponsible "sorcerer's apprentices" who have set in motion a force they do not know how to stop. Much more attention should be directed to the influence exerted on the growth of underprivileged populations by the social and economic infrastructure derived from other Western influences. For example, more efficient transportation facilities make for better distribution of food and thereby increase population size, as illustrated by the role of the English-built railway system in India. Everywhere, also, better roads and more convenient means of transport facilitate rapid migrations of people from one region into another, and especially into urban centers, resulting in population increase where the economic opportunities are a little greater and the food supply a little less erratic. The modern technologist, rather than the physician and public health officer, has played the largest role in accelerating population growth.

It seems appropriate to quote here from a prescient paper written by Benjamin Franklin in 1751 and published in Boston in 1755, entitled *Observations Concerning the Increase of Mankind and the Peopling of Countries*. Here Franklin estimates that the population of the American Colonies doubles every 25 years and that within 100 years more Englishmen will be west of the Atlantic Ocean than east of it.

THE ONLY GENERALIZATION that can be safely made at the present time is that population growth is the fastest in some of the areas that have the least adequate food supplies, the worst sanitary conditions, and especially the most deficient medical facilities. It is important to emphasize that modern medicine and public health have played but a limited part in the population avalanche because health improvement is, in fact, one of the essential conditions of birth control.

Even in areas where the recent phase of population growth has been accelerated by medical advances, there is no proof that the economic and social difficulties posed by overpopulation have been as greatly increased thereby, as is commonly believed. The special case of Ceylon is worth considering in some detail because it is the one most often quoted as evidence that the population avalanche is a simple and direct consequence of disease control—in this case, the virtual elimination of malaria through the widespread use of insecticides.

It should be emphasized at the outset that the lowering of death rates in Ceylon antedates the control of malaria by DDT spraying. The Ceylon death rate (all causes) has been falling almost continuously since 1905, the downward trend having been interrupted only twice—once in 1935 after a disastrous drought and once again during the latter part of the Second World War. Admittedly, the rate of change became more striking as a result of the systematic DDT campaign. Mosquito control was followed by a sharp reduction in the incidence not only of malaria but also of infant diarrhea. As a result, the overall death rate dropped almost one-half; and furthermore, the birth rate, already high, became even higher. The population of Ceylon had risen from 2.4 million in 1871 to 8 million in 1950, corresponding to an average yearly increase rate of 1.7 percent, but this rate jumped to 2.8 percent after the DDT campaign.

While the figures mentioned above leave no doubt that insect control accelerated markedly the rate of population growth, the interpretation of this fact is not as simple as is usually assumed. The population figures that are quoted, such as those given in the preceding paragraph, refer to the island as a whole and not to the restricted areas that were already heavily populated two decades ago. However, the antimosquito campaign did more than increase the population density in the areas that were already settled; it had the even more important effect of making once more habitable parts of the island that had been very productive and populated in the past but had been abandoned during the last century because of malaria. In other words, the DDT campaign reopened new lands into which the population could expand, much as drainage had done by facilitating human habitation in the malarious forests and lowlands of Europe during the Middle Ages.

In the light of what has happened in Ceylon and elsewhere, the population avalanche should be described in terms somewhat different from those commonly used. To a very large extent, it represents the acceleration of a process that has been going on ever since the emergence of man—namely, the progressive filling up of all areas of the world by human populations. Throughout history, new agricultural and industrial processes have made it possible to produce food, process raw materials, and therefore establish civilization in areas previously considered out of bounds. The unpleasant fact that the whole globe will soon be completely inhabited is not so much a consequence as a cause of the population avalanche.

Drainage and then insecticides have rendered new regions available for man by ridding them of malaria and of other insect-transmitted diseases. Because water can be brought almost everywhere under sanitary conditions and because any remote region can be readily supplied from the outside with food and the raw materials required for specialized industries, deserts now provide acceptable and even pleasant conditions for work and for everyday life. The recent population increase in the American Southwest was made possible by the technological advances that made water available everywhere and thus permitted the transformation of desert lands into productive areas for both agriculture and industry. Other technological innovations are now beginning to make the frozen north also habitable for man.

Thus it is grossly misleading to identify the increase in world population with increase in population density. Large congested cities have long been part of human civilizations; in fact, it is probable that congestion has existed ever since the beginning of recorded history. But it was a highly localized congestion, as illustrated by the life of the cliff dwellers and especially of the artisans and laborers in the medieval walled cities. The striking and really new phenomenon of our time is that the *totality* of the globe is rapidly becoming populated. Needless to say, this process cannot go on forever; indeed, it will not continue much longer, since such a large percentage of the earth is already occupied. A biological disaster would therefore be inevitable if the population growth were to continue at the present rate. The colonization of oceans and of outer space need not be considered here, since it is in the domain of science fiction rather than a practical possibility.

Despite the dire affirmations of the prophets of gloom, however, there are several reasons to be hopeful, the most important being that, progressively but surely, most human groups are becoming industrialized and urbanized. In the past, industrialization and urbanization have had a two-phased effect on population growth—first accelerating it, then retarding it. As we shall see, the retarding influences are now beginning to operate in some of the overpopulated areas of the world where industrialization is in the process of changing the social order, just as happened in Europe a century ago. The growth of the human population has now been shown to be subject to control by the willful action of human individuals.

The large fluctuations in birth rates in the countries of Western civilization during modern times bear witness to the fact that family size is determined by a multiplicity of social factors involving willful action, but they are so ill defined that they have not yet been identified. Surveys made among middle-income populations living in prosperous suburbs have revealed that the average number of children desired by young couples has almost doubled during the past three decades. In fact, unexplained fluctuations in birth rates have repeatedly occurred all over the Western world during historical times.

In France, the population level and average family size reached a plateau during the late nineteenth century and remained essentially unchanged during the first four decades of the twentieth century. Then immediately at the end of the Second World War (but not after the First), the birth rate increased markedly and remained high until 1950, even though France was then in a state of political confusion and the country's economic future looked very bleak indeed.

All predictions concerning demographic changes have so far proved erroneous, but a few general remarks concerning past events may be justified in order to illustrate how complex and obscure are the human factors that determine birth rates. In the countries of Northern and Western Europe, and in the other areas peopled by their emigrants, the trend toward smaller families began almost a century ago and has persisted until very recently. During the early postwar period, however, birth rates increased almost everywhere in the Western world and reached levels much above those of the 1930s. In some countries—including the United States, Australia, New Zealand, and Canada—they have remained close to the postwar level, although a new downward trend is now becoming evident. In other countries, especially France and Norway, birth rates seem to have become stabilized for the present at a position intermediate between the immediate prewar and postwar levels. In most other European countries, they have drifted down to the 1940 levels. In Finland, for example, the birth rate fell from 28 per 1,000 population in 1947 to 18 in 1958.

The rapid and marked shifts in birth rates during recent decades in the countries of Western civilization can hardly be explained by changes in the availability of food, in knowledge of contraception, or in religious beliefs. For lack of these customary explanations, efforts have been made to search for more subtle determinants of human behavior.

Certain sociologists have attributed the remarkable stability of the population level in France from the late part of the nineteenth century until the Second World War to the essential stability of the social and economic structure. The bourgeois desire to transmit an unchanged state of affairs to the following generation made it undesirable to divide the family estate among many children. This conservative social attitude, it is said, vanished when the disasters of the Second World War shattered faith in the French national economy as well as in the bourgeois social values, and when inheritance taxes made it almost impossible to pass on accumulated wealth to following generations. The deeper biological urges then took the upper hand and children became a value in themselves, irrespective of any concern for the uncertain future.

Some American economists have suggested a different social motivation for the postwar baby boom in the United States and for its continuation longer than had been expected. In the words of one of them, "Americans have behaved in the past decades as if diminishing relative marginal utility sets in, after a point, for durable consumer goods; and they have chosen, at the margin, larger families." In other words, automobiles, washing machines, and the various forms of conspicuous wealth having lost much of their symbolic value, children have taken the place of material goods as symbols of prosperity and happiness. Furthermore, so the claim goes, the American population shows a tendency to "reimpose the strenuous life by raising the birth rate." It has been suggested also that when birth control is still a new idea, keeping up with the Joneses means having fewer children. Now that small families no longer convey an invidious distinction in prosperous countries, having a large family has come to represent a new kind of status symbol, a form of conspicuous consumption.

The various explanations offered to account for the higher postwar birth rates in the countries of Western civilization are entertaining and suggestive, even though not entirely convincing. Whatever their validity, however, they serve to illustrate the range of human factors that can be invoked to explain choices with regard to family size. The unadorned facts, in any case, clearly establish two points of great practical importance. One is that birth rates can be profoundly affected by factors that are neither biological in the ordinary sense of the word nor related to simple economic necessities. The other is that population growth cannot be checked merely by further education in contraceptive techniques. In the world as a whole, one of the most guilty social groups from the point of view of the population avalanche is the prosperous American suburbanite—hardly an innocent in matters of birth control.

The problem is different in the underprivileged countries. There the birth rate is much higher, as a rule, than in the Western world; furthermore, it has not yet shown any significant tendency to decrease among rural people, except in a very few special situations. As infant and childhood mortality is decreasing (although not as much or as fast as generally assumed), high birth rates naturally result in very high growth rates. From 1950 to 1960, the excess of births over deaths averaged 31.4 per 1,000 per year in Taiwan, 26.8 in Mauritius, 27.7 in Albania, 31.8 in Mexico, 33.9 in El Salvador, and 37.3 in Costa Rica. Such figures acquire their full and somewhat frightening significance when it is realized that, with an annual increase of 30 per 1,000, a population will double itself in twenty-three years!

It is widely assumed that the rate of population growth in the underprivileged parts of the world would be rapidly slowed down if inexpensive and convenient contraceptive devices were made available to low-income populations. In reality, however—and granted, of course, the urgent need for improving the techniques and knowledge of contraception—it is unlikely that this approach alone can have a significant effect on birth rates. What is needed first is to create a genuine desire for smaller numbers of children, and a belief that this goal is both desirable and possible. In other words, there has to be a basic change in attitudes before couples take the willful action to reduce fertility and to exercise the care required for its control.

Advocates of birth control naturally find it difficult to enlist the cooperation of destitute people who regard children as the one worthwhile aspect of their lives. Anyone inclined to criticize the Africans, Asians, and Latin Americans for their failure to make the efforts required for birth control might ponder the unwillingness of Western people to change their own ways with regard to cigarette smoking, overeating, or lack of physical exercise, despite the wide publicity given to the relation between these practices and various forms of illness. And it bears repeating that the United States is one of the countries where the population is increasing the fastest. Among us, as in the underdeveloped countries, it is difficult to sacrifice the pleasure of the present or the immediate future for the sake of a distant future that is but dimly perceived.

Population-control programs are plagued by the fact that the poorer the community, the more important is the role played by children in its daily life. Under restricted conditions of existence, children usually constitute the only hope of reward. They provide labor on the farm and insurance against the solitude and trials of old age; they are the most reliable and often the only source of deep emotional satisfaction; finally and probably most important, they symbolize hope and eternity. Men and women playing with children amid poverty or destruction proclaim faith in mankind, whatever the present trials of life. As Plato wrote in *Symposium*: "Marvel then not at the love which all men have for their offspring; for that universal love and interest is for the sake of immortality."

The first need and greatest difficulty in population control is therefore to create values and motivation based on the ability to visualize the future. Human beings must be taught to sacrifice the satisfaction of the present for the sake of a form of life vaguely envisioned but not factually experienced. In this light, the prospects of population control appear rather discouraging, since nothing is more difficult to change than values and motivation. On the other hand, history shows that industrialization always brings about a rapid fall in birth rates, irrespective of religious allegiance. Italy and Japan are two of the countries in which the industrial upsurge after the war was immediately followed by a marked fall in birth rate.

Through mechanisms that are ill understood and complex, but highly effective, industry brings about a non-Malthusian check on birth rate, a check based not on poverty and limitation of food but on economic and social progress. The Reverend Richard Jones, who was Malthus's immediate successor at the East India College, was one of the first to suggest that the most effective brake on population increase would be not primary wants of food but the secondary wants stimulated by civilized life, which he thought capable of indefinite extension. Between 1900 and 1962, the birth rate in Italy, a Catholic nation, fell from 33 to 19 per 1,000, and there is reason to believe that the change was related to marked gains in literacy and technological development. In fact, the curtailment of childbearing all over Europe might have occurred even somewhat faster if it had not been slowed down by the official opposition of governments, churches, and all "right-thinking" people. Individual couples began to practice birth control against the advice of their leaders as soon as the social and economic structure put a premium on smaller families.

For historical reasons, the population problem in the underdeveloped countries today has little in common with what happened in Western countries during the first Industrial Revolution. In the West, mortality rates declined and population increased only after industrialization was well on the way; wealth was being created faster than people were being born. Moreover, the empty lands of America and Africa were providing additional sources of food as soon as larger amounts were needed. In contrast, the underdeveloped countries are now in a state of accelerated population growth, but efforts to modernize and industrialize them have hardly begun. The result is a conflict between the demands of the people for higher living standards and the need to set aside capital for agricultural and industrial development.

The pessimists believe that the conflict between demographic growth and the economic requirements for industrialization cannot be resolved before the population has reached a catastrophic level. The optimists, while admitting that excessive population growth is a hindrance to industrial development, nevertheless believe that there is still enough time before an irreversible stage is reached. According to them, living standards can be raised through industrialization even while the world population continues to grow. Historical precedents and a blind faith in the human condition are my only justification for selecting from this controversy examples that support the optimistic attitude.

The voluntary control of family size that has accompanied industrialization in the past is not a phenomenon peculiar to people of European origin. It occurred also in Japan, and the present population trends in Lebanon give a picture of what will probably happen in other parts of the world. Until very recent times, the Lebanese family, whether Moslem or Christian, exhibited the traditional high, uncontrolled fertility found in all rural areas of low socioeconomic status. Lebanon has now begun a process of urbanization, and the traditional family pattern is rapidly being replaced by the Western pattern, with controlled lower fertility brought about by later marriages, recourse to induced abortion, and the earlier use of contraception. Although the trend is most pronounced among educated city women, it is gradually spreading through the other sections of the Lebanese community as their economic and social status approaches that of European people.

A study carried out among Indian villagers in 1954 revealed that fertility first tended to increase when people on a bare subsistence level moved to a slightly higher standard of living. Fertility reached a maximum at a "critical level" of living, then fell rather rapidly with increasing economic status.

Thus it seems likely that the population experience of Western

Europe will be repeated in the rest of the world. Europeans utilized every possible means of birth limitation, including abortion, abandonment of children, and even infanticide, once they were sufficiently motivated to limit the size of their families. Admittedly, interest in family control is still lacking today among most underprivileged peoples. Frustrating poverty and shortages of food tend to make for an unplanned existence, focused almost exclusively on the experience of today with little thought of tomorrow.

But aspirations for a new kind of life are now spreading everywhere in the world, and this will almost certainly change attitudes toward family size. There is even a possibility that the change will happen sooner than anticipated and that other people will be bolder than Western countries have been in their acceptance of various methods for conception control. For example, several national groups have no ethical or religious scruples against voluntary abortion; witness its widespread use in Japan and probably in many other countries. Voluntary sterilization of men and women is popular in Puerto Rico.

It is necessary at this point to open a parenthesis and discuss attitudes toward the various methods used for the limitation of births, since these methods constitute at present the *sine qua non* of population control. Ignorance of contraceptive techniques or unwillingness to use them is usually held responsible for excessive population growth wherever it occurs, especially in the underdeveloped parts of the world. Religious objections to the very concept of artificial contraception, among people of Catholic and other religious faiths, are also considered an important contributing factor. There are many reasons to believe, however, that these explanations deal with but minor aspects of the overpopulation problem.

Many forms of contraception have long been known and practiced among primitive people. The Ebers papyrus (1550 B.C.), the oldest known Egyptian compendium of medical writings, describes the formula for a medicated tampon designed to prevent conception; it includes honey and the tips of the shrub acacia, a mixture now assumed to yield the spermicidal agent lactic acid as it undergoes fermentation. In Europe, the use of the condom was already well known during Malthus's time and became so widespread in the early nineteenth century that it was banned by the pope in 1826. When Francis Place launched the birth control movement in 1822, he recommended several of the contraceptive techniques still in use today. Finally, conception control can be achieved by several methods other than contraception, and most of these have long been known and continue to be used all over the world.

The influence of religious doctrines on birth control, while real, is probably much smaller than usually assumed. The demographic data for different countries of Western civilization reveal no relation whatever between the dominant religion of a country and its birth rates. For example, Italy, Belgium, and France, three countries where Roman Catholicism is the dominant faith, have birth rates significantly smaller than those of Northern Ireland, Scotland, New Zealand, and the United States, where the non-Catholics vastly outnumber the Catholics. In Holland the average birth rate among Catholics is smaller than among Protestants. True enough, birth rates in Canada are higher among Catholics than among Protestants, but religious faith is not the only determining factor in this particular case. A large percentage of Canadian Catholics live under a type of rural economy that is associated everywhere in the world with birth rates higher than those prevailing in urban industrial areas, irrespective of religious faith. Moreover, the desire of the French Canadians to achieve the "revenge of the cradle" by outbreeding the English-speaking majority may also play some role in their higher birth rates. As to the Catholic countries of Latin America, their birth rates are extremely high, but not more so than those of many Oriental countries where other religions prevail.

Surveys carried out in the United States indicate that at least 90 percent of white couples with no fertility impairment use some form of contraception when the wife is over thirty; to a very large extent, this applies to Catholic families as well as to those of other religious faiths. Extending birth control to the remaining small minority of couples who do not exercise effective voluntary limitation of fertility would therefore have at most a very slight effect on the national birth rate. Fertility is high at present in the Western world, and especially in the United States, simply because couples deliberately choose to have more children than they did several decades ago. To a very large extent, the rapid population increase in the Western world since the end of the war had its origin in social mores and fashions, rather than in failure to control fertility through lack of convenient contraceptive techniques or through neglect of their practice.

Many different contraceptive devices and other methods of conception control have long been available, and many new ones are being introduced at the present time. But whatever their convenience, safety, and effectiveness, they will not help in checking population growth unless individual couples really want to limit the size of their own families. The problem of excessive population growth is not peculiar to people of darker skins or of lower economic status. It will not be solved unless it becomes the concern of everybody, everywhere, white as well as dark-skinned people, not only in the tropical slums but also in our own luxurious suburbs.

# Hygeia and
# Asclepius

THE WORD "HYGIENE" now conjures up smells of chlorine and phenol, pasteurized foodstuffs and beverages in cellophane wrappers, a way of life in which the search for pleasurable sensations must yield to practices that are assumed to be sanitary. Its etymology, however, bears no relation to this pedestrian concept. "Hygiene" derives from the cult of Hygeia, the lovely goddess who once watched over the health of Athens. Hygeia was probably an emanation, a personification of Athena, the goddess of reason. She was identified with health, but she was not involved in the treatment of the sick. Rather, as the guardian of health, she symbolized the belief that men could remain well if they lived according to reason. There is in the Museum of Athens a lovely marble head, probably originating in Tegea, in Arcadia, about A.D. 380. It shows Hygeia as a serene, benevolent maiden, personifying health by her balanced and reasonable demeanor.

Throughout the classical world, Hygeia continued to symbolize the virtues of a sane life in a pleasant environment, the ideal of *mens sana in corpore sano*. In Greece she eventually came to be more closely identified with mental health, and in Rome she was known as Salus, a divinity of well-being in general. But in reality Hygeia was not an earthbound goddess of ancient origin. Her name derives from an abstract word meaning health. For the Greeks she was a concept rather than a historical person remembered from the myths of their past. She was not a compelling Jeanne d'Arc but only an allegorical goddess Liberty, and she never truly touched the hearts of the people. From the fifth century B.C. on, her cult progressively gave way to that of the healing god, Asclepius.

To ward off disease or recover health, men as a rule find it easier to depend on healers than to attempt the more difficult task of living wisely. Asclepius—the first physician, according to the Greek legend—achieved fame not by teaching wisdom but by mastering the use of the knife and the knowledge of the curative virtues of plants. In contrast to Hygeia, the name Asclepius is of very ancient origin. Apparently, Asclepius lived as a physician around the twelfth century B.C. He was already known as a hero during Homeric times and was created a god in Epidaurus around the fifth or sixth century B.C. His popularity spread far and wide, even beyond the boundaries of Greece. Soon Hygeia was relegated to the role of a member of his retinue, usually as his daughter, sometimes as his sister or wife, but always subservient to him. In most of the ancient iconography from the third century on, as well as in all subsequent representation, Asclepius appears as a handsome, self-assured young god, accompanied by two maidens: on his right Hygeia and on his left Panakeia. Unlike Hygeia, her sister Panakeia became omnipotent as a healing goddess through knowledge of drugs either from plants or from the earth. Her cult is alive today in the universal search for a panacea.

The myths of Hygeia and Asclepius symbolize the never-ending oscillation between two different points of view in medicine. For the worshipers of Hygeia, health is the natural order of things, a positive attribute to which men are entitled if they govern their lives wisely. According to them, the most important function of medicine is to discover and teach the natural laws that will ensure a healthy mind in a healthy body. More skeptical or wiser in the ways of the world, the followers of Asclepius believe that the chief role of the physician is to treat disease, to restore health by correcting any imperfection caused by the accidents of birth or of life.

In one form or another these two complementary aspects of medicine have always existed simultaneously in all civilizations. It is written in the Yellow Emperor's *Classic of Internal Medicine* that "the ancients followed Tao and the laws of the seasons under the guidance of their sages who were credited with the realization of the value of education in the prevention of disease." Whatever the precise meaning of this statement, it certainly implies that ancient Chinese medicine embodied rules of behavior thought essential to the maintenance of health. But Chinese medicine also developed a very evolved system of therapeutics, with complex surgical procedures and many useful drugs.

A similar coexistence of hygienic wisdom in the affairs of daily life and of valuable surgical and medical lore is found among most primitive peoples. Taboos, religious practices, and ancestral customs that appear meaningless to us had in many cases a definite health function at the time they were formulated. The great leaders of men in the past—the Moses or Mohammed of the ancient world—owed part of their success to the sanitary discipline that they enforced in nomadic life. As is beginning to be realized, there is more to environmental sanitation than the technical plumbing of Westernized cities. Hygiene involves a social philosophy that must take into consideration the human and economic aspects of the cultural pattern of which it is designed. Just as the cult of Hygeia idealized the Greek way of life, many rules of conduct represent the attempts of peoples to achieve an adaptation to their environment compatible with physiological needs and emotional urges.

Needless to say, this adaptive state often breaks down, and for many reasons. Men will rebel and transgress, undeterred by the consequences of their actions for themselves and their group. Furthermore, empirical rules of conduct lose their usefulness when applied under biological or social conditions different from those under which they have evolved. They are solutions reached by trial and error, to meet special circumstances, but are rarely applicable to other conditions. No habitat or rule of conduct, whatever its wisdom, can take care of antisocial behavior or unforeseeable accidents. As disease and other failures of adaptation are obvious and often dramatic, whereas health and fitness are considered the "normal" state and therefore unnoticed, it is not surprising that the cult of Hygeia tends to be neglected and that the skill of Asclepius looms large and bright in the mind of man. In our societies the school of public health always plays second fiddle to the school of medicine.

Most civilizations very early developed a class of specialists possessing great therapeutic skill. They practiced massage, bloodletting, dry cupping, cauterization; they performed astonishing surgical feats, from the treatment of fractures to the removal of kidney stones and the intrusion into the skull called trephining. Some of the techniques are very remarkable indeed—for example, the suturing of wounds with termites as practiced in India, East Africa, and Brazil. In brief, the procedure consists in bringing the edges of the wound close together, having termites bite through them, and thereupon cutting their heads off! Primitive people have also recognized the virtues of many effective drugs, most of which are still in use today, and have applied them wisely to the relief of human suffering. Opium, hashish, coca, cinchona, podophyllin, and ephedrine are but a few of the natural products that have come to us as a heritage from primitive medicine. That more rediscoveries can be expected is shown by the fact that extracts of the plant Rauwolfia, a drug long known to Hindu physicians, have recently found an important place in Western medicine as a tranquilizer and for the treatment of certain mental diseases. Thus an immense amount of useful knowledge of therapeutics had accumulated long before the so-called scientific era. Indeed, it can be said that the sciences of anatomy, physiology, and in part of chemistry found their raw material in the discoveries of the disciples of Asclepius and of his counterparts all over the world. In contrast, it is not apparent that the cult of Hygeia contributed much to scientific development, unless a life of reason be considered a prerequisite to science. While Asclepius is, in Luther's words, only "God's body patcher," the serene loveliness of Hygeia in the Greek marble symbolized man's lofty hope that he can someday achieve a state of harmony within himself and with the surrounding world.

# PART V

# Reason and Will

We are still on our way, renewing and enriching ourselves by moving on to new places and experiences. Wherever human beings are involved, social adaptations make it certain that trend is not destiny. Life starts anew for all of us, with each sunrise.

# Science as
# a Way of Life

I SHALL PREFACE my remarks by acknowledging that for those who take it seriously, a life in science is very demanding indeed. Few are the evenings or the holidays during which I do not find it necessary to devote a good deal of my time to the study or the preparation of scientific material. This necessity has compelled me, of course, to neglect some other occupations and amusements that I might have otherwise enjoyed. But in reality, this neglect has never taken the form of real sacrifice. Rather, it has involved choices among several types of activities that I could have pursued. What is certain is that it has never made me feel that I was divorcing myself from normal human pursuits.

Every sensible man now recognizes that science is as much a part of culture as are the subjects referred to as humanities. In the modern world, no one can claim to be cultured who does not have some understanding of scientific facts and principles. Moreover, it is certain that the increasing importance of science in public affairs is compelling scientists to become deeply involved in all forms of human activities. In a curious but very real way, scientific technology has established a much-traveled bridge between the world of cold facts and the throbbing life of the human being of flesh and bone.

From *The Unseen World* (New York: Rockefeller University Press, 1952), pp. 106–10. Reprinted by permission of The Rockefeller University Press.

Despite common belief, the interplay between science and the rest of society is not a new phenomenon. True enough, there is a tendency at present to regard science as an activity peculiar to our times, and to assume that it began acquiring great social importance and captivating public concern only after the discovery of the miracle drugs, the explosion of the atomic bomb, and the excitement caused by Sputnik and space exploration. In reality, however, public interest in science has deeper and far more interesting origins. During the second half of the eighteenth century and throughout the nineteenth century, the general educated public of Europe and America was keenly interested in theoretical science and well aware of its practical implications. The success of the Christmas lectures at the Royal Institution in London during the nineteenth century reflected an attitude that was fairly common in most countries of Western civilization, as illustrated by the fact that scientific lectures and demonstrations attracted everywhere large and fashionable audiences. Books on "natural philosophy," as science was then called, were found in every well-appointed private library and were widely read and discussed among nonspecialists.

I have introduced here the old-fashioned expression "natural philosophy," because it corresponds to an attitude toward science that deserves to be cultivated more than ever today. Many of the greatest scientists cultivate philosophy, play music, draw or paint, write poetry, and participate actively in local or world politics. It is true, of course, that some scientists become narrow specialists, but I have seen no evidence that this makes them more competent or more productive in their field of specialization. On the other hand, scientists who assert that a scientific knowledge is the only form of culture worth cultivating might profit from reading what Charles Darwin wrote in his autobiography.

For many years I cannot endure to read a line of poetry. I have tried lately to read Shakespeare, and found it so unendurably dull that it nauseated me. I have also almost lost my tastes for pictures and music. . . . My mind seems to have become a kind of machine for grinding general laws out of large collections of facts. But why this should have caused the atrophy of that part of the brain alone on which the higher tastes depend I cannot conceive. A man with a mind more highly organized or better constituted than mine would not I suppose have suffered; and if I had to live my life again I would have made a rule to read some poetry and listen to some music at least once every week; for perhaps the parts of my brain now atrophied could thus have been kept active through use. The loss of these tastes is a loss of happiness, and may possibly be injurious to the intellect, and more probably to the moral character, by enfeebling the emotional part of our nature.

Darwin's remarks point to one aspect of scientific life that caused much concern to some people and made them question the wisdom of devoting one's life to science. Obviously, some of the richest human values have remained almost completely outside the fold of orthodox science. Certainly the arts and classical philosophy seem at first sight to come much closer than does science to many of the problems of existence that have always haunted mankind. Again speaking for myself, I shall confess that time and time again I too have felt some discouragement from realizing that science does not provide clear-cut answers to the questions that preoccupy us most deeply: the place of man in the cosmos and the meaning of life. Often also, I have felt the urge to turn to some other form of activity, artistic perhaps, or philosophical, that would liberate me from the exacting discipline of the scientific method and allow an uninhibited and more total expression of my personality. But on the other hand, there are large compensations in scientific pursuits, and taken together they satisfy me and give me confidence that I have made a good choice for my life.

First, science provides a feeling of intellectual and emotional security, because however limited the philosophical significance of its achievements, these have a lasting value and constitute evidence that mankind is progressing. I might be permitted to quote here the words of the very great microbiologist Louis Pasteur, who cannot be accused of having been a coldhearted scientist because in fact he repeatedly acknowledged in public that the feelings of the heart were for him as important as the acquisition of knowledge. "The experimental method," Pasteur wrote, "rarely leads astray and then only those who do not use it well. . . . The charm of our studies, the enchantment of science, is that everywhere and always we can give the justification of our principles and the proof of our discoveries." Happy are those who can experience "the serene peace of laboratories and libraries!"

Science, it is true, has not yet given a final answer to the questions that most preoccupy mankind, but as a scientist I am proud of taking part in an exciting and extraordinary adventure that began long before me, and that will continue long after me. Again in Pasteur's words, "Laboratories . . . are the temple of the future. There it is that humanity grows, becomes stronger and better. There it learns to read the works of nature, symbols of progress and of universal harmony; whereas the works of man are too often those of fanaticism and destruction."

As a conclusion the best I can do, it seems to me, is to answer the questions of my readers by a statement of my faith.

I believe that by the exercise of science as well as of other intellectual pursuits, mankind grows continuously into some higher form, and that in some mysterious way it is in the process of transcending itself. While my own contribution to this upward trend will, of course, be very small, it has an immense value nevertheless, because it becomes part of a spiritual structure that is endlessly emerging from amorphous matter. Science is not only an effort to gather knowledge and develop techniques for achieving mastery over nature. As Aristotle wrote two thousand years ago in his *Ethics*, science is above all the search for understanding. Aristotle's words still convey today the very spirit of the scientific way of life. While it may never be possible to reach absolute truth, nevertheless each one of us adds a small stone to the structure of knowledge, and from all these efforts there emerges a certain grandeur.

# Science and Man's
# Nature

WORDS HAVE dictionary meanings, but more important, they have
undertones that are determined by the history, beliefs, and hopes of the
people who use them. The word "culture," for example, denotes very
different attitudes and contents depending on the kind of civilization to
which it is applied. For civilizations of the Arcadian type, based on the
belief that life was happy in the past, the role of culture is to preserve
and transmit experience and traditions as faithfully as possible. In
contrast, civilizations of the Utopian type, which believe that happiness can be realized only in the New Jerusalem, demand that culture
prepare man for the mastery of nature and for the creation of a better
world.

Most people, in any period of history, have been at times Arcadian
and at times Utopian. There is no doubt, however, that the world as a
whole is now losing its belief in Arcadia and that the concept of culture
is changing accordingly. Whereas traditional civilizations put a premium on the transfer of beliefs and customs from one generation to
another, modern societies tend to regard the heritage of the past as but
a matter of entertainment for leisure time, and to consider that the
forces that are creating the world of tomorrow are the really serious

*Daedalus*, vol. 94 (1965), pp. 223–44. Copyright © 1965 by American Academy of Arts and
Sciences. Reprinted by permission.

concern of culture. One of the consequences of this shift of emphasis has been the progressive recognition that the natural sciences constitute as legitimate a component of culture as the traditional knowledge of humanity, of our history, and of our artistic creations.

It goes without saying that many varied social forces other than science have played and continue to play an immense role in shaping modern life. The invention of tools and of agriculture by prehistoric people, the emergence of social groups and especially of large cities, and the development of laws and of the various religions are but a few among the nonscientific forces that have determined the evolution of human nature and of the ways of life. Today, however, science and the technologies derived from it constitute the forces that affect most profoundly the environment in which men have to function and to evolve. Either by choice or from necessity, the cultural evolution of man will be molded in the future by scientific concepts and technological forces. Even more important, probably, is the fact that science is accelerating the rate of environmental and conceptual changes.

The horse remained the most rapid means of locomotion until the invention of the railroad, but we have moved from the propeller to the supersonic aircraft in one generation. All civilizations have until recently considered the earth as the center of the universe and man as the highest form of life, but we now seriously think about ways of communicating with other thinking and highly evolved creatures that we assume to exist in many parts of the universe. Science is the most characteristic aspect of our civilization precisely because it provides the mental and physical apparatus for rapid changes in our ways of life and even more, perhaps, in our conceptual views of creation. Indeed, the tempo at which man changes the environment and his views of himself is now so rapid that the rules of conduct for the good life must be changed from one generation to the next. In many fields, the wisdom of the parents is now of little use to the children.

The immense role of science in the practical affairs of the modern world is recognized by all, even by its detractors, but surprisingly its influence on culture is often questioned, even by its champions. The following statement is typical of this skeptical attitude concerning the modern mind as it confronts science: "Our lives are changed by its handiwork, but the population of the West is as far from understanding the nature of this strange power as a remote peasant of the Middle Ages may have been from understanding the theology of Thomas Aquinas." I shall attempt later in this essay to consider some of the factors that contribute to the estrangement of the scientific enterprise from the human condition. But it may be useful to emphasize first that science has influenced modern thought and culture much more profoundly than is usually admitted. In fact, it is probable that most educated men have now incorporated concepts derived from theoretical science in their daily thoughts even more effectively than medieval or Renaissance Europeans ever incorporated Thomas Aquinas in their cosmologies or their ethics.

The rate of acquisition of new knowledge was so slow in the distant past, and indeed until the advent of experimental science, that ancient civilizations found it difficult to conceive of the possibility of progress. Men whose lives depended entirely on the course of natural events were bound to be more aware of the recurrence of daily and seasonal phenomena, year after year, than of the continuous process of change that we now take for granted. Seeing that natural events repeat themselves endlessly, they tended to extrapolate from these cosmic cycles to human history. For them, the myth of eternal return seemed to apply to the affairs of man just as it did to the cycles of nature and the motions of stars. The known conditions of the present seemed to them but one stage in the endless ebb and flow of events.

It is difficult, of course, to determine with precision at what time the myth of eternal return was displaced in the Western mind by the concept of progress—namely, by the belief in a continuous process of change toward a new state different not only from the present but also from anything in the past—and, it is hoped, better. The philosophical teachings of the Renaissance and of the Enlightenment certainly helped to formulate the concept and make it intellectually acceptable. But there is no doubt that the philosophy of progress became part of collective consciousness in the Western world approximately at the time when experimental science first began to prosper. Men like Condorcet and Franklin wrote of progress as a theoretical possibility and placed their hopes for its realization in the future developments of science. However, it was the doctrine of biological evolution that eventually provided the theoretical basis for the concept of progressive historical change. The doctrine of evolution therefore provides one of the most striking examples of the influence of scientific knowledge on modern culture.

Few laymen, it is true, have an exact understanding of the scientific mechanisms involved in biological evolution. Nevertheless, practically all of them now accept as a fact that everything in the cosmos—

heavenly bodies as well as living organisms—has developed and continues to develop through a process of historical change. In the Western world, most great religions have come to accept a progressive historical view of creation.

Enlightened laymen tacitly apply evolutionary concepts not only to living organisms and to man but also to his social institutions, his customs, and his arts. Yet the general acceptance of this evolutionary view is rather recent, dating only from the post-Darwinian era. Evolutionary concepts were still ignored or ridiculed, and almost universally opposed, less than one hundred years ago. In contrast, they appear so obvious today that most orthodox churches, political parties, and schools of sociology, history, or art teach them and indeed make them the basis of their doctrines. It can be said without exaggeration that theoretical biology has thus introduced into human thought a new element that pervades all aspects of traditional culture.

Cosmology, or the physicochemical sciences, could probably be used just as well as the theory of evolution to illustrate how much modern thought is being influenced by scientific knowledge. But since I am a biologist ignorant of these fields, I must act here as a representative of the lay public, whose views concerning the cosmos and the structure of matter are progressively being transformed by a kind of knowledge that I do not really understand. Like every human being, for example, I have been puzzled by the concept of the divisibility of matter. I cannot imagine that the division of matter into smaller and smaller fragments can come to an end since I can always carry out one further dividing operation in my mind. Fortunately, I begin to sense that this paradox is not entirely beyond human comprehension. Although I know nothing of the theories or practices of elementary particle physics, I can apprehend that when sufficient energy is applied to elementary particles in the big accelerators, the particles are changed not by a process of true division but by a transmutation of energy into matter; any particle can be transformed into any other if the energy applied is sufficiently great.

In the preceding paragraph, I have mentioned on purpose a kind of phenomenon completely foreign to my knowledge in order to illustrate the manner in which science becomes incorporated into the cultural tradition. Science shapes culture not necessarily through its technical aspects, but rather by providing new points of view and by facilitating new attitudes. That the earth is round and that all living creatures that we know have a common ancestry are not obvious either to my senses or my common sense, yet these concepts have become integrated in my daily thoughts and thus constitute part of the fabric of my culture. It would be surprising if the general concepts of elementary particle physics and of relativity theory did not in some way become integrated in the general culture of the next generation.

The integration of scientific knowledge into general culture will probably be accelerated by the fact that there is a wide public awareness of some of the basic assumptions of science. Many lay people have come to realize that each particular field of science develops as if it were a self-contained structure, with its own body of facts and its own inner logic. Students of matter investigate elementary particles and the laws that govern the primordial stuff of which these particles might be but the transient manifestation; their information is derived from recent experiments in high-energy physics carried out with the aid of complex hardware. Students of human evolution trace the origin of man, step by step, to some small creature that lived in trees at the beginning of the Paleocene period; their conclusions are derived from the comparative study of ancient fossils found here and there in many parts of the world. It is obvious enough that the structure of matter and the evolution of man constitute two fields of science that have developed independently, each with its own techniques, points of view, and goals. In this light, it would appear as if there were no such thing as science but only a multiplicity of unrelated fields of knowledge. But while it is a fact that each field of science has its own characteristics and displays its own pattern of development, it is also true, and probably far more important, that no incompatibility has ever been found between one field of science and another; the laws of one do not violate the laws of the other.

The remarkable compatibility between all fields of science, whether they deal with inanimate objects or with living things, has implications that affect deeply the culture of our times. The validity of these implications is supported by the fact that the various scientific disciplines strengthen each other when, perchance, they can establish contact. Despite the immense diversity of creation, we all accept that there exists in nature a profound underlying unity. The search for this unity provides the motivation for the lives of many different men—some who, like Einstein, search for it in general natural laws and others who, like Teilhard de Chardin, would trace cosmic evolution to a divine origin.

So general is the belief in the unity of nature, and in the power of the scientific approach, that this method is now applied to most areas of human concern, from the natural sciences to the historical sciences, from the analysis of the human fabric to the appreciation of human arts, naïve as it may be to hope that methods developed for the study of inanimate objects can be applied to the much more complex and qualitatively different problems of social human life. But despite their premature character, the attempts to apply the scientific method as used by the natural sciences to problems for which it is not suited are of interest because they reveal a general awareness that we have under cultivation only a small area of the fields that can be exploited by science.

Since the various scientific fields include all the subjects on which reasonable people can converse objectively and exchange verifiable information, it is difficult, if not impossible, to state in words where science ends and where the humanities begin. The paradox, however, is that this semantic difficulty hardly ever causes any confusion in human behavior. The immense majority of the lay public shows by its reading habits that it sharply differentiates between science and non-science; this differentiation also appears in the fact that concert halls and art museums have more popular appeal than science exhibits. The "two cultures" may be an illusion, but in practice science is still regarded in our communities as a kind of foreign god—powerful and useful, yes, but so mysterious that it is feared rather than known and loved.

It is healthy to acknowledge that scientists themselves generally behave like the lay public when they function outside their areas of professional specialization. The student of plasma physics or of plasma proteins is not likely to select books on marsupials for his bedside reading, nor is the organic chemist inclined to become familiar with problems of population genetics. Most scientists, it is true, are interested at present in radiation fallout and in the hidden surface of the moon, but so are many members of the Rotary Club. Winston Churchill, Pablo Picasso, and Ernest Hemingway are much more frequently discussed at the luncheon tables of scientific research institutes than are the Nobel Prize winners in physics, chemistry, or biology of the same generation. And if Linus Pauling or Robert Oppenheimer is mentioned, it is less likely with regard to either's achievements as chemist or physicist than because their behavior makes them interesting and vital human beings. In brief, while scientists are deeply committed to their own specialized fields, they generally turn to nonscientific topics when they move outside their professional spheres.

The priority of general "human" concerns over purely scientific interests acquires particular importance in education. Whatever historians and philosophers of science may say concerning the fundamental similarities between science and the humanities as intellectual and creative pursuits, the high school or college student soon discovers from his personal experience that the two kinds of learning and activities are different as far as he is concerned. He will probably like one and despise the other, and science commonly loses in the comparison. A recent study of high school students selected for extremely high scholastic aptitude (only 1 percent of the total student population) revealed that the percentage of those selecting science decreased from 37.77 percent in 1958 to 28.87 percent in 1963. Even more serious was the finding that among those who had originally selected science, 55.2 percent of the males and 58.9 percent of the females changed to other fields during their college years. The significance of these figures becomes the greater when it is realized that the trend away from science occurred during a period when great social pressure was being exerted on young people to induce them to go into scientific careers.

The difficulty of scientific courses, and the shortage of gifted scientific teachers devoted to the training of undergraduates, may account in part for this disturbing rejection of science. But to be satisfied with such obvious explanations seems to be unwarranted and unwise. At the risk of oversimplifying the problem and exaggerating its gravity, I incline to the view that the attitude of the lay public and of many young people toward science is at bottom one of hostility arising from anxiety. In my opinion, this anxiety is in part the result of a breakdown in the system of relationships between human nature and the scientific creations of man.

Throughout this essay, the expression human nature is used in the French sense of *nature humaine*, which encompasses much more than does the English phrase. By human nature I mean not only the instinctive, psychological, and moral attributes that are characteristic of all of us but also all the physiological needs and urges that are woven into our very fabric and that we have retained from our evolutionary past. In other words, I shall have in mind our total nature rather than the limited aspects of it usually denoted by the expression "human nature." In the light of this larger view of our nature, it may be easier to understand how scientific knowledge, although it enables us to manipulate our environment, paradoxically leaves us outsiders in the world we are creating. While we are progressively mastering nature, our own nature has not so far surrendered to the scientific and technological onslaught.

Mankind has, of course, always known anxiety. The doctrine of original sin may well be merely a symbol for the uneasiness we experienced when we first realized that we were alienating ourselves from the rest of creation. From ancient times, many have been those who believed that the world is out of joint, and it is not at all certain that their percentage numbers are larger than in the past. What is beyond doubt is that the gap between our nature and the rest of nature is constantly becoming wider, hence the ambivalent attitude of modern students toward science. They want the benefits of scientific technology but feel uneasy and indeed apprehensive about scientific knowledge per se. Despite much writing on the miracles of science, public fear and mistrust of scientists is probably on the increase and is certainly becoming more vocal. More and more frequently, the emphasis is on the potential dangers of technological innovations, and even on horror stories concerning them.

The attitude of uneasiness has been increased, of course, by the fear of nuclear warfare, and of certain technologies that threaten our health. Popular articles entitled "The truth about . . ." almost uniformly refer to the dangers of medical and technological procedures and hint at the social irresponsibility of scientists. However, the origins of the anti-science movement are more complex and more profound than would appear from recent developments. There was already much talk of the "bankruptcy" of science during the nineteenth century. Science was then accused of destroying religious and philosophic values without substituting for them any other guide to behavior or any convincing picture of the universe and of human destiny. This dissatisfaction is pungently expressed in John Dewey's warning that "a culture which permits science to destroy traditional values, but which distrusts its power to create new ones is destroying itself." The malaise has now extended to the scientific community itself, as recently acknowledged in a public lecture by a distinguished professor of chemistry in the United States. "Science is only one branch of philosophy. . . . If we do make claims for support because of our rather immediate relation to industrial technology, we may well be making value judgments concerning technology that we are, by virtue of our training, ill-equipped to make."

Admittedly, the meaning of the word "value" is so poorly defined that most scientists would probably deny that it has any usefulness as a basis either for discussion or for action. Yet the word is so charged with the hopes of mankind, and its impact on the relationships between the world of science and the rest of society is so great, that it must be recognized as a real force. I would not presume to formulate values or propose a solution to the dilemma stated by Dewey. I shall instead limit myself to a consideration of several aspects of the scientific enterprise that contribute to its progressive estrangement from the human condition, and thereby to incoherence in modern life.

A symposium entitled "Man and His Future" was held in London in 1963. Its purpose was to examine the consequences of the fact that "research is creating and promising methods of interference with natural processes which could destroy or could transform every aspect of human life which we value."

The participants in the symposium found it rather easy to discuss the role of science in several current problems, such as: how to feed the billions of hungry people in the world; how to maintain an adequate supply of raw materials and of energy; how to accelerate the process of learning; how to prepare man for space travel. There was a tacit agreement among them that by using the proper scientific approach, "almost everything one can imagine possible will in fact be done, if it is thought to be desirable." In contrast, the participants found no basis for common discourse when the discussions turned to the physical, psychological, emotional, cultural, or ethical traits that are desirable for human betterment. Indeed, the sheer diversity of views concerning what constitutes the good life led one of them to conclude that the only possible social policy for science, as well as for human institutions, was "piecemeal social engineering," that scientists must forgo ambitious social plans and dedicate themselves instead to limited goals.

History shows, however, that human institutions cannot merely drift if they are to survive. Each civilization is characterized by the special kind of problems it elects to emphasize. Furthermore, all societies operate on certain assumptions and move toward certain goals. Despite our pathetic attempt at objectivity, we as scientists are in fact highly subjective in the selection of our activities, and we have goals in mind when we plan our work. We make *a priori* decisions concerning the kind of facts worth looking for; we arrange these facts according to certain patterns of thought that we find congenial; and we develop them in such a manner as to promote social purposes that we deem important. The most sweeping assumption in our communities at the present time is that the good life will automatically emerge if we focus our scientific efforts on the production of things and on the manipulation of the body machine, even though a large percentage of scientists probably believe that such an attitude is responsible for incoherence in technological civilization.

One might argue, of course, that incoherence is not objectionable per se, that incoherence may even be a symbol of intellectual integrity, and a necessary condition for the evolutionary development of mankind, since no one knows how to formulate either the ultimate truth, or the good life, or even the intermediary goals on the way to these ideals. In practice, however, there are limits to the amount of incoherence that humanity and its societies can tolerate; the popular success of anti-utopian and antiscientific literature at the present time may indicate that we are approaching the breaking point.

I shall attempt in the following pages to discuss several disturbing aspects of the interplay between our nature and the environment created by scientific knowledge. First to be considered will be the fact that while the external environment and our ways of life are being revolutionized by technology, our biology remains fundamentally the same as when we emerged from our animal past. Outwardly, we make adjustments to the new conditions of life; inwardly, however, we have so far failed to make true adaptations to them, and this discrepancy creates physiological and psychological conflicts that threaten to become increasingly traumatic.

Another cause of incoherence in our societies is that modern knowledge, especially scientific knowledge, relates less and less to human experience. In many cases, the technical apparatus of knowledge reaches into aspects of reality that are beyond human grasp. There is a disjunction between scientific knowledge and direct human experience.

Because science and technology are now advancing without the guidance of a well-thought-out philosophy of natural and social values, they achieve results and produce effects that in many cases no longer correspond to real human needs. Man, through science, has released disruptive forces he has not yet learned to control. In front of his eyes, these forces are undermining the relationships slowly built through evolutionary processes between nature, the works of reason, and the hidden aspects of man's nature.

H. G. Wells pointed out in *A Modern Utopia* that ours is an adaptive civilization, incompatible with static social structures. Since we transform the external world through technology, we must also change our societies and ways of life, because the maintenance of adaptive fitness is as essential for the survival of institutions as it is for the survival of living things. As presently formulated, however, evolutionary and social concepts give but an inadequate picture of man's relation to his environment. Their inadequacy comes from the fact that human societies and ways of life are rapidly changing, while certain fundamental components of man's nature remain essentially unaltered.

Ever since the Neolithic Revolution, human beings have become increasingly proficient in controlling the external world—beasts, forests, floods, climate, and many other natural forces. They have also developed enough knowledge of their own bodies and behavior to exercise some measure of control over certain aspects of their lives. Indeed, our confidence that we can modify and improve not only external nature but also our own nature constitutes the rationalistic basis for modern technological civilization. In Western countries, at least, technology has transformed the external world, medicine is learning to manipulate the body and the mind, social institutions are striving to establish universal respect for human dignity. Thus ways of life are undergoing profound adaptive changes in an attempt to keep the *social* human being in tune with the rapid changes in the environment that are brought about by technological innovations.

In contrast, many important aspects of our fundamental nature are not changing at all, or are changing so slowly that they are out of phase with the modern world. Biological evolutionary mechanisms are far too slow to keep pace with social evolution. For example, most functions of the body continue to exhibit diurnal and seasonal cycles, as well perhaps as cycles of other periodicities. Even though the ideal of technology is to create a constant and uniform environment, physiological functions still undergo cyclic changes, because they are likened to the cosmic forces under which human evolution took place. When modern life carries the day into the night, maintains the same temperature and food supply throughout the year, and imposes rapid changes of longitude in a jet aircraft, it creates physiological conflicts because our body machine continues to function according to the cosmic order. People who travel by jet aircraft have a direct perception of the physiological disturbances caused in their bodies by the change of longitude. The immediate effects of the conflict between our paleolithic constitution and the exigencies of modern life can be documented by chemical, physiological, and psychological measurements, but little is known of their long-range consequences. There is no doubt, however, that many physiological disturbances have their origin in the conflict between the modern environment and the paleolithic ordering of physiological functions.

The so-called fight-or-flight response constitutes another manifestation of very ancient hidden forces that are still operating in us today. It consists in a series of physiological and chemical processes that are rapidly mobilized in the body under conditions of threat and were certainly useful in the past. When prehistoric man encountered an enemy or a wild beast, a variety of hormonal processes placed his body in readiness either for combat or for running away. Today the same processes are still set in motion under circumstances that modern man symbolizes as a threat—for example, during social conflicts at the office or at a cocktail party. The physiological consequences of the fight-or-flight response, however, are no longer useful and indeed are probably noxious, since the proprieties of civilized life require the subjugation of the direct physical response and thus prevent the expenditure of physical energy.

Many other ancestral mechanisms that persist in the modern human being must find some outlet, even though they no longer correspond to a necessity of life. Just as a kind of hunting activity remains a need for the house cat even when it is well fed at home, similarly we have retained from our evolutionary past certain needs that no longer have a place in the world we have created, yet they must be satisfied. Ancient civilizations were aware of the profound effects that hidden physiological and psychological forces exert on human behavior, and they commonly symbolized these forces by a ferocious bull struggling against reason. In fact, most people have developed empirical procedures to let these occult forces manifest themselves under somewhat controlled conditions. The Dionysian celebrations, the Eleusinian mysteries, and many other myths and rituals served as release mechanisms for fundamental human urges that did not find adequate expression in the rational and classical aspects of Greek life; even Socrates found it wise to participate in the Corybantic rites. Many such ancient traditions still persist in the advanced countries of Western culture, though in a distorted form. In the most modern city, as among the hills of Arcadia three thousand years ago, men and women perceive in springtime that nature is awakening and at work in their bodies, just as it is in the beasts and trees. Carnival is still celebrated when the sap starts running.

Scientific knowledge of the persisting ancestral aspects of our nature hardly goes beyond a vague awareness of their existence. Limited though it is, this knowledge is nevertheless sufficient to make it clear that medical and social philosophies are based on assumptions that should be reexamined. Some of these assumptions have come to light in their simplest and perhaps crudest forms during discussions of the medical problems posed by the necessity to make man more effective in the technological age, and also to prepare astronauts for life in space capsules.

At the London symposium, the participating scientists each had his or her own formula for modifying the human being by mechanical prostheses, organ grafting, drug action, or eugenic control. But they hardly concerned themselves with the effects of these alterations on the aspects of our nature grouped under the adjective "irrational." A similar indifference appears in a recent article by a physician who has specialized in problems of space medicine. According to him, the sensible solution of these problems is to modify man drastically; the easiest approach being, in his view, to replace certain organs by mechanical parts more efficient for dial reading and better suited to electronic control. Natural ordinary man could thus be converted into an "optiman."

Needless to say, the efficiency that biotechnologists aim at fostering in the various forms of "optiman" has little to do with the ancient but still vigorous biological human urges. Commentators in the daily press and in magazines have pointed out in many humorous or scornful articles that some scientists appear to be unaware of these fundamental needs of our nature. The lay public has pragmatically recognized that we retain from our ancestral past certain needs and drives that, even though scientifically ill defined, nevertheless cry out for some form of expression.

There are also many tacit assumptions in the belief that the goal of technology, including medicine, should be to provide us with a sheltered environment in which we are protected as completely as possible from traumatic experiences. This assumption is dangerous because of the fact that many important traits of our nature cannot develop normally, or remain in a healthy state, without constant stimulation and challenge. Life at a constant temperature through air conditioning, learning made effortless through mechanical aids, avoidance of conflicts through social adjustment—all are examples of the means by which modern life eliminates or minimizes physiological or psychological effort but by the same token causes an atrophy of man's adaptive mechanisms. Thus, while protection from stresses and effort may add to the pleasure or at least comfort of the moment, and while emotional neutrality minimizes social conflicts, the consequences of an excessively sheltered life are certainly unfavorable in the long run. They are even dangerous in that the human jellyfish becomes adjusted to a particular place and time but loses his ability to readjust as surroundings change.

In contrast with the arts, science is usually identified with logic and reason. Indeed, a large part of scientific history obviously consists in the progressive unfolding of a logical process; each particular field of science has its own inner logic, which makes one fact derive from another. It is also true, on the other hand, that the growth of science presents many aspects that are essentially independent of logic. At any given period, scientists are profoundly influenced by the assumptions they accept as a basis for their work and by the goals they pursue consciously or, more often, unconsciously. To a large extent, these assumptions and these goals are those of the social community as a whole.

The most influential assumption of modern science is that the best and indeed the only scientific approach to the study of natural phenomena and of living organisms is to divide them into fragments and to investigate elementary structures and properties in greater and greater detail. While it is repeatedly, and properly, pointed out that this analytical approach has been immensely fruitful in discoveries, there is far too little recognition of the disturbing fact that it has led to the neglect of other fields of science. Although everyone recognizes that the very existence of natural phenomena and of living organisms is the manifestation of the interplay between their constituent parts under the influence of environmental factors, hardly anything is known of the mechanisms through which natural systems function in an integrated manner.

In the course of reductionist analysis, scientists tend to become so involved intellectually and emotionally in the elementary fragments of the system, and in the analytical process itself, that they lose interest in the organism or the phenomenon that had been their first concern. For example, the student of mankind who starts from a question singled out because of its relevance to human life is likely to progress seriatim to the organ or function involved, then to the single cell, then to the cellular fragments, then to the molecular groupings or reactions, then to the individual molecules and atoms; and he would happily proceed, if he knew enough, to the elementary particles where matter and energy become indistinguishable. Problems of great interest obviously arise at each step in the disintegration of the original phenomenon. But in practically all cases the phenomenon itself is lost on the way, and the knowledge acquired in the course of its analysis usually throws little light on its determinants and modalities, let alone on the approach to its control. Scientists might find it useful now and then to evaluate their professional activities in the light of Kant's admonition, "To yield to every whim of curiosity, and to allow our passion for inquiry to be restrained by nothing but the limits of our ability, this has an eagerness of mind not unbecoming to scholarship. But it is wisdom that has the merit of selecting from among the innumerable problems which present themselves, those whose solution is important to mankind."

Loss of interest in phenomena as they occur in nature is found in practically all fields of science. It would be out of place to discuss here the consequences of this aspect of scientific professionalism for the advancement of knowledge. But it is relevant to the present theme to suggest that therein lies in part the cause of the estrangement of the general public from science. The primary interest of the public is in the phenomena of nature or in the living organisms, whereas the deepest commitment of professional scientists is to the results of their analytical processes. In consequence, scientists generally lose their public as they lose sight of the original problem.

Furthermore, whereas science was at first a method to deal with the world of matter and of life as we perceive it through our senses, much of the scientist's knowledge is now acquired through technical and mental processes that operate outside the range of immediate human experience. Étienne Gilson stated in his William James Lectures at Harvard: "Every scientist naturally has the temper and the tastes of a specialist. . . . The natural tendency of science is not towards unity, but towards an ever more complete disintegration." This statement certainly describes a state of affairs that is increasingly prevalent, but it does not, in my opinion, deal with the most important aspect of the problem. A more disturbing aspect of modern science is that the specialist himself commonly loses contact with the aspect of reality that was his primary concern, whether it was matter, life, or humanity.

In their own experience of the physical world, physicists do not use their specialized knowledge for a richer or more subtle contact with reality; nor are biologists rendered capable of perceiving the living experience more acutely because they are familiar with intermediated metabolism or X-ray diffraction patterns of contractile fibers. Theoretical physicists apparently find it difficult to convert the mathematical formulas on which they depend into experiences of thought meaningful to their own senses and reason. General biologists find no trace of the creativeness of life in the macromolecules they isolate from the cell. The student of consciousness cannot relate the operations of the sense organs or of the nerve impulse to the emotion elicited by a fragrant rose or a romantic sunset.

There has been much talk during recent years of the lack of communication between the humanistic and the scientific aspects of knowledge. In reality, however, this disjunction is not so critical as is often suggested. We all can and do learn many facts and concepts pertaining to areas of knowledge totally different from the ones in which we are specialists. The breakdown in communication is complete only when the concepts cannot be related to human experience. The physicist, the biologist, the humanist, and the lay person can all find a common ground for discourse if they talk about matter, life, or humanity as perceived by the senses or as apprehended in the form of images, analogies, and responses. But discussions of matter in terms of mathematical symbolism, or of life and humanity in terms of disintegrated components, cannot be related by any form of direct experience. Specialists must return to the original human basis of their work if they want to converse with mankind.

Just as scientific knowledge is becoming alienated from human experience, so are its technological applications becoming increasingly alienated from human needs. Although modern technology appears at first sight but a spectacular extension of what it started out to be in the eighteenth and nineteenth centuries, in reality it is moving toward other goals. This change of focus is contributing to the disjunction between science and mankind.

The natural philosophers and sociologists of the Age of Reason were concerned with a few well-defined problems of obvious importance for the welfare of the human race. Everywhere they saw misery and disease caused by acute shortages of food and of elementary conveniences. They observed that ignorance of the natural forces generates terror, superstitions, and often acts of cruelty. The task they set for science was therefore to abolish the threat of scarcity and to gain enough knowledge to help humanity face the natural world without fear. These goals were within the range of human experience. By making it possible to reach them, science was truly acting as a servant of mankind.

In contrast, science and the technologies derived from it now often function as forces independent of human goals. In many cases, as we have seen, knowledge creates concepts that we cannot restate in terms of our experience, and increasingly technology creates services and products that we do not really need. All too often, knowledge and technology pursue a course that is not guided by a predetermined social philosophy. The knowledge of ionizing radiations and of atomic structure was developed by men with the highest ideals who can be regarded as saints of science, yet immense harm has come from their creations. The guilt for this harm cannot be placed on villains with selfish interests or bent on hurting mankind; it results rather from a political and social process that allows science to move blindly in the social arena.

Even though dangers are also inherent in the knowledge concerning automation, synthetic chemicals, or almost any other new technology, surprisingly little is done to evaluate the possible social consequences of these innovations. One dramatic illustration of this negligence is the research budget of the State Department. Science, lavishly endowed by public funds, produced nuclear weapons—the means by which man can now destroy himself. The problem of preventing this catastrophe is primarily the State Department's responsibility. Yet its total budget for policy research studies is negligible. Indeed, there is very little federal support for any kind of scholarly work on the explosive international issues now facing the world. Nor is there much recognition of the fact that the recent advances in medicine have created vast new problems that are essentially social, political, and economic rather than scientific. As E. M. Forster predicted in "The Machine Stops," technology moves on but not on our lines; it proceeds but not to our goals. It is urgent that science and technology be given goals of significance and value to us lest the sorcerer's apprentice be converted from a literary symbol into a terrifying reality.

The Industrial Revolution, with mass production of energy and its rapid injection into all aspects of social life, is everywhere beginning to disrupt the great dynamic processes that have so far maintained the earth in a state compatible with human life. Disruption of the water cycle is speeding water on its way to the sea and increasing its destructive action on land surfaces; denudation of the soil is creating dust bowls all over the earth; pollution of the air and of water is beginning to upset the biological balance and to damage human health. The medical sciences themselves are becoming so effective that they can affect unfavorably the fate of immense numbers of people and of their descendants, often creating new pathological processes as they control old diseases. Their greatest impact will probably be not so much on the size of the world population as on its genetic qualities and on its other qualitative characteristics.

Needless to say, there is nothing fundamentally new in the fact that technology alters the relationship between man and nature. For many thousand years, we have modified our environment by using fire, farming the land, building houses, opening roads, and even controlling our reproduction. The all-important difference, however, is that many modern applications of science have nothing to do with human biological needs and aim only at creating new demands, even though these be inimical to health, to happiness, or to the aspirations of mankind. Technology allowed to develop for its own sake often acts as a disruptive force that upsets the precarious relations upon which civilizations have been built in the past. It creates new environmental conditions to which we find it difficult to adapt and which destroy some of the most valuable human attributes.

A process of adaptation is, of course, going on continuously between humanity and the new world it is creating. As we have seen, however, some important traits that are built into the fabric of our nature are not likely to be eliminated, or significantly modified, despite all the changes that occur in our societies and ways of life. Even when we become automated city dwellers, our physiological processes remain geared to the daily rotation of the earth around its axis and to its annual rotation around the sun. The paleolithic bull that survives in our inner self still paws the earth whenever a threatening gesture is made on the social scene. The tragic paradox is that science fosters ways of life and manners of response that are often determined by technological expediency, whereas it hardly concerns itself with the fundamental characteristics and needs of our nature.

While most human beings believe that the proper study of mankind is man, the scientific establishment has not tooled itself for this task. The great scientific institutions are geared for the analytical description of the body machine, which they approach in much the same spirit as they do simple inanimate objects. They pay little heed to the scientific study of man as a functioning entity, exhibiting all the complex responses that living entails. Nor do they pay much attention to the environmental factors that condition the manifestations of human life.

The disjunction between our nature and the creations of science and technology inevitably manifests itself in social disturbances. In principle, these disturbances are not beyond the scope of scientific study; in practice, however, they have a low order of priority in the world of learning. The study of humanity as an integrated unit, and of the ecosystems in which it functions, is grossly neglected, because it is not in the tradition that has dominated experimental science since the seventeenth century. Such a study would demand an intellectual approach, as well as research techniques and facilities, different from those that are fashionable and professionally profitable in the academic establishment.

Two historical reasons account for the tendency of scientists to neglect the problems posed by the complex situations found in the real world. One is that the simpler problems are more likely to yield clear results and rapid professional advance. The other reason is that until recently, the applications of science were direct and on the whole beneficial. Only during the past few decades has science become such a powerful force that any technological intervention affects simultaneously many aspects of human life.

It is therefore a moral obligation for the scientific establishment to devote itself in earnest to the study of ecosystems, both those of nature and those created by human beings. But ecosystems cannot be studied by the use of the oversimplified models that constitute the stock-in-trade of orthodox experimental science.

The urgency to escape from the shackles of the scientific past is particularly apparent when attention turns to humanity itself. One of the strangest assumptions of present-day biology is that knowledge of the living human being will automatically follow from so-called fundamental studies of the elementary structures and reactions of fragments derived from living things. In reality, a very different kind of knowledge is needed to understand the nature of the cohesive forces that maintain humanity in an integrated state—physically, psychologically, and socially—and enable it to relate successfully to its environment. Hardly anything is known of our adaptive potentialities, of the manner in which we respond to the stimuli that impinge on us early in our development and throughout our lives, of the long-range consequences of these responses not only for ourselves but for our descendants. There

THE WORLD OF RENÉ DUBOS

are countless problems ranging from those posed by the earlier sexual maturity of children to those involved in urban planning, which should and could be studied scientifically yet have hardly any place in the curriculum of universities or research institutes.

Incoherence implies the breakdown of integrative relationships. One remedial measure is, of course, to establish better understanding and communication within the scientific community itself and between it and the public. But there is no knowledge of how this can be done effectively. At most, it is known that a few scientific books of distinction have been widely read, or at least have had a wide influence and are often quoted. A study of the reason for their success might provide some insight into the determinants of the public response to science, and indirectly into the aspects of science that have human values.

There are good reasons to believe that conceptual views of the world, even if purely theoretical, can have as much general appeal as utilitarian applications, and it is obvious, of course, that the appeal is even greater when the facts have some relevance to the problems that have always preoccupied mankind, whether these be concerned with our place in the cosmos or with our survival and welfare. But in any case, scientific communication demands more than the description of facts or the reporting of news. In science, just as in any other field, we can communicate with one another only through the channels of shared experiences, or still better, through mutual hopes.

Through its emphasis on oversimplified models, the scientific community is betraying the very spirit of its vocation—namely, its professed concern with reality. Nature exists only in the form of complex ecosystems, and these constitute the environment that we perceive and to which we respond. As human life becomes more dependent on technology, it will become more vulnerable to the slightest miscarriage or unforeseen consequence of innovations, hence the need for studies directed to the problems of interrelationships within complex ecosystems. Science will remain an effective method for the acquisition of knowledge meaningful to us, and consequently for social service, only if its orthodox techniques can be supplemented by others that come closer to the human experience of reality and to a kind of social action designed for fundamental human needs.

The study of natural and man-made ecosystems, as well as of our responses to environmental forces, has as much intellectual dignity and deserves as much academic support as the study of isolated particles and elementary reactions. Only through a scientific knowledge of our own nature and of the ecosystems in which we function can technology be usefully and safely woven into the fabric of society. Indeed, a truly human concept of technology might well constitute the force that will make science once more part of the universal human discourse, because technology at its highest level must integrate knowledge of the external world and of our own nature.

Since each particular field of science has its inner logic of growth, the scientific enterprise can long continue to move on its own momentum even though it becomes increasingly indifferent to humanity. Lacking worthwhile social goals, however, science may soon find itself floundering in a sea of irrelevancies. Eventually, it might even be rejected by ordinary people if they were to decide that its values are irrelevant and dangerous. "It seems to me entirely possible," stated recently a Sigma Xi lecturer, "that our society, which, for whatever motives, has invested not only immense sums of money but large amounts of spiritual faith in what it uninformedly conceives science to be, may become as thoroughly disillusioned and rebellious toward scientific and technological authoritarianism as early societies became rebellious toward regal authoritarianism."

Despite its spectacular successes, science is not yet firmly established in the human mind. Its increasing alienation from the problems that are of deepest concern for mankind might well transform the anti-utopian outbursts so characteristic of our time from a literary exercise into an antiscience crusade. In its mildest form, such a crusade will at least continue to clamor for a moratorium on science, under the pretext that knowledge is accumulating faster than it can be digested and therefore is becoming dangerous. In reality, of course, there cannot be any retreat from science. Rather, public apprehension and hostility point to the need for and enlargement of science. Scientists must take more to heart the questions that deeply concern human beings; they must learn to give greater prominence to large human values when formulating their problems and their results. Fortunately, this is probably easier than is commonly believed, because as emphasized earlier, history shows that the broad implications of science can become integrated in the intellectual fabric of modern societies. Human cultures, like organisms and societies, depend for survival on their internal integration, an integration that can be achieved only to the extent that science remains meaningful to the living experience of humanity.

# Genetic
# Engineering

GENETIC ENGINEERING is not new. It began in 1930—almost half a century ago—when a technique was developed at the Rockefeller Institute Hospital to modify in the test tube the hereditary characteristics of the microbes that cause lobar pneumonia. This achievement led to the demonstration that the substance now known as DNA is the carrier of heredity. Although I was present at the birth of genetic engineering, I never worked in the field and can only marvel at the new techniques of recombinant DNA that now make it possible to transfer genes from any kind of living thing to any other kind.

In reality, it is misleading to state that "scientists are now able to create new forms of life." The genetic engineering of today means only the introduction into fairly simple microbes of a few genes derived either from other microbes or from higher forms of life, including *Homo sapiens.* However, the very fact that such genetic recombination is possible has created hope and anguish—hope that the technique will be used to beneficial purposes, anguish at the thought that it might generate new diseases and lead to the manipulation of human nature.

For a long time, I had a quasi-religious hostility to experiments combining genes from different organisms, because I felt that this was contrary to the ways of nature. Like other biologists, I used to believe that gene exchange does not take place in nature, except during sexual

*The New York Times*, April 21, 1977.

conjugation between creatures of the same species. I now realize, however, that genetic exchange occurs frequently under natural conditions. For example, harmless bacteria readily incorporate gene fragments from other bacteria and thus become able to produce toxins, to resist antibiotics, to cause cancer in plants.

Contrariwise, virulent bacteria can lose the genes that make them dangerous. It is likely that bacteria also can incorporate DNA fragments from the animals and plants in which they reside.

Since gene exchange occurs widely in nature, I now feel that it is proper to do it experimentally under controlled conditions.

Even though human genes can be incorporated into bacteria and other organisms, changing human nature by genetic engineering seems to me impossible except, perhaps, for the correction of a few genetic maladies. Furthermore, my long experience in the field of infectious diseases has convinced me that laboratory techniques are most unlikely to produce strains of microbes that will start worldwide epidemics of new forms of disease. Billions upon billions of microbes exist everywhere in nature, constantly undergoing genetic changes, yet only very few can cause disease, and even then only when the conditions are just right.

The great epidemics of the past and the increase in certain forms of cancer among us can be traced more to environmental factors than to new strains of microbes or viruses. For example, the severity of the 1918 flu pandemic was largely due to the conditions created by World War I.

I doubt that gene recombination in the laboratory will create microbes more virulent than those endlessly being created by natural processes. In any case, we know a great deal about handling dangerous microbes. I have been in daily contact with investigators working on smallpox, rabies, typhus, plague, cholera, tuberculosis, and so on, and yet I have witnessed very few laboratory infections, and never one responsible for starting an epidemic.

Like all human enterprises, genetic engineering may entail some unpredictable risk. I can only state that this is an acceptable risk, because the potential benefits are large and the dangers purely hypothetical. Needless to say, countries will differ concerning what they regard as acceptable risk. Some ban DDT and saccharin, others consider that the benefits derived from these substances justify their use.

The American people may decide that the safest course is a moratorium on DNA recombinant research, or regulations limiting it to a few institutions. Such policies would paralyze research in the United States but would not affect it in other countries.

DNA recombinant research can be carried out almost anywhere, because it requires only simple equipment, unless put into a cumbersome straitjacket by unreasonable safety measures.

DNA recombinant research will go in many places for several reasons. It enables even poor countries to engage in the most sophisticated field of biological science. It promises practical applications in medicine, agriculture, and industry. It is one of the most exciting areas of knowledge, with large philosophical and scientific implications for the understanding of life.

# The Pursuit of
# Absurdity

MOST CIVILIZATIONS have been finally destroyed by military conquest, but in practically all cases they had been weakened by internal disturbances long before external enemies gave them the *coup de grace*. The usual pattern is that a particular civilization develops to the point of absurdity certain characteristics that had contributed to its initial success and then to its power—just as certain animal species overdevelop organs in their evolution. Civilizations commonly behave as if they have become intoxicated with their technological and social proficiency and lost critical sense in dealing with their own creations. This tendency is exemplified by the fate of Gothic architecture.

The architects of the twelfth and thirteenth centuries had such confidence in their technical skills that they built higher and higher cathedrals with more and more flamboyant ogives. In 1163, the vault of the nave in Notre Dame de Paris achieved the world record with a height of 110 feet. This record was broken by Chartres in 1194 with 114 feet, then by Rheims in 1212 with 125 feet, then by Amiens in 1221 with 140 feet. Competition among cities eventually became as strong a motivating force in architectural design as was the glorification of God.

Even though the nave of the Amiens cathedral was so high that it gave a sense of insecurity, its splendor and boldness stirred the people

*Audubon*, March 1972, pp. 106–7.

of Beauvais to jealousy. When they began to build their own cathedral, in 1227, they vowed to raise its vault 13 feet higher than that of Amiens. The Beauvais choir was brought to the promised height, but it had hardly been roofed when it fell. The Beauvais people rebuilt the choir, and once more it fell. A third time they built it, this time to 154 feet from the ground, but then they ran out of funds, and the church was left without transept or nave for two centuries. Eventually, in 1500, the gigantic transepts were begun, and in 1552, a lantern tower was raised over the transept cross to a height of 500 feet. In 1573 the tower collapsed, bringing down with it large sections of the transept and choir. This was the end of the great period of Gothic architecture, and in any case the Gothic style had become less and less meaningful because it was no longer the spiritual expression of the age of faith. The Gothic experience provides a symbol for what has happened to many civilizations in the past, and for what is now happening to our own.

Like architectural styles, successful social structures have often been developed to a point of absurdity. The administrative genius of the Roman Empire in using the populations and the natural resources of the countries it conquered eventually caused its failure by making it completely dependent on these countries and, even more, by allowing the empire to grow beyond manageable size. The concentration of political power in the French monarchy helped to make France the greatest nation in Europe, but it reached the point of absurdity in Louis XIV's formula "L'État c'est moi" (I am the State), which prepared the ground for the Revolution.

Our own civilization is also threatened by the absurd development of characteristics that were highly desirable when they first emerged. Thus the escape from physical drudgery has degenerated into contempt for physical work; the struggle for equality of rights has led to the belief that there is equality of talents; the use of the automobile for greater freedom of movement has turned into a compulsion; efficiency has become an end unto itself, destructive of diversity and of the quality of life; economic growth, which originally produced more goods for more people, is now largely pursued for its own sake, even when it means ecological degradation.

The ultimate form of the growth myth, which would be comical if it were not suicidal, is the affirmation, endlessly repeated from a myriad of official platforms, that our survival and the quality of our lives depend on the production of more and more electric power. It is claimed that continuation of progress demands that the production of electricity continue to increase at a rate of some 6 percent a year, whereas in fact the population increases at a rate of only 1 percent a year.

For many years, there was not a truer slogan than "Better life through electricity." But the use of electricity now constitutes one of the best illustrations of a good thing overdeveloped to an absurd point. In urban areas, a very large percentage of electricity is used for obnoxious and absurd advertising, for raising high-speed elevators to absurd heights, and for absurd air-conditioning practices. In most parts of the country, windows that could be opened to provide cross-ventilation would greatly decrease the need for air conditioning. This, in turn, would decrease the amount of heat generated at the site of the power plant where the electricity is produced, and reduce temperatures in the city, where heat is released by air conditioners. What is needed is not more electricity for air conditioning but saner architectural design. The problem of air conditioning is important in itself, because it accounts for a large percentage of the demand for electricity in urban areas; it also provides an outstanding example of the fact that social needs can be satisfied by techniques other than more and more electric power, provided we escape from the obsession that everything in life depends on such power.

In a recent issue of the *Bulletin of the Atomic Scientists*, Manson Benedict, professor of nuclear engineering at Massachusetts Institute of Technology, advocated the rapid development of fast breeder reactors because, in his words, "An abundant supply of electricity . . . is essential to civilized society." Yet countless highly civilized societies developed before electricity was used or even recognized. Furthermore, even though the consumption of electric power per capita in the United States was very much smaller in 1940 than it is now, there is no evidence that the present American society is more civilized or happier than it was then. Nor are European people less civilized than American people because they consume only half as much electricity per capita. What Benedict really meant is that an ever-increasing supply of electricity is essential for a society that measures civilization by power and therefore by the amount of electricity it consumes—a circular argument. Whether this is the most desirable kind of society is far from obvious, and in fact is doubted by increasing numbers of people, including many professors of engineering.

Industrial efficiency has generated immense economic wealth, but it is making Western civilization dependent on technological and social structures so complex they are almost out of control—witness the power blackouts all over the land. Through specialization in knowledge, in management, and in technical skills, our society has succeeded in achieving fitness between the social forms of life and the kinds of environment it creates. But fitness and efficiency impose limitations on freedom. For example, there is such an intricate reciprocal relationship in the United States between working habits, automobile transportation, the packaging industry, and other aspects of life that modifying any component of the system is likely to cause serious social disturbance. The result is a fundamental conservatism that substitutes endless manipulation of details for significant change.

Biology shows that the most specialized and the most efficient forms of life commonly find it difficult to undergo rapidly enough the necessary adaptive modifications when adaptability decreases with increasing specialization.

# The Willed Future

SCIENCE and the technologies derived from it can best contribute to civilization not through a further expansion of the megamachine but by helping in the maintenance of the ecological balance and in the development of man's potentialities. This will be made difficult by the attitudes we have inherited from the nineteenth and early twentieth centuries. We have trained our social reflexes for technological "advances," however trivial their goals and deleterious their long-range effects. Instead of conveying a technological quality, the word "progress" now means just moving on, even though the forward motion is on a road that leads to disaster or despair. Worthwhile social goals for progress must first be formulated before planning can provide a desirable and enjoyable structure for the human effort.

Normative planning is not concerned with forecasting a future that is inevitable but rather with "constructing" or "inventing" desirable futures—to use expressions associated with the writings of Pierre Massé and Dennis Gabor. This means anticipating a desired state of affairs and acting on the present conditions to bring it about. There is a "logical" future, which is the expression of natural forces and antecedent events. On the other hand, there is also a "willed" future, which comes into being because man makes the effort to imagine it and to build it. H. G. Wells wrote in *A Modern Utopia*, "Will is stronger than Fact; it can mold and overcome Fact. But this world has still to discover its Will." What H. G. Wells meant by "Will" is the image of a future that is not only desired but also possible. In this light, long-range normative planning is similar to the design of utopias, except that it implies the specification of the means required to reach the utopian state.

Concern with the future used to be expressed in the form of literary exercises, or at best in the form of purely social utopias, formulated on the basis of certain theological, political, or economic beliefs shared by the members of the utopian group. Utopias are no longer fashionable today, partly because we lack a stable ground of generally accepted values to provide the hard foundation on which to construct viable social systems. It may be also that the eclipse of man's normative functions results from the acceptance by many scientists and sociologists of the view that the world of science and technology sets its own "arising ends." A tired resignation to the imperatives of economies and scientific technology along with the collapse of the old metaphysics may account for this acceptance. In any case, the tendency during recent decades has been to limit planning to the here and now. The future is imagined not as a really new venture but as a mere extension of the past.

To escape from this static and paralyzing view of civilized life, it will be necessary to construct multiple models of possible futures different from the present state of affairs and to imagine courses of action that would bring such futures into being. Since anticipations govern the policies of change, they paradoxically, but very effectively, become the causative agents of change. Causative anticipations differ from predictions in that the future they describe must not only be "possible" but also embody considerations of the "desirable." They imply value judgments as to what is desirable or not, good or bad, and thus inevitably give a direction to the social and scientific enterprise.

In an inspired passage in *Science and the Modern World* Alfred North Whitehead suggests that the order of nature as conceived by scientific determinism has now taken the role of Fate in the Greek tragedy. The great tragedians of the modern world are the scientists, "with their vision of fate, remorseless and indifferent, urging and incident to its inevitable issue. . . . This remorseless inevitableness is what pervades scientific thought. The laws of physics are the decrees of fate." Fortunately, the applications of science to human affairs do not have as high a degree of inevitability as do the laws of nature. Contemporary man seems to be poised between passive acceptance of scientific technology for its own sake, violent rejection of it, and conscious use of it for some ultimate concern. The social ferment that is beginning to agitate the community of scientists gives hope that man still has a chance to control his destiny by imposing a direction on the scientific endeavor and, in particular, by consciously planning the scientific technology that will shape the modern world.

# PART VI

# Man in the Biosphere

We cannot escape from the past, but neither can we avoid inventing the future. With our knowledge and a sense of responsibility for the welfare of humankind and the earth, we can create environments that are ecologically sound, esthetically satisfying, economically rewarding, and favorable to the continued growth of civilization.

# The Wilderness
# Experience

UNTIL THE AGE of twenty-seven, I knew of the earth only some of its most humanized environments, in France, Italy, England, and the eastern coast of the United States. My first direct contacts with the wilderness were during the late 1920s and the 1930s, when I drove several times across the North American continent and discovered—a true emotional discovery for me—the New Mexico mesas from the Raton Pass and the Pacific Ocean from a primeval forest in Oregon. Around 1930, these environments were still essentially wild.

I now realize how much my life would have been enriched by longer and more intimate contacts with the wilderness. The experience of nature in a native prairie, a desert, a primeval forest, or high mountains not drowned with tourists is qualitatively different from what it is in a well-tended meadow, a wheat field, an olive grove, or even in the high Alps. Humanized environments give us confidence because nature has been reduced to the human scale, but the wilderness in whatever form almost compels us to measure ourselves against the cosmos. It makes us realize how insignificant we are as biological creatures and invites us to escape from daily life into the realms of eternity and infinity.

In one of Kyoto's Zen temples, I have seen men and women who have the impression of achieving this escape by looking at a distant hill in an attitude of reverence. We can also perceive some of the cosmic values of the wilderness by contemplating the great spectacles of nature—for example, simply by looking down into the Grand Canyon of the Colorado. But the real experience of the wilderness probably requires the participation of all our senses, in a manner that calls to mind Paleolithic ways of life.

The hunter-gatherers of the Old Stone Age were conditioned physically and mentally by the features of their immediate surroundings: the lay of the land, the rocks, and the soil; the springs, river, and lakes; the various forms of animal and plant life; the sunshine and rainfall—all the natural phenomena they experienced directly. Their bodily responses were conditioned and their mental processes were informed by the environmental stimuli they perceived through their senses. They thereby acquired an empirical knowledge that was more holistic than analytic but so precise and so well fitted to their local environment that it enabled them to cope effectively with the various aspects of the wilderness in which they lived, much as wild animals do in their native habitats.

Ever since the development of agriculture in the Neolithic period, the immense majority of human beings have lived in environments they have transformed. As a result, few of us really desire to inhabit the wilderness permanently and even fewer could long survive in it. This is not because we are genetically different from the Stone Age hunter-gatherers, but because humanized environments do not provide the opportunities for the expression of certain human potentialities that are still in us but can be expressed only under conditions similar to those of Paleolithic life.

Even among people today, the really experienced hunters or fishermen perceive with their whole body the layout of the landscapes and waterscapes in which they practice their particular sport. They come to know almost instinctively the habits of the animals that interest them and how these habits are affected by the seasons, the vagaries of the weather, and other aspects of the environment. In *Meditations on Hunting*, José Ortega y Gasset reports how the hunter "instinctively shrinks from being seen" and "perceives all his surroundings from the point of view of the animal." For the hunter, "wind, light, temperature, ground contour, minerals, vegetation, all play a part. They are not simply there . . . as they are for the tourist or the botanist, but rather they function, they act." These words of Ortega's convey how human beings can still learn to function as organic parts of a given environment instead of simply observing it passively, as do most people when looking at scenery. Human beings can even learn about nature from animals. A naturalist who had raised two wolves and was in the habit of taking long walks with them in the wilderness described how the behavior of his animal companions made him perceive aspects of nature—smells, sounds, and sights—that he had not noticed before. Thus although we are no longer adapted to life in the wilderness, this is not due to changes in our genetic nature but to social and cultural forces that inhibit the expression of some of our potential.

From the beginning of recorded history and even in prehistoric legends, the word "wilderness" has been used to denote barren deserts, deep forests, high mountains, and other inaccessible or harsh environments not suited to human beings, cursed by God, and commonly occupied by foul creatures. Such forms of wilderness evoked a sense of fear for a good biological reason. They are profoundly different from the environmental conditions under which our species acquired its biological and psychological characteristics during the Stone Age.

The word "wilderness" occurs approximately three hundred times in the Bible, and all its meanings are derogatory. In both the Old and New Testaments, the word usually refers to parched lands with extremely low rainfall. These deserts were then, as now, unsuited to human life, and they were regarded as the abodes of devils and demons. After Jesus was baptized in the Jordan River, he was "led up by the Spirit into the wilderness to be tempted by the devil." The holy men of the Old Testament or of the early Christian era moved into the wilderness when they wanted to find a sanctuary from the sinful world of their times. Thus while some great events of the Judeo-Christian tradition occurred in the desert, this environment was at best suitable for spiritual catharsis.

In Europe, the word "wilderness" applied chiefly to primeval forests, high mountains, and marshes, because these parts of the continent were uninhabitable. According to Marjorie Nicolson, people until the eighteenth century regarded mountains as "nature's shames and ills . . . warts, blisters, and imposthumes" on the otherwise fair face of the earth. When the Puritans arrived in the New World, the huge forests that covered the Atlantic coast at that time similarly appeared to them as a "heidious and desolate wilderness full of wilde beastes and wilde men." The majority of immigrants who settled in the rest of the American continent during the following two centuries also regarded the primeval forest with fear and contempt.

Ecologists define as wilderness any environment that has not been disturbed by human activities, but in the popular mind the word still has a deep resonance with a feeling of alienation and insecurity. It is used to denote almost any place, natural or artificial, in which people feel lost or perplexed. In the past, nature in the wild has been usually regarded as alien and cruel, the site of evil and witchcraft. Now many people in industrialized societies use the word "wilderness" to denote huge anonymous urban agglomerations that appear to them hostile and corrupt.

Humankind has always struggled against environments to which it could not readily adapt; in particular, it has shunned the wilderness or has destroyed much of it all over the world. Contrary to what is often stated, this is just as true of Oriental as of Occidental people.

The admiration of wild landscapes expressed in Oriental arts and literature probably reflects not so much the desire to live in them as the intellectual use of them for religious or poetic inspiration. The ancient Chinese, especially the Taoists, tried to recognize in nature the unity and rhythm that they believed to pervade the universe. In Japan, the followers of Shinto deified mountains, forests, storms, and torrents and thus professed a religious veneration for these natural phenomena. Such cultural attitudes were celebrated in Chinese and Japanese landscape paintings more than a thousand years before they penetrated Western art, but this does not prove that Oriental people really identified with the wilderness. Paintings of Chinese scholars wandering thoughtfully up a lonely mountain path or meditating in a hut under the rain suggest an intellectual mood rather than life in the wilderness. The Chinese master Kuo Hsi wrote in the eleventh century that the purpose of landscape painting was to use art for making available the qualities of haze, mist, and the haunting spirits of the mountains to human beings who had little if any opportunity to experience these delights of nature. Much of the Chinese land had been grossly deforested and eroded thousands of years before, and the Taoist movement may have been generated in part by this degradation of nature and as a protest against the artificialities of Chinese social life.

In the Christian world, also, there has been a continuous succession of holy men, poets, painters, and scholars who did not live in the wilderness but praised it for its beauty and its ability to inspire noble thoughts or actions. Saint Francis of Assisi was not alone among medieval Christians in admiring and loving nature. The Swiss naturalist Konrad Gesner wrote in 1541 that "he is an enemy of nature, whosoever has not deemed lofty mountains to be most worthy of great contemplation." After Jean Jacques Rousseau, the many romantic writers, painters, and naturalists of Europe became more than a match for the Chinese poets and scholars of the Sung period. But like the Chinese, they wrote of the wilderness in the comfort of their civilized homes, as intellectuals who preached rather than practiced the nature religion.

In Europe, the shift from fear to admiration of the wilderness gained momentum in the eighteenth century. The shift was not brought about by a biological change in human nature but was the consequence of a new social and cultural environment. Fear of the wilderness probably began to decrease as soon as dependable roads gave confidence that safe and comfortable quarters could be reached in case of necessity. There were numerous good roads in western Europe by the time Jean Jacques Rousseau roamed through the Alps and Wordsworth through the Lake District. In the New World, access was fairly easy even to the High Sierras when John Muir reached them from San Francisco.

Appreciation of the wilderness began not among country folk who had to make a living in it, but among city dwellers who eventually came to realize that human life had been impoverished by its divorce from nature. People of culture generally wanted to experience the wilderness not for its own sake but as a form of emotional and intellectual enrichment. In Europe, Petrarch is the first person credited with having deliberately searched mountain and primeval forest for the sheer pleasure of the experience. His account of his ascent of Mount Ventoux in 1336 is the first known written statement of the beauty of the Alps under the snow, but he reproached himself for letting the beauty of the landscape divert his mind from more important pursuits. By the early Romantic period, however, the wilderness came to be seen not only as the place in which to escape from an artificial and corrupt society but also as a place to experience the mysterious and wondrous qualities of nature. The wilderness experience became a fashionable topic of conversation as well as of literature and painting and thus rapidly changed the attitudes of the general public toward nature.

Until the eighteenth century, for example, the Derbyshire peak region in England was considered wild and unfit for human eyes. In 1681, the poet Charles Cotton described it as "a country so deformed" that it might be regarded as "Nature's pudenda." Travelers in those days were advised to keep their coach blinds drawn while traversing the region so as not to be shocked by its ugliness and wildness. Within a few decades, however, the very same region came to be regarded as so attractive that it inspired lines of extravagant praise by nineteenth-century poets. The Derbyshire hills are now considered rather tame, since they do not exceed 2,000 feet in elevation; later poets shifted their admiration to wilder and more rugged sceneries, such as the Lake District in England, the Alps, and high mountains in general. In less than two centuries, new emotional and intellectual attitudes thus completely changed the relationships between English people and their natural environment.

People who express love for the wilderness do not necessarily practice what they preach. In 1871, Ralph Waldo Emerson refused to camp under primitive conditions when he visited John Muir in the Sierras and elected instead to spend the night in a hotel. When Thoreau delivered the lecture with the famous sentence "In Wildness is the Preservation of the World," he was living in Concord, Massachusetts, a very civilized township where the wilderness had been completely tamed. He loved the out-of-doors but knew little of the real wilderness. His cabin by Walden Pond was only two miles from Concord; woodchucks were the wildest creatures he encountered on his way from the pond to town, where he often went for dinner. In fact, Thoreau acknowledged some disenchantment when he experienced nature in a state approaching real wilderness during his travels in the Maine woods.

As pointed out by Aldous Huxley in his essay "Wordsworth and the Tropics," the sceneries that inspired Thoreau and nineteenth-century Romantic poets were very different from the wilderness that has frightened people throughout the ages. "To us who live beneath a temperate sky and in the age of Henry Ford, the worship of Nature comes almost naturally. It is easy to love a feeble and already conquered enemy. . . . There are . . . wild woods and mountains, marshes and heaths, even in England. But they are there only on sufferance, because we have chosen, out of our good pleasure, to leave them their freedom." For us, now, "the corollary of mountain is tunnel, of swamp an embankment; of distance, a railway." In the real wilderness, however, "rivers imply wading, swimming, alligators. Plains mean swamps, forest, fevers."

As did their Oriental counterparts, Christian advocates of the wilderness discovered its beauty while trying to escape from their social environment in search of a better way of life. They valued it as a symbol of anticorruption at least as much as for its own sake. The European pro-wilderness movement gained momentum in the nineteenth century from the reaction against the brutalities of the Industrial Revolution.

Appreciation of the wilderness was later enhanced by science. Instead of regarding deserts and marshes as the abode of evil spirits and mountains as ugly deformities of the earth's surface, educated people learned to look at these phenomena as expressions of a natural order different from the creations of the human order but with a beauty of their own. Most people probably still experienced awe in the face of wilderness, but they also had a sense of sublimity at the prodigious creativeness of nature and a feeling of reverence for the laws—divine or natural—that link humankind to the rest of creation.

Increasingly during recent years, interest in the wilderness and the desire to preserve as much of it as possible have been generated by an understanding of its ecological importance. It has been shown, for example, that the wilderness accounts for some 90 percent of the energy trapped from the sun by photosynthesis and therefore plays a crucial role in the global energy system. The wilderness, furthermore, is the habitat of countless species of animals, plants, and microbes; destroying it consequently decreases the earth's biological diversity. This in turn renders the ecosystem less resistant to climatic and other catastrophes and less able to support the various animal and plant species on which we depend. Undisturbed natural environments— including forests, prairies, wetlands, marshes, and even deserts—are the best insurance we have against the danger inherent in the instability of the simplified ecosystem created by modern agriculture. From a purely anthropocentric point of view, we must save as much wilderness as possible because it constitutes a depository of genetic types from which we can draw to modify and improve our domesticated animals and plants.

Admiration of the wilderness can thus take different forms. It can lead to direct and prolonged experience of the natural world, as in the case of John Muir. For many more people, it derives from a desire to escape from the trials and artificialities of social life, or to find a place where one can engage in a process of self-discovery. Experiencing the wilderness includes not only the love of its spectacles, its sounds, and its smells, but also an intellectual concern for the diversity of its ecological niches.

Above and beyond these considerations, however, are moral ones that also favor wilderness preservation. The statement that the earth is our mother is not a sentimental platitude. Our species has been shaped by the earth, and we feel guilty and somewhat incomplete when we lose contact with the forces of nature and with the rest of the living world. The desire to save forests, wetlands, deserts, or any other natural ecosystem is an expression of deep human values. Concern for the wilderness does not need biological justification any more than does opposing callousness and vandalism. We do not live in the wilderness, but we need it for our biological and psychological welfare. The experience of the quality of wildness in the wilderness helps us to recapture some of our own wilderness and authenticity. Experiencing wildness in nature contributes to our self-discovery and to the expression of our dominant potentialities.

The human species has now spread to practically all parts of the earth. In temperate latitudes, although not in tropical or polar regions, we have enslaved much of nature. And it is probably for this reason that we are beginning to worship the wilderness. After having for so long regarded the primeval forest as an abode of evil spirits, we have come to marvel at its eerie light and to realize that the mood of wonder it evokes cannot be duplicated in a garden, an orchard, or a park. After having been frightened by the ocean, we recognize a sensual and mystic quality in its vastness and in the ebb and flow of its waves. Our emotional response to the thunderous silence of deep canyons, to the frozen solitude of high mountains, and to the blinding luminosity of the desert is the expression of aspects of our fundamental being that are still in resonance with cosmic forces. The experience of wilderness, though indirect and transient, helps us to be aware of the cosmos from which we emerged and to maintain some measure of harmonious relation to the rest of creation.

# The Resilience
# of Nature

WHEN THE UNITED NATIONS CONFERENCE on the Human Environment convened in Stockholm in 1972, its main themes were expressed in phrases such as "pollution is making the earth unsuited to life"; "rivers and lakes are dying"; "deserts are on the march"; "natural resources are being depleted." This pessimistic view of the world's condition reflected an awareness on the part of the general public that human activities are now causing extensive environmental damage all over the earth. Deforestation, erosion, and salination are lowering agricultural productivity in many places. Chemical pollutants are spoiling the quality of air, water, and other aspects of the environment, with deleterious effects on all forms of life. Human activities decrease the wealth of the earth by wasting its natural resources and bringing about the extinction of many living species. Aldo Leopold's words about prairie vegetation could apply just as well to many other ecosystems now threatened by human activities:

> No living man will see again the long-grass prairie, where a sea of prairie flowers lapped at the stirrups of the pioneer. We shall do well to find a forty-acre patch here and there on which the prairie plants can be kept alive as species. There were a hun-

dred such plants, many of exceptional beauty. Most of them are quite unknown to those who have inherited their domain.

The fact that lovely wildflowers that used to be common in our woods are becoming extremely rare—the fringed gentian and the trailing arbutus, for example—testifies to the impoverishment of the native flora in many places during the past few decades. Concern for endangered species focuses chiefly on animals and plants that are well known because of some obvious attribute, but the gravest losses may be of species that are essentially unknown yet play an important role in the ecology of tropical or other fragile ecosystems.

Many people believe that much of the damage done to the earth is so profound that it is now irreversible. Fortunately, this pessimism is probably unjustified, because ecosystems have enormous powers of recovery from traumatic damage.

Ecosystems possess several mechanisms for self-healing. Some of these are analogous to the homeostatic mechanisms of animal life; they enable ecosystems to overcome the effects of outside disturbances simply by reestablishing progressively the original state of ecological equilibrium. More frequently, however, ecosystems undergo adaptive changes of a creative nature that transcend the mere correction of damage; the ultimate result is then the activation of certain potentialities of the ecosystem that had not been expressed before the disturbance.

Numerous examples of such environmental recovery occur either through homeostatic response or through adaptive changes of a creative nature. I shall describe a few of them, selected because they illustrate environmental problems in different climatic zones and different technical approaches to environmental improvement.

Anyone who has established a home on abandoned farmland in the temperate zone is painfully aware of nature's ability to restore the forest vegetation that existed before the advent of agriculture. This has been my own experience in the Hudson Highlands forty miles north of New York City, where endless struggle is required to prevent the return of the type of forest that once covered that part of the world.

A recent bulletin from the University of Rhode Island Agricultural Experimental Station provides a typical illustration of the restorative ability of nature in the temperate zone. Two centuries ago, 70 percent of the land in Rhode Island had been cleared of the forest that once covered it almost completely. The primeval forest had been transformed into agricultural land by the original white settlers. During the late nineteenth century, however, the less productive farms were abandoned, and trees returned so rapidly that less than 30 percent of the state remains cleared today. Nature provided the mechanisms for a spontaneous step-by-step restoration of the original ecosystem. Similarly, forest is reoccupying abandoned farmlands in many other areas of the eastern United States. For example, although Massachusetts is one of our most heavily populated states, it has now become one of the most heavily forested. The return of the trees is not peculiar to the Atlantic coast. In Michigan, the Porcupine Mountain forest, which had been badly damaged by mining during the nineteenth century, has now recovered so well that it is called the Porcupine Wilderness State Park.

Deforestation began in western Europe during the Neolithic period and probably reached its peak a century ago, but brush and trees take over as soon as agricultural land is abandoned for economic reasons; the original ecosystem may become reestablished even on land that has been cleared and cultivated for more than a thousand years!

When the Korean War ended in 1953, a demilitarized zone (DMZ) of 2.5 miles width was agreed upon by North and South Korea. The DMZ was then a wasteland pockmarked with bomb craters and shell holes, yet it has now become one of Asia's richest wildlife sanctuaries. Abandoned rice terraces have turned into marshes used by waterfowl; old tank traps are overgrown with weeds and serve as a cover for rabbits; herds of small Asian deer take refuge in the heavy thickets. Korean tigers and lynx now roam in the mountains of the eastern part of Korea. Birds prosper throughout the DMZ, because they are almost completely out of reach of guns; pheasants are so plump that they have difficulty getting off the ground; the rare Japanese ibis has recently been spotted; the monogamous Manchurian crane, a white, black, and red bird with a majestic wingspan of eight feet, can be watched performing its elaborate mating ritual, which consists of bows, wing flapping, and leaps into the air.

Although trees in the temperate zone are the most obvious manifestation of ecological recovery, they are not the only ones. Animals also reestablish themselves as soon as they have a chance. Deer multiply to a nuisance level where they find an adequate supply of food; wild turkeys have once more been sighted in all counties of New York State; coyotes and even wolves are on the increase in those parts

[ 265 ]

of the northeastern states that are reacquiring some wilderness characteristics.

The reintroduction of beavers in Sweden provides a picturesque illustration of nature's ability to reestablish the natural order after it has been destroyed by human intervention. In that country, the last of the original population of beavers was shot in 1871, at a time when the species had disappeared from most of its habitats. However, when a few beavers from the surviving Norwegian stock were reintroduced in Sweden between 1922 and 1939, they rapidly multiplied to such an extent that they caused extensive damage to forest and arable land. There are now once more vociferous demands for an open season on beavers and even for their complete eradication.

In the temperate zone, a forest area of some hundred acres containing a suitable mix of species and habitats can maintain itself under conditions of heavy use and can recover even from severe damage. But this is not the case in tropical, desertic, or arctic regions, or even for areas that have been strip-mined in Ohio, Pennsylvania, and elsewhere in Appalachia. In many parts of the world, ecologic recovery requires extremely long periods of time and is possible only if very large areas are protected from further damage.

Despite their massive grandeur and seemingly stark immutability, the Himalayas, the Andes, and the East African mountains are among the most fragile ecosystems on earth. Their steep slopes deteriorate rapidly and often irreversibly when erosion follows such overuse as excessive wood cutting, grazing, or cropping. Semidesertic areas and tropical rain forests also are extremely susceptible to environmental insults. All over the earth, deserts are indeed on the march. Yet even some of the most fragile ecosystems can recover under special circumstances. Recovery can take place when the proper species reach the damaged ecosystem either by accidental transportation or by active migration.

In 1883, Krakatoa, an island in the Sunda Strait near the Malay Peninsula, was partly destroyed by a tremendous volcanic eruption that killed all its forms of life. Experts have estimated that the explosion had the violence of a million hydrogen bombs. The seismic wave it generated reached 135 feet above sea level, destroying seaside villages in Java, Sumatra, and other neighboring islands. Ash and gases rose 50 miles into the sky, blocking out sunlight over a 150-mile radius. Vast quantities of pumice hurtled through the air, defoliating trees and clogging harbors. When the eruption ended, what was left of Krakatoa was covered by a thick layer of lava and was completely lifeless.

The wind and the sea currents, however, soon brought back some animals and plants, and life once more took hold on the lava. More than thirty species of plants were recognized as early as 1886. By 1920, there were some 300 plant species and 600 animal species, including birds, bats, lizards, crocodiles, pythons, and, of course, rats. Today, less than a century after the great eruption, the plant community on Krakatoa is fairly complex, although it has not yet reached the composition of the climax forest in the rest of the Malay Archipelago.

Many examples of resurgence of life have been observed under other conditions. Even Bikini and Eniwetok, pulverized and irradiated by fifty-nine nuclear blasts from 1946 to 1958, are said to be reacquiring a complex biota, despite the destruction of their topsoil.

The most recent illustration of nature's biological power is the rapid establishment of living things on Surtsey, the new island created by a submarine volcanic eruption on November 14, 1963, off the coast of Iceland. Within less than ten years after its emergence, Surtsey had acquired from the neighboring islands and from Iceland itself a biota that makes it an almost typical member of the Icelandic ecosphere.

The introduction of biota from an exterior source is not always needed for the recovery of a fragile ecosystem. Many plants or their seeds can persist in a dormant state for long periods of time and prosper again as soon as conditions are favorable for their development. The Wadi Rishrash region of the Eastern Desert in Egypt, for example, was shut off to grazing in the 1920s. Within a few years, the vegetation was so dense that it resembled an irrigated oasis; desert animals took refuge in it during the breeding season. With its new biota, the region appears almost out of place in its barren surroundings.

In Greece and the African Sahel, similarly, a diversified vegetation reappears spontaneously when the land is protected against grazing by cattle, goats, and rabbits; even trees grow in areas that had long been almost desertic. In a particular Sahelian ranch of one-quarter million acres, the land changed spontaneously from the state of desert to pasture when a barbed-wire fence was installed to prevent uncontrolled grazing and when cattle were allowed to graze in each area of the ranch only once in five years.

Recovery of a damaged ecosystem occurred recently in west Texas near the city of San Angelo, at the confluence of the three Concho rivers. The process began with Rocky Creek, which dried up thirty years ago but now makes an important contribution to the municipal water supply of San Angelo. At the turn of the century, Rocky Creek was a never-failing clear stream that ran through a valley of tall grasses, dotted occasionally here and there by mesquite or some other form of brush. Fish and waterfowl were abundant in the stream; deer and smaller game sought refuge from summer heat under the trees of its banks. Throughout the early decades of the twentieth century, however, brush increasingly invaded the floor of the valley and hillsides. Rocky Creek became progressively narrower and shallower and eventually ceased to flow during the drought of the 1930s. Fish, waterfowl, deer, and other game virtually disappeared.

While the drought contributed to the impoverishment of Rocky Creek, most of the damage seems to have resulted from changes in land use. Before the white settlements, herds of buffalo and other grazing animals periodically migrated down from the plateaus. They were so numerous that they left in their wake a hoof-scarred land almost denuded of grass, but the damage was only temporary, because they stayed for a relatively short time; they did not return to the same place for a year, or perhaps for several years, thus allowing grass to grow back. The situation changed when white ranchers made a practice of enclosing cattle within barbed-wire fences and keeping them in the same area year after year. As a result of overgrazing, the better types of native grass progressively disappeared and were replaced by mesquite and other brush. The deeply growing roots of these plants sapped the underground water that had formerly found outlets into creeks and rivers and had permitted the growth of desirable varieties of grasses.

Around the middle of the twentieth century, a few ranchers began to change their grazing practices in order to protect their cattle against the drought. They reduced the number of livestock so that the level of grazing enabled tall grasses to return, and they started a program of brush destruction by herbicides.

The result was beyond expectation. In 1964, a half-forgotten spring began to flow for the first time in some thirty years. Its flow progressively increased, and soon Rocky Creek also came back to life. As more and more brush was eliminated, new seeps and springs began to flow in the valley. Many of them continued to yield clear water even during a hot, dry summer. Rocky Creek has flowed the year around since the late 1960s, all the way to the Middle Concho. Fish, waterfowl, deer, and other game are once more part of the scenery. Other programs of brush control now conducted by the University of Texas in collaboration with ranchers show that, as was done in the Rocky Creek area, it is possible in other areas to bring back to life numerous seeps and springs that have been dried up for several decades.

While deserts are on the march over much of the earth, they can be made to retreat. In the words of Mohamed El-Kassas, the Egyptian expert on desertification:

> The desertification process can be reversed. It has been in a number of countries. In the 1930's, the United States experienced droughts that were just as damaging as the Sahel's of the 1970's. In the 1950's, the U.S. faced equally serious droughts, but almost no damage was done. Why? Because meanwhile the Americans had adopted correct land use policies, proper environmental management and the right legislation.
>
> The most important thing is to build up each country's indigenous capacities. This is more important than outside help in the form of food and money. Of course, research is useful, but the basic technologies are already known and, again, it is more important to apply existing knowledge than to enlist more experts. The situation is not at all hopeless . . . if we use our resources.

The recovery of lakes and waterways polluted by industrial and household effluents is another manifestation of the restorative ability of nature. In several parts of the world, damage caused by water pollution has been completely or partially corrected, not by treating the polluted ecosystem but simply by interrupting further pollution and letting natural forces eliminate the accumulated pollutants. The results achieved for the Thames in London, the Willamette River in Portland, Oregon, Lake Washington in Seattle, and Jamaica Bay in New York City are but a few among the many examples of improvement in water quality achieved by antipollution measures during the past decade.

In the London area, the Thames River has long been extremely polluted, as attested to by Michael Faraday's much publicized letter to the *Times* in 1855. The abundance and variety of fish had started to decrease almost two centuries before in the Thames estuary, and only eels survived in certain areas by 1855. As of 1976, however, there were eighty-three species of fish in the estuary, and even salmon were caught in London for the first time in approximately 150 years. In the Connecticut River, the Atlantic salmon was reintroduced in 1977 after 200 years' absence and seems to be able to persist.

A few details concerning Jamaica Bay in New York City illustrate the improvement that can be achieved even under the least promising conditions.

Jamaica Bay is a large Atlantic bay adjacent to John F. Kennedy Airport. It used to be the site of an important shellfish industry and offered refuge to hundreds of thousands of migrating waterfowl during the spring and fall, but it suffered extensive damage as a result of its proximity to the large population of New York City and later to the airport. Sand was dredged from its bottom; its water was polluted by discharges from more than 1,600 sewers; the marshes on its periphery were filled with garbage that formed artificial islands.

During the past two decades, however, attempts have been made to save the bay. Water pollution control facilities have been established; the dumping of garbage has been discontinued; grasses and shrubs have been planted on the existing islands of garbage. As a result, shellfish, fin fish, and birds are once more abundant. The center of the bay has become a wildlife refuge. The bird population is remarkable not only for its abundance but also for its diversity and for the presence of a few unusual species. There are large numbers of wading shore birds such as sandpipers, dowitchers, and green herons. Migration time brings wave upon wave of scaup and brandt, mallards and canvasbacks, Canadian geese and teal. The glossy ibis and the Louisiana heron also have come back, as well as the snowy egret, a bird that was almost extinct in this region in the 1920s.

The return of the glossy ibis to Jamaica Bay, of the wild turkey and the peregrine falcon to their old habitats of the eastern United States, of the salmon to the Willamette River and more recently to the Thames illustrates that once disturbing influences have ceased, some of the original ecological order reestablishes itself spontaneously. Similar phenomena of ecological recovery have been observed in many other parts of the world, particularly in North America and Europe. It is probable, therefore, that environmental degradation can be interrupted in many cases and that the rate of improvement can often be more rapid than is commonly believed. With good management and human commitment, nature often takes over and heals itself.

. . .

NATURAL ECOSYSTEMS are profoundly different from those of earlier geological times, and even from those of more recent times when the earth's climate had become essentially what it is today. Ecosystems constantly evolve under the influence of physicochemical forces that are poorly understood but are known to be much more powerful than those unleashed by human activities. Long before the human presence, for example, stupendous dust storms repeatedly occurred on earth, as they have recently been found to occur on the planet Mars. Climatic changes, volcanic eruptions, earthquakes, hurricanes, fires of natural origin, and the activities of animals and plants have also played their part in the formation of natural ecosystems. During the first half of this century, the evolution of ecosystems was commonly regarded as occurring through an orderly succession of plant and animal species following each other in a fairly well-defined order. According to this view, the end result is a climax population that remains fairly stable until affected by some major disturbance. Reality, however, is far more complex and more interesting than suggested by this simplistic picture of systematic succession and climax. Even without human intervention, many random events influence the evolution of ecosystems in ways that are not predictable.

Fire, for example, was considered for a long time to have only destructive effects, but it is now known to be essential for the development of certain plant species. Small fires prevent catastrophic wildfires. Small fires also release mineral nutrients from organic debris and make them available for further plant growth. The National Park Service has recently adopted a policy of letting fires of natural origin run their course almost unchecked in certain wilderness areas and even starting controlled fires wherever necessary for the maintenance of certain species of trees or for the health of the land.

Fires have contributed profoundly to the evolution of ecosystems in several parts of the world by interfering with the spread of the forest or destroying it where it existed. This is particularly true for the Great Plains of North America, where preagricultural Indians set fires to facilitate the hunt and thereby prevented almost completely the growth of trees and shrubs. The short-grass prairie might have emerged spontaneously in the Far West, since trees have difficulty in maintaining themselves in areas of low and erratic rainfall, but fire was essential for the creation of the tall-grass prairies in the eastern part of the North America grassland.

Another essential element in the development of the prairie ecosystem was its animal population. Until the turn of the century, immense herds of buffalo trampled open spaces in the grass and at the same time richly manured the soil. In the words of a nineteenth-century observer, the buffalo "press down the soil to a depth of 3-4 feet. . . . All the old trees have their roots bare of soil to that depth." The spaces opened in the grass by the buffalo were utilized by smaller animals. Prairie dogs, for example, supported predators such as the black-footed ferret and also turned over enormous quantities of earth by their incessant burrowing activity.

Whatever the factors involved in the evolution of prairie vegetation, the final result was a balanced system of luxuriant and tall grasses, numerous species of wildflowers, and a black sod more than 10 feet deep in certain places. So many random events contributed to the emergence of the American prairie that we probably could not recreate it today even if all its plants were known. The flora could not be reestablished in their original state without the participation of all the former fauna and other natural forces, including the trampling of the soil by immense herds of buffalo.

Thus human beings have probably never been in real "balance" with their environment except under conditions where population density is extremely low, as in the polar regions or the Australian desert. Where the land has long been continuously occupied, the analogues of natural ecological communities have progressively emerged over many generations by a trial-and-error method usually guided by unconscious human values.

Most of these communities have undergone profound changes in the course of time as a consequence of wars, epidemics, new agricultural practices, and the conscious or accidental introduction of new animal and plant species.

The region of England now known as the Downs, for example, has experienced several very different ecological states during historical times. This region was completely wooded before human occupation, but Neolithic farmers began to cut down the trees almost five thousand years ago, using fire and stone axes, and most of the forest was progressively converted into farmland. During the middle of the fourteenth century, however, large areas of arable land were abandoned as a result of the plague (Black Death) that decimated the human population. If the epidemic had occurred in earlier Saxon times, when the land was cultivated by individual farmers, many fields would certainly have returned to the original forested state, but the feudal system created a different situation. Shepherds with flocks of sheep could deal with much more land than plowmen with ox teams. This change in agricultural practice enabled the lords to keep their land in productive use and free of trees, even where labor was in short supply. Sheep grazing, unlike the munching of cattle, crops the grass into a lawnlike texture. It stimulates the growth not only of grass but also of many wildflowers— rock rose, wild thyme, scabious, and the like—that make the Sussex Downs smell, in the words of Rudyard Kipling, "like dawn in paradise." A multitude of insects, especially butterflies, also flourish on these sheep-grazed plants. Even now, trees come back spontaneously whenever sheep and rabbits are removed from the Downs, but in practice these animals are present almost everywhere and prevent the return of the forest. Thus in this case, as in the case of the American prairies, the creation and maintenance of an artificial yet highly desirable ecosystem is dependent on a multiplicity of random factors resulting in the control of tree growth by the animal population.

Other desirable ecosystems, in contrast, have emerged from the proliferation of certain trees. For example, the Adriatic coast, from the Po valley to south of Ravenna, used to be covered with oak and beech. During the fourth and fifth centuries, monks introduced *Pinus pinea* for its nuts and for esthetic reasons. The pines thrived, escaped, and established themselves on the hills. Thus was created the harmonious mixture of broadleaf trees and pines that Dante describes in *Purgatorio*.

Rainfall, wind, and drought have, of course, exerted an enormous influence on the natural evolution of soils—for example, in the "dust bowl" of the southern Great Plains. It had been feared that the agricultural value of the land would be destroyed by the tremendous dust storms of the 1930s, but in fact the dust bowl region has produced bumper crops during the past two decades, in part as a result of wiser agricultural practices but also because of somewhat greater rainfall. As mentioned earlier, dust storms have occurred repeatedly under natural conditions in the past and they certainly will occur again in the future. Rainfall is one of those random events that has an unpredictable influence.

Other factors in the evolution of natural ecosystems are changes that have occurred in the very chemical composition of their soils, chiefly but not exclusively as a consequence of agricultural use. In many places, particularly in what used to be the American prairie, the soil has lost much of its organic matter since it has been put under cultivation, but there are other places, in contrast, where agricultural practices have brought about an increase in soil organic matter. European farmers recognized long ago that most of their soils (of the gray-brown podzolic types) have to be manured for satisfactory crop yield. Similarly, early colonists of New England learned from the Indians to put a fish into each hill of corn. Many gray-brown podzolic soils of Europe and perhaps of the United States now seem richer in organic matter and are more fertile than they were in their original forested state as a consequence of fertilization. Agricultural practices, and the general policies of land management, may now play a role as important as that of natural forces in the evolution of ecosystems.

In most parts of the earth, ecosystems have thus continuously evolved, first through the influence of random natural events, then as a side effect of human activities, and increasingly because of deliberate social choices.

# Creating Farmland
# Through Science

CONTRARY TO general belief, farmland is not a "natural" resource. It had to be created out of some form of wilderness, at some time in the past, and once created it has to be maintained in a fertile condition. In many parts of the world, including the United States, large areas of good farmland are being lost, in part by being used for nonagricultural purposes, in greater part as a result of unwise agricultural practices. At the same time, however, new farmland is being created elsewhere, on a large scale, as I saw during a recent visit to Brazil.

The name "Brazil" usually calls to mind the dense tropical rain forest of the Amazon Valley. But a very large percentage of Brazil's territory consists, in fact, of elevated semidesert savannas, or plains, that go under the general name *cerrados*. Until recently, most *cerrados* were considered unsuited to productive agriculture.

I was in Brazil twenty-two years ago and remember well the aridity of the *cerrado* around the emerging city of Brasilia. I returned to Brasilia in September to participate in the celebrations of the twentieth anniversary of the city as Brazil's new capital, and of its university. To my great surprise, I discovered from the plane and in the course of driving around the countryside that the Brasilia region I had known as a semidesert savanna in 1959 now has intensive, highly diversified agriculture, as well as some densely wooded areas.

*The New York Times*, Oct. 20, 1981.

The rainfall is abundant in the Brasilia region, some 60 inches a year, which is more than the annual rainfall in the New York City area (40 inches), but it is restricted to a very few months, the balance of the year being essentially rainless. Such conditions are almost incompatible with production of agricultural crops by conventional methods. Furthermore, it was discovered that the Brasilia *cerrado* was somewhat deficient in phosphorus and lacked some chemical elements that were essential but needed only in minute amounts. New agricultural methods have been developed to overcome these handicaps. For example, Brazilians have taken advantage of the water table's remaining at a fairly constant level despite the lack of rainfall during much of the year: crops that have roots that reach wet soil throughout the growing season have been used, and minerals have been added to correct chemical deficiencies in the soil. In fact, a great variety of crops, among them wheat and soybeans, are now successfully cultivated around Brasilia.

Brazil is not the only country experimenting with the creation of new farmland. The countryside near Adelaide, Australia, used to be known as "the 90 miles of desert," because it supported only scant vegetation. Australian scientists demonstrated that the region was semidesert not by reason of a lack of water but because its soil contained virtually no phosphorus, zinc, copper, or nitrogen. After the first three of these elements were added to the soil, nitrogen-fixing legumes could be cultivated, and it became possible to develop agricultural practices that have now converted the "90 miles of desert" into rich farmland.

Many Third World countries are situated in semitropical savannas. Conditions differ, of course, from one type of savanna to another, but the agricultural development of poor countries could probably be accelerated through the kind of ecological knowledge that has provided a rational basis for new agricultural practices around Brasilia and in the "90 miles of desert" of Australia.

According to Dr. Mario G. Ferri, professor of botany at the University of São Paulo, knowledge of the ecological peculiarities of particular Latin American *cerrados* will eventually make it possible to create large areas of new fertile farmland and this greatly increased agricultural production will lead to a decrease in the pressure to exploit the Amazon forest through exportation of its valuable lumber. Most of the efforts to use deforested areas of the Amazon Valley as pastures or croplands have led to ecological disasters. Hundreds of ranches already have been abandoned, and even the huge ones developed by European and American corporations are in trouble, despite efforts to manage them scientifically.

The creation of rich farmland in the *cerrados*, according to Dr. Ferri, could provide the respite of at least fifty years that is needed to acquire the knowledge of Amazonian ecology necessary for determining what areas can be safely exploited, and most important, what parts should be maintained as wilderness reserves.

A book published in the United States this year scornfully speaks of Brasilia as a city built on a "red dirt plateau where nobody lives or wants to live." This statement may have been largely true at the time of my first visit, in 1959, yet Brasilia appeared quite satisfied with the physical appearance of the place and with the living conditions.

# Symbiosis of the Earth
# and Humankind

THE FARMING COUNTRY of the Île de France north of Paris, where I was born and raised, has been occupied and profoundly transformed by human beings since the late Stone Age. Before it was inhabited, the region was covered with forests and marshes, and it would return to this state of wilderness if it were not for the human presence. Now that it has been humanized, however, it consists of a complex network of prosperous farmlands, tamed forests and rivers, parks, gardens, villages, towns, and cities. It has long been heavily populated and has continuously supported various forms of civilization. While it has repeatedly experienced destructive wars and social disturbances, it has remained ecologically diversified and economically productive. From the human point of view, it is more satisfying visually and more rewarding emotionally—for me and most people—than it would be in the state of wilderness. It provides a typical example of symbiosis between humankind and the earth.

The historical development of the region where I was raised has certainly conditioned my ecological philosophy. It has convinced me that human beings can profoundly alter the surface of the earth without desecrating it and they can indeed create new and lasting ecological values by working in collaboration with nature.

I know, of course, that many human interventions into nature have

*Science*, vol. 193 (Aug. 6, 1976), pp. 459–62. Copyright © 1976 by American Association for the Advancement of Science. Reprinted by permission.

been destructive; history is replete with ecological disasters. I know also that many industrial and agricultural practices of our times have distressing ecological effects and are likely to have frightening consequences in the future. However, I do not find it useful to elaborate on these dangers, because they are well known. Instead of describing the manifestations of the ecological crises and of repeating once more that further environmental degradation can be minimized only by conservation measures, I take a more constructive view of the interplay between humankind and the earth. I shall consider how the practices of environmental conservation might be complemented by prospective policies of environmental creation.

For thousands of years, human beings have been engaged in creative transformations of the wilderness and of humanized environments, but the process has been greatly accelerated and intensified since the nineteenth century. One of the psychological effects of the Industrial Revolution was to encourage the belief that any kind of change was justified if it was economically profitable—even if it caused a degradation of human life and of environmental quality. During recent decades, however, there have been signs of a reversal in this psychological attitude. For the sake of convenience, I take the middle of the twentieth century as the watershed in the social view of the relationships between human beings and the earth.

In 1933, the city of Chicago held a World's Fair to celebrate its hundredth anniversary. The general theme of the fair was that the increase in wealth and in the standard of living during the "Century of Progress" had been brought about by scientific technology. The guidebook to the exhibits had a section entitled "Science discovers, Industry applies, Man conforms," and the text proclaimed "Individuals, groups, entire races of men fall into step with . . . science and technology." There could not be a more explicit statement of the then prevailing belief that the real measure of progress is industrial development, regardless of the consequences.

Scientific technology is even more creative in 1976 than it was in 1933. Yet no one would dare state today that humankind must conform to, or fall in step with, scientific or technological dictates. The present view is rather that industry must conform to human nature and be managed within strict ecological constraints. The desire for technological innovation and for industrial expansion is now checked by an equally strong concern for the long-range consequences of human interventions into nature.

The following examples illustrate that the concern for social and ecological consequences is not incompatible with creative human interventions into natural systems.

Among people of Western civilization, the English are commonly regarded as having a highly developed respect and appreciation of nature; but the English landscape, admirable as it is, is far different from what it was in the state of wilderness. It is not the native landscape but one that has become familiar because it has been progressively shaped from the primeval forest by centuries of human intervention. Roadsides and riverbanks are trimmed and grass-verged, trees no longer obscure the views but appear to be within the horizon, foregrounds contrast properly with middle distances and backgrounds. Much of the English landscape is indeed so humanized that it might be regarded as a park or a vast ornamental farm.

In England, as in many other parts of the world, the prodigious and continuous efforts of settlers and farmers have created an astonishing diversity of ecosystems that appear natural only because they are familiar but are really of human origin. For example, the patchwork of semirectangular fields so characteristic of East Anglia was created in the eighteenth century to facilitate certain types of agricultural improvements. At that time, the farming country was divided by law into plots, each 5 to 10 acres in area, often without much regard to the natural contour of the land. The fields were divided by drainage ditches and straight lines of hawthorn hedges, and trees were planted in rectangular rows. This famous landscape is thus a very artificial human creation. When it first came into being, in fact, it greatly shocked farmers, nature lovers, and landscape architects. Within a very few generations, however, it has evolved into a pleasing and highly diversified ecosystem; its ditches and hedges harbor an immense variety of plants, insects, song birds, rodents, and larger mammals. It has come to be regarded as a "natural" environment.

Developed as it was for a certain kind of agriculture, this landscape is poorly suited to modern practices. As a result, ditches, hedges, and trees must now go, in order to make possible the creation of larger tracts of land more compatible with the use of high-powered agricultural equipment. This change is destroying the habitats for the many kinds of wild animals and plants that lived in the hedged-in fields, but the open fields will certainly develop their own fauna and flora and, furthermore, have the advantage of permitting large sweeps of vision.

Thus the ecological characteristics of an environment are determined not only by geographic and climatic factors but also by sociocultural imperatives. In addition, the genius of the place is profoundly affected by purely cultural values, as is illustrated by the great English parks created in the eighteenth century.

The English landscape architects transformed the humanized land of East Anglia by taking their inspiration from bucolic but imaginary landscapes painted by Claude Lorrain, Nicolas Poussin, and Salvatore Rosa. They obviously did not believe that "nature knows best" but instead tried to improve on it by rearranging its elements. They eliminated vegetation from certain areas and planted trees in others; they drained marshes and channeled the water into artificial streams and lakes; they organized the scenery to create both intimate atmospheres and distant perspectives. In other words, they invented a new kind of English landscape based on local ecological conditions but derived from the images provided by painters.

The English parks are now the envy of the world. However, as can be seen from eighteenth-century illustrations, they were then far less attractive than they are now. The planted trees were puny, the banks of the artificial streams were bare and raw, the masses of vegetation were often trivial and, in any case, were poorly balanced. The marvelous harmony of scenic and ecologic values that is now so greatly admired did not exist in the eighteenth century except in the minds of the landscape architects who created the parks. The sceneries composed from the raw materials of the earth acquired their visual majesty and came to fruition only after having matured with time. Their present magnificence symbolizes that human interventions into nature can be creative and indeed can improve on nature, provided that they are based on ecological understanding of natural systems and of their potentialities for evolution as they are transformed into humanized landscapes.


EVERY PART of the world can boast of humanized lands that have remained fertile and attractive for immense periods of time. From China to Holland, from Japan to Italy, from Java to Sweden, civilizations have been built on a variety of ecosystems that have been profoundly altered by human intervention. Many of these artificial ecosystems have proved successful even in regions not highly favored by nature. In Greece, for example, a large olive grove in a valley near the Delphi site has been under continuous cultivation for several thousand years; many rice paddies of tropical Asia also have been successful for millennia. Israel, which was once the land of milk and honey, then became largely desertic after Roman times, has once more achieved agricultural prosperity as a result of skillful ecological management, including irrigation and reforestation.

In our own times, the development of the world's arid regions will continue to require the creation of new artificial ecosystems. The oil countries of the Middle East are now wallowing in petrodollars, but the wealth underground will virtually disappear within thirty to forty years. To prepare for the future, the income now derived from oil must be invested in the development of human and material resources that will remain productive after the wells have dried up. To this end, some Arab countries have initiated programs aimed at determining what kinds of crops and livestock suitable to semidesertic conditions can be introduced and improved. Giant irrigation programs, focused on desalinated water, are also being considered in the hope of converting several million acres of sand into agricultural land.

Since irrigation projects of such magnitude will probably be ecologically unsound, it has been suggested that the Middle Eastern nations create in the desert self-contained cities so designed as to be able to grow their own food, perhaps in greenhouses located on the roofs of buildings. The economy of these hypothetical cities would be based not on scarce and unreliable water supplies but on the abundant sunlight that can be used to produce solar energy for the development of intensive agriculture and of certain specialized industries. By concentrating agriculture and industry in a limited area with a fairly high population density, most of the desert could be kept as wilderness—a natural resource that may be much in demand in a more densely populated world.

The most interesting aspects of these approaches to the development of arid regions is not their technical boldness but a vision of the future in which a transient form of natural wealth—oil—would be converted into agricultural, industrial, and social creations of lasting value. Whatever the financial resources available for these projects, however, the ultimate success of any venture will depend on the creation of artificial ecosystems designed within the constraints of local environmental conditions.

. . .

A CENTURY AGO, wood was the fuel used to heat most homes, as well as to fire steam engines and even locomotives. In our times, fossil fuels and nuclear fuels have almost completely displaced wood for such uses, and several other sources of energy are under consideration. It is not impossible, however, that trees and other plants will again become important sources of energy; they may also come to compete with petroleum and coal as a source of raw materials for the chemical industries. The potentialities of these uses can be surmised from the magnitude of the role played by the vegetation of natural areas (wilderness) in the economy of the earth.

Only 3 percent of the incident solar energy on the earth is fixed by the photosynthetic activity of plants, yet the amount of energy produced by the total vegetation of natural areas in any given year vastly exceeds the total amount used by humankind for its daily life and for driving even its most extravagant technologies. The precise figures are not available, but what matters is the magnitude of the difference.

It has been estimated that organic materials equivalent to 840 trillion kilowatt-hours are produced yearly on the whole surface of the earth by photosynthesis. Of this grand total, about two-thirds is produced by the land vegetation, especially the forests; the other third is fixed by the vegetation growing in water, especially the various wetlands, the marine estuaries, and the areas of ocean plankton. Surprising as it may seem, the contribution of agriculture to the energy derived from photosynthesis is rather small—much smaller than one-tenth the contribution of the natural areas. Cultivated lands produce only the equivalent of 50 trillion kilowatt-hours per year, and from this must be deducted the enormous amounts of energy used in the form of fossil fuels by modern agricultural techniques.

In contrast to the 840 trillion kilowatt-hours produced yearly by photosynthesis in natural areas, the total energy consumption by humankind was only 70 trillion kilowatt-hours in the year 1973. Another way of formulating this relationship is to say that the present annual production of biomass on the land areas alone is of the order of 100 billion tons (dry weight), with an energy equivalent about six times greater than the current utilization of energy by all human activities. These figures indicate that the energy needs of the United States and even of the world might be met in theory by devoting only a small fraction of the land areas to this purpose—as could the production of organic materials derived from plants to serve as feedstocks for the chemical industry. In practice, of course, many agricultural and chemical techniques have to be developed or refined before vegetation can be used on a significant scale to provide a renewable source of energy and of substitutes for petrochemicals. But the problems as a whole have been sufficiently well defined to warrant some long-range ecological speculation.

Plant materials have one obvious advantage over coal and petroleum: they are renewable. Furthermore, their use as sources of energy and of chemicals would probably result in less environmental contamination than the use of fossil fuels, especially with regard to sulfur compounds and carbon dioxide—an environmental hazard of unknown magnitude. Since plants use this substance for their growth, the result is a closed cycle instead of overload of the natural cycles, as is the case with organic fossil fuels.

ONE OF the objectionable aspects of vegetation as a source of energy and chemicals is that it is more diffusely distributed and more difficult to transport than coal or petroleum. This difficulty will probably require that the biomass be handled in fairly small industrial units, a limitation that has some advantages. One of them is that it may favor social decentralization. Another is that decentralization will facilitate the return to the land of the waste products from plant materials, which can then serve as plant nutrients.

Granted that the techniques for production of energy and chemicals by photosynthesis are still in a primitive stage, the ecological prospects are sufficiently encouraging to justify a vast program of research in fields pertaining to the production and utilization of plant materials, such as photosynthesis, plant physiology, plant genetics, including the production of new artificial species, ecological association of different plant species, and development of techniques for the fermentation of plant materials to produce methane and for their hydrogenation to produce combustible liquids. While the new technologies that could thus be developed are not urgently needed in the United States, they might be of immediate practical importance in some countries that have abundant vegetation but lack other resources. Furthermore, the production of energy and materials by photosynthesis points the way to long-range global solutions based on biological techniques compatible with the ecological health of the planet.

. . .

THERE ARE different kinds of satisfactory landscapes: on the one hand, the various types of wilderness still undisturbed by human intervention; on the other, the various humanized environments created to fit the physiological, esthetic, and emotional needs of modern human life.

There will be less and less wilderness as the world population increases, but a strenuous effort must be made to preserve as much of it as possible, for at least two different reasons. The wilderness is the greatest producer of renewable sources of energy and of materials—as well as of biological species—and is therefore essential to the maintenance of the ecosystems of the earth. Furthermore, human beings need primeval nature to reestablish contact now and then with their biological origins; a sense of continuity with the past and with the rest of creation is probably essential to the long-range sanity of the human species.

In practice, however, most people spend most of their time in humanized nature. They feel most at ease in landscapes that have been transformed in such a way that there exists a harmonious interplay between human nature and environmental forces, resulting in adaptive fitness. The quality of this interplay requires a constant expenditure of effort, because any environment, left to itself, is no longer adapted to the physiological and mental needs of modern humanity. Even though a landscape has been economically productive and esthetically attractive for many generations, it will be invaded by brush and weeds as soon as it is neglected. The rapid degradation of abandoned gardens, farmlands, or pastures is evidence that humanized nature cannot long retain its quality without constant human care. Conservation practices are as essential for the maintenance of humanized nature as they are for the protection of the wilderness.

The stewardship of the earth, however, goes beyond good conservation practices. It involves the creation of new ecosystems in which human interventions have caused some changes in the characteristics of the land and in the distribution of living things, to take advantage of potentialities of nature that would remain unexpressed in the state of wilderness. Throughout history and even prehistory, humankind has tampered with blind ecological determinism. Forests have been cut down or managed, certain swamps have been drained, and agricultural productivity has been increased by practices designed to modify the physical structure, chemical components, and microbial life of soils. The fauna and flora have also been managed by introduction of new plant and animal species, selection and improvements of strains, crop rotation, control of weeds. Ever since Neolithic times, human life has taken place in managed environments.

Experience shows that most natural situations can be converted into several different ecosystems involving different kinds of relationships to humankind. Thus, East Anglia was at first completely forested, then it was cultivated in open fields, then the fields were converted into hedged plots, and the tendency is now to return to large open fields. In the American Southwest the Navajos, the Zuñis, and the Mormons have established viable relationships with nature based on very different ways of livelihood and different social relationships. These three groups relate to the same kind of soil under the same sky but march to different social drums in their own artificial ecosystems. Until our times, the photosynthetic activity of plants has been used chiefly for the production of food, fibers, and building materials, but there are now projects to use it for the production of various kinds of fuel and of feedstocks for the synthetic chemical industries.

Nature is like a great river of materials and forces that can be directed in this or that channel by human intervention. Such intervention is justified because the natural channels are not necessarily the most desirable, either for the human species or for other species. It is not true that "nature knows best." It often creates ecosystems that are inefficient, wasteful, and destructive. By using reason and knowledge, we can manipulate the raw stuff of nature and shape it into ecosystems that have qualities not found in wilderness. Many potentialities of the earth become manifest only when they have been brought out by human imagination and toil.

Just as the surface of the earth had been transformed into artificial environments, so have these in turn influenced the evolution of human societies. The reciprocal interplay between humankind and the earth can result in a true symbiosis, being used here in its strong biological sense to mean a relationship of mutualism so intimate that the two components of the system undergo modifications beneficial to both. The reciprocal transformations resulting from the interplay between a given human group and a given geographical area determine the characteristics of the people and of the region, thus creating new social and environmental values.

Symbiotic relationships mean creative partnerships. The earth is to be seen neither as an ecosystem to be preserved unchanged nor as a quarry to be exploited for selfish and short-range economic reasons, but as a garden to be cultivated for the development of its own potentialities for the human adventure. The goal of this relationship is not the maintenance of the status quo but the emergence of new phenomena and new values. Millennia of experience show that by entering into a symbiotic relationship with nature, humankind can invent and generate futures not predictable from the deterministic order of things, and thus can engage in a continuous process of creation.

# To Cultivate Our
# Garden

BOTANICAL GARDENS and arboreta once wielded enormous influence in the world. At the end of the eighteenth century, the Swiss physician and botanist Konrad von Gesner estimated that there were more than 1,600 botanical gardens and arboreta in Europe. A few of these were on estates of the rich, but most had been created for the cultivation of medicinal plants. Until our day, plants were practically the only sources of drugs, and as a result, professors of medicine like Gesner were also botanists, who used university gardens under their supervision for the training of medical students.

Nor were medicines the only product of these gardens. Some botanists also made it a practice to cultivate, disseminate, and study exotic plants received from explorers around the world, and many of these plants later assumed enormous economic importance. In the 1850s, cinchona seeds sent from the Amazon to the botanical garden of Java enabled Dutch colonists there to create plantations that became the world's chief source of cinchona bark, from which quinine is derived.

Natural rubber is one of the most spectacular examples of the influence that botanical gardens can exert on the fate of an industry or a

The New York Academy of Science, *The Sciences*, April 1982, pp. 10–12, 14. From keynote address to international conference on the future of botanical gardens and arboreta at New York Botanical Garden, October 1980.

region. The tree *Hevea brasiliensis* grows naturally in several parts of the Amazon valley, and the rubber obtained from it was shipped to industrial nations through the Brazilian port of Manaus. Although Manaus lies in the heart of the Amazonian rain forest, the rubber trade was so intense between 1890 and 1920 that this relatively small city become one of the richest and most highly developed in the world. It was the first Latin American city to have electric light. Majestic buildings and homes, churches and cathedrals, and a complex system of sewers and floating docks were built there nearly overnight. The year 1896 saw the dedication of a large, ornate opera house built of Italian marble and crowned with a cone of polychromatic tiles imported from Alsace. On its opening night, the Italian tenor Enrico Caruso sang before a full house of 1,400 spectators.

In the meantime, English botanists learned to cultivate *H. brasiliensis* in greenhouses and began distributing seeds and seedlings to several Southeast Asian countries through the Kew Gardens of London (officially known as the Royal Botanic Gardens). Plantation rubber was so readily produced in Malaysia that large quantities of it could be exported as early as 1910. Shortly after, it completely displaced the natural rubber of Brazil, and Manaus became a ghost town.

Today, directors of botanical gardens and arboreta no longer engage in activities so economically urgent as the preparation of medicinal drugs and the transfer of cinchona and hevea trees from one tropical country to another were in their times. In our era, their contributions could never make or break the fates of cities or countries. These days, the gardens simply try to appeal to the general public by displaying plant species under the most attractive conditions at suitable times of year.

While these traditional contributions to science and to the public are important, and deserve appreciation, botanical gardens and arboreta could serve an even more essential purpose by involving themselves more directly in solving certain contemporary problems, a task for which they have unique qualification. Indeed, they could yet become as vital to the world as they were in the time of Gesner or in the heyday of Manaus.

There are clear signs that several botanical gardens and arboreta have already begun to evolve in this way. At Kew Gardens, for example, the emphasis has long been on the collection of wild plant species (Kew boasts the world's largest herbarium) and on taxonomy.

But the new director of Kew, Arthur Bell, is a biochemist who has stated that one of his main concerns will be to use the garden's facilities for improving patterns of agriculture in developing countries. Again, at the New York Botanical Garden, the traditional herb garden is now being complemented by what has been called a chemurgic garden, the beds of which display economically important plants—those of industrial, medicinal, and cosmetic value, as well as those used for fuels, dyes, and flavorings. And in Washington, D.C., the Herb Society of America is helping to develop, at the U.S. National Arboretum, a national herb garden that will include not only herbs used in the home but also those used in agriculture and industry.

Ever since Neolithic times, human beings have cultivated plants with a few very practical purposes in mind—for production of food, lumber, textile fiber, drugs, and ornament. Plants that do not fit these categories generally have been regarded as weeds. It is rather shocking to realize, for example, that just thirty plant species provide 80 percent of the world's food supplies, even though many thousands of other species possess desirable nutritional properties. Botanists have searched for new plant varieties mainly out of scientific curiosity. This scientific policy must, of course, be continued, but botanical gardens might supplement it with a more utilitarian motive: the search for socially useful species. For such an approach to succeed, techniques must be developed to evaluate (or at least to detect) not only a plant's properties in its natural habitat but also its potentialities under other conditions. The search for plants with desirable properties always involves two independent considerations: proper genetic endowment and the environmental conditions required for its phenotypic expression.

The second consideration can be almost as significant as the first. For example, most herb gardens in this country and in Western Europe consist of a few aromatic species, almost everywhere the same. But the aromatic characteristics of the plants of a particular species or variety differ markedly from garden to garden, even under the same climatic conditions. I know from simple "nose tests" of crushed leaves that plants grown in the herb garden of the New York Botanical Garden differ aromatically from those grown in Central Park, or in the Brooklyn Botanic Garden—all in New York City. On many occasions in the 1920s and 1930s, I visited villages of southeastern France, near Grasse, the capital of the French perfume industry. Three of these villages specialized in the cultivation of jasmine, because, according to specialists, jasmine plants grown there have qualities most desirable for the manufacture of perfumes. Similarly, while roses grow readily in many parts of the world, certain limited regions of Asia and eastern and southern Europe seem to be best suited for the production of attar of rose. It is also known that the yield of a particular medicinal drug by a given plant species is profoundly influenced by methods of cultivation, as well as by environmental conditions.

Clearly, if industrial civilization were to turn, as it may yet, to the earth's biomass for fuel and feedstocks for the chemical industry, the criteria for selection of plant varieties would be very different from those that apply to the production of food, lumber, or fiber. For example, we should search out plants with the highest possible photosynthetic activity, as well as those capable of growing on soil or in waters not suitable for the production of food or for other valuable crops. Many plant species currently ignored should be investigated for their ability to produce hydrocarbons or other substances that could be put to use in the chemical and pharmaceutical industries.

There are many other fields of endeavor for the new botany, and one of the most urgent is the study of injured ecosystems. While much ecological damage is taking place all over the earth, it is also true that ecological recovery can often occur spontaneously when insults to the ecosystem are ended. After the First World War, the Verdun region of France was a wasteland; now its indigenous vegetation has returned, along with its birds, rabbits, deer, and even boars. Spontaneous ecological recovery can take place under seemingly unfavorable conditions, provided the areas are protected from grazing animals. Little is known of these natural recovery processes, though such knowledge would greatly help in the formulation of ecologically sound policies of land use and reclamation.

In most cases, damaged ecosystems will require more direct human intervention for their successful recovery. This is already happening in Israel, but the reclamation of strip-mined areas in this country will certainly present problems of greater complexity and magnitude. As elsewhere, the tendency in such work is to use plant species already well known, even though obscure species might prove more suitable, at least during the early phases of reclamation.

Moreover, it is probably a mistake to assume, as many do, that the "best" environment is an untouched stretch of virgin land and that reclaiming a wasteland necessarily means returning it to its original state. Practically all existing ecosystems that human beings find desirable were produced by profound transformations of nature or even by the creation of entirely artificial ecosystems. The eighteenth-century English naturalist William Marshall believed

> Nature knows nothing of what we call landscape because this word refers to habitats manipulated by human beings for their own purpose. . . . No spot on this island [England] can be said to be in a state of Nature. There is not a tree, perhaps not a bush, now standing of the face of the country which owes its identical state to Nature alone. Wherever cultivation has set its foot, Nature has become extinct. . . . Those who wish for a Nature in a state of total neglect must take their residence in the woods of America.

The expression "total neglect" seems to imply that nature can achieve perfection, or at least fully develop its potential, only as a result of human management. The truth is, however, that many aspects of human life conflict with natural ecosystems, and indeed usually result in their destruction. All farming activities constitute a violent struggle against natural ecological conditions. Farmland had to be created out of wilderness, usually at great cost of energy—to cut down trees, drain wetlands, irrigate dry lands, and also destroy wild forms of life and their habitats. Successful farming, like flower gardening, is usually incompatible with the kind of ecological equilibrium that would exist under completely natural conditions.

In the past, artificial ecosystems like farms, estates, and villages evolved over long periods of time, and this slow development enhanced their chances of success by allowing for the play of corrective forces— natural and human—and thus for the satisfactory orchestration of their different components. As human intervention becomes increasingly rapid and violent, the trial and error of the past must be replaced by scientific knowledge. Studies are needed to determine the amount of energy required for maintaining the ecological stability of artificial ecosystems; the comparative abilities of different types of vegetation to trap solar energy for synthesis of different organic substances and maintenance of soil humus; and the evolution of artificial ecosystems under different geological and climatic conditions—a problem of crucial importance for the utilization of tropical lands.

Urban ecosystems present their own special problems. For more than fifty years, I have watched from my windows on the Rockefeller University campus the lawns that we try to maintain, at immense costs of water, energy, and human labor—and usually without much success. Lawns were originated in Great Britain, where the climate is favorable for their development and where labor conditions were once compatible with their maintenance. As seventeenth-century French Prince de Ligne said of the English: "Their verdure they owe to their fogs." English lawns are out of place, not only on the Rockefeller campus, or in Central Park, but in most of the United States. There seems to be a national ambition to create, against all odds, lawns that resemble championship golf courses. Botanical gardens should collaborate with landscape architects in the development of new kinds of ground cover suited to the various climates in this country and to different kinds of human uses as well.

Much also remains to be learned concerning the effects of air and water pollution, as well as of pesticides, on the growth and lives of plants. It seems that fewer and fewer plant species are being used, either for shade, ornaments, or the muffling of noise, both in urban and suburban centers. There is need for more knowledge of flowering plants, trees, grasses, and other kinds of ground cover that can thrive under the conditions—natural and social—that prevail in each particular region. Such knowledge might help to correct the monotony and drabness of plant life in cities, and thereby decrease somewhat the desire to escape from the city every weekend.

Surprising as it may sound, the time may soon come when certain kinds of foodstuffs will once more be widely grown in urban areas. It is probably true that citrus fruits, artichokes, pineapples, and other such crops with exacting climatic requirements can best be produced on a large scale only in special parts of the country. Food plants less perishable than these also can be produced most economically under special climatic and soil conditions: Why grow apples, tomatoes, and carrots in New York State if they can be obtained at low cost from Washington, California, or Texas? However, there are great ecological and social dangers inherent in such excessive concentration and specialization of food production. Complete dependence on food that must be hauled over long distances is probably not a wise policy. Rather, each urban area should strive once more toward partial self-sufficiency, especially in the case of perishable foodstuffs. The phenomenal increase in the price of vegetables and fruits, as well as the lamentable deterioration of their taste, may spur a renewal of food production in urban areas—if only to make fresh and tasty fruits and vegetables once more available to the city dweller.

There exist in many cities examples of successful gardening and farming, even in environments that appear extremely uninviting. Local children from Manhattan public schools, organized under the Dome Project, have turned a rubble-strewn lot on West Eighty-fourth Street into a very attractive vest-pocket vegetable garden. In San Francisco, unused land under a city freeway exchange has been transformed into a farm where urban children have the opportunity to raise animals and learn gardening. This project has been so successful that the city has purchased five adjoining acres to enlarge the farm.

I myself have done enough old-fashioned gardening to know the ordeals and frustrations of trying to produce significant amounts of food on a small patch of soil, using only conventional methods. On the other hand, it appears that more convenient methods of cultivation can be developed scientifically for the production of many different kinds of valuable foodstuffs, at least on a small scale, under completely controlled conditions.

Clearly, botanical gardens and arboreta have missions that transcend their traditional scientific concerns. The availability of plant collections, and more precise knowledge of the properties of plants, will be increasingly needed in the management of environmental and social problems. Botanists, ecologists, and environmentalists may criticize these proposals for being almost completely human-centered, but while acknowledging the truth of this, I do not think it is a valid criticism. Even when we attempt to look at the external world objectively, we see it with human eyes, evaluating it and using it on the basis of human needs, values, and aspirations. As Ralph Waldo Emerson wrote long ago, we call a plant a weed only when we have not yet discovered a way to use it to our own ends.

# A Theology of
# the Earth

HOW DRAB AND GRAY, unappealing and insignificant, this planet would be without the radiance of life.

The earth is one of the nine planets in the solar system, third in distance from the sun, fifth in size, and with a radius of less than 4,000 miles—a mere speck in space. Judged in these terms, it is a trivial astronomical object, one of the smallest among the celestial bodies that gravitate through the limitless universe. But while the physical measurements worked out by astronomers give a quantitative picture, they do not give a complete picture, because they do not take biological characteristics into consideration.

The German philosopher Georg Wilhelm Hegel pointed out more than a century ago that *Richtigkeit*, correctness, is not the same thing as *Wahrheit*, the truth. It is correct to define the earth by quantitative studies, but the more interesting and significant truth about it transcends measurements concerning its size, motions, and place in the cosmos. The earth is unique in the solar system because it possesses qualities derived from the myriad forms of life it harbors. Being a living organism, it is more varied, more changeable, more unpredictable than inanimate matter, and also more delicate.

[ 295 ]

The early aviators, flying at relatively low altitudes and low speeds, had the opportunity to discern the bones of the earth beneath its covering of living flesh. They could recognize that the covering of vegetation is in many places so tenuous as to appear like a little moss in the crevices that could readily be destroyed. But they realized also that this covering, thin and fragile as it is, creates the green of the forest, the brilliance of flowers, the varieties of blue in atmosphere and ocean, and most remarkably the phosphorescence of human thought.

It was worth the many billions of dollars spent on the manned space program to obtain further evidence that the earth is unique by virtue of the sensuous appeal it derives from its green and blue mantle and by virtue of the intellectual vibration it derives from man. The Apollo missions may not have yet discovered much of theoretical interest and practical importance concerning outer space, but they have enabled us to see with our own eyes that the surface of the moon is pockmarked, dusty, gray, and drab. The photographs taken from the Mariner space-craft have furthermore destroyed any illusion about the existence of Martians and their canals. The soft glow of the moon and the brooding redness of Mars are not attributes inherent in these lifeless bodies but the qualities bestowed on them by human eyes, looking at them through the atmosphere of the earth. In contrast, the accounts of the astronauts have helped us to experience on a cosmic scale how colorful, warm, inviting, and diversified the earth is against the bleakness and coldness of outer space. These qualities originate exclusively from the activities of living things.

All ancient civilizations have expressed, each in its own way, won-derment at the beauty of the earth. Aristotle tried to imagine how men who had spent all their lives under luxurious conditions but in caves would respond when given for the first time the chance to behold sky, clouds, and seas. Surely, he writes, "These men would think that gods exist and that all the marvels of the world are their handicrafts." The visual evidence provided by space travel now gives larger significance to Aristotle's image. Although the earth is but a tiny island in the midst of vast reaches of alien space, it derives distinction from being a magic garden occupied by myriads of different living things that have pre-pared the way for self-reflecting human beings.

When the earth took form in the collapse of a cosmic dust cloud into the star we call the sun, about 4.5 billion years ago, the atmosphere consisted chiefly of the gases hydrogen, ammonia, and methane, but not free oxygen. The burning surface was exposed to fierce ultraviolet radiation and had no water. Such an environment was obviously incompatible with the existence of any form of life, let alone human life.

The various other planets of the solar system had at first a structure not unlike that of the earth. They underwent profound changes on different courses and at different rates, depending on their relative size and position with regard to the sun. Only on earth did these changes result in conditions that eventually permitted the emergence of life.

During the first half billion years of the earth's existence, hydrogen progressively escaped from the atmosphere, and carbon dioxide and water were released from the crust through intense volcanic activity. Some of the chemical ingredients now present in all living cells were produced by solar radiation acting on the components of the primordial atmosphere. By the end of that period, the oceans had formed, and sugars, purines, pyrimidines, amino acids, and other organic substances produced out of the atmosphere's components by the solar irradiation had begun to accumulate in the surface waters. And then, by unknown processes, self-reproducing protoplasma became organized from these simple organic materials. Life had begun, and from then on living things increased in complexity and diversity through evolutionary processes. Eventually, after another billion or two billion years, the earth's atmosphere came to consist chiefly of nitrogen gas, to which was added the free oxygen released from carbon dioxide by the photosynthetic activities of primitive organisms.

For an immense period of time, life could probably exist only beneath the oceans' surface, where it could be protected against excessive ultraviolet radiation emanating from the sun. As the water was rich in nutrients, one may assume that once life had started, the oceans soon teemed with primitive organisms. Progressively, these organisms evolved into more complex forms as the conditions changed. What is certain in any case is that blue-green algae very similar to the ones that exist now have been found in Precambrian deposits that are two billion years old. Such algae have been and remain to this day among the most effective producers of the oxygen that is essential for the existence of animals and men.

Life as we know it has thus emerged and evolved in response to the consecutive occurrence of a multiplicity of different conditions: the gases of the primordial atmosphere were replaced by the nitrogen-oxygen mixture; liquid water accumulated on the land surface; and a proper temperature range came to prevail. While it is certain that the earth is the only part of the solar system to have achieved this state of compatibility with life, similar conditions may exist elsewhere in the cosmos. This, however, is a matter for speculation, unsupported by factual knowledge.

The emergence of life requires such an extraordinary combination of circumstances that it constitutes an event with a very low order of probability—so low, indeed, that it may have occurred only once. Certain scientists, however, believe that since there may be many planets in other systems that have had an evolutionary development similar to that of the earth, life must have emerged repeatedly. According to them, "We are not alone" in space. Whether this is true, one must agree with the physicist and theologian William Pollard of Oak Ridge Associated University that there may not be

> another place like the Earth within a thousand light years of us. If so, the Earth with its vistas of breathtaking beauty, its azure seas, beaches, mighty mountains, and soft blanket of forest and steppe is a veritable wonderland in the universe. It is a gem of rare and magic beauty lying in a trackless space filled with lethal radiations and accompanied in its journey by sister planets which are either viciously hot or dreadfully cold, arid, and lifeless chunks of raw rock. Earth is choice, precious, and sacred beyond all comparison or measure.

The adjective "sacred" may be surprising in a description of the characteristics of this planet, and yet it expresses an attitude that has deep roots in the human past and still persists. The very fact that the word "desecration" is commonly used to lament the damage human beings are causing to the environment indicates that many of us have a feeling that the earth has sanctity, that man's relation to it has a sacred quality.

In common usage, the meaning of the word "nature" is extremely limited. It does not refer to the earth as shaped by cosmic forces but almost exclusively to the living forms on which men depend and to the earth's atmosphere and surface, which are the creations of life. The interdependence between man and the other forms of life is so complete that the word "nature" usually has biological connotations, even when referring to inanimate substances. In practice, we do not live on the planet earth but with the life it harbors and within the environment that life creates.

The oxygen we breathe is a product of life. It was first released into the atmosphere in a free form by primitive organisms that lived more than 2 billion years ago. It is still being produced by most members of the plant kingdom and by the microscopic algae of ocean plankton, as well as by the most gigantic trees. Microbes and plants are thus absolutely necessary for the existence of animals and human beings, not only because they produce food but also because they literally create a breathable atmosphere.

Like the atmosphere, the present surface of the earth is also a creation of life. Everywhere, under natural conditions, the topsoil is alive with insects, grubs, earthworms, and microbes, which find shelter in it, feed from it, and in so doing transform it chemically and physically. This is true whether the soil supports forests, prairies, tundras, grasslands, farmlands, gardens, or parks. Organic gardeners have legitimate scientific reasons to claim that earthworms contribute as much as fertilizers to the fertility of the soil. In fact, the microbial forms of life that are invisible to the naked eye are at least as important as earthworms and insects. Every speck of humus contains billions of living microbes belonging to countless different varieties, each specialized in the composition and transformation of one or another type of organic debris derived from animals, plants, or other microbes. The expert can often detect the activities of microbes in the soil simply by handling and smelling it when warm and humid weather increases the intensity of microbial life. Surprising as it may seem, soil microbes account for a large percentage of the total mass of the living stuff of the earth.

Experience shows that under usual conditions the remnants of animals and plants do not accumulate in nature. Very rapidly they are consumed by microbes and thereby taken through a chain of chemical alterations that breaks them down step by step into simpler and simpler compounds. The microbes themselves eventually die, and their bodies are also transformed by microbial action. In this manner, the constituents of all living things are returned to nature after death. Reduced to simpler forms, they are available for the creation of new microbial and plant life, which is eventually consumed by animals and men. Microbes thus constitute indispensable links in the chain that binds inanimate matter to life.

The eternal movement from life to dead organic substances, then to microbial bodies, and finally to simple chemical molecules that are converted back into plant and animal life again is a physical manifestation of the myth of eternal return. During the late Roman Republic, the Epicurean philosopher Lucretius untiringly reiterated in his poem *De*

*Rerum Natura (On the Nature of Things)* that nothing arises except as a result of the death of something else, that nature remains always young and whole in spite of death at work everywhere, and that all living forms are but transient aspects of a permanent substance. It is literally true that all things come from dust and to dust return, but to a dust eternally fertile. Throughout the living world and particularly in the soil, all organisms constantly enact the famous phrase of Lucretius's poem: "Like runners in a race, they hand on the torch of life."

The soil is thus a truly living organism, because its chemical composition and its texture at each particular site are constantly regenerated from the primeval rock by the activities of living things. Every site, furthermore, accommodates a multiplicity of different kinds of organisms, each of which occupies a localized, special niche that it modifies to a form even more suitable for its needs. Social bees have an environment that differs from that of solitary bees living in the very same field—in part because the two do not use the same kind of resources, and even more because the social bees create their own microclimate inside the beehive. The soil under an oak forest differs from what would have developed in the same rock formation under a pine forest, because these two species of trees have different root systems. As pine needles accumulate, furthermore, they produce a surface layer different from the humus into which oak leaves are transformed when they die and decompose. In addition, the quality of light under an oak tree is different from what it is under a pine tree. All living things thus create microenvironments that enrich the diversity of the earth's surface.

In nature, most changes elicited by the interplay between a particular organism and its total environment are in the long run beneficial to both. The changes that result from these reciprocal effects account for the immense diversity of places and living things on earth. They also explain the exquisite fitness and interdependence between all aspects of creation so commonly encountered in undisturbed environment.

Fitness and interdependence, however, are not static properties. Slowly but inexorably, all aspects of the earth are changing, and this requires of living things that they also change in order to maintain their compatibility with environmental conditions. The ability to evolve is therefore an essential attribute of life; evolutionary changes constantly alter the manifestations of fitness and interdependence. These changes, furthermore, progressively result in the production of new forms of life from old forms, thus increasing in a continuous manner the diversity of biological systems and of their activities. Diversity accounts

in large part for the self-repairing processes that tend to occur spontaneously when accidents disturb the natural order of things—hence the
adaptability and resilience of the living earth. It accounts also for the
adaptability, resilience, and richness of human life.

When human beings emerged in their present biological form
150,000 or so years ago, they must have been fitted for the conditions
prevailing around them. Since fitness in the biological sense implies
suitable interrelationships between the organism and the total environment, the environment was fit also and ready for us when we appeared
on earth. For Walt Whitman, from the point of view of the poet and
humanist, the "primal sanities" of nature were the qualities of the earth
that make for a rich human life.

Whitman's primal sanities refer to the conditions under which we
evolved and to which our biological constitution is still adapted. But
while our biological nature has remained much the same since the
Stone Age, our surroundings and ways of life have changed profoundly.
Civilization is often in conflict with primal sanities, as evidenced by the
present ecological crisis. This conflict accounts for the unfortunate fact
that the science of human ecology, which would be concerned with all
aspects of the relationships between human beings and the rest of
creation, has come to be identified almost exclusively with the problems of disease and alienation resulting from environmental insults. Yet
there is much more to human ecology than this one-sided view of the
relationships between humanity and the external world.

We are still of the earth, earthy. The earth is literally our mother,
not only because we depend on her for nurture and shelter but even
more because the human species has been shaped by her in the womb
of evolution. Each person, furthermore, is conditioned by the stimuli
he receives from nature during his own existence.

If we were to colonize the moon or Mars—with abundant supplies
of oxygen, water, and food, as well as adequate protection against heat,
cold, and radiation—we would not long retain our humanness, because
we would be deprived of those stimuli that only earth can provide.
Similarly, we shall progressively lose our humanness even on earth if
we continue to pour filth into the atmosphere; to befoul soil, lakes, and
rivers; to disfigure landscapes with junkpiles; to destroy the wild plants
and animals that do not contribute to monetary values; and thus to
transform the globe into an environment alien to our evolutionary past.
The quality of human life is inextricably interwoven with the kinds and
variety of stimuli we receive from the earth and the life it harbors,

because human nature is shaped biologically and mentally by external nature.

Admittedly, certain human populations have functioned successfully and developed worthwhile cultures in forbidding environments, such as the frozen tundras or the Sahara. But even the most desolate parts of the Arctic or the Sahara offer a much wider range of sensations than does the moon. Eskimo life derives exciting drama from ice, snow, and water, from spectacular seasonal changes, and from the migration of caribou and other animals. The nomadic Tuareg have to cope with blinding and burning sand, but they also experience the delights of oases. Being exposed to a variety of environmental stresses and having to function among them is far different from living in a spacesuit or a confining space capsule, however large it may be, in which all aspects of the environment are controlled and extraneous stimuli are almost completely eliminated.

Participation in nature's endless changes provides vital contact with the cosmic forces, which is essential for sanity. In *The Desert Year*, the American drama critic turned naturalist Joseph Wood Krutch pointed out that normal human beings are not likely to fare well in areas lacking visible forms of life. For example, they rarely elect to stay long in the deserts of the American Southwest, as if this kind of scenery, magnificent as it is, were fundamentally alien to mankind.

> Wherever, as in this region of wind-eroded stone, living things are no longer common enough or conspicuous enough to seem more than trivial accidents, man feels something like terror. . . . This is a country where the inanimate dominates and in which not only man but the very plants themselves seem intruders. We may look at it as we look at the moon, but we feel rejected. It is neither for us nor for our kind.

We seek contact with other living things probably because our own species has evolved in constant association with them and has retained from the evolutionary past a biological need for this association.

Human nature has been so deeply influenced by the conditions under which it evolved that the mind is in some ways like a mirror of the cosmos. Some of the early Church fathers had a vision of this relationship, as illustrated by Origen's exhortation to man: "Thou art a second world in miniature, the sun and the moon are within thee, and also the stars." More than a thousand years later, the British biologist Sir Julian

Huxley reformulated Origen's thought in modern terms and enlarged it to include his own concepts of psychosocial evolution:

> The human type became a microcosm which, through its capacity for self-awareness, was able to incorporate increasing amounts of the macrocosm into itself, to organize them in new and richer ways, and then with their aid to exert new and more powerful influences on the macrocosm.

Sir Julian's statement implies two different but complementary attitudes toward the earth. The fact that man incorporates part of the universe in his being provides a scientific basis for the feeling of reverence toward the earth. But the fact that he can act on the external world often makes him behave as if he were foreign to the earth and its master—an attitude that has become almost universal during the past two centuries.

The phrase "conquest of nature" is certainly one of the most objectionable and misleading expressions of Western languages. It reflects the illusion that all natural forces can be entirely controlled, and it expresses the criminal conceit that nature is to be considered primarily as a source of raw materials and energy for human purposes. This view of man's relationship to nature is philosophically untenable and destructive. A relationship to the earth based only on its use for economic enrichment is bound to result not only in its degradation but also in the devaluation of human life. This is a perversion that, if not soon corrected, will become a fatal disease of technological societies.

The gods of early man were intimately connected with the earth, and belief in them generated veneration and respect for it. But respect does not imply a passive attitude; early human beings obviously manipulated the earth and used its resources. Primitive religion was always linked with magic, which was an attempt to manage nature and life through the occult influences that were assumed to lurk in the invisible world. There is a fundamental difference between religion and magic. In the words of the anthropologist Bronislaw Malinowski, "Religion refers to the fundamental issues of human life, while magic turns round specific concrete and detailed problems." Our salvation depends on our ability to create a religion of nature and a substitute for magic suited to the needs and knowledge of modern man.

The problems of poverty, disease, and environmental decay cannot be solved merely by the use of more and more scientific technology.

Technological fixes usually turn out to be procedures that have unpredictable consequences and are often in conflict with natural forces. Indeed, technological magic is not much better than primitive magic in dealing with the fundamental issues of human existence, and in addition, it is much more destructive. In contrast, better knowledge of our relationships to the earth may enable us to be even more protective of the natural world than were our primitive forebears; informed reason is likely to be a better guide for the management of nature than was superstition or fear. We do know scientifically that the part of the earth on which we live is not dead material but a complex living organism with which we are interdependent; we also know that we have already used a large percentage of the resources that have accumulated in the course of its past. The supply of natural resources, in fact, presents a situation in which the practical selfish interests of mankind are best served by an ethical attitude.

For most of its geological history, the earth had no stores of fossil fuels or concentrated mineral ores. These materials, which are the lifeblood of modern technology, accumulated slowly during millions upon millions of years; their supply will not be renewed once they have been exhausted. They must therefore be husbanded with care—for immediate reasons and also for the sake of the future. The natural resources that we now gouge out of the earth so thoughtlessly and recklessly certainly should not be squandered by a few greedy generations.

From the beginning of time and all over the world, our relationship to nature has transcended the simple direct experience of objective reality. Primitive people are inclined to endow creatures, places, and even objects with mysterious powers; they see gods or goddesses everywhere. Eventually, human beings came to believe that the appearances of reality were the local or specialized expressions of a universal force; from belief in gods, we moved up to belief in God. Both polytheism and monotheism are losing their ancient power in the modern world, and for this reason it is commonly assumed that the present age is irreligious. But we may instead be moving to a higher level of religion. Science is at present evolving from the description of concrete objects and events to the study of relationships as observed in complex systems. We may be about to recapture an experience of harmony, an intimation of the divine, from our scientific knowledge of the processes through which the earth became prepared for human life and the mechanisms through which human life relates to the universe as a whole. A truly ecological view of the world has religious overtones.

The earth, as I have said, came to constitute a home suitable for us only after it had become a living organism. The sensuous qualities of its blue atmosphere and green mantle are not inherent in its physical nature; they are the creations of the countless microbes, plants, and animals that it has nurtured and that have transformed its drab inanimate matter into a colorful living substance. Human beings can exist, function, enjoy the universe, and dream dreams only because the various forms of life have created and continue to maintain the very special environmental conditions that set the earth apart from other planets and generated its fitness for life—for life in general and for human life in particular.

We are dependent on other living things and like them must be adapted to our surroundings in order to achieve biological and mental health. Human ecology, however, involved more than interdependence and fitness as these are usually conceived. Human beings are influenced not only by the natural forces of their environment but also and probably even more by the social and psychological surroundings they select or create. Indeed, what they become is largely determined by the quality of their experiences. Henry Beston wrote in *The Outermost House*:

> Nature is part of our humanity, and without some awareness and experience of that divine mystery man ceases to be man. When the Pleiades, and the wind in the grass, are no longer a part of the human spirit, a part of very flesh and bone, man becomes, as it were, a kind of cosmic outlaw, having neither the completeness and integrity of the animal nor the birthright of a true humanity.

These words convey one aspect of the ecological attitude that must be cultivated to develop a scientific theology of the earth.

But there are other aspects, based on the fact that we are rarely passive witnesses of natural events. We manipulate the world around us and thus set in motion forces that shape our environment, our life, and our civilizations. In this sense, we make ourselves, and the quality of our achievements reflects our visions and aspirations. Human ecology naturally operates within the laws of nature, but it is always influenced by conscious choices and anticipations of the future.

The relationships that link humankind to other living organisms and to the earth's physical forces thus involve a deep sense of engagement with nature and with all processes central to life. They generate a spirit of sacredness and of overriding ecological wisdom that is so universal and timeless that it was incorporated in most ancient cultures. One can recognize the manifestations of this sacredness and wisdom in many archaic myths and ceremonials, in the rites of preclassical Greeks, in Sung landscape paintings, in the agricultural practices of preindustrial peoples. One can read it in Marcus Aurelius's statement that "all living things are interwoven each with the other; the tie is sacred, and nothing, or next to nothing, is alien to ought else." In our time, the philosophical writings of Alfred North Whitehead have reintroduced in a highly intellectualized form the practical and poetical quality of ecological thought.

Human ecology inevitably considers relationships within systems from the point of view of our privileged place in nature. Placing humanity at the pinnacle of creation seems at first sight incompatible with orthodox ecological teachings. Professional ecologists, indeed, are prone to resent the disturbing influence of human intervention in natural systems. If properly conceived, however, anthropocentrism is an attitude very different from the crude belief that human beings are the only value to be considered in managing the world and that the rest of nature can be thoughtlessly sacrificed to our welfare and whims. An enlightened anthropocentrism acknowledges that in the long run, the world's good always coincides with our own most meaningful good. We can manipulate nature to our best interests only if we first love it for its own sake.

While the living earth still nurtures and shapes us, we now possess the power to change it and to determine its fate, thereby determining our own fate. Earth and humanity are thus two complementary components of a system that might be called cybernetic, since each shapes the other in a continuous act of creation. The Biblical injunction that man was put in the Garden of Eden "to dress it and to keep it" (Genesis 2:15) is an early warning that we are responsible for our environment. To strive for environmental quality might be considered as an eleventh commandment—concerned, of course, with the external world but also encompassing the quality of life. An ethical attitude in the scientific study of nature readily leads to a theology of the earth.

# Gaia and Creative
# Evolution

I HAVE always disliked the expression "Spaceship Earth" to designate our planet, and I believe that it has led to faulty thinking about environmental problems. The word "spaceship" calls to mind a mechanical structure carrying a limited supply of fuel for a defined trip and with no possibility of significant change in design. The earth, in contrast, has many attributes of a living, evolving organism. It constantly converts solar energy into innumerable organic products and increases in biological complexity as it travels through space. I was therefore captured by the idea James Lovelock put forward in *Gaia: A New Look at Life on Earth*: that the surface of the earth behaves as a highly integrated organism capable of controlling its own composition and its environment. He used the name of the Greek earth goddess Gaia to symbolize this complex biological behavior of the earth. I shall first briefly summarize its factual contents, then formulate a few questions in the hope that they will lead to a further development of the hypothesis.

It is not the first time that the earth has been regarded as a living organism. In a book entitled *The Land Problem*, Otis T. Mason, one of the early American environmentalists, wrote in 1892, "Whatever our theory of its origin, the earth may be discussed as a living, thinking being. . . . We are in the presence of something . . . that has come to be

Unpublished review of *Gaia: A New Look at Life on Earth*, written Sept. 14, 1979.

what it is, has grown, that can be sick and recover." The Gaia hypothesis is more concrete and can best be formulated in Lovelock's own words:

> The physical and chemical condition of the surface of the Earth, of the atmosphere and of the oceans has been and is actively made fit and comfortable by the presence of life itself. This is in contrast to the conventional wisdom which held that life adapted to the planetary conditions as it and they evolved their separate ways.

The Gaia concept has its origin in the fact that the chemical composition of our atmosphere is profoundly different from what it would be if it were determined only by lifeless physicochemical phenomena. For example, it would produce an atmosphere containing approximately 98 percent carbon dioxide with very little if any nitrogen and oxygen, whereas the corresponding figures for our atmosphere are approximately 0.03 percent, 79 percent, and 21 percent. Lovelock presents numerous other examples of such profound departures from chemical equilibrium and postulated the existence of a global force that is able to bring about and keep fairly constant a highly improbable distribution of molecules. He believes that this hypothetical global force consists in the countless forms of life that create and maintain disequilibrium situations through cybernetic systems. Since I do not have the competence to evaluate the validity of Lovelock's physicochemical arguments, I shall restate the problems he discusses in biological terms with which I am more familiar.

The fitness of an organism to its environment is, of course, an essential condition of its biological success and even survival. All living things seem to be endowed with a multiplicity of mechanisms that enable them to achieve fitness by undergoing adaptive changes in response to those of the environment—genetic changes that occur during the evolution of the species, and physiologic and anatomic changes that occur during the existence of each particular organism. In higher species and especially in humankind, these biological mechanisms are supplemented by adaptive social forces.

On the other hand, many present forms of life would certainly be annihilated if the surface of the earth were very different from what it is now. They could not adapt rapidly enough if the salinity, the acidity, the relative proportions, gases, minerals, and organic substances—or any of the other physicochemical characteristics of the earth—were to deviate far from their present values for any length of time. In other words, the present environment does indeed exhibit fitness for the present forms of life but it would have been unsuited to those of the distant past. An atmosphere with 21 percent oxygen, for example, would have been extremely toxic for the earliest forms of life. During the past 3.5 billion years, the global environment has progressively changed, probably as a consequence of the activities of living things, and living things also have undergone corresponding changes through a feedback process. The Gaia system postulated by Lovelock thus appears to be a result of co-evolution. Instead of listing the chemical examples of this creative process discussed by Lovelock, I shall quote a picturesque phrase taken from one of his recent articles: "The air we breathe can be thought of as like the fur of a cat and the shell of a snail, not living but made by living cells so as to protect them against an unfavorable environment."

A few years ago, theoretical discussions were conducted by NASA to consider the possibility of making the planet Mars suitable for human life—which meant providing water, oxygen, moderate temperatures, protection from ultraviolet radiation, and so on. The general conclusion was that Mars could be made habitable only through the progressive introduction of living species capable of creating, over an immense period of time, more and more complex ecosystems similar to the ones that have evolved on earth during more than 3 billion years. This analysis has helped us recognize the profound and innumerable changes that life had to bring about on the surface of primitive earth to create, for present living things, the fitness of the terrestrial environment that L. J. Henderson had taken as the normal state of affairs.

According to the Gaia hypothesis, the earth's biosphere, atmosphere, oceans, and soil constitute a feedback, or cybernetic, system that seeks an optimal physical and chemical environment for life on this planet. At any given time, this system results in a relative constancy both in the composition of the environment and in the characteristics of living things. Repeatedly throughout his book, Lovelock refers to this equilibrium situation as "homeostasis"—a word invented by the Harvard physiologist Walter B. Cannon to denote the remarkable state of constancy in which living things can maintain themselves despite changes in their environment.

The word "homeostasis," however, does not do full justice to the Gaia concept, which implies in addition that living things have profoundly transformed the surface of the earth while themselves undergoing continuous changes, in a co-evolutionary process. Practically all the examples that Lovelock discusses refer, in fact, to creative evolution rather than to homeostatic reaction. For example, the accumulation of oxygen in the air, which became significant 2 billion years ago (a result of biological photosynthetic activities), probably destroyed many forms of life for which this gas was poisonous. In Lovelock's words, however, "Ingenuity triumphed and the danger was overcome, not in the human way by restoring the old order, but in the flexible Gaian way by adapting to change and converting a murderous intruder into a powerful friend." Cybernetic mechanisms progressively brought about the emergence of biological species capable of living in the presence of oxygen and of using it for the production of energy. In this case, as in most other environmental changes, the Gaian way was not an automatic homeostatic reaction but a creative co-evolutionary response.

It seems worth considering that the Gaian control results in global homeostasis only over a period of time that is short on the evolutionary scale. One figure will suffice to illustrate the magnitude of the terrestrial changes that are continuously caused by life. In their aggregate, all the green plants now fix approximately 840 trillion kilowatt hours of solar energy per year in the form of biomass. This is more than ten times the amount of energy that all of humankind uses annually, even with its most extravagant technologies. Who can doubt that this continuous turnover of organic matter and energy must have modified the surface of the earth and goes on changing it? Furthermore, Lovelock himself points out that the process of change may pick up speed and complexity as a result of human interventions, and he appropriately quotes me in stating that on a local level, profound co-evolutionary changes have occurred in certain terrestrial environments and in their biological systems during historical times.

In the last chapter of his book, Lovelock has the courage to explore the relevance of the Gaian hypothesis to the effects of human interventions into nature. I agree with him when he states that environmentalists often shoot at the wrong targets because the resiliency of the earth, considered as an organism, probably makes ecosystems more resistant to pollution than commonly believed.

I hope that in the next edition of his book, Lovelock will emphasize not only the homeostatic aspects of the Gaia hypothesis but also its creative aspects. This would be in the spirit of his statement that the Gaia concept is an alternative to the "depressing picture of our planet as a demented spaceship, forever traveling driverless and purposeless, around an inner circle of the sun."

# PART VII
# The Built Environment

We expect more of the environment in which we live
. . . than conditions suitable for our health, resources to run the economic machine, and whatever
is meant by good ecological condition. We want to
experience the sensory, emotional, and spiritual satisfaction that can be obtained only from an intimate
interplay, indeed from an identification, with the
places in which we live.

# Life in the City

THE EXPRESSIONS "CITY" and "urban agglomeration" are commonly used as if they were interchangeable. When a difference of meaning between them is acknowledged, it refers only to a question of magnitude, the phrase "urban agglomeration" being used for a very large city or for an association of contiguous cities. But there are differences of a more qualitative nature between the two expressions, as becomes clear when one considers the problems posed by attempts to create new cities during the past few decades. The spirit of a real city has subtle qualities more difficult to understand—let alone to create at will—than the quantitative aspects of an urban agglomeration.

Planners are primarily concerned with the technological efficiency of the urban system with regard to industrial, economic, and political activities. They pay less attention to the psychological and emotional needs of city dwellers or to the relation between city life and civilization.

While the technological aspects of the urban system are fairly well understood and can be manipulated, little is actually known about the influence that cities have exerted on the development of human potentialities and therefore on the emergence of civilized life. Civilizations have flourished in cities for more than 5,000 years, but they have difficulty in surviving in the huge urban agglomerations of the contemporary world.

"Urban planning" can be used as a generalized term because its principles are much the same everywhere and have changed little in the course of time. Some 2,000 years ago, Livy had already recognized that Rome's geographical situation had played an immense part in its economic and political success.

Not without cause did gods and men select this place for establishing our City—with its healthful hills; its convenient river, by which crops might be floated down from the midland regions and foreign commodities brought up; its sea, near enough for use, yet not exposing us, by too great propinquity, to peril from foreign fleets; a situation in the heart of Italy—a spot, in short, of a nature uniquely adapted for the expansion of a city.

Livy's statement is still surprisingly applicable to modern urban agglomerations. Their success depends upon ease of internal and external contacts through the efficiency of means of communication, and these are now based on the same technologies all over the world.

Whereas all urban agglomerations exhibit technological similarity, each true city has its own brand of civilization, the distinctive characteristics of which are derived not only from topography and climate but also and even more from a certain quality of human relationships. In ancient Greece, Sparta and Athens symbolized two different attitudes concerning the relationships between the citizen and society. During the fourteenth century, the conservatism of Siena led to a way of life and a type of civilization somewhat different from that fostered by the more adventurous spirit of Florence. Even today the similarities of conveniences, stresses, and population structures in all the great cities of the Western world do not erase their differences in mood. When judged by the spirit of the place, New York is as different from San Francisco and Los Angeles as London is from Paris and Rome.

Granted these differences of spirit between cities, the success of city life nevertheless depends on qualities that are universal. *A priori*, it seems reasonable to assume that a sense of safety is a fundamental need, whether in cities, towns, or villages. But in fact, safety has rarely been a significant concern in the selection or design of human settlements. Populations that have been compelled to abandon areas devastated by floods, earthquakes, or volcanic eruptions commonly return to these areas even when warned of future dangers. The smoke escaping from the fumaroles of Vesuvius or Etna does not discourage Italian peasants from cultivating the slopes of these volcanoes. The island of Santorini (Thera), in the Aegean Sea, was the site of a stupendous volcanic eruption 3,500 years ago and has experienced multiple other eruptions during recent times, yet populations have come back after each disaster—as they have in Martinique after the destructive eruption of Mount Pelée in 1902 had killed more than 30,000 people.

Indifference to danger can be observed in all parts of the world at the present time. A few years ago, the inhabitants of Tristan da Cunha, in the South Atlantic, were compelled to abandon the island after a volcanic eruption destroyed their village. Two years later most of them had returned, despite the hospitality given them by the English government. The young people who eventually went back to England did so not to escape danger but because they had acquired a taste for urban life. Vestmannaeyjar, the largest fishing harbor in Iceland, was destroyed in 1972 by a volcanic eruption that lasted six months. A program for the modernization and enlargement of the harbor was formulated as soon as the volcanic activity began to subside. While in Japan late in 1973, I experienced two significant earthquakes in the region of Nagoya; the inhabitants took the matter quietly, even though seismologists have predicted that a very severe earthquake is due in the very near future. Smog does not make the inhabitants of Los Angeles abandon their city. Nor do New Yorkers abandon theirs because the multiplicity of its problems gives the impression that it has become unmanageable.

Young people the world over are barely conscious of the dangers to which they are exposed. I have seen small Navajo children herd sheep in the solitude of the Arizona desert. I have also seen small Taiwanese children play in the narrow streets of Taipei amidst wild automobile traffic that appeared unconcerned with their presence. Normal children and teenagers are more interested in adventure than they are concerned with safety. And this is also true for many adults. People of all ages willingly sacrifice comfort for a chance to participate in the adventures and spectacles of city life. The movement from the country to the city is often motivated by purely economic reasons; the first cities probably started as places for the exchange of goods. Evidence for trade in salt, obsidian, soapstone, copper, lapis lazuli, and iron ore can be traced back 10,000 years, to even before the advent of agriculture. Then, trade made facilities for defense necessary, along with structures for administration. Shrines and systems of worship were also early features of city life. But the continued success of cities depended on the excitement they provided.

During the Middle Ages, cities offered protection in time of war and against robbers, but much of their appeal was probably in the fact that they made everyday life more interesting than was possible in the country. They were the sites of the ceremonies conducted by the church, the nobility, and the various professions—ceremonies that added color and glamour to medieval life. In the Moslem world, the market and the mosque each Friday are the centers of collective life; the requirement that a minimum of forty men be present for the noonday prayer on Friday tends to associate religious practices with fairly large population centers. One hundred years ago, the large European cities were crowded and unhealthful, but their atmosphere was electrified by the hopes emerging from the Industrial Revolution. Modern cities are the stages for most of the great happenings of the present epoch; they give the impression that each person can participate in these events to the extent that he wishes.

One of the greatest contributions of cities is that they have provided mechanisms for making the presence of the stranger tolerable and for facilitating his integration into the social body. The Italian piazza, the Spanish plaza, the French mall have long played a role analogous to that of the agora in the ancient Greek cities. People of all classes and origins meet in these public places and can become acquainted without having to commit themselves to personal relationships. Throughout history, it has been in the public places that the resident has first become aware of the stranger, observing him critically but also with curiosity, becoming used to his mannerisms before engaging in nodding acquaintance with him, and finally seeking his company. In the miserable sections of Calcutta, the public places available for the activities of daily life bring about casual contacts among people belonging to different religions or social classes and thus facilitate collaboration in neighborhood activities of people who would otherwise have little if any chance of becoming acquainted.

Public places emerged spontaneously in all cities of the Old World. But although the role they have played in the past is well understood, their establishment in new cities has rarely been successful. It is easy to design attractive public places where people can assemble, but it is difficult to generate the human warmth that comes from collective activities. A real city environment depends on an atmosphere in which the human presence is active rather than passive. Public places are elements of social interaction only to the extent that they encourage and facilitate the kinds of activities identified with the words "happening" or "occurrence," events that emerge spontaneously and almost unconsciously.

The quality of the townscape therefore involves much more than natural and architectural features. People rarely visit the city or settle in it to look at parks or monuments, however beautiful these may be. They go to the city for the sake of human encounters and of all that comes from them—social contacts, business and employment opportunities, intellectual and artistic satisfactions. Only when these social expectations have been satisfied do people become really concerned with the physical amenities of the environment. In fact, environmental amenities can probably be usefully defined only in terms of the contributions they make to the human encounter. People are more likely to gather where something is happening that interests them, moves them emotionally, or gets them socially involved. The popularity as meeting places of railroad stations in the past and of airports now does not come from the physical pleasantness of this kind of environment but from the fact that it is associated with adventure through travel and human contacts. The shops of artisans or tradesmen also have been popular meeting places throughout the ages, because they provide displays of human enterprise.

The situations that have the greatest appeal are the ones in which the spectator can take an active part in the act. The piazzas, malls, and open-air cafés in Europe are examples of such situations. For complex historical reasons, public places have not been popular in the United States since the end of the nineteenth century, and even the village greens of New England have lost much of their social function. But increasingly during recent years, the doorsteps of old houses and the low walls surrounding the fountains in front of new skyscrapers are used as seats by strollers, workers, lovers, and bums even in the busiest New York thoroughfares. Watching the life of the city as it goes by provides endless entertainment for the spectator, who himself contributes to the spectacle by his attitudes and his remarks.

The biological limitations of the human brain make it difficult to know really well more than a few hundred persons. A group of this magnitude therefore constitutes the most comfortable unit of social life, but in most types of human settlements, this comfort is bought at a high price. Life in the tribe, the village, or the small neighborhood can offer only a narrow range of human associations, and it imposes behavioral constraints that limit personal development. In contrast, the city offers both a wider range of choices and greater freedom of action. The variety of places of work and of entertainment, as well as of such specialized groups as churches and clubs, provides a broad spectrum of activities and relationships among which the city dweller and visitor can choose. Even more important, the streets, plazas, or malls, the cafés, restaurants, and places of entertainment provide the opportunity for chance encounters that are at times extremely rewarding, precisely because they add unexpected components to life. As these encounters do not commit the participants to continued associations, they give time for deliberate choices to those who wish to escape from an accustomed social milieu. The hope that one's horizon will be enlarged by accidental contacts contributes everywhere to the appeal of city life.

Civilizations owe a great deal to the chance encounters that have enabled persons of different origins and talents to enrich themselves reciprocally and to formulate together new modes of life, of artistic expressions, and even of scientific knowledge. The interplay of thoughts in the agoras of ancient Greek cities helped to sharpen philosophical and political concepts. In Europe during the seventeenth century, the search for new ways to manipulate the physical world led to the creation of academies and thus accelerated the development of science and technology. The revolt against the academic painting of the nineteenth century became an organized movement through a few artists who met in the art centers of Europe. Impressionism might not have developed into a full-fledged movement if Claude Monet, Auguste Renoir, Alfred Sisley, and Frédéric Bazille had not met in 1862, first in the stultifying art classes of the École des Beaux-Arts and then in the Paris cafés and restaurants. The history of modern art is largely the history of chance encounters that developed into irreversible historic trends. The Impressionist school and the other schools that followed it arrived at their philosophies of art not by abstract thought but as a result of personal contacts between congenial souls. Humankind has progressively discovered its intellectual and emotional wealth through the unpredictable encounters and confrontations made possible by life in the city.

Most human beings desire to participate in the adventures and spectacles of collective life, but they also want to make a unique creation of their own life. All share the ecological endowment of the human species; all retain some psychological aspects of the Paleolithic hunter, of the Neolithic farmer, and of the urban dweller who has experienced the splendors and miseries of civilizations; all are at the same time Don Quixote and Sancho Panza, Dr. Jekyll and Mr. Hyde, the Tartarin of Tarascon who dreams of hunting lions in Africa and the one who loves his cup of chocolate in bed. Yet with so much in common, each one knows that he is a unique specimen of the human species.

Genetic constitution and the accidents of life make each person different from all those who have lived before, who live now, or who will live in the future. Furthermore, the freedom to move into new environments constitutes a mechanism for self-discovery and self-realization. Each human being first imagines what he would like his life to be. Then he tries to shape it by taking advantage of the options open to him, and especially by seeking the environments that seem to him most suitable for the fulfillment of his dreams. We do not react passively with environmental factors; we actively move toward them and we respond to them creatively. The teachers of the young Napoleon Bonaparte predicted in his school records, *"Ira loin si les circonstances le favorisent"* ("Will go far if circumstances favor him"). But in a large measure, it was Bonaparte himself who selected or created the circumstances that enabled him to go far and to become known as Napoleon.

The chief merit of the city may be to provide a wider range of options to act out one's own way of life. In this respect, it is important to note that while the child born and raised in the slums is theoretically as free as the privileged child, his range of choices and his ability to move are so limited that he becomes almost a prisoner of biological determinism. The diversity of the environment is therefore more important than its efficiency or its beauty, because it provides a wider range of circumstances for individual development. Environmental diversity helps each human being to discover what he is, what he can do, and what he wants to become. The great cities of the world acquired a great diversity from their historical past, and this is one of their greatest assets. It may be exhausting to live in New York, London, Paris, or Rome, but each of these cities, as well as others that readily come to mind, offers an immense range of intimate atmospheres and public spaces that provide stages on which to create one's own self-selected persona while functioning as an organic part of a social group.

# Shelters: Their
# Environmental Conditioning
# and Social Relevance

IN THE WILD, each of the different animal and plant species lives in one special type of environment to which it is biologically adapted; this environment is its natural habitat. In contrast, human beings have settled in most parts of the earth, including many places where physicochemical conditions are unsuited to the biological characteristics of the human species. Even the so-called temperate zones of the earth are not naturally favorable to human life. Few of us could survive in them if our societies had not developed artifacts that enable us to resist food deficiencies and weather inclemencies. We depend on artificial methods of food storage and on the use of clothing, fire, and an immense diversity of shelters. Furthermore, since practically all our crops belong to sun-loving plant species, large areas of the temperate regions had to be deforested before they could accommodate large human populations.

The cradle of the human species was probably the plateau of East Africa, which used to be and still is now a subtropical land of alternating rainy and dry seasons, associated with periods of growth and dormancy. The sparsity of trees in this savanna region allows ready visual access to the horizon, and all human beings are still biologically adapted to such a subtropical environment.

In James M. Fitch, ed., *Shelters: Models of Native Ingenuity* (Katonah, N.Y.: The Katonah Gallery, 1982), pp. 9–15. Courtesy of The Katonah Gallery.

[ 322 ]

As far back as the Old Stone Age, however, our precursors began moving to other parts of the earth, thereby developing minor biological differences as a result of genetic drift and exposure for many generations to different physical surroundings and ways of life. But despite these changes, all human groups are still fundamentally identical in their physiological requirements and probably also in their psychological drives and emotional needs.

From the physiological point of view, all human beings have remained semitropical animals to such an extent that they cannot truly adapt biologically to either very cold or very hot climates. This is true even of the Eskimos, who arrange their lives so that their bodies are in a semitropical environment most of the time; their skin remains warm throughout the Arctic winter, thanks to the insulating properties of the clothing they wear outdoors and thanks to the high temperature they maintain in their igloos or other shelters. People living in hot dry regions escape the effects of the scorching sun by wrapping themselves in protective clothing, such as the burnoose of the Bedouins, and by living in settlements where the streets are narrow and wisely oriented to provide shade. In human equatorial regions, people have learned to take full advantage of natural breezes. Thus, millennia before the advent of air conditioning, human beings all over the earth had learned empirically to adjust the temperature of their immediate environment between 70 and 80 degrees Fahrenheit. In other words, they had created microclimates suitable to their semitropical biological nature through the proper use of clothing and shelters.

Stone Age people probably first occupied deep caverns and other more or less natural shelters protected by overhanging rocks. As far back as thousands of years ago, however, they began to build shelters of different sizes and shapes—round, octagonal, hexagonal, or square—with walls, ceilings, and floors of different materials, textures, and colors. Such diversity suggests that many different types of shelter design can be adapted to the universal traits of human nature.

Erik Erikson once wrote that "roundness surrounds you more nicely than squareness," and many of the Stone Age rooms were indeed round—for example, those built in Moldavia, on the U.S.S.R.– Rumanian border, some 50,000 years ago. But square and rectangular rooms have come to prevail all over the world. Neither climate nor biological necessity can explain the change in the size or shape of shelters and rooms. In the American Southwest, for example, the Navajos lived until recently in round hogans, consisting of a single room large enough to house some twenty people. Most of these people, however, have now moved or are moving into conventional houses. In the Southwest also, the Pueblo people have long lived in adobe buildings consisting of many very small rectangular rooms as different as possible in shape and material from the hogans formerly used by their Navajo neighbors. Diversity in types of shelters is very striking even on Easter Island, which is only 117 square kilometers, the size of a small U.S. township. Some of the rooms built there in the past and still occupied two centuries ago were only 2 meters in diameter, whereas others were 100 meters long! Eventually, however, the traditional building practices of Easter Island were replaced by others that favored rectangular rooms of sizes and shapes similar to the ones prevalent in most of the Western world. Everywhere on earth, cultural and historical forces have thus been at least as influential in design as the natural conditions of the environment.

The type of room most prevalent now in the countries of Western civilization is rectangular with vertical walls that are 3 to 8 meters in length and width, and 2.5 to 4 meters in height. As already mentioned, these dimensions are not the consequence of biological imperatives, and it is probable that they have been determined by technical aspects of construction and by facility of use by the occupants.

Since the physiological needs and psychological attributes of all human beings are fundamentally similar and still reflect the conditions experienced by our precursors in the semitropical savanna, it should be possible in theory to define an environment—a shelter—with characteristics that are ideal for *Homo sapiens*. But in practice ethnic groups and individual people differ profoundly, not in what they need but in what they want. Furthermore, social wants are much more variable and therefore less well defined than biological needs, because they reflect historical influences, contemporary social forces, and aspirations for the future. What people want is so largely determined by traditions and expectations that no type of shelter can be universally acceptable even if it satisfies completely all the biological needs of human beings.

The design of shelters must therefore be carried out within the constraints imposed by the biological invariants of human nature and must also fit the demands of a particular group or person. Furthermore, it must take into account the fact that individual and social tastes change. It may be useful, nevertheless, to consider some broad principles of building that have long been empirically discovered and widely practiced over a long period of time.

Pretechnological civilizations began very early to rely on thick-walled buildings, perhaps to save on fuel or because fire was difficult to control, and probably also because this type of construction has multiple advantages. Not only is it resistant to storm, fire, and flood, but it has, in addition, desirable acoustic and thermal properties. During cold weather, thick walls store the heat produced by fireplaces or furnaces and release it slowly at night after heating has been discontinued. During hot weather, in contrast, thick walls absorb the solar heat, thus retarding the temperature increase in the interior of the house. After sunset they radiate the stored heat into the house and slow down the rate of cooling. Having lived during the summer and winter seasons in old, well-built adobe houses of Arizona and New Mexico, I have experienced the superiority of their physical comfort over that of modern motels, even those equipped with sophisticated heating and air-conditioning equipment. The same quality of "natural" temperature control through wise design of thick-walled buildings can still be experienced in many ancient houses of Southern Europe.

Massive wall construction became ingrained in most ancient architecture but had to undergo adaptive changes to meet local climatic conditions. In humid tropical regions, for example, glazed windows admitted light but kept out rain; overhanging roofs intercepted the direct sun but did not shut out light; louvered grills provided for ventilating air but prevented visual intrusions. Other practices naturally developed in very hot, dry countries. Dry heat can be made bearable and even pleasant in shaded courtyards such as those of the Spanish tradition or in buildings where massive walls and relatively small openings insulate the indoor areas.

In most parts of the world, however, thick walls are now considered obsolete because their building is labor-intensive and the control of temperature and humidity is thought to be more readily achieved by modern air-conditioning techniques. It is of interest to note in passing that wherever air conditioning is used, the temperature is set at approximately 70 to 75 degrees Fahrenheit, thus providing technological evidence for the view that all human beings fundamentally have the same temperature requirements.

[ 325 ]

Le Corbusier seemingly had biological justification when he asserted that the circulating air of modern buildings should be maintained at a constant temperature around 70 degrees Fahrenheit, but in reality, the biological requirements with regard to temperature are more complex than this figure would indicate. Even under conditions of health, the body temperature exhibits diurnal and seasonal fluctuations that reflect cosmic forces and are inscribed in the genetic constitution of the human species. Conditioning the air at temperature and humidity levels that remain constant throughout the day and the year is therefore not likely to create optimal environmental conditions. Unfortunately, little is known about a possible ideal range of conditions.

It can be argued, on the one hand, that air conditioning should be geared as closely as possible to the diurnal and seasonal fluctuations woven into our biological fabric. On the other hand, perfect adjustment to environmental temperature and humidity may not provide sufficient stimulation for the full development of human potentialities. Our bodies and minds possess remarkable mechanisms for adaptation to environmental changes and are indications that adaptive responses to environmental challenges commonly have creative effects and contribute to a sense of well-being. According to certain geographers and historians, vigorous civilizations are more likely to develop in parts of the world where climatic changes are sufficiently pronounced to cause stimulation but not so violent as to overpower human adaptive mechanisms.

A century ago, the considerations thought to be of major importance in the design of shelters were problems of light, temperature, and the avoidance of "miasmas" and bad smells assumed to be responsible for disease. It was furthermore recognized that environmental requirements differ with age and occupation and are not the same in health and in disease. For example, the sick and the young should be sheltered from traumatic experiences, and workers have to be protected from unhealthful atmospheres. To stimulate the development of human values, however, the environmental control of shelters must go beyond this commonsense wisdom and exclusive concern for protection. It should aim also at the production of stimuli capable of favoring the expression of human potentialities. In other words, human beings should live under conditions that keep their adaptive mechanisms in a state of readiness and provide them with the challenges necessary for creativity.

Architectural traditions have commonly led to the neglect of certain spatial experiences and cultural influences that may greatly contribute to physical and mental well-being and development. Nomadic people, who usually live in temporary shelters or tents, tend to group their activities around some external focus—a water hole, a shade tree, a campfire, or the abode of a wise man. For them, open space is, therefore, an important part of their experience. In contrast, people who live in permanent buildings tend to have only restricted visual contact with space, bounded as their daily life is by walls, floors, and ceilings.

The vast majority of people spend a large percentage of their time indoors, yet hardly anything is known about the effects of such room characteristics as size, height, shape, and color on human comfort, happiness, and performance. In the countries of Western civilization, most dwellings now consist chiefly of a few types of rooms, which, irrespective of esthetic criteria, probably satisfy a few universal human needs. For example, rooms must, of course, be well lighted and well ventilated; their overall dimensions must allow for comfortable and safe motions of the body; design must take into account that most people dislike to have their vision restricted to a very short distance. There are probably physiological reasons for the fact that few people like their working area to face the wall and that children are put in a corner for punishment. Beyond these commonsense requirements, however, few are the characteristics of enclosures that have been proved to be essential for biological needs, except perhaps—and this is questionable— the need for visual contact with open space. Most other criteria used for evaluating the quality of a room deal with values and tastes that are culture-bound and therefore vary with place and time. Two examples will serve to illustrate how the suitability of dwellings can be affected by sociocultural factors that seemingly have no direct biological influence.

The so-called bubble of individual space—namely the most comfortable distance between persons during social contact—is usually much greater among Anglo-Saxon people than among Mediterranean people. A purely cultural difference of this nature has to be reflected within the shelter in the level of togetherness that is considered objectionable or desirable in a given social situation.

Human behavior is also affected by the technological equipment in the room. Until this century, rooms were individually heated, either by fireplaces or stoves; light was provided at first by candles, and later by lamps using kerosene, acetylene, or gas. Since these techniques were somewhat dangerous, children had to spend their evenings in rooms occupied by adults. The phrase "family circle" probably originated from the grouping of children and parents around the hearth and the lamp. But the situation changed with the introduction of central heating and electric lighting, which were sufficiently convenient and safe so that children could have their own living quarters and indulge in greater freedom of behavior. The trend toward "a room of one's own" is therefore an outgrowth of sociocultural forces rather than the expression of biological imperatives. But it may have social consequences. In the past, the necessity to function for several hours in intimate contact with a diversified social group imposed a rather strict social discipline, which may have conditioned the later life of the child.

Since most shelters are built with practical ends in view, their designers commonly overlook considerations that do not appear of practical importance yet may contribute to the quality of life. Such seemingly unimportant factors are perhaps most readily perceived from the point of view of a child. A few years ago, for example, a group of French children were given the opportunity to "invent rooms in which they would like to live." Their initial response was to imagine and build conventional rooms crowded with furniture and gadgets, similar to what they saw in their communities or in popular magazines. Progressively, however, the children produced designs less influenced by their local conditioning and better suited to their own tastes and interests. In particular, they invented rooms having certain special characteristics best suited for particular functions. Bedrooms had few and small windows; playrooms were free of interference and wide open; rooms for telling secrets had unusually low ceilings.

These peculiarities of design should not be dismissed as childish fantasies. Most people, adults as well as children, seem to take a special interest in rooms with an unusual shape and size. Barns, attics, cellars, closets, hiding places behind the stairs or under large pieces of furniture seem ideal places in which to engage in hobbies or fanciful imaginings. This search for unorthodox places may have its origin in the instinct for exploration and adventure. The fanciful irregularity of ancient human settlements—such as those common around the Mediterranean, in the Near East, and in many parts of Asia—rarely fail to attract visitors who, when at home, live in rooms and settlements that are comfortable and efficient but from which no real secret is expected because everything has been carefully planned from the point of view of a practical way of life.

Until recent times, the work of successful planners and builders was guided by ecological wisdom derived from empirical experience. Local constraints made it necessary for them to develop architectural styles suited to the natural conditions of the place where they worked and to the building materials that were readily available. Thus came into existence all over the world types of dwellings wonderfully adapted to local conditions: the snug, well-oriented houses of New England; the breezy plantation houses with broad porches in the South; the thick adobe-walled haciendas in the American Southwest. And everywhere, from the northern climates to the sun belts of Europe and America, there appeared roofs of different slopes, depending upon the amount of rain or snow in the region. The diversity and beauty of this "architecture without architects" arose empirically, almost subconsciously, through a process of natural selection determined by the environmental constraints and by the availability of local building materials.

Ever since antiquity, there have been many treatises devoted to the theoretical and practical aspects of the plastic arts in general and of architecture in particular. Charles Blanc published in 1876 an influential book called *Grammaire des Arts du Dessein*, in which he advocated that the various styles should aim at expressing the fundamental moods of the human mind—the sublime, the beautiful, the pretty, the sad, the endearing, the frightening, and so on. According to him, furthermore, each particular style should be suited to the historical and regional mood of the place. Just as the massiveness of Egyptian temples expressed a religious attitude different from that of Gothic cathedrals, so should every aspect of shelter design convey the social status and lifestyle of the occupants. In his *Grammaire*, Charles Blanc emphasized almost exclusively the technical and artistic aspects of architecture; he barely discussed the effects of shelters on health and comfort, obviously considering these problems of a lower order than those of esthetic appearance and spiritual meaning.

In 1864, Pasteur had been appointed to teach a course of physics, chemistry, and biology at the very École des Beaux-Arts, in Paris, of which Charles Blanc was one of the intellectual leaders. In his teaching, Pasteur formulated original views concerning the design, building, and operation of shelters; he even devised experiments to illustrate that exposure to undesirable physical environments had dangerous consequences for health. However, his teaching at the École des Beaux-Arts lasted only three years, and no other scientist was appointed to replace him when he resigned in 1867. It is obvious that the Beaux-Arts administration represented the orthodox architectural thinking of the time and considered that the physicochemical and biological aspects of the building process were of minor importance and that architecture should be taught primarily as an art, expressed through conventional building techniques.

At the end of the nineteenth century, the traditional philosophy of architecture began to be questioned in England by William Morris, who advocated simpler, unadorned vernacular styles. Morris's ideas were developed in France by Le Corbusier and in Germany by the Bauhaus school of design under the leadership of Walter Gropius. The Bauhaus substituted for conventional styles of architecture a rational style based on the use of modern technology. Fifty years after the publication of Charles Blanc's *Grammaire des Arts du Dessein*, the classical styles were being replaced by a method of construction employing an interior framework of steel, which eliminated the need for supportive walls and accommodated curtain walls of glass. This type of architecture came to be called the International style, because it was based on modern international technology; it was also called functional, because it rejected needless ornamentation. All over the world, many buildings, large and small, testify that the austere simplicity of the International functional style can generate beautiful architectural designs that are expressive not of the place where they are located but of the period during which they were built.

The originators of the International functional style expressed their theories in a few arresting formulas. The phrase "form follows function," attributed to the Chicago architect Louis Henri Sullivan (1856–1924), conveys the view that the physical appearance of a building should reveal the function of each of its parts without any unnecessary adornment. Mies van der Rohe's "less is more" implies the belief that the very simplicity of a design contributes to its esthetic quality. When Le Corbusier referred to apartment houses and private dwellings as *machines à habiter*, he meant that the design of buildings, whatever their purpose, should primarily aim at efficient function, as is the case for the other machines of modern technology.

The International functional style in architecture emerged in the 1920s from a few European centers. It has now spread all over the world in the form of steel-framed, glass-faced, geometrical buildings that have been assumed to provide rational environments for the pursuit of business, administration, industry, and family life.

However, many people, including famous architects of our times, have come to believe that modern buildings are defective from both the human and technical points of view. They are now said to provide poor living and working conditions for their occupants; they generate a monotonous and depressing atmosphere not only for the people who live in them but also for the people who look at them; and they are extremely wasteful of energy.

The present hostility to many aspects of modern architecture and to the various forms of shelters can be explained in large part by the fact that the statement "form follows function" is not as meaningful as it sounds. In its usual architectural meaning, the word "function" is commonly limited to the physical structure and the service systems of the buildings. From the occupants' point of view, however, the functions of a building refer chiefly to biological and social uses—to the satisfactions of the mind and the comforts of the body, at least as much as to the physical aspects of design. If all human needs and values were taken into account, the meaning of the word "functionalism" would be so broad and vague that it could not provide specific guides for design. In practice, form is selected according to the particular kind of function the designer has elected to emphasize, the result being, unfortunately, that most buildings of the so-called functional school do not do justice to the human functions they are expected to serve. The present rebellion against "functionalism" is largely an effort to reintroduce human and ecological factors into the architectural equation.

A century ago, Charles Blanc's *Grammaire des Arts du Dessein* symbolized the almost exclusive concern of architects for the aesthetic aspects of their profession. Half a century ago, the Bauhaus school emphasized the technological aspects of building. In his recent book, *American Building: The Environmental Forces That Shape It*, James Marston Fitch analyzes, in contrast, the relationships between human beings and buildings in the course of daily life. The initial sections of his book deal with physiological processes as they are affected by environmental factors, and the early chapters discuss how the quality of a building depends not only on visual perceptions but also on the responses of the organism as a whole.

The word "shelter" implies practical considerations for the design, construction, and use of buildings. But important as they are, these considerations fail to take into account the powerful symbolic meanings that have always and everywhere been associated with the words "shelter" and "home." Since it is difficult to verbalize these symbolic values in precise terms, let alone to express them quantitatively, a large aspect of shelter design will probably remain in the domain of the architect as an artist rather than becoming part of precise architectural science. There is here an analogy with the art of medicine, which, though less well defined than the science of medicine, is nevertheless as important for the welfare of the patient.

In the final analysis, the first and most important steps in design are those that involve choices about human ways of life rather than about technical problems. One does not function the same way in the austere simplicity of a Japanese house, in the disciplined elegance of a classical European living room, or in the sloppy comfort of modern overstuffed furniture. Before designing shelters, we must therefore ask ourselves some basic questions concerning how we want to live, what we want to become, and how we want our societies to evolve.

The sophistication and durability of many structures, both large and small, from ancient civilizations testify to the fact that some of our ancestors had practical knowledge of building materials and techniques, as well as a subtle appreciation of the psychological effects of form. The design of shelters has been affected by an immense diversity of social factors—in particular, by fashion. As mentioned earlier, eminent architects of the International style are now bored by what they believed to be its aesthetic virtues only a generation ago.

Now, as in the past, style is determined as much by choice, nostalgia, or caprice as by knowledge, resources, or necessity. The coldness and ugliness of our shelters and cities is the concrete expression of our social ills. Our systems of values and ways of life account for the fact that modern industrial buildings are commonly more imaginative from the architectural point of view than are the monuments we build for social relationships or religious worship. If there is reason for hope in the design of better shelters, it is in our increasing awareness that ethical, social, and cultural considerations are as important as materials and techniques in the creation of desirable environments, because these inevitably affect our ways of life.

# The Fitness of the Environment

*The Fitness of the Environment* is the title of a book written a half century ago by Lawrence J. Henderson, a philosophical physician at Harvard who was drafted from the Medical School to serve in the Faculty of Arts and Sciences. The phrase expresses very precisely the point of view that I shall take in discussing the effects that environmental factors exert on human life in technological societies. In Henderson's words:

> Darwinian fitness is compounded of a mutual relationship between the organism and the environment. Of this, fitness of environment is quite as essential a component as the fitness which arises in the process of organic evolution.

The ideal of fitness that Henderson had in mind seems, unfortunately, to be almost completely forgotten by environmentalists. They are concerned less with fitness of the environment than with social and biological dangers arising from modern life—such as pollution, the behavioral disturbances caused by crowding, the pathological consequences of exposure to excessive and unnatural stimuli, the thousand devils of the ecological crisis. For most lay people and not a few scien-

*The Rockefeller University Review*, July–August 1968, pp. 2–11. Copyright © 1968 by The Rockefeller University. Reprinted by permission.

tists, the word "environment" evokes not fitness but a world of night-mares.

Our societies are slowly becoming aware of the environmental problems created by the social mismanagement of technology and may succeed in developing techniques for controlling some of them. How-ever, while the kind of piecemeal social engineering that environmen-talists are now developing will be useful, it will not go far toward solving the ecological crisis or its attendant threats to the quality of human life. The technological fix amounts to little more than putting a finger in the dike, whereas what modern societies need is a coherent philosophy of man in his environment.

If the goal of technological civilization is merely to do more and more of the same, bigger and faster, tomorrow will be but a horrendous extension of today and will almost inevitably lead us to disasters. What is presently called "environmental improvement" consists of palliative ad hoc measures designed to retard or minimize the depletion of resources, the rape of nature, the loss of human values, the violent forms of social unrest. Such programs are the expressions of fear rather than of constructive thought. At best, they constitute shortsighted corrective responses to acute crises, but they never go to the heart of the problem.

The phrase "fitness of the environment" provides a framework for a much broader concept of environmental science. It suggests that sud-den and drastic changes are likely to disrupt adaptive fitness and therefore to disturb physical and mental health. More interesting, it implies also that what is written in our genes and its realization in the body and mind of each of us are both shaped by the adaptive responses that human beings make to their environment.

In the long run, most forms of adaptation to the environment involve genetic changes. In this essay, however, I shall be concerned with the problems of the immediate future and I shall consequently emphasize the effects of the environment on the phenotypic expres-sions of mankind.

The awareness that human characteristics are determined by envi-ronmental forces was highly developed among the Greek philosophers and physicians. In a striking passage of his treatise on "Airs, Waters, and Places," Hippocrates asserts boldly that climate, topography, soil, food, and water affect not only physical stature and health but also behavioral patterns, military prowess, and even political structures.

In confirmation of Hippocrates' perception, there has been observed a trend toward earlier maturation of children for many decades in most Westernized countries. Growth is not only being accelerated; the final adult heights and weights are greater as well. Some fifty years ago, maximum stature was not being reached in general until the age of twenty-nine; commonly now it is reached at about nineteen in boys and seventeen in girls.

Little if anything is known of the long-range consequences of the rate of maturation, but it can be assumed that being early or late in development influences many aspects of behavior. In this regard, it is disturbing that our society increasingly tends to treat young men and women as children and to deny them the chance of engaging in responsible social activities, paradoxically at a time when their biological development is accelerated.

The acceleration of anatomical and sexual development and the increase in adult size have been at least as pronounced in the city as in the country—perhaps even more so. Yet the view still prevails that life in the country is more healthful than life in the city because it is more natural. This belief may have been justified in the past. Now, however, the differences between country and city life are rapidly disappearing in most parts of the Western world. Whether living in a city, a suburb, or on a farm, the modern human being acquires certain characteristics that are almost universally distributed, because they are determined by technological imperatives. Life expectancy and health problems— the so-called diseases of civilization—are much the same among city dwellers in New York, London, Paris, Moscow, or Sydney as among farmers, lumberjacks, or fishermen in any part of the world where their activities have been technicized.

The transformation of the ways of life and environment by technology is so recent that its long-range biological consequences cannot be predicted. Nevertheless, some of the problems inherent in this change can be stated even now, at least in the form of questions for which relevant knowledge could be obtained by pointed biological research.

Humanity, having evolved under the influence of cosmic forces, has been "imprinted" by the many rhythms of nature—ranging from those of the mother's heartbeat to those associated with the daily and seasonal cycles. During the past two decades, a large variety of physiological rhythms have been described for animals and man. They affect such different characteristics as blood levels, urine excretion, adrenaline output, mitotic activity, activity of the plasma, deep body temperature, and limb blood flow. Of special interest is the fact that circadian rhythms persist even in regenerating tissues.

The essential characteristics of the internal environment in animals and man naturally remain within narrow limits; nevertheless, some of the most important biochemical activities exhibit marked seasonal variations. A striking example of such seasonal periodicity is provided by the levels of fasting ketonuria in rats kept without food for 48 hours. When measured from May to October in the United States or in England, the amount of acetone bodies excreted by these animals as a result of fasting was many times greater than it was during the winter months. Excretion of acetone bodies remained at a low level during the winter even when the rats were placed in a room maintained at summer temperatures. It is clear, therefore, that factors other than heat were responsible for the higher level of fasting ketosis observed during the summer months. The amount of glycogen in the liver of rats after 24 hours of fasting also varied according to a seasonal pattern, being much higher in the winter than in the summer.

Biological rhythms are unquestionably the outcome of the shaping of human physiology by the cosmic environment. However, they are not immutably set and can be altered by changes in ways of life or in geographical location. Such changes usually cause profound disturbances, as experienced by workers who go from day to night shift, or by people moving long distances by jet aircraft. Several of these disturbances have been related to changes in certain physiological functions—for example, in endocrine activity.

Technology enables us to eliminate from the environment some of the rhythmic changes under which human evolution took place, but it does not thereby eliminate the rhythms that were woven into the human fabric during evolution. This dissociation of the two kinds of rhythms is a recent experience for the human race. Its long-range effects cannot be predicted *a priori*, but they could be studied in appropriate experimental models.

Air conditioning, uniform exposure to light throughout the year, isolation from climatic and seasonal changes, and other aspects of life in the technological environment generate physiological problems involving such factors as cosmic cycles, biological rhythms, and hormonal changes that could be integrated in experimental models. The study of these problems is essential to the development of rational methods for environmental management. For example, knowledge of the physiological responses to temperature changes at different seasons of the year could certainly help in developing more rational and effective air-conditioning practices.

One of the consequences of technology is that during the next few decades, most people will live in large urban areas. Crowding and constant exposure to noise and other stimuli are accompaniments of urbanization commonly regarded as among the most serious threats of the modern environment.

Although it is fashionable to complain about crowding, the fact is that countless human beings appear to have elected to live among crowds throughout historic and even prehistoric times. The Neolithic settlements, Rome during the Imperial period, the medieval fortified towns, and the cities of the Industrial Revolution all exhibited population densities that have not been exceeded in our own times. Modern cities are larger, but generally they are less crowded than those of the past.

It can be assumed that human beings will become even better adapted to crowding as a result of being increasingly exposed to city life during the early phases of their development. Eventually this adaptation may involve genetic changes in the human race, but at present it is largely determined by the experiences of individual life.

In most cases, the deleterious effects of crowding result not so much from high population density as from the social disturbances associated with sudden increases in density. The appalling amount of physical and mental disease during the first phase of the Industrial Revolution had several different causes—such as poor sanitation and malnutrition—but one of the most important factors was certainly that immense numbers of people from nonurban areas migrated within a few decades to the centers of the industrialization. They had to live and function in the crowded tenements and shops of the mushrooming industrial cities before they could make physiological and emotional adaptation to their new ways of life. Yet it took but a few more decades to convert these rural populations into urban ones, which now find satisfaction in the crowds that generated disease a century ago. You cannot get the boys back on the farm now that they have seen the big city.

The effects of crowding cannot be estimated from the levels of population density; they depend on the social organization and on the nature of interrelationships between individual people. Hong Kong and Holland are among the most crowded areas of the world, yet their populations enjoy good physical and mental health, because from long experience with crowding, they have slowly developed patterns of human relationships that minimize social conflicts and allow people to retain a large measure of individual freedom. This does not mean that we can indefinitely increase the density of our populations but only that the safe limits have not been determined.

For most people in the world today, contact with hordes of human beings has come to constitute the normal way of life. This change has certainly brought about all kinds of individual adaptations to social environments that constituted biological and emotional threats in the past. However, the long-range consequences of this adaptation are not known. If constant and extreme crowding has pathological effects, these will have an insidious course, their expressions being determined not by the initial effect of the crowding stimulus on a particular target organ but rather by the complex secondary responses evoked from the whole organism and from the social group.

Responses to population density involve phenomena so purely human that they cannot be completely duplicated in animal populations. Yet certain aspects of the crowding problem can be studied in experimental models. For example, in animals, as in human beings, crowding affects the secretion of various hormones, but the extent of the effects depends on the conditions under which high population density is achieved. If adult animals (young or old) are assembled in one area from different sources, they exhibit aggressive behavior. In contrast, if they are born and allowed to multiply within a given enclosure, they achieve a social organization that minimizes violent conflict. From now on, the proper utilization of space for human habitation will constitute an important aspect of environmental science. Although the experimental studies so far directed to this problem are few in number and small in extent, they have greatly contributed to a better understanding of the effects that crowding exerts on human beings. Most important, they have made clear that what determines whether a given population density constitutes a pleasant, an annoying, or a dangerous experience includes many factors other than population density.

One can readily visualize the development of a science of space utilization based on the study of physiological characteristics such as hormonal responses, changes in fertility, or acquisition or loss of certain behavioral patterns. The interpretation of the findings will have to take into consideration the historical development of the experimental model. At all levels of population density, the history of the individual organism and of his group conditions the manner in which space is experienced.

I have selected the problems of biological cycles and utilization of space to illustrate two aspects of environmental science in which the responses of the organism to environmental stimuli are most markedly conditioned by the history of the species and of the group. I shall now turn to nutrition and to environmental pollution for examples in which the response to environmental stimuli is more sharply the expression of the individual organism's own characteristics.

Undernutrition and deficiency states are no longer as prevalent in the industrialized countries as they used to be. However, there has appeared all over the Western world a new form of malnutrition that is definitely related to certain characteristics of life in technological societies.

The fundamental metabolic requirements of man are, of course, unchangeable, but quantitatively they are influenced by environmental factors. Nutritional requirements were determined two generations ago from metabolic studies made on vigorous and physically active young adults. The values thus established are probably very different from those that would be obtained for people living in the modern automated and sheltered environment. Despite our sophisticated knowledge of intermediate metabolism, we are grossly ignorant of the kind of nutrition that would be suited to the ways of life in technological societies.

One aspect of this problem directly relevant to our discussion is that the nutritional regimens characteristic of technological societies appear to be dangerous when they are associated with certain habits and stimuli also prevalent in these societies. The endless discussions on the etiology of vascular diseases are confusing even to experts, because they must take into consideration many factors other than food. For example, although high consumption of lipids appears to be correlated with a high incidence of vascular diseases, nutrition is but one part of a complex chain in the causation of those diseases. Genetic factors, lack of physical effort, the so-called tensions of competitive life, and probably a host of other unrecognized agencies condition the manner in which a person responds to a given nutrition regimen. The influences that affect development during intrauterine and early postnatal life may be among the factors that play a role in the genesis of vascular diseases.

The acceleration of anatomical and physiological maturation observed in Westernized countries is probably due in large part to changes in the nutritional management of early life and to the control of childhood diseases. No one doubts that malnutrition and infection are objectionable, but it is also possible that extremely rapid maturation may have undesirable results in the long run. The large baby who becomes a big teenager does not necessarily become a healthy adult.

It has been suspected from observations in man, and demonstrated by experimental studies in animals, that a rich and abundant nutrition during early life so conditions metabolic and behavioral characteristics that the nutritional demands of the organism remain large thereafter, perhaps throughout life. For people living in a sheltered and automated world, the nutritional imprinting resulting from large food intake early in life may well have undesirable metabolic and behavioral consequences.

In this case again, experiments in laboratory animals have provided models that make it possible to analyze the mechanisms through which early nutritional regimens affect lastingly the fate of the organism.

All forms of environmental pollution, including noise and other excessive stimuli, are obviously objectionable aspects of the technological environment. In fact, they are commonly as bad outside as inside the city—for example, on heavily traveled highways or on bodies of water crowded with motorboats. Sewage, organic chemicals, and mineral fertilizers such as phosphates and nitrates pollute not only city water supplies but also all natural waterways and lakes. Exhausts from motorcars, factories, and incinerators are incorporated in smogs that are almost as intense over suburbs as over cities. In fact, smogs are progressively spreading all over the land and even over the ocean masses.

No systematic studies have been made concerning the biological activities of the various kinds of air and water pollutants. Much has been written about the oxides of sulfur and nitrogen, and about carbon monoxide. In contrast, little attention has been paid, for example, to the colloidal particles released from automobile tires grinding on pavement, or to the asbestos released from brake linings and from materials used for insulation in the building trade. Yet these particulate materials constitute a very large percentage of the total mass of air pollutants and are of a size that allows them to penetrate deeply into the pulmonary tract.

The experience with ionizing radiations and with cigarette smoking has made it clear that many effects of environmental pollution are extremely slow in developing. In many cases, this almost rules out the possibility of establishing convincing etiological relationships between cause and effect. As a result, it is difficult to create the kind of social pressure necessary for environmental improvement.

Since most kinds of environmental pollutants produced by modern technology did not reach significant levels until one or two decades ago, their worst effects are yet to be recognized.

Judging from past experience, one can predict some general trends in public approach to environmental control. Wherever convenient, chemical pollution of air, water, and food will be sufficiently controlled to prevent the kinds of toxic effects that are immediately disabling and otherwise obvious. Human beings will then tolerate without complaint concentrations of environmental pollutants that are low enough not to interfere with social and economic life. Continued exposure to such low levels of toxic agents will, however, result in a great variety of delayed pathological manifestations that will not be detected at the time of exposure and may not become evident until several decades later.

In a recent experiment, it was found that if during the neonatal period, mice received a single injection of particulate pollutants common in urban air, a very high incidence of liver tumors was produced during their adult life. This observation suggests that the worst effects of the kind of pollution we are now experiencing may become apparent only in the future. But the larger significance of the experiment is to point out that the young organism is far more susceptible to environmental insults than is the adult.

The responses to environmental stimuli made by the organism during the very early phases of its development, including the intra-uterine phase, deserve special emphasis because they exert profound and lasting effects on the physical, physiological, and behavioral characteristics of the adult. Often, indeed, such effects are so lasting that they can be regarded as a general expression of a biological imprinting mechanism analogous to emotional scarring in Freudian pathology.

Experiments have revealed that in animals, too, early influences condition growth, longevity, behavior, resistance to stress, and learning ability. The effects exerted on human life by early influences can therefore be studied through the use of experimental models, much as is being done for other types of biological problems.

When I invoke the term "environment," I usually couple it to the word "human," for I am not concerned with the environment per se but rather with how environmental factors affect human life. I have emphasized in particular that the physiological as well as the behavioral effects of the environment are conditioned by the organism's evolutionary and individual past and by its adaptive state. A temperature of 55 degrees Fahrenheit feels balmy in midwinter and cold in midsummer. A sky that appears blue to the New Yorker will be perceived as muddy by the Montana rancher. Main Street in Gopher Prairie, Minnesota, may appear oppressively crowded to the visiting farmer, whereas it will seem deserted to an inner-city dweller.

Environmental factors not only affect well-being and productivity at the time they are experienced. More important, they also condition future responses to almost any stimulus. Time is therefore an essential factor in the evaluation of environmental effects. By acting on the child during his formative stages, the environment shapes him physically and mentally, thereby influencing what he will become and how he will function as an adult. For this reason, environmental planning plays a key role in enabling human beings to actualize their potentialities.

Although I have focused my remarks on the shaping of physical and mental attributes by environmental forces, this does not imply that I regard man as the product of a kind of predestination. Rather, I wanted to emphasize that choosing or creating an environment is an act that not only affects us in the here and now but also imposes a pattern on the future. In this light, the concept of an optimum environment is unrealistic, because it implies a static view of man. Value judgments largely determine where we want to go and what we want to become; in consequence, they are as important as objective, measurable parameters in evaluating the quality of the environment.

Admittedly, it is possible to rear and train children for life in oversocialized conditions—even to such an extent that they do not feel safe and happy outside a crowd of their own kind—but this does not invalidate the view that there is potential danger in our level of overcrowding today. Children and adults can be trained to accept as desirable almost any form of perversion—physiological, behavioral, or intellectual.

In the final analysis, the human environment means what is experienced by human beings, and it is the quality of this experience that gives value to life. For this reason, I feel sorrow and indignation at seeing the children of American cities being conditioned by noise, ugliness, and garbage in the street—and thereby conditioned to accept public squalor as the normal state of affairs.

A personal experience has taught me the wisdom of Winston

Churchill's words "We shape our buildings, and afterwards, our buildings shape us." I spent my school years in Paris, until the age of twenty-four. At that time, the historic buildings of Paris were dark, covered with black soot. We used to believe that this somber tonality—caused by dirt!—gave antique refinement to the Parisian atmosphere. Indeed, there was an outcry of anger when André Malraux proposed that the Paris buildings should be washed. Then a miracle happened. When the soot was removed from the eighteenth-century monuments, their surfaces revealed the golden hue of the building stone, as subtle and warm as young human flesh. For more than a century Parisians, and the rest of the world, had become accustomed to the gloomy mood created by the soot and dirt of the Industrial Revolution. Sensitive life had been impoverished by this conditioning. How I wish now that as a young boy I had seen the Gothic cathedrals when they were still white and the eighteenth-century buildings when they proudly displayed colorful stones and pink marble steps.

Human beings are so adaptable that they can survive, function, and multiply despite malnutrition, environmental pollution, excessive sensory stimuli, ugliness and boredom, high population density, and its attendant regimentation. But while biological adaptability is an asset for the survival of *Homo sapiens* considered as a biological species, it can undermine the attributes that make human life different from animal life. From the human point of view, the success of adaptation must be judged in terms of values peculiar to humanity.

The purely biological aspects of our interplay with our environment can be studied both in the field and in laboratory models by the methods of experimental science. It is obvious that the knowledge thus acquired will not be sufficient to formulate environmental policies, because science per se cannot define or impose values to govern behavior. Science can, however, go far toward predicting the likely biological consequences of technological practices, and therefore can contribute to the development of values by providing a more factual basis for options. Environmental science will come of age when technological and biological knowledge is used to anticipate the distant consequences of human responses to surroundings and events, thereby helping humanity make itself as it makes its environment.

# The Netherlands, a Horizontal Country

THE PLANNERS of Imperial Rome certainly did not consider the small area of northwestern Europe now occupied by the kingdom of the Netherlands as a promising place for the development of civilization. Few parts of the world have been as poorly endowed by nature with regard to climate, soil fertility, and other resources. Julius Caesar did take an interest in the Low Countries, and Roman legions occupied much of them at the beginning of the Christian era, but only for military reasons. The Low Countries were in a strategic position for the defense of the Empire's western provinces, as they straddled the route by which the barbarians from the German forests could penetrate the rich agricultural lands of Gaul and Southern Europe.

To Mediterranean eyes, the Low Countries must have appeared most undesirable at that time, just a desolate area of heath, fetid swamps and dank woodlands, unsuited to agriculture and with no mineral resources. The North Sea climate is commonly at its worst in this region—cold, humid, foggy, and with winds that are almost constant and at times extremely violent. The country was nevertheless extensively and intensively developed early during the historical period to such an extent that even before Spanish occupation, much land had to be protected by a complex system of dikes, levees,

*Celebrations of Life* (New York: McGraw-Hill, 1981), pp. 96–110. Copyright © 1981 by The René Dubos Center for Human Environments, Inc.

and pumps against inundation by the waters of the North Sea and the rivers.

Peat bogs abound throughout the Netherlands and much of the land is below sea level. The greatest part of the remainder of it is made up of low sandy plains with occasional hill ridges rarely exceeding 45 meters in elevation. In practically all parts of the country, the soil can be used for agriculture only after elaborate techniques of reclamation and fertilization. Even though the Netherlands had become one of the richest countries in the world at the time of Spanish occupation, in the sixteenth and seventeenth centuries, with an extremely productive agriculture, there was some justification for the remark attributed to the Duke of Alba, who had tried to overcome the Dutch rebellion against Spain, "Holland is as near hell as possible." There is much truth, however, in another remark attributed to a Frenchman, "God created the world, but the Dutch made Holland." The word "made" is appropriate, because the Netherlands provide the most spectacular example of humankind's ability to transform the surface of the earth and to create out of it artificial environments in which animals and plants can prosper and civilization can develop—a process that I have called elsewhere "the wooing of earth" by humankind, or creative symbiosis between earth and humankind.

My purpose now is to give a brief account of the steps by which the Dutch have succeeded in creating extraordinary sceneries and a prodigious civilization on what sociologists have facetiously called a bad piece of real estate. A few details of ancient history and even prehistory will show that the unique features of urban settlements in the Netherlands have progressively emerged from very primitive techniques of land management.

Uninviting as the natural conditions appear to be for human life in the Low Countries, Homo sapiens had nevertheless become established along the coast more than 10,000 years ago. Farming and the keeping of cattle were already carried out during Neolithic times, and the early settlers burned over the heaths to encourage new, tender growth for their flocks of animals. This practice and overgrazing progressively destroyed much of the vegetation and exposed vast tracts of the underlying sand. Under the influence of the wind, much of that sand was pushed inland, where it created dunes in many areas.

Long before the Roman era, people originating from Germany and other parts of Eastern Europe had built fairly extensive settlements on salt marshes barely one-third meter above sea level, especially in the northern areas that are now the provinces of Groningen and Northern Friesland. As these settlements were dangerously susceptible to flooding, they were repeatedly heightened by layers of turf sod and of clay. Such refuge mounts, commonly designated terpens, became more numerous. They were at first just spacious enough to protect a single farmstead or hamlet, or to serve as a refuge for livestock during times of flood. As terpens progressively increased in size and height, they provided a pattern for the future development of most Dutch towns. The population must have increased considerably even before the Christian era, as indicated by the fact that the single Germanic Batavi tribe, which had settled in the northern part of the Netherlands, could supply 100,000 men as auxiliaries to Julius Caesar's Roman legions.

Roman rule vanished completely in the Netherlands around A.D. 350, leaving little trace except for a few settlements and some faint evidence of the grid pattern in the countryside. During the troubled centuries that followed the Roman withdrawal, people from eastern Europe—Friesians, Saxons, and Franks—established themselves all over the Netherlands; the Dutch population largely stems from them. Like the rest of Europe, the Netherlands suffered from invasions by Vikings and other Nordic people during the Dark Ages.

Relative peace and order began to prevail after the end of the Nordic invasions, and this permitted rapid agricultural and economic development. Since much of the land is protected from the North Sea only, and ineffectively, by the sand dunes, strict control of the water from the sea and from the river was essential almost everywhere. What the early settlers learned in building terpens as refuges for their families and cattle against storm tides and river floods was to secure villages and towns against the flood. The technique was sufficiently developed in the eighth or ninth century for cities such as Leiden and Middleburg to be established along the western coast on artificial mounds 100 or so meters in diameter and some 15 meters high—real hills in this very flat country.

In most places, the ground is so wet that the only way to put up a new building is to prepare a special site for it. While onerous, this necessity has had the advantage of preventing haphazard growth and urban sprawl. In contrast to the disorderly urban development all over the United States and in much of Europe, the Netherlands offer a crisp break between town and country and this makes possible ready access from urban settlements to bucolic scenes. A ten-minute drive from almost any town leads to a place beside a river or canal where one can sit on the grass, admire wildflowers, and watch more kinds of birds than one is likely to see in other Western industrialized countries. Protection against water depends largely on dikes. The first substantial ones were built in the eighth or ninth century. Most parts of the coastal belt had thus been protected against the sea and the river by the end of the thirteenth century.

Time and time again, however, villages were devastated and whole areas of agricultural land ruined as a consequence of flooding from the rivers or after the bursting of dikes. On the night of November 18, 1421, for example, a great storm tide backed by a fierce westerly wind attacked and breached the dikes at Brock and destroyed much land north and south. Early accounts speak of seventy-two villages destroyed and 100,000 people drowned. Modern studies suggest that these figures may have been exaggerated, but the destruction was so great nevertheless that many people, including the nobility, had to go begging, and their plundering raids made the region unsafe for several years. This is but one example among the countless disasters caused by wind and water throughout the history of the Netherlands. The disastrous floods of January 1916 and February 1963, to which I shall return later, show that the threat is always present and especially dangerous in the Holland and Zeeland areas. Throughout history, new dikes were built constantly and rapidly to replace the ones that had been destroyed, an enterprise that became and has remained a national commitment. The motto of the arms of the province of Zeeland, *Lucto et Emergo* (I strive and arise), symbolizes the spirit of the Netherlands as a whole.

As already mentioned, the early settlers found little good fertile soil. Agricultural land was created at first from peat bogs, especially until the nineteenth century, when peat was the chief fuel used in the Netherlands. A spectacular feat of such land reclamation took place from an extensive peat bog in the northwestern part of the country. Beginning in the seventeenth century, the peat was dug up, then the sterile sandy subsoil was progressively changed into rich farmland by the addition of manure and artificial fertilizers.

However, the most typical and picturesque type of artificial farmland is the polder, which is created from completely submerged areas. Lakes, whether of salt or fresh water, are pumped dry after having been surrounded by a dike and, in the dike, a wide canal. The canal is dug first and the soil removed from it is used to build the dike around the area to be converted into a polder. The water is then pumped into the canal, which carries it to a river or to the sea. Polders are usually crisscrossed by small ditches, which keep them well drained. The layout of their meadows or crops, cut into regular strips by the ditches, calls to mind a Mondrian painting, or more prosaically the gridiron pattern of a city, the streets of which would have no traffic. Standing below in the polder itself provides the sight, extraordinary in the strong etymological sense of the word, of boats in the encircling canal silhouetted against the sky as they move above the land.

Most of the tremendous tasks involved in the construction, maintenance, and repair of the dikes, the development of levees along the canals and rivers, and the creation of land from peat bogs and in the polders were originally carried out with simple tools. Spades and matlocks sufficed for most construction work; heavy pile drivers, operated by teams of thirty to forty men, were used to build levees and dams. Large wicker baskets, sleds, and ox-drawn carts served for the transport of material, such as clay for the dikes, or timber piles and mattresses of willow wands to reinforce the water defenses. The wheelbarrow was not introduced until fairly late.

Pumping out the water was naturally the crucial part of the reclamation, and this used to be done by thousands of windmills, the thatched roofs and moving sails of which became a picturesque and endearing feature of the Dutch landscape. The use of windmills, however, is of more recent origin than commonly believed. For many centuries the only methods for removing excess water from the polder were by gravity drainage, the counterbalanced bailing bucket, and the horse- or man-powered scoop wheel. The first two records of wind-driven water mills date from 1408 and 1414. These first windmills were small and inefficient. Larger and more efficient ones, working on the principle of the Archimedean screw and able to lift water for 2 to 4 meters, did not become common until after the beginning of the seventeenth century. They are the water mills made familiar by pictures of the Dutch scenery.

Needless to say, the control of water and the creation of land demanded tremendous efforts that exceeded the abilities of a single family or small group of families. The building of houses in areas artificially protected from water required much sand carrying and pile driving, and implied not only communal participation but also a high level of social organization and discipline. In the Middle Ages, severe laws were enforced to help win the battle against water. "No feuds were allowed once the dikes needed repairs," writes Dr. J. van Deen, the historian of Dutch reclamation. Breaking the dike peace could mean being sentenced to death. "In some parts, any man refusing to do his share could be buried alive in the breach with a pole stuck through his body. The people who lived farther inland had to come and work at the dike. "Dike or depart" was the old saying. Any man who was unable to repair the breach in his own section of the dike had to put his spade in the dike and leave it there. This was the sign by which he gave his farm to any man who pulled the spade out of the dike and who felt powerful enough to close the breach. This was the "Law of the Spade." Eventually there arose administrative structures that derived their authority from their service to the common good. The personal and social disciplines that were essential conditions for water control must account in large part for the complementary spirits of independence and of democratic tradition that have contributed so much to the Dutch ways of life and to the greatness of the Netherlands.

Despite incessant struggle against the elements and in spite of incredibly complex political difficulties both at home and abroad, most semi-independent parts of the Low Countries had achieved great prosperity at the time they became part of the Spanish Empire. A measure of their power is that they eventually achieved freedom from Spain, which was then the greatest and wealthiest military power in Europe. The Dutch even established six new universities in different parts of the country during and immediately after the Spanish wars.

The phenomenal achievements of the Netherlands are the more striking when it is realized that, at the time of the Spanish wars, the population was only of the order of 3 million people grouped in more or less independent municipalities within seven provinces. These become the "United Provinces" for the purpose of eliminating Spanish domination, but they were otherwise in constant conflict about religious, economic, and almost any other matters. The religious aspects of these rivalries are especially entertaining because they involved not only Catholics against Protestants, and Calvinists against Lutherans, but even bitter conflicts of doctrine between different groups of Calvinists.

The Netherlands thus had a form of government that was part oligarchic, part republican, unique in its diversity, and for this reason seemingly far less effective than the surrounding European monarchies, from both the political and the administrative points of view. The success of the Netherlands in the face of so many internal and external difficulties provides evidence that the local management of affairs is usually more effective than national or global management.

The sixteenth and seventeenth centuries have been called the Golden Age of the Netherlands. The western part of the country—that is, Holland proper, and Amsterdam in particular—were then the envy of Western Europe. The 3 million people of the Seven United Provinces, which had been so poorly endowed by nature, had not only triumphed over Spain, they also dominated the maritime trade of the world and managed much of its finance. Their merchant marine was ten times greater than that of France and three times greater than that of England; indeed, it was greater than those of England, Spain, and France combined. The commercial enterprise of the Dutch carried their merchant vessels from Recife to Nagasaki and from Archangel to the Cape of Good Hope.

The Netherlands was also the leader in practically all fields of culture. Rembrandt the painter, Spinoza the philosopher, and Dr. Nicholas Tulp all lived in Amsterdam at the same time. Dr. Tulp is of special interest to me for two different but related reasons. He taught the then unorthodox doctrine that the chief role of the physician is not to administer drugs but to help the patient mobilize the natural defense mechanisms that are essential to the control of disease. He was painted on several occasions by Rembrandt, who also made of him an etching that I regard as the most perceptive portrait of the ideal physician. In nearby Delft, there also lived at that time Anton van Leeuwenhoek (1632–1723), the first scientist to develop a microscope that enabled him to see and follow the activities of bacteria and other microbes. Several illustrious foreigners also lived in the Netherlands during the Golden Age. Tsar Peter (later, the Great) of Russia came to study shipbuilding and went home to model his capital (now Leningrad) on Amsterdam, with canals for thoroughfares. The French philosopher René Descartes found Amsterdam the best place in which to think freely in the midst of great comfort. As he wrote in one of his letters, "What other country could one choose where all the conveniences of life and all the exotic things one could desire are to be found as readily? Where else could one enjoy a freedom so complete?" Amsterdam was then truly the city of Europe.

The agricultural productivity, as well as the expansion of industry, commerce, and overseas trade had all been achieved despite extreme paucity in natural resources and against great handicaps created by natural and political conditions. They were the results of human efforts, intelligence, and daring symbolized in two paintings by Frans Hals. These paintings capture contrasting aspects of the Dutch character, both of which contributed to the success of the Netherlands at that time. One conveys the Puritan sobriety of the Governors of the Old Men's Home at Haarlem and epitomizes the industriousness that then prevailed in all Dutch towns. The other shows the roistering cavaliers of the St. Jorisdoelem—the swashbuckling adventurers who carried the Dutch flag around the world. The capacity for assiduous toil and daring spirit can also both be recognized in the urban architecture of that time—the staid simplicity of most churches and almshouses contrasting with the splendor and the self-assurance of town halls and merchant dwellings.

The qualities of Dutch life are evoked by Albert Camus in his novel *La Chute* (*The Fall*).

You take these good people for a tribe of syndics and merchants counting their gold crowns with their chance of eternal life, whose only lyricism consists in, occasionally, without doffing their broad-rimmed hats, taking anatomy lessons. You are wrong. . . . Holland is a dream, monsieur, a dream of gold and smoke—smokier by day, more gilded by night. . . . Holland is not only the Europe of merchants but also of the sea, the sea that leads to Cipango, and to those islands where men die mad and happy. I like these people swarming on the sidewalks, wedged into a little space of houses and canals hemmed in by fogs, cold lands, and the sea steaming like a wet watch. I like them because they are double. They are here and elsewhere.

They are "here" because, since the beginning of time, the Dutch have lived in environments they have created, almost entirely by themselves, out of nature; they are in consequence integral parts of these environments. But they are also "elsewhere" for two different reasons. On the one hand they became early part of the whole world not only because their ships made them the greatest international carriers of merchandise but also because their technical proficiency in many fields gave them the opportunity to work in the most unexpected places—draining the English fens and the Russian marshes, popularizing and selling almost everywhere tulip and other bulbs originally derived from the Orient, converting the Philips industrial plant in Eindhoven into a center for electronic research with branches in many parts of the world. On the other hand, the Dutch have long lived in such crowded environments that they can remain sane as they have most of the time only by spending much of their lives within their own thoughts, aware of the external world, of course, but concerned at least as much with their own private, internal world.

The wind-driven water-pumping mills that made possible the great reclamation schemes of the seventeenth century and were so typical of the Dutch landscape during the Golden Age began to be replaced by steam pumps at the end of the eighteenth century. But it was the introduction of the electric pump at the beginning of our own century that made possible the draining of the Zuider Zee, one of the greatest technological achievements of modern times.

The Zuider Zee used to be a very shallow body of water, silted with rich alluvions from the several rivers that empty themselves into the North Sea. Plans to drain it and convert it into farmland had been formulated in the seventeenth century but were then beyond the possibilities of technology. More precise schemes were put forward during the nineteenth century, and the one submitted by the engineer Dr. Cornelis Lely was adopted in principle by the Dutch parliament in 1901. A great storm tide in 1916 and the food shortages caused by the First World War finally led to passage of the act for the closure of the Zuider Zee in 1918. The scheme was to throw a dam across the whole mouth of the Zuider Zee in order to cut it off completely from the North Sea and then to proceed gradually with the draining operations. The scheme had three objectives: to reclaim some 555,000 hectares of dry land (i.e., approximately one-tenth of the agricultural area of the Netherlands!) in several great polders; to reduce the coastline by 300 kilometers; and to provide a freshwater reservoir of 296,000 hectares. One of the polders (Wieringermeer) was completely drained in 1930, two years before the dam was completed.

Work on the project was begun in 1923, and the last gap on the dam was sealed on May 28, 1932. A monument on this spot reads: *Een Volk dat leeft bouwt aan zijn toekomst* ("a living nation builds for its future"). Faced with interlocking blocks of Rhineland basalt, the dike crown rises 7.5 meters above mean sea level. It is 32 kilometers long and carries a wide motorway that links Friesland to North Holland. It has locks for ships to pass in and out. There are sluices and a large pumping station that regulates the level of the water inside the dam. What was once the Zuider Zee now consists of four polders and a freshwater lake, the Ijsselmeer. The latter supplies drinking water to the human settlements on the polders and also water for irrigation in periods of drought.

It was taken for granted in the 1930s that all the reclaimed land would be used for agriculture, and two of the Zuider Zee polders are indeed devoted to farming. In the Netherlands as in many other countries, however, economic prosperity is taking people out of agriculture, changing their habits, and increasing their expectations. Fewer and fewer people want to live in the small hamlets typical of the old polders. Motorcycles and cars make it possible for them to live in larger places that provide more services and attractions. Furthermore, now that the Netherlands are part of the Common Market, they can obtain certain crops more cheaply from Italy and France than from national agriculture. Fewer and fewer Dutch people are engaged in farming, and more and more of the reclaimed land is being used for new towns, industry, and various forms of recreation.

The reclaimed Zuider Zee remains in any case an almost miraculous example of the transformation of the surface of the earth by human ingenuity and effort. I visited the area in the fall of 1969, on a rather stormy day. Listening to the violent wind and to the waves lashing on the dam, it was difficult for me to imagine that only two decades earlier, there was only salt water inside the dam, with fishing boats and screaming gulls where I now saw substantial farms and handsome villages, with religious buildings around the village square. (As I recall, Protestant, Catholic, and Jewish congregations had to be represented in each village.)

For many decades now, some 2 percent of the national income of the Netherlands has been spent on dredging, draining, and reclaiming for the creation and protection of dry areas. Much land has been thereby made available for agriculture and other human activities, including the enjoyment of "nature." But the environment is called "nature" only for lack of a more accurate word, since most of the surface of the earth has been profoundly transformed by human intervention. Two figures will suffice to illustrate the magnitude of this transformation. In 1840, the salt coastline of the Netherlands was 1,979 kilometers long. It will be reduced to 676 kilometers after completion of the system of dams, sluices, storm barrages, and strengthened dikes along the vulnerable coastline of the Rhine-Maas-Scheldt delta. "The Dutch have truly made Holland" by transforming nature through the bold use of technology, and what is even more remarkable is that the process of transformation of the bodies of water and of land continues to go on at an accelerated pace in many parts of the country.

The recent feats of land reclamation are technological miracles of the twentieth century, but their very complexity makes certain human settlements even more vulnerable than in the past to violent storms and to accidents of human origin. For this reason, watch is kept constantly along the dikes, and weather forecasts are announced twice daily in winter.

On January 31, 1953, the wind became increasingly violent during the day, and at 11:00 P.M. the radio warned that the following day would bring "severe northwesterly gales . . . unsettled weather, showers, hail, and snow." On February 1, the northwest gales increased the tides, which are in any case normally highest at that time of the year, and pushed a huge mass of water through the North Sea. The sea rose higher than it ever had in human memory, washing over the dikes in some protected areas and smashing through them in many places. Close to 1,280 kilometers of dikes were destroyed. Miles of railroad track were washed off the top of a dike 10.4 meters above sea level. The seawater came to cover more than 400,000 acres of farmland and villages; almost 2,000 people lost their lives; tens of thousands of animals were drowned; similar numbers of buildings were destroyed or damaged; the soil was poisoned by the sea salt. The dikes were repaired within a year, at the stupendous cost of 6 percent of the national budget, but it took seven years before Dutch agricultural production fully recovered from the February 1953 disaster.

After the 1953 catastrophe, a delta commission was organized to explore the possibility of sealing off the Scheldt and Rhine estuaries and of shortening the southern shoreline. The Delta project was adopted in 1957 and when completed, during the 1980s, should greatly enhance the safety of the southwestern Netherlands. Its main purpose is not, as was the case for the Zuider Zee, to reclaim new land but to increase the country's freshwater resources, to check the penetration of salt into existing agricultural land, and to make the islands in the delta more accessible. These islands could then be used for industry, more intensive agriculture, or residential and recreation areas, which are much needed in the southern Netherlands. The delta project was altered by an act of Parliament in 1976 under the pressure of environmentalists who pointed out that the initial plan would irreversibly change the ecological character of the estuary. The controversies on the merits of the new, much more expensive plan continue and thus make it clear that the Dutch are still in the process of making Holland, still hoping that the eastern Scheldt will be closed to the ravages of the North Sea in 1985.

Another spectacular project still in the process of development is along the 35 kilometers of waterfront that separate Rotterdam from the North Sea. Although Rotterdam was practically destroyed by the German air raid of May 1940, its harbor was rapidly rebuilt after the war. More important, it has been modernized and enlarged to such an extent that it is now the largest, busiest, and most modern harbor in the world, thanks to its location close to the highly industrialized and densely populated areas of Western Europe, with some 250 million people within a radius of 500 kilometers. Everything seems to be the biggest and most modern in the Rotterdam area: the world's largest container loading and unloading facilities; one of the highest capacity grain terminals; and accommodations for the largest tankers.

The new harbor section is properly called Europort, because it serves as a European processing center for handling and redistributing grain and oil as well as for the production and distribution of countless chemicals. Oil storage tanks, refineries, and chemical plants extend for many kilometers out of Rotterdam. But the most impressive aspect of the enterprise is the extent to which the city, as well as the harbor and industrial facilities of Europort, are new, artificial—a purely human creation that has completely transformed the natural environment.

The phenomenal density of population and intensity of industrial growth in the western Netherlands would have resulted in massive environmental degradation if it were not for the local peculiarities of urban development. With some 6 million inhabitants, this area has some 1,000 people per square kilometer. If the United States were as densely populated as the Netherlands, the total American population would be as large as that of the whole world today—more than 4 billion people. In the Netherlands, furthermore, six out of ten people live on land that is below sea level. At the present time, 27 percent of the Dutch people dwell on 5 percent of the country's area, and it is all but certain that the population will continue to increase. Most people, furthermore, live in a horseshoe-shaped belt of towns, cities, and suburbs called the Randstad (Ring City), located in the Holland province. The base of the horseshoe is on the North Sea dunes, and its open end faces southeast. It is about 48 kilometers across, would be 177 kilometers long if straightened out, and runs from Dordrecht through Rotterdam, Delft, The Hague, Leiden, and Haarlem to Utrecht. Its population density is four times higher than the average for the country as a whole.

Despite this extreme level of industrialization, urbanization, and crowding, most Dutch people enjoy excellent health, with a long expectancy of life and a low crime rate. There are still small stretches of open space between most of the cities and towns of the Randstad, but the most remarkable and uniquely Dutch aspect of this conurbation is that its core retains a rural appearance.

The horseshoe area between the towns and the North Sea—or rather between the mounds on which the towns are built and the dikes and dunes that separate them from the North Sea—is rich agricultural land with well-tended farms. Cows, ducks, swans, herons, lapwings, and of course, the water of the canals and rivers can be seen everywhere. As mentioned earlier, this happy situation is due to the fact that human settlements have had to be built on mounds and therefore cannot sprawl, as they do in the industrialized areas of other countries. In consequence, cities, towns, and even villages have to be sharply separated from the country, where grass and flowers are stirring with the wind.

The wind itself contributes to the diversity of landscapes and waterscapes. It blows almost constantly, brushing over the dunes and across towns and meadows, bringing low clouds and rains from the Atlantic in all seasons. It carries now and then the summer warmth or the freezing cold from Central Europe; it bends trees and also turns the few surviving working windmills. Seen from a low-flying airplane, this tiny region, which is so tight and tense, busy and booming in the human settlements of the Randstad, appears, nevertheless, more comfortable than other countries better endowed by nature. Its agricultural core of meadows, cultivated fields, and water might well serve as a model for social organization and land management in rich urbanized industrial countries.

Recent developments in the city of Amsterdam will illustrate the extent to which the Randstad landscape and waterscape are completely managed. The Amsterdam Forest Park, called "The Bos"—or more colloquially, "the Woods"—was created southwest of the city in 1934 by sacrificing three polders 4 meters below sea level. An extensive network of drainage pipes had to be laid to maintain a water level compatible with the development of the roots of the trees to be planted. Lakes created by the drainage are used for swimming and canoeing. The shapes of the steep polder dikes were softened into gentler slopes and an artificial hill was created. All sorts of trees common to northwestern Europe were planted over 1,000 of the total 2,230 acres. The Bos, now almost half a century old, consists of long wooded slopes, lakes, and canals where people walk, ride bicycles, fish, or paddle their canoes. Icelandic ponies can be seen ambling through the trees, but this bucolic picture acquires a less idyllic aspect when more than 100,000 people come to the woods on summer weekends.

Paradoxically, the most disturbing aspects of the Netherlands future may originate not from shortages in resources or from economic difficulties but from the very successes of the Dutch people in shaping their country and from the consequences of these successes for the safety and the quality of future Dutch life.

For example, the growth of Amsterdam has required the development of huge dormitory cities. On the west side, the creation of Slotervaart, Slotermeer, Osdorp, and Geuzenveld involved raising the subsoil level by at least 1.8 meters. This was done by sacrificing and excavating the huge Sloterplas polder over an area approximately 1.6 kilometers long and 0.4 kilometers wide, to a depth of 27.4 meters. The rich polder topsoil was used to create parks, lawns, and recreation land; the 19.9 million cubic meters of sand that was excavated from beneath served to prepare the building site. The excavation site itself was turned into a lake.

All these new housing developments differ from the traditional cities and towns of the Netherlands, and from central Amsterdam in particular, in offering large open areas either of land or of water. This change, however, is considered undesirable by many people who regard the dormitory towns as too orderly, too inflexible, with no pleasurable surprises. The absence of Dutch coziness suggests that even though the buildings and parks may be of high technical quality, they are the kinds of settlements that municipal authorities design for "other people" but in which they themselves rarely elect to live.

The city of Rotterdam also symbolizes both the triumphs of technology and their threats to the quality of life. Rotterdam can legitimately boast of having the largest and most modern harbor facilities of Europe and perhaps of the world, but this technologic and economic success has been achieved at the cost of many other values. The deeper the New Waterway is dredged, the larger the amounts of salt and toxic substances that enter from the sea and that contaminate not only the drinking water but also the soil of the agricultural Westland. This trend will continue even if, as is claimed, the delta plan increases the volume of Rhine water that will flow through the New Waterway.

Air pollution from oil refineries and from chemical industries is constantly increasing. The oil spillage from the tankers is contaminating most North Sea beaches. Tar contamination is so common that people make it a practice to keep a bottle of gasoline with a rag at the entrance of their house to clean the soles of shoes before walking in. Many Dutch people are beginning to doubt that there is a real economic or other justification in one more oil tank, one more distillery, or one more plant for the manufacture of plastics. They are asking themselves whether they really want more growth or whether they are continuing to build not out of necessity but simply because they know so well how to build.

Perhaps more important in the long run, however, is the threat to the coziness of the environment in the Netherlands, and particularly to the intimate relationship between people and things that used to be such an appealing aspect of Dutch life. Will the exciting environments now being created by modern technology ever have the appeal of the exquisite atmospheres conveyed in the paintings by Rembrandt, Jan Vermeer, Pieter de Hooch, and the other masters of the past—atmospheres that made the rest of the world so envious of Dutch life during the Golden Age of the Netherlands?

# Vertical Manhattan

THE TRAVELER approaching New York City from the ocean first perceives Manhattan as an ethereal mass slowly emerging from the water. He long remains unaware of the confusing and overpowering mass of steel and of stone, and he can imagine a luminescent spirit ascending into the sky. The illusion creates different moods, depending on the weather and the hour of the day. At times the island seems to float mysteriously in clouds or in the mist, as if it were some holy mountain in an ancient Chinese scroll; often it shimmers in precious pinks and blues like one of William Blake's visions come to life; at dusk or at night, it glows like a flaming torch. Never does it evoke only brute force and material wealth.

The spiritual quality of the spectacle makes one forget the crudeness of its material origin. Yet these rising towers that so deceptively reflect the splendors of heaven are, in fact, bound to hard bedrock and are built of harsh materials; they represent wealth and arrogance. Each and every one of the tall buildings is the product of materialistic urges and was erected not as a contribution to a concerted common task but as a display of power and pride. How did it happen that this uncoordinated effort, motivated by ruthless ambition, could have engendered so spiritual a silhouette against the sky? Through what mysterious alchemy did the random interactions of gross individual strivings bring into existence, in the course of half a century, one of the most unexpected and grandiose architectural symphonies of the world? The Manhattan skyline thus symbolizes a very perplexing aspect of human life— the fact that mankind can convert crude appetites into the splendors of civilization and transmute greed into spirituality. Throughout historical times, man has created better than he planned and than he knew. Works of lasting value have often emerged from efforts aimed at the satisfaction of immediate and material urges.

Entering Manhattan by the Brooklyn Bridge also contributes to this schizophrenic view of mankind. Both sides of the bridge are crowded with tense human beings, aggressive and often cruel, bent on extracting money from each other and obsessed with the pursuit of gross sensual pleasures. As judged from their behavior, most of them appear unaware of the sky; they seem undisturbed by the brutality of the noise, by the harshness of the artificial lights, by the uncouthness of the environment in which they function. Automobiles, trucks, and electric trains generate on the pavement of the bridge a deafening vibration, creating a metallic kind of hell in which men seem condemned to move mechanically and endlessly. But the bridge itself is like a gigantic diaphanous web stretched across the sky, indeed like a lyre on the strings of which light plays at all hours of the day and of the night, singing the poesy of industrial civilization.

The massive pillars of the Brooklyn Bridge evoke ancient temples in which profound mysteries were once enacted. This illusion seems to become reality at night, when Manhattan sparkles and vibrates through millions of illuminated windows, each one of them a symbol of man's passionate struggle for power and for creation. And there comes to mind the memory of J. A. Roebling, the architect of the bridge, who died from a wound received during the first stages of the construction, and his son Washington Roebling, who continued the task. Washington Roebling's health broke under the crushing load of responsibilities, but though paralyzed, he continued to supervise the work from his bedroom window. The Roeblings' lives, thus dedicated to the construction of this poetical masterpiece of steel and stone, show man at his highest—more concerned with worthy creation than with health and comfort.

It is clear that the most profoundly different attributes still coexist today in all men, as well as in their works—from greed and cruelty to asceticism and self-sacrifice, from natural earthiness to the highest aspirations, from materialistic achievements to spiritual ecstasy. This pluralistic character of human nature makes the science of humanity much more complex than the sciences concerned with matter or with other living things, and it poses to sociology and to human medicine problems vastly different from those of veterinary medicine and of general biology.

# The Genius of Design

I HAVE COME to this conference because it deals with a problem that is at the heart of my profession as a biologist. Like you, I would like to learn how human beings and all other living things can live and function effectively on the earth. I say on this earth because despite what may happen next month, when astronauts will land on the moon, we have not been designed to live and function anywhere but on this earth. Furthermore, all of us become so shaped by the environment in which we have been born and in which we function that we cannot deny our origins and reject our past without losing a part of our essential biological and mental being.

You see: I am a biologist!

During the past three days, I have had a feeling that we are attending not a conference on design but a conference on antidesign. Our discussions have proceeded with a tacit assumption that if we could correct a few of the ills of our society, everything would be all right. Society and technology could then proceed on their own course without the positive and creative intervention by which human beings determine what they want the world to be.

I take a very positive and personal attitude toward design. I would define design as the incarnation—the word "incarnation" implies here

"The Rest of Our Lives," *Proceedings* of the International Design Conference in Aspen, Colorado, June 1969, pp. 57–63.

putting flesh on ideas—of one's faith in one's vision of the world. Design implies that a person wants to create a world that fits his own genius.

I shall probably use the word "genius" several times in the course of these remarks. I shall apply it to human beings, I shall apply it to animals, and I shall apply it to the landscape and to nature, because I shall use it in its etymological sense. In the traditional Greco-Roman sense, the word "genius" means the array of attributes that defines the person and makes the person be what he should become. It is the attributes that make a landscape different from other landscapes, that impose constraints upon what we can do with that landscape. Design implies the recognition that each person, each place, each time has its own genius defined by the array of attributes that makes him or it different from anything that has happened before or that will happen again. Design implies a conscious attempt that demands courage and the willingness to integrate these attributes in a new structure that reflects the genius of the designer.

I do not use the word "genius" to denote some extraordinary quality but only to denote the courage to be oneself, to put one's signature on one's own life and on one's own creations.

A corollary of this genius is the humility to grant other people the right to be what they are and become what they choose to be. Throughout all my remarks, I will affirm who I am and what I want the world to be. But in a complementary way, I am obliged to encourage you to do the same, even though I may disagree with your vision.

Design thus demands from each and every one of us an attempt to isolate from the immense welter of experiences and impressions that impinge on us those experiences and impressions that fit our genius and can be integrated into that picture, that reality, that is our individual reality.

Whoever will organize another conference of this sort should have in mind mottoes that come from William Blake in "The Marriage of Heaven and Hell." One is: "Everything possible to be believed is an image of truth." The other is: "What is now proved was once only imagined." These statements affirm that humanity's dignity and power come from our ability to imagine the world so as to have it become what we want it to be. The world can become what you want only if you have the courage to act on what you imagine.

Another motto might be taken from Shelley's "Defense of Poetry." "We want the creative faculty to imagine that which we know." The word "imagine" as used by Shelley has a very powerful meaning—namely, that we must organize the facts as we know them into an image of our own: in other words, into a design.

One can readily develop a philosophy of design out of these mottoes, but it must be based on the unchangeable biological nature of man and on the ecological characteristics of the earth environment. At all costs, we must respect the identity of each individual component of the system with which we work. We may select among those components, but we must respect their individuality. This is essential to mental sanity as well as to biological sanity. It imposes the recognition of variety as an essential component of design.

There is another aspect of design that appears in contradiction with the need for variety and variability, yet is equally valid because it is complementary. No system can survive, whether a human society or an animal society, without achieving the kind of unified structure that makes every component relate to every other. There has to be some kind of internal coherence that imposes constraint on the designer, whatever he is concerned with.

There comes to my mind, as I speak, another phrase that might serve as a useful guide for the planning of a conference on design. It comes from Marianne Moore's definition of poetry. According to her, the poem is "an imaginary garden with real toads." The imaginary garden is that concept of reality that we create out of the bewildering confusion of reality; the real toads are the actual components of life that are there in the living structure of the garden.

Why have I felt so disturbed by the discussions of the past three days? Perhaps I can explain by calling to mind the poster announcing the conference. You will recall that it shows a pyramid, a cube, and a sphere—in other words, well-defined structures—covered by a cloth that half-conceals their form, and little men standing on top of the cloth to lift it. I take this poster as a symbol of the illusion—an illusion that has been expressed time and time again during the past three days—that the rest of our lives, the future, the world in which we live our own lives is more or less predetermined. Those cubes, those spheres, and those pyramids represent the structure of our society, and all those little men will lift the cloth to unveil that predetermined future.

I hate to be placed on top of all these structures as one of the little men. The most important component of the drawing should be a big man, big in size, big in illusions, big in courage: willing not only to unveil the future but to destroy what is under the cloth if it does not fit his faith, his image of what he wants the world to become. In any case, it is very unscientific.

Why should I use the word "scientific"? It is just plain nonsensical to believe that the world is shaped, that the future is determined, by what is already present under the cloth.

The future has never been the predictable consequence of antecedent events but rather of the choices and decisions by individual men. Jesus and his followers upset, within fifty years, the powerful administrative structure of the Roman Empire. A century ago, the Bohemians upset the academic art and bourgeois conventions of Paris. France and the world have been different places ever since.

Those structures under the cloth can be destroyed by those who have conviction and courage enough to state what they do not like and what they want to happen.

The slogan "Make love not war" may be getting a little thin and worn out. Nevertheless, it will remain important in the history of mankind not for what it means literally but because it is proving right now a powerful factor in determining international politics—as powerful as Einstein's formula of the equivalence of man and energy. The slogan "Make love not war" is a force that Washington has to take into consideration just as much as the availability of nuclear weapons. It provides a telling example of how human beings who have convictions can change the course of events against all the power of technology and the power of political structures.

The shapes under the cloth are irrelevant to the future of our lives for other more concrete reasons. Those who speak about the future assume that the mechanical, technological forces that have been set in motion will inevitably shape our lives. That is not the way things happen historically. There is quite another force to be reckoned with here: this is the fact that our needs, potentialities, and limitations have not changed for 100,000 years. The genetic endowment of humankind that determines how we function has not changed since the late Stone Age. Each and every one of us, whatever the outward expressions of his daily mood may be, continues to function with the same inner forces, the same biological needs, that existed in the Paleolithic hunter and the Neolithic farmer.

Most of the problems that disturb us today—the college crisis, the fact that the natural world is being degraded, the disturbance in human relationships—all these problems have well-defined biological components that are rooted in man's unchangeable nature.

If human life, our societies, and the quality of our environment are to be saved, it will be through mechanisms very different from those described by the futurologists, who pretend they can give a picture of what the world will be like in the year 2000. I have in mind the book by Herman Kahn and Anthony Wiener, of which Tony Wiener gave you an abstract at this conference. It is a scholarly work except that it deals only with the trivialities of our times. It does not touch on any of the problems that concern you now or will concern you in the future—the problems that have to be solved in order to make the world really different from what it is today, not just more of the same. The book does not even touch on any of the obvious environmental problems that have to be solved within the next twenty years if we are to survive.

Tony Wiener must, actually, share many of my concerns, because at every point in his presentation, he expressed doubt whether the facts he was reporting were really as important as is commonly thought. At the end of his presentation—as, by the way, at the end of their book—he made the explicit statement that after all, the technological miracles predicted might not be very important, because human beings are more deeply concerned about other things.

Now to return to that poster. The cloth that covers the pyramid, the cube, the sphere looks like a shroud, and is indeed a shroud. It's right that it should look like a shroud, because the structures underneath are dead—or dying, at least. I hope that young people among you are going to destroy them.

Why should it be that so many intelligent people have spoken on this platform during the past three days and have made statements that seem to imply acceptance of the fact that the rest of our lives is going to be what futurologists tell us? I think it's because nobody tells the truth. Not that the speakers have lied, but those who have provided them with so-called information have not told the whole truth.

Why should there be all these errors of fact and misuse of words among intelligent people? First of all, there is the fact that, contrary to what is being said, communication has not improved and, in fact, is breaking down. The technology of communication has nothing to do with the ability of human beings to perceive and to integrate the information that they receive through mechanical means. What the technology of communication does is to transmit certain signs devoid of all the rich connotations and overtones that any one of those signs should have. The technology cannot cure the intellectual dishonesty that burdens its channels today.

It is intellectual dishonesty that makes promises that are not warranted, only in the hope of stirring up interest and, perhaps, obtaining a handsome research grant from some office in Washington or some wealthy foundation.

Even more dangerous and more universal is intellectual escapism, the attempt to escape the real problems around us. Typical is the endless discussion among humanists as well as scientists about the prospect of manipulating man's genetic endowment. This is a wonderfully entertaining, titillating kind of science fiction. We organize meetings about it in all sorts of pleasant places to talk about it, and that saves us from the responsibility of walking across the street, where 100,000 children are being poisoned every day by lead in paint. A large part of mental retardation in our city population comes from something as trivial as lead poisoning from paint. Something can be done immediately about this problem, but it is not being done because it is not of sufficient interest or as exciting intellectually as talking about changing the genetic nature of man.

Let me restate in a few simple words what I regard as the biological determinants and constraints of design. The first point is that the human being has not changed genetically and will not change in the foreseeable future. Our biological equipment is still the same as that of the Paleolithic hunter and the Neolithic farmer. Through cultural processes, the activities of our mind have changed but not our genetic constitution.

The second point is that each person is unique. Each one of you certainly believes that he is different from everybody else in this room, but biological and mental uniqueness goes even beyond what you realize. To begin with, each of us differs from other human beings in genetic constitution, except in the case of identical twins. Statistically, it is impossible that at any time in the past there has been anyone identical with you genetically and that there will be anyone identical with you in the future. Each person is unique, unprecedented, unrepeatable.

Mention of identical twins raises another aspect of the singular, unrepeatable identity of each of us. It is true that identical twins are endowed with the same array of genes. What people become, however, is not determined only by the genes they inherit from their parents. Genes govern the person's responses to environmental stimuli, but the effects of these responses on the individual are different. Because environmental stimuli differ from person to person in the unique developmental history of each of us, we become different people through the responses we make to the environment and to all the stimuli that impinge on us throughout our lives. Most important are the environmental forces that act on the child during the first five or six years of life, including prenatal life. This fact imposes on us an enormous responsibility to learn more about the manner in which the environment shapes young people and thereby influences their future. It also has large implications with regard to our concept of freedom.

I believe in individual freedom, in free will. Freedom, however, is something that you can exercise only if conditions are right. Children born and raised in a slum have, in theory, as much freedom, free will, as those who haven't been raised in a slum. But in practice, they are conditioned, both in a negative and in a positive way, by the slum environment that shaped the expressions of their genetic endowment. Slum children are not entirely free because they do not have the chance to develop at the critical time those components of their potential individuality that would make it possible for them to become something else, to choose something else.

In fact, I am not thinking only about slum children. The most deprived children in the world today may be the children born and raised in the pretentious suburbs of New York City, where the range of their stimuli is so narrow, and especially where the quality of those stimuli is so cheap. As you see, I am beginning to link the total environment, the way we design it, with what human beings have become. I have spoken of the genius of each person, that which is unique to him. But there is also the genius of the place. All ancient literatures have embodied the concept of genius or spirit of the place in the forms of gods and goddesses. The spirit of the place determines what the place can become. The formal gardens of Italy and France fit well in certain parts of Italy and France, whereas the magnificent parks of England would not do well under the same conditions.

Let me try to convey to you the sense of what I'm trying to say by quoting a letter of Horace Walpole. Walpole was very influential in formulating the theory of the English park. He had gone to France at a time when it was fashionable in France to imitate everything English. In that letter home, he wrote: "The French will never succeed in having trees, parks, and lawns as beautiful as ours until they have as rotten a climate."

This is a profound statement. For each type of country, for each type of climate, for each type of landscape, we must learn to recognize the genius of the place, and we must work with it. There is a feedback from environment to us. It is this feedback that permits us to discover what we are, discover what the environment is capable of becoming, and thereby create the integrated structure that is the mark of all great civilizations.

What we need is faith in ourselves. The ability to create that imaginary garden demands not only intelligence and knowledge but also courage. The courage I urge you all to seek and to possess was well designed by Albert Camus. First I shall try to make his point in English: "I have always thought that if a man who has hope in the human condition is a fool, then a man who despairs of events is a coward." The word "events" is of great importance; what Camus wanted to convey was not just a literary faith in man but a sense of commitment, the willingness to do something concrete for what you believe in. The original French is more concise: *"J'ai toujours pensé que si l'homme que esperait dans la condition humaine etait fou, celui qui desperait des evenements etait un lache."*

I have looked at many young faces during the past three days. I have admired your faces. I perceive what richness there is in them. But I have a feeling that you are being betrayed, that you are not being told what you can do and, worse, that confidence in yourself is being destroyed. I have rapidly improvised my speech this morning in the faith that despite power structure, soulless technologies, and the mechanization of life, we will prevail because we can remain the architects of our future.

# PART VIII

## Think Globally,
## Act Locally

Whereas most important problems of life on earth
are fundamentally the same everywhere, the solutions to these problems are always conditioned by
local circumstances and choices.

# Local Solutions to
# Global Problems

ON AMERICAN and Canadian college campuses where I recently lectured, most students were intensely concerned with environmental and social problems, but chiefly in their large-scale aspects, and preferably at the national and global levels. Faculty as well as students were surprised and somewhat annoyed when I suggested that instead of being exclusively concerned with the nation or the world as a whole, they should first consider more local situations—for example, the messiness of public rooms on their campus and the disorder of their social relationships. My message to them was that thinking at a global level is a useful and exciting intellectual activity but no substitute for the work needed to solve practical problems at home. If we really want to contribute to the welfare of humankind and of our planet, the best place to start is in our own community, and its fields, rivers, marshes, coastlines, roads, and streets, as well as with its social problems.

I had many occasions to ponder on the local aspects of global problems while participating directly or indirectly in the huge international conferences organized during the 1970s under the auspices of the United Nations to discuss the contemporary problems of humankind. There was a pattern common to these megaconferences. They all began with resounding statements of global concern and with clarion calls for

*Celebrations of Life* (New York: McGraw-Hill, 1981), pp. 83–87. Copyright © 1981 by The René Dubos Center for Human Environments, Inc.

international thinking and action. As the meetings went on, however, discussions of concrete issues soon became hopelessly diluted in a flood of ideological verbiage unrelated to practical action. At the end of the conference, the efforts to set down a statement of consensus yielded resolutions so broad and so vague in meaning that few of them could be converted into action programs. As a result of these observations, I came to believe that such international conferences are a waste of time.

I have now changed my mind, for two different reasons. On the one hand, the megaconferences of the 1970s generated a global awareness of certain dangers that are now threatening all nations, the rich as well as the poor. This is not a small achievement, because thinking globally is not easy for human beings. As a species, *Homo sapiens* has evolved in small social groups and in limited physical environments, so that our intellectual and emotional processes are not biologically adapted to global or long-range views of any situation. It is only when people from all parts of the world have the opportunity to listen to each other's problems that they realize, even though with difficulty and slowly, how crowded we are on our small planet, how limited are its resources, and how multifarious are the dangers to which we are all increasingly exposed.

The megaconferences of the 1970s had the additional merit of bringing to light the diversity of physical and social conditions on our planet and of dramatizing the consequences of this diversity. While there was much posturing during the conferences, the official delegates learned from representatives of other countries that global problems appear in a different light depending on local situations.

The environmental purists of the Western world discovered, for example, that abject poverty is the worst form of pollution and that many poor countries have legitimate reasons to be more interested in economic development than in the ecological gospel. At the 1976 U.N. Conference on the Habitat, in Vancouver, the poor nations naturally complained of being exploited by the rich industrialized countries, but they also realized that they had much to learn from Western civilization concerning advanced technologies applicable to such problems as water supply, low-cost housing, or sustainable rural development—let alone industrial development.

The most valuable achievement of the international conferences was probably, however, to reveal that the best and commonly the only possible way to deal with global problems is not through a global approach but through the search for techniques best suited to the natural, social, and economic conditions peculiar to each locality. Our planet is so diverse, from all points of view, that its problems can be tackled effectively only by dealing with them at the regional level, in their unique physical, climatic, and cultural contexts. Three examples will suffice to illustrate the necessity of the local approach to global problems.

The recommendations of the Vancouver Habitat Conference were explicit with regard to the fact that all people need clean water and decent shelters. The techniques required to meet these obvious biological necessities, however, must be designed to fit local conditions, such as the density of the human settlements, the topographical, geographical, and climatic conditions, and of course, the economic resources. The design of shelters is further complicated by local social habits and tastes. The recommendations concerning cultural matters or quality of life had to be even less specific, because these values have intense local and historical characteristics that transcend scientific determinism and definitions.

The word "desertification" refers not to natural deserts but to areas that are being rendered desertic by human activities, especially by overgrazing and by the use of wood as fuel. Since desertification is a problem of increasing gravity in many parts of the world, the United Nations Environment Programme (UNEP) first attempted to control its spread with projects that were transnational, in the sense that they dealt with vast continuous areas stretching across several countries. However, this transnational approach had to be abandoned, because the social and agricultural practices leading to desertification differ from country to country. The desert unit of UNEP has recently decided that before receiving international help, the individual countries must formulate their own projects fitted to their particular agricultural and social practices.

Until 1973, the low cost of petroleum and natural gas, and the ease with which these fuels could be shipped and used anywhere in the world, created the illusion that fairly uniform technological policies could be formulated for the planet as a whole. However, petroleum and gas are becoming much more costly and soon will be in short supply. For this reason, plans are being made to replace them with coal, which is much more plentiful, and eventually by different kinds of renewable sources of energy, such as nuclear fission (and perhaps fusion), solar radiation, the wind, the tides, the waves, and the different kinds of organic materials grouped under the name of biomass. Each one of these sources of energy has advantages and objections peculiar to it, and unlike petroleum and gas, each one is much better suited to one natural or social situation than to others. For example, coal is not available everywhere; its shipment over long distances is costly and its mining results in types of environmental degradation that differ from region to region. Solar radiation has a better chance to be developed on a large scale in regions of intense insolation; the wind, where it blows in a fairly dependable manner; the biomass, in densely wooded areas; nuclear fission, in industrialized countries that are deficient in other energy resources and where the public is therefore more likely to accept the risk of massive unpredictable accidents.

Just as the shift from hydroelectric power to coal, then to petroleum and gas, made certain heavy industries move from New England to the Appalachians and to Texas, so we can anticipate that future industrial developments will differ from one place to another when local solutions to the global energy problem have been worked out.

In my opinion, it is fortunate that practical necessities will compel different local solutions to global problems. Globalization inevitably implies more standardization and therefore a decrease in diversity, which in turn would slow down the rate of social innovation. Another danger of globalization is that in excessive interdependence, systems may fail to function properly as a result of accident or sabotage. Finally, we may soon reach a point, if we have not reached it already, at which technological, economic, and social systems become so huge and so complex that they cannot be readily adapted to new conditions and cannot continue to be really creative. The human mind cannot cope with the comprehension, let alone the management, of systems that are too large or too complex, even when these are of human origin. In contrast, there is a better chance for adaptability, creativity, safety, and manageability in multiple fairly small systems, aware and tolerant of one another but jealous of their autonomy.

Skepticism concerning the value of globalization does not imply isolationism. The ideal for our planet would seem to be not a World Government but a World Order, in which social units maintain their identity while interplaying with one another through a rich communications network. This is beginning to happen through the specialized agencies of the United Nations (there are at least sixteen of them at the present time), such as the World Health Organization, the International Labor Office, the Food and Agricultural Organization, the World Meteorological Organization, and the United Nations Environment Programme. Their existence and success justify the hope that we can create a new kind of global unity out of the ever-increasing diversity of social structures.

Focusing on a local problem is thus very different from retreating into isolationism. In fact, it necessarily requires the operation of several kinds of social networks involving scientists, industrialists, politicians, and private citizens. Controlling water pollution in the Great Lakes is making some progress through the enactment of multiple complex agreements at industrial and political levels between the United States and Canada. Similar progress has also been made in the case of the Rhine to the point that the four nations involved—Switzerland, France, Germany, and Holland—have formulated and actually put into action a system of fines to be paid by the industries that pollute the river. The fate of the Mediterranean appeared hopeless a few years ago but now, after decades of incredibly complex negotiations involving all the Mediterranean countries, there is some hope that this highly local problem can be progressively solved through agreements concerning the control of domestic and industrial discharges.

# Franciscan Conservation vs.
# Benedictine Stewardship

HISTORY IS REPLETE with ecological disasters; the most flourishing lands of antiquity seem to have been under a malediction. Mesopotamia, Persia, Egypt, West Pakistan were once the sites of civilizations that remained powerful and wealthy for great periods of time but are now among the poorest areas of the world. Their lands are barren deserts, many of their ancient cities abandoned, most of their people so poor, malnourished, and diseased that they have no memory or even awareness of their magnificent past. Since the same situation is true for much of India, China, Southeast Asia, and Latin America, it would seem that all civilizations are mortal.

Civil strife, warfare, famine, and disease certainly contributed to the demise of ancient Eastern civilizations, but the desolate appearance of their lands today would seem to indicate that the primary cause of the decline was the depletion of the soil caused by prolonged occupation by large numbers of people. Exhaustion or destruction of water resources probably followed and dealt the final blow. Babylonian civilization, for example, disappeared after its system of irrigation was destroyed by the Mongols, but its environment had begun to degenerate long before this final disaster.

Reprinted with permission of Charles Scribner's Sons, an imprint of Macmillan Publishing Company, from A God Within, pp. 153–74. Copyright © 1972 by René Dubos.

The English archaeologist Sir Mortimer Wheeler has examined in detail the fate of Mohenjo Daro, the archaeologically famous city-civilization that flourished from 2500 to 1500 B.C. on the plains of the Indus River in present-day Pakistan. This civilization, which prospered some four thousand years ago, at the same time as Mesopotamian and Egyptian civilizations, differed from them in its architecture, art, and technology. Like them, however, it disappeared, because, in Wheeler's words, it was "steadily wearing out its landscape." In modern ecological jargon this means that its environment was being destroyed by overuse or misuse. Pessimists have therefore much historical evidence for their thesis that civilizations inevitably ruin their environments.

There is, however, another side to the question. The American geographer C. O. Sauer is of the opinion that "the worn-out parts of the world are the recent settlements, not the lands of old civilizations." For more than a thousand years, Japanese agriculture has remained highly productive without decreasing the fertility of the soil or spoiling the beauty of the landscape. In Western Europe also, many areas opened to agriculture by the Neolithic settlers remain fertile today after several thousand years of almost continuous use. This immense duration of certain cultivated landscapes contributes a sense of tranquillity to many parts of the Old World; it inspires confidence that mankind can survive its present ordeals and learn to manage the land for the sake of the future.

These contrasting views of the relationships between civilization and the land may not be as incompatible as they appear. All the great Eastern civilizations that wore out their soil were located in and around semiarid and arid zones. Under such climatic conditions, which prevail over approximately 35 percent of the world's land mass, productive agriculture depends on irrigation, and damage to the soil can be rapid and irreversible in the time scale of human life. In contrast, Western Europe, Japan, and certain other parts of Asia are blessed with a greater and especially a more constant rainfall, which enables their soils to recover fairly rapidly after they have been damaged by ecological mismanagement. Climatic conditions, however, cannot account entirely for the fate of the world's civilizations. They do not explain the sudden disappearance of the Maya, Khmer, and other great civilizations that once flourished in humid countries. In Mexico, the end of the Teotihuacan culture occurred suddenly, around A.D. 800, during a moist period. The primary cause was probably the fact that the protective forests of the region had been cut. The erosion that ensued, coupled with the destructive effects of cultivation, was apparently sufficient to offset the blessings of returning moisture. Ecological mismanagement was also responsible for the deterioration of agriculture around the Mediterranean basin in the ancient world and is now creating similar problems in many temperate regions, including the United States. The land has remained fertile under intense cultivation only where farmers have used it according to sound ecological principles. Unwise management of nature or of technology can destroy civilization in any climate and land, under any political system.

Environmental degradation in the modern world is commonly blamed on modern technology, but the roots of the problem go far deeper. When George Perkins Marsh visited the Near East in the middle of the nineteenth century, he was shocked to find deserted cities, silted harbors, and wastelands instead of flourishing civilizations. "Technology" could not then be blamed for soil turned barren, forests destroyed, and ancient bodies of water replaced by salt and sand flats. Marsh properly concluded that sociological errors discouraging good agricultural practice had led to the deterioration of agriculture in the Mediterranean countries, and he recognized also that good agricultural practices had preserved the quality of the land in other parts of the world. His book *Man and Nature*, first published in 1864 and revised in 1874 under the new title *The Earth as Modified by Human Action*, advocated conservation practices but chiefly from the agricultural point of view.

While Marsh emphasized the quality of agricultural lands, another aspect of ecological concern was taking shape in the United States—the efforts to save the quality of nature. One of the most articulate spokesmen of the new movement was the American ecologist Aldo Leopold (1887–1948), whose primary commitment was to wildlife and to undisturbed wilderness. Leopold advocated an ecological conscience in all aspects of man's relation with nature; as one of the founders of the Wilderness Society, he was influential in securing government approval for the protection of America's first wilderness area at the head of the Gila River in New Mexico. He preached a "land ethic" in his book *A Sand County Almanac*, which has become the Holy Writ of American conservationists.

Marsh's influence was not great, probably because he wrote at a time when the methods of modern agriculture were producing enormous increases of crop yields, and his teachings therefore seemed irrelevant. In contrast, Leopold rapidly gained a large following because the obvious damage done to nature by the new technologies had created a public mood receptive to his plea for a new ethic of man's relation to nature.

A curious expression of the present public concern for the environmental crisis has been the theory, which became academically fashionable during the 1960s, that the Judeo-Christian tradition is responsible for the desecration of nature in the Western world. This view seems to have been publicized for the first time around 1950 by the Zen Buddhist Daisetz Suzuki. But it was given academic glamour by Lynn White, Jr., professor of history at the University of California at Los Angeles, in a much publicized lecture entitled "The Historical Roots of Our Ecologic Crisis." It is a measure of its popular success that this lecture has been reproduced *in extenso*, not only in learned and popular magazines but also in *The Oracle*, the multicolored, now defunct journal of the hippie culture in San Francisco. Whether valid or not, White's thesis demands attention because it has become an article of faith for many conservationists, ecologists, economists, and even theologians.

The thesis runs approximately as follows: The ancient Oriental and Greco-Roman religions took it for granted that animals, trees, rivers, mountains, and other natural objects can have spiritual significance just like people and therefore deserve respect. According to the Judeo-Christian religions, in contrast, humanity is apart from nature. The Jews embraced monotheism, but with a distinctly anthropomorphic concept of God. The Christians developed this trend still further by shifting religion toward an exclusive concern with human beings. It is explicitly stated in Chapter 1 of Genesis that man was shaped in the image of God and given dominion over creation. This chapter has provided the excuse for a policy of exploitation of nature, regardless of the consequences. Christianity developed, of course, along different lines in different parts of the world. In its Eastern forms, its ideal was the saint dedicated to prayer and contemplation, whereas in its Western forms it was the saint dedicated to action. Because of this geographical difference in Christian attitudes, the most profound effects of humanity's impact on nature have been in the countries of Western civilization. To a large extent, furthermore, modern technology is the expression of the Judeo-Christian belief that we have a rightful dominion over nature. Biblical teachings thus account for the fact that Western man has had no scruples in using the earth's resources for his own selfish interests or in exploring the moon to satisfy his curiosity, even if this means the raping of nature and the contamination of the lunar surface.

Since the roots of the environmental crisis are so largely religious, the remedy must also be essentially religious: "I personally doubt," White writes, "that ecologic backlashes can be avoided simply by applying to our problems more science and more technology." For this reason, he suggests that the only solution may be a return to the humble attitude of the early Franciscans. Francis of Assisi worshiped all of nature and believed in the virtue of humility, not only for the individual person but for man as a species. We should try to follow in his footsteps, so as to "depose man from his monarchy over creation, and abandon our aggressive attitude toward Nature." "I propose Francis as a patron saint of ecologists" is the conclusion of White's essay.

In my opinion, the theory that Judeo-Christian attitudes are responsible for the development of technology and for the ecological crisis is at best a historical half-truth. Erosion of the land, destruction of animal and plant species, excessive exploitation of natural resources, and ecological disasters are not peculiar to the Judeo-Christian tradition and to scientific technology. At all times, and all over the world, thoughtless human interventions into nature have had a variety of disastrous consequences, or at least have changed profoundly the complexion of nature.

The process began some ten thousand years ago, long before the Bible was written. A dramatic extinction of several species of large mammals and terrestrial birds occurred at the very beginning of the Neolithic period, coincident with the expansion of agricultural man. His eagerness to protect cultivated fields and flocks may account for the attitude "if it moves, kill it," which is rooted deep in folk traditions over much of the world. Nor was the destruction of large animals motivated only by utilitarian reasons. In Egypt, the pharaohs and the nobility arranged for large numbers of beasts to be driven into compounds where they were trapped and then shot with arrows. The Assyrians, too, were as vicious destroyers of animals—lions and elephants, for example—as they were of people. Ancient hunting practices greatly reduced the populations of some large animal species and in some cases led to their eradication. This destructive process has continued throughout historical times, not only in the regions peripheral to the eastern Mediterranean but also in other parts of the world. In Australia, the nomadic aborigines, with their fire sticks, had far-reaching effects on the environment. Early explorers commented upon the aborigines' widespread practice of setting fires, which, under the semi-arid conditions of Australia, drastically altered the vegetation cover, caused erosion, and destroyed much of the native fauna. Huge tracts of forest land were thus converted into open grasslands, and the populations of large marsupials were greatly reduced.

Plato declared his belief that Greece was eroded before his time as a result of deforestation and overgrazing. Erosion resulting from human activities probably caused the end of the Teotihuacan civilization in ancient Mexico. Early peoples, aided especially by that most useful and most noxious of all animals the Mediterranean goat, were probably responsible for more deforestation and erosion than all the bulldozers of the Judeo-Christian world.

Nor is there reason to believe that Oriental civilizations have been more respectful of nature than Judeo-Christian civilizations. As shown by the British scientist and historian Joseph Needham, China was far ahead of Europe in scientific and technological development until the seventeenth century A.D. and used technology on a massive and often destructive scale. Many passages in T'ang and Sung poetry indicate that the barren hills of central and northern China were once heavily forested, and there is good reason to believe that there, as elsewhere, treelessness and soil erosion are the results of fires and overgrazing. Even the Buddhists contributed largely to the deforestation of Asia in order to build their temples; it has been estimated that in some areas temple building was responsible for much more than half of the timber consumption.

The Chinese attitude of respect for nature probably arose, in fact, as a response to the damage done in antiquity. Furthermore, this respect does not go as far as artistic and poetical expressions would indicate. The classic nature poets of China write as if they had achieved identification with the cosmos, but in reality most of them were retired bureaucrats living on estates in which nature was carefully trimmed and managed by gardeners. In Japan, also, the beautifully artificial gardens and oddly shaped pine trees could hardly be regarded as direct expression of nature; they constitute rather a symbolic interpretation of an intellectual attitude toward scenery. Wildlife has been so severely reduced in modern Japan that sparrows and swallows are the only kinds of birds remaining of the dozens of species that used to pass through Tokyo a century ago.

One of the best-documented examples of ecological mismanagement in the ancient world is the progressive destruction of the groves of cedars and cypresses that in the past were the glory of Lebanon. The many references to these noble evergreen groves in ancient inscriptions and in the Old Testament reveal that the Egyptian pharaohs and the kings of Assyria and Babylon carried off enormous amounts of the precious timber for the temples and palaces of their capital cities. In a taunt against Nebuchadnezzar, king of Babylon, the prophet Isaiah refers to the destructive effects of these logging expeditions. The Roman emperors, especially Hadrian, extended still further the process of deforestation. Today the few surviving majestic cedars are living testimony to what the coniferous forests of Lebanon were like before the ruthless exploitation that long preceded the Judeo-Christian and technological age.

All over the globe and at all times in the past, people have pillaged nature and disturbed the ecological equilibrium, usually out of ignorance, but also because they have always been more concerned with immediate advantages than with long-range goals. Moreover, they could not foresee that they were preparing for ecological disasters, nor did they have a real choice of alternatives. If we are more destructive now than we were in the past, it is because there are more of us and because we have at our command more powerful means of destruction, not because we have been influenced by the Bible. In fact, the Judeo-Christian peoples were probably the first to develop on a large scale a pervasive concern for land management and an ethic of nature.

Among the great Christian teachers, none is more identified with an ethic of nature than Francis of Assisi (1182?–1226), who treated all living things and inanimate objects as if they were his brothers and sisters. His tradition has continued to express itself in many forms among Judeo-Christian people—as, for example, in the philosophical concept that all living things can be arranged in a continuous series, the Great Chain of Being; in Albert Schweitzer's reverence for life; in the semitranscendental utterances of writers such as Wordsworth, Thoreau, and Walt Whitman. The Darwinian theory of evolution provided a scientific basis for the intuitive belief in the brotherhood of all living things. Most modern men have come to accept or at least to tolerate the thought, so disturbing a century ago, that we belong to a natural line of descent that includes all animals and plants. It is not unlikely that the Franciscan respect for nature—in its various philosophical, scientific, and religious forms—has played some part in the emergence of the doctrine of conservation in the countries of Western civilization and its rapid spread during the past century.

While it is easy to believe that wilderness should be preserved wherever possible, the reasons generally given to advocate the maintenance of undisturbed ecological systems and the preservation of endangered species are not entirely convincing. Despite what the conservationists say, nature will go on even if whooping cranes, condors, or redwoods are exterminated, just as it has gone on after the extinction of millions of other species that have vanished from the earth in the course of time. The fossil beds, with their myriad of long-vanished forms, testify to the fact that man is not the first agency to alter the ecological composition of the earth.

Environments that are being upset by smogs, pesticides, or strip mining are not destroyed thereby; they will become different by evolving in directions determined by these challenges. We may not like the consequences of these changes for ethical, esthetic, or economic reasons, but it is nevertheless certain that the disturbed environments will eventually achieve some new kind of biologic status, as has been the case in the past after all great ecological disasters.

Changes occur even under natural conditions, because nature continuously evolves. The classical concept of "ecologic climax" is a postulate that tends to replace reality. Climax assumes the end of change, but the ecological reality is a dynamic state; the biological equilibrium is never reached, because natural and human influences continuously alter the interplay between the various components of the ecosystem.

Final or stable communities are exceptional in nature, and they are impossible wherever there is human activity. Every form of agriculture, even the most primitive, involves the creation of artificial ecosystems. Since most of the temperate world has now been transformed by human beings, the balance of nature is at best an artificial and static concept unrelated to the conditions that prevail in most of the world.

Although the need to maintain the balance of nature cannot provide a valid case for conservation, there are other strong reasons for protecting environmental quality and preserving as much wilderness as possible. Some of these reasons were cogently stated in the 1860s by George P. Marsh:

> It is desirable that some large and easily accessible region of American soil should remain as far as possible in its primitive condition, at once a museum for the instruction of students, a garden for the recreation of lovers of nature, and an asylum where indigenous trees . . . plants . . . beasts may dwell and perpetuate their kind.

It has now become obvious that the pollution of rivers and lakes is creating grave economic problems, because the United States is coming close to a shortage of water for home and industrial needs. Polluted air damages buildings and vegetation; automobile exhausts kill evergreens and dogwoods along the highways, as well as the celebrated pines of Rome. In all its forms air pollution is deleterious to human health and increases medical problems.

A scientific justification for taking a conservative attitude toward changes in nature is that the long-range outcome of human interventions into natural ecosystems cannot be predicted with certainty. Past experience has shown that many of these interventions have resulted in unforeseen ecological disturbances, often disastrous for man himself.

Another justification is that the progressive loss of wilderness decreases biological diversity. This, in turn, renders ecological systems less stable and less likely to remain suitable for a variety of species, including us. Conservation of natural systems is the best guarantee against irrevocable loss of diversity and the simplest way to minimize ecological disasters. Consider what might happen if—as has been seriously suggested by some "experts" in lumbering companies— native forests were completely replaced by artificial forests. This could certainly be accomplished by planting seedlings of the few desired species and growing them under controlled conditions with generous use of fertilizers and protective sprays. The artificial forest would probably be economically profitable for years or decades, but if such tree farms became victims of infection or other ecological accidents, and if there were no sizable natural forest communities left in the climatic and soil regions where the artificial ones had been established, starting the reforestation process anew would be extremely difficult. Undisturbed native marshes, prairies, deserts, and forests are at present the best assurance against the potential hazards inherent in the truncated, oversimplified ecosystems that are being created by the monocultures of a few strains selected for specialized properties, especially in view of the fact that these strains require massive use of chemical fertilizers, plant hormones, pesticides, and other synthetic products. The prospect of vast blighted zones choked with weeds and scarred by erosion is more than a Wellsian fantasy.

Above and beyond the economic and ecological reason for conservation, there are esthetic and moral ones that are even more compelling. The statement that the earth is our mother is more than a sentimental platitude: we are shaped by the earth. The characteristics of the environment in which we develop condition our biological and mental being and the quality of our life. Even were it only for selfish reasons, therefore, we must maintain variety and harmony in nature. Fortunately, as ecologists have estimated, the amount of ecological reserves needed in North America approximates 10 million acres, which is far less than 1 percent of the total land area of the continent. But even if the economic impact were greater than this statement suggests, the conservation of wilderness would be justified for a number of spiritual values on which we cannot put a dollar sign. The ever-increasing popularity of the national parks, the presence of aquariums and plants in city apartments, may indicate that pigeons, dogs, cats, and even people do not suffice to make a completely satisfying world. Our separation from the rest of the natural world leaves us with a subconscious feeling that we must retain some contact with wilderness and with as wide a range of living things as possible. The national parks contribute a value that transcends economic considerations and may play a role similar to that of Stonehenge, the Pyramids, Greek temples, Roman ruins, Gothic cathedrals, the Williamsburg restoration, the Gettysburg battlefield, and the holy sites of various religions.

Ian McMillan, a California naturalist, has written of the struggle to save the California condor: "The real importance of saving such things as condors is not so much that we need condors as that we need to save them. We need to exercise and develop the human attributes required in saving condors; for these are the attributes so necessary in working out our own survival." Conservation is based on human value systems; its deepest significance is in the human situation and the human heart. Saving marshlands and redwoods does not need biological justification any more than does opposing callousness and vandalism. The cult of wilderness is not a luxury; it is a necessity for the protection of humanized nature and for the preservation of mental health.

Francis of Assisi preached and practiced absolute identification with nature, but even his immediate followers soon abandoned his romantic and unworldly attitude. They probably realized that we have never been purely worshipers of nature or passive witnesses of our surroundings and natural events. Human life was naturally close to nature during the Stone Age, but Paleolithic hunters and Neolithic farmers altered their environment. By controlling and using fire, domesticating animals and plants, clearing forests, and cultivating crops, they began the process that eventually humanized a large percentage of the earth. Every form of civilization, each in its own way, has since contributed to the shaping of the earth's surface and thus altered the composition of the atmosphere and the waters. Even people who thought they were returning to the ways of nature usually transformed their environment more than they knew. "Sometimes as I drift idly along Walden Pond, I cease to live and I begin to be," Thoreau wrote in his journal. But he used a canoe to drift on the pond and he cleared an area along its shore to grow beans and construct his cabin.

Thus, human life inevitably implies changes in nature. Indeed, we shape our humanness in the very process of interacting constructively with the world around us and milking nature to make it better suited to our needs, wishes, and aspirations. Stonehenge, Angkor Wat, the Parthenon, the Buddhist temples, and the countless other places of worship created by humanity before the Judeo-Christian era represent forms of human intervention that exacted as large a toll from nature as did the construction of the Judeo-Christian shrines or the immense American bridges and industrial plants.

Christianity acknowledged early that human beings differed in their spiritual needs and aspirations; each of the important saints symbolizes a different approach to the human problem. In the article quoted earlier, Lynn White, Jr., suggests that Saint Francis's example can help mankind to achieve a harmonious equality with the rest of creation, as if animals, plants, and even inanimate objects were really our brothers and sisters. This doctrine is not quite congenial to me, because I like gardening and landscaping and therefore tend to impose my own sense of order upon natural processes.

Benedict of Nursia, who was certainly as good a Christian as Francis of Assisi, can be regarded as a patron saint of those who believe that true conservation means not only protecting nature against human misbehavior but also developing human activities that favor a creative, harmonious relationship between ourselves and nature.

When Saint Benedict established his monastery on Monte Cassino during the sixth century, his primary concern was that he and his followers should devote their lives to divine worship. However, though he was an aristocrat, he knew the dangers of physical idleness, and he made it a rule that all monks should work with their hands in the fields and in shops. As a result, the Benedictine monks achieved an intimate relationship with the world around them. One of the still dominant aspects of the Benedictine rule is that to labor is to pray. Saint Benedict had not intended his monks to become scholars. But in the course of time a great tradition of learning and of artistic skills progressively developed in the Benedictine abbeys.

Lynn White, Jr., the very historian who has advocated that ecologists take Saint Francis as their patron saint, has also emphasized the social importance of the fact that "the Benedictine monk was the first scholar to get dirt under his fingernails." For the first time in the history of human institutions, the Benedictine abbeys did not immediately launch into scientific investigations; they encouraged, instead, the combination of physical and intellectual work, destroying the old artificial barrier between the empirical and the speculative, the manual and the liberal arts. This created an atmosphere favorable for the development of knowledge based on experimentation.

The first chapter of Genesis speaks of our dominion over nature. The Benedictine rule in contrast seems inspired rather by the second chapter, in which the Good Lord placed man in the Garden of Eden not as a master but rather in a spirit of stewardship. Throughout the history of the Benedictine order, its monks have actively intervened in nature—as farmers, builders, and scholars. They have brought about profound transformations of soil, water, fauna, and flora, but in such a wise manner that their management of nature has proved compatible in most cases with the maintenance of environmental quality. To this extent, Saint Benedict is much more relevant than Saint Francis to human life in the modern world, and to the human condition in general.

The Benedictine rule was so successful during the early Middle Ages that its monasteries burgeoned over Europe, and their numbers reached many thousands. They differed somewhat in their interpretation of the rule, but all were organized along similar religious and social patterns. All the Benedictine monks and nuns accepted the cloistered life and regarded manual labor not as a regrettable necessity but as an essential part of spiritual discipline. They practiced a democratic administrative system of home rule and tried to achieve a living relationship with the physical world around them. The monastic rule was so broadly human that it permitted different attitudes toward nature and man. For example, while the original Benedictines generally settled on the hills, the monks of the Cistercian branch of the order preferred the valleys. This topographical variation in the location of the monasteries proved to be of great economic and technological significance because it broadened the influence of the Benedictines in the development of Europe.

The Cistercians played a social role of particular importance precisely in this regard, because they established their monasteries in wooded river valleys and marshy lands that were infested with malaria and therefore ill suited to human occupation. With their lay helpers, they cleared the forests and drained the swamps, thus creating, out of the malarious wilderness, farmlands that became healthy and prosperous. They achieved such great fame in the control of malaria by eliminating the swamps that they were entrusted with the task of draining the Roman Campagna.

Cistercian life was, of course, not motivated by the desire to create agricultural lands. A mystic attitude toward nature certainly played a role in their selection of secluded places for the worship of God. Saint Bernard was sensitive to the poetic quality of the site when he chose to establish his Cistercian monastery in Clairvaux:

> That spot has much charm, it greatly soothes weary minds, relieves anxieties and cares, helps souls who seek the Lord greatly to devotion, and recalls to them the thought of the heavenly sweetness to which they aspire. The smiling countenance of the earth is painted with varying colors, the blooming verdure of spring satisfies the eyes, and its sweet odor salutes the nostrils. . . . While I am charmed without by the sweet influence of the beauty of the country, I have not less delight within in reflecting in the mysteries which are hidden beneath it.

Saint Bernard believed that it was the duty of the monks to work as partners of God in improving his creation or at least in giving it a more human expression. Implicit in his writings is the thought that labor is like a prayer that helps in recreating paradise out of chaotic wilderness. While the primary commitment of the monks was to divine worship, they devoted much effort and inventiveness to practical problems, as Arthur O. Lovejoy observed:

> Cistercian monks were so devoted to the Virgin that every one of their hundreds of monasteries was dedicated to her; yet these White Benedictines seem often to have led the way in the use of power. Some of their abbeys had four or five water wheels, each powering a different workshop.

All types of Benedictine monasteries, in fact, were involved in technological activities. The monks developed windmills as sources of power on their holdings. This power was used for the conversion of their agricultural products into manufactured goods—leather, fabrics, paper, and even liqueurs such as Benedictine and Chartreuse, which achieved worldwide fame. Thus these medieval monasteries prepared the ground for the technological era in Europe.

When practiced in the true spirit of the Benedictine rule, monastic life helped the monks to establish close contact with the natural world through the daily and seasonal rituals and through works that were coordinated with cosmic rhythms. The Benedictine rule also inspired a type of communal organization that was both democratic and hierarchic, because each monk or nun had rights in the monastic organization but also had to accept a certain place in the social order. This complex social structure found its expression in an architectural style beautifully adapted to the rituals of monastic life and to the local landscape. Benedictine architecture, in its several various forms, thus achieved a functional beauty that made it a major artistic achievement of Western civilization.

Many human interventions into natural systems have been destructive. Technological man in particular uses landscapes and water, mountains and estuaries, and all types of natural resources for selfish and short-range economic benefits. But his behavior in this regard is not much worse than that of the people whose activities caused erosion in West Pakistan, in the Mediterranean basin, in China, or in Mexico. The solution to the environmental crisis will not be found in a retreat from the Judeo-Christian tradition or from technological civilization; rather, it will require a new definition of progress, based on better knowledge of nature and on a willingness to change our ways of life accordingly. We must learn to recognize the limitations and potentialities of each particular area of the earth, so that we can manipulate it creatively, thereby enhancing present and future human life.

Conservation, according to Leopold, teaches what a land can be, what it should be, what it ought to be. Although this aphorism has much appeal, it is misleading, because it implies a questionable philosophy of ecological determinism and of our relation to nature. It assumes that some invisible hand is guiding biological processes to the one perfect state of ecological harmony among the different components of a particular environment, whereas experience shows that different satisfactory ecosystems can be created out of the same set of environmental conditions. The aphorism seems to suggest, moreover, that we should not interfere with the natural course of ecological events, a view that does not square with the existence all over the world of successful parks, gardens, agricultural fields, and managed forests.

Francis of Assisi's loving and contemplative reverence in the face of nature survives today in the awareness of our kinship to all other living things and in the conservation movement. But reverence is not enough, because man has never been a passive witness of nature. He changes the environment by his very presence and his only options in his dealings with the earth are to be destructive or constructive. To be creative, man must relate to nature with his senses as much as with his common sense, with his heart as much as with knowledge. He must read the book of external nature and the book of his own nature, to discern the common patterns and harmonies.

Repeatedly in the past and under a great variety of religious traditions and social systems, man has created from wilderness new environments that have proved ecologically viable and culturally desirable. Because of my own cultural tradition, I have chosen to illustrate this creativeness by the Benedictine way of life—its wisdom in managing the land, in fitting architecture to worship and landscape, in adapting rituals and work to the cosmic rhythms. An Australian aborigine, a Navajo Indian, a Buddhist, or a Moslem would have selected other examples, taken from their respective traditions, but the fundamental theme is universal because it deals with man's unique place in the cosmos. Human life implies choices as to the best way to govern natural systems and to create new environments out of wilderness. Reverence for nature is compatible with willingness to accept responsibility for a creative stewardship of the earth.

# Noblesse Oblige

THE DANGERS of human intervention into nature have been repeatedly analyzed by modern scholars, most trenchantly, perhaps, by the American ecologist David Ehrenfeld in his recent book *The Arrogance of Humanism*. Ehrenfeld gives to the word "humanism" a broader meaning than the usual one. He uses it scornfully to denote the belief, almost universal in the countries of Western civilization, that we can engineer the future according to our whims, by arranging and rearranging the natural world in any way we see fit. We operate on the belief that we can fully understand natural processes and therefore predict the consequences of our interventions into nature. With numerous examples taken from contemporary life, Ehrenfeld has no difficulty in showing that this human conceit has generated dangerous situations that could not have been predicted, that probably cannot be corrected, and that may eventually destroy the most "humanistic" of modern societies.

Our arrogance, in Ehrenfeld's sense, is still very much at work—and not only in the United States. For example, plans are under discussion in the U.S.S.R. to redirect toward the south the course of certain Siberian rivers that naturally flow north, so that their water can be used to irrigate vast areas of semidesertic land. Similarly, the presi-

Reprinted with permission of Charles Scribner's Sons, an imprint of Macmillan Publishing Company, from *The Wooing of Earth*, pp. 149–57. Copyright © 1980 by René Dubos.

dent of a famous Japanese research institute has proposed, under the title "A Dream for Mankind," eight gigantic projects of environmental management that might go far, he thinks, toward solving the world's energy and food problems. One of these projects would be to dam the Congo River in central Africa so as to create an immense lake that would "improve" natural conditions. Another project would be to build a barrier across the Bering Strait, between the United States and the U.S.S.R., to interrupt the sea currents from the Arctic Ocean and thus make the Pacific climate more temperate. A third project would be to dam the Sampo River on the upper reaches of the Brahmaputra between China and the Indian province of Assam; the water would then be allowed to flow to India through a tunnel across the Himalayas to operate the largest hydroelectric power plant in the world.

It is easy to imagine the local benefits that may be derived from such enormous enterprises, but it is certainly impossible to predict their effects on the global ecosystem. This does not mean, of course, that they should not be undertaken. The Suez and Panama canals also constituted great ecological risks when they were built. If the modification of the surface of the earth is a form of arrogance, it has been a feature of human life for immense periods of time. In fact, as I have said before, people have no choice but to transform the surface of the earth, since they are not biologically adapted to most of the natural environments in which they live.

Ehrenfeld discusses some of the environmental values that are "being lost" as a result of present human activities. "British hedges and small fields, European farms and vineyards, North American urban and suburban parks and farms, and gardens everywhere are either being destroyed or altered in the name of efficiency." All the ecosystems mentioned in this passage are, in his word, "cultured landscapes," and some of them are of recent origin. Objecting to the destruction or alteration of these artificial ecosystems merely because of opposition to any change is an expression of the attitude that I have labeled "environmental ambivalence" or, more simply, the desire to keep everything as it was during one's youth. Change will continue because it is an inevitable condition of life. But it must be based on good reasons. I believe with Ehrenfeld that destroying or altering existing ecosystems, whether natural or artificial, in the name of "efficiency" can often have unfortunate consequences.

Since manipulating nature is an inevitable aspect of the human condition, it is a natural attitude and not a manifestation of arrogance, especially when efforts are made to base action on knowledge and judgment of values. After a conference at Princeton University, where Ehrenfeld and I expressed our different views concerning human interventions into nature, Rufus E. Miles, senior fellow at the Woodrow Wilson School there, wrote to say:

> I would much have preferred to have you mention the concept of noblesse oblige as man's appropriate role at the top of the animal kingdom. A person of noble birth and outlook learns to accept his elevated status and knows that others will serve him, yet he treats them with thoughtfulness and kindness. He accepts a reciprocal responsibility toward them. This is a far cry from arrogance. Do you not think it would be well to preserve the word "arrogance" for its intended usage, which is a vain, condescending, and unkind form of behavior by a person in a position of power toward other persons or fauna or flora?

Noblesse oblige seems to me an admirable way of expressing the attitude with which we should approach all environmental problems. We shall continue to intervene into nature, but we must do it with a sense of responsibility for the welfare of the earth as well as of humankind, and we must therefore attempt to anticipate the long-range consequences of our actions. Human modifications of the earth can be lastingly successful only if their effects are adapted to the invariants of physical and human nature. Fortunately, such constraints are compatible with diversity; there are many ways to deal with nature that accord with natural laws. A forest in the temperate region lends itself to the creation of parks as different in style as those of England, France, and Japan. In England, the so-called New Forest has been under constant management since 1079, and different parts of it are treated according to different ecological formulas—some left *au naturel*, some carefully pruned, some reserved for recreational activities, and so on. The individuality of a cultural environment is achieved through the choices made by a particular culture among the several options available to it at a given time in a given place.

Until recently, options were provided almost exclusively by the natural world, and choices were made by caprice or empirical wisdom. Increasingly now, options and choices are affected by scientific knowledge. In many countries of Western civilization, for example, the higher yields of scientific agriculture have led to the abandonment of marginal farmland. It may soon be economically possible to use this abandoned land for the production of rapidly growing trees or other vegetation that can serve as sources of energy and of raw material for chemical industries. On the other hand, it will be more desirable in other places to keep the land clear of brush so as to use it for recreational purposes or for esthetic pleasure. Depending on the circumstances, this can be done by keeping animals grazing on it, by annual mowing, or by treatment with chemicals.

Knowledge enlarges the range of options through different mechanisms. It enters the public domain in the form of verifiable facts and laws. It generates innovations that can help to achieve chosen ends. It constantly surprises and subverts, because new discoveries and applications are largely unpredictable. Knowledge thus makes people more receptive to new attitudes and more willing to change their ways. Who would have predicted two centuries ago that the soybean and the potato would come to occupy such a large place in the economy of Western nations, or that population control would first become possible on a large scale through the use of a contraceptive prepared from a seemingly trivial plant growing wild in Mexico!

However, while knowledge increases the range of options, it cannot be the sole basis for decision making, because it is always incomplete and therefore cannot describe all aspects of the world that bear on human life and environmental quality. Knowledge is more effective as a generator of possibilities than as a guide to choice and as a source of ethics. In the final analysis, the management of the earth must be value-conscious and value-oriented. Human systems are different from natural systems in that they are teleological as well as ecological. Each human society has its own images of the future that influence its policies. The extent of our interventions into nature is inevitably influenced, for example, by social attitudes concerning natural resources.

Although technological civilization depends on abundant supplies of metals and energy, opinions differ as to the priority connected with obtaining these supplies in a wider context. Large reserves of copper exist in Cascades National Park, but their exploitation would require a huge open mine that would spoil a wonderful wilderness area. Titanium could be obtained from the sand of Cape Cod, and various other metals as well as uranium from the granite of the White Mountains, but at the expense of the esthetic appeal of these humanized landscapes. In these cases, then, the "limits to growth" are determined not by availability of raw materials but by the choices society makes concerning other factors affecting the quality of life.

The present supplies of fossil fuels will eventually be depleted, but practical techniques will certainly be developed within a few decades to produce energy from renewable sources—nuclear or solar or perhaps both. The selection of methods for the production and use of energy will involve choices, however, based not only on scientific knowledge and cost-benefit analysis but also on judgments of value. For example, the development of nuclear energy will inevitably require enormous generators that will lead to strict technological and social controls. Similarly, trapping solar energy in orbiting satellites and beaming it to earth in the form of microwaves that will be used to generate electricity will require a high degree of social organization and centralization. In contrast, the first steps in the use of conventional sources of solar energy will have to be carried out in fairly small units—a necessity that will favor social decentralization. Many people, perhaps the great majority, will prefer abundant electricity without giving thought to its origin, its environmental effects, and its indirect social costs. Other people will prefer instead small-scale technologies compatible with social decentralization and regional and cultural pluralism. The final outcome will probably be a mix of centralized and decentralized sources of energy, selected to fit the environmental and social characteristics of each given situation and facilitating the expression of the multiple aspects of human nature.

The production and use of resources and energy are not only factors that will affect management of the earth. Whatever types of intervention into nature are being contemplated, the main concerns of their proponents have so far been productivity and efficiency, because these are the measures of technical perfection and economic reward. Yet the really significant end products of the changes resulting from human interventions are their long-range effects on the quality of human life and the environment. Efficiency and productivity have been identified with progress, because they have contributed to wealth, but we now realize that they are often achieved at great human and environmental cost. The squalor of Coketown in Dickens's *Hard Times*; the misery of the people, the land, and the streams in Appalachia; and all the other horror stories of the present ecological crisis make it clear that the words "productivity" and "efficiency" can serve as a measure of real success only if they incorporate, along with their purely technical connotations, concern for biological and social applications and values.

From the point of view of human and environmental quality, diversity and flexibility are probably more valuable than productivity and efficiency. Natural ecosystems are characterized not by high productivity but by resilience and flexibility, attributes that enable them to persist in the face of climatic disturbances and other uncertainties. Ecosystems are more likely to be durable when they contain a great diversity of species and when these are linked in complex symbiotic relationships. Furthermore, biological progress through evolutionary mechanisms tends to be more rapid when the total population is subdivided into colonies that are sufficiently small and separated to permit the survival of mutant forms, yet sufficiently interconnected to permit interbreeding.

Human societies differ from natural ecosystems in that they are influenced by teleological considerations at least as much as by environmental conditions. There are, nevertheless, suggestive analogies between human and natural systems. Just as biological diversity facilitates Darwinian evolution, so is cultural diversity essential for social progress. It is probably fortunate in this regard that all over the world, ethnic and regional groups are asserting their identity and beginning to recapture some autonomy. This process might help increase cultural diversity and thereby the rate of creative social change.

Even if the trend toward social decentralization is successful, however, there will probably occur simultaneously an increasing globalization of certain types of human activities—in particular, those dealing with transportation and other forms of communication, and those dependent on large-scale complex technologies. We may thus gradually move toward a dual type of human relationship between humankind and earth—on the one hand an increasingly centralized management based on the use of highly automated technologies derived from sophisticated science, and on the other hand a decentralized management dealing at the local level and on the human scale with the more intimate aspects of life. The general formula of management for the future might then be: Think globally and act locally!

Global thinking and local action both require understanding of ecological systems, but ecological management can be effective only if it takes into consideration the visceral and spiritual values that link us to the earth. Scientifically defined, ecology is nothing more than the study of interrelationships between living things and their environment; it is therefore ethically neutral. These relationships, however, are always influenced by the human presence, which introduces an ethical component into all environmental problems. Since the nature of our activities determines the extent and direction of environmental changes, ecological thinking must be supplemented by humanistic value judgments concerning the effect of our choices and actions on the quality of the relationship between humankind and earth, in the future as well as in the present.

Noblesse oblige.

# The Five E's
# of Environmental
# Management

AT THE TURN of the century, John Muir and his associates in the Sierra Club opposed any human intervention into nature, especially in the areas of majestic wilderness. Their ideal was the preservation of nature, undisturbed by human activities. During the same period, the professional environmentalist Gifford Pinchot introduced the word "conservation" to denote not the absolute preservation of nature as advocated by Muir but its scientific management for the benefit of humankind.

Such very different attitudes concerning human relationships to nature have persisted side by side among the militant environmentalists of the 1960s, but the differences were concealed by the emotional force of the movement. The differences in attitude were very much in evidence, however, during the ceremony organized at the White House in 1980 to celebrate "the second environmental decade." One of the events of the ceremony was a proclamation by President Carter changing the name of Alaska's Arctic National Wildlife Range to the William O. Douglas Arctic Wildlife Range. This event symbolized Justice Douglas's commitment to preservation and glorification of the wilderness in the spirit of John Muir. In contrast, another event at the same ceremony was the presentation by the newly created Environmental Industry Council of an award to President Carter for his "leader-

From a lecture delivered at Princeton University on the tenth anniversary of Earth Day, April 22, 1980.

[ 400 ]

ship . . . in the realm of environmental protection and environmental improvement in all its facets, economic, geographic, political and technological" in agreement with Pinchot's belief in the scientific management of nature.

There are very different rooms in the mansion of the environment movement!

We have just celebrated the tenth anniversary of the first Earth Day, the environmental event charged with emotion that occurred in April 1970. With ten years of experience behind us, we are under the illusion that we can now formulate sound and comprehensive environmental policies. We believe, on the one hand, that we should preserve the wilderness wherever possible and protect it from human encroachment. But we realize, on the other hand, that we must carefully manage and improve the areas—by far the greatest percentage of the surface of the earth—where human beings have settled and which they have transformed to satisfy their needs. For example, we should minimize as much as possible all forms of pollution and of environmental degradation; we should develop safe and renewable sources of energy; we should oppose the Army Corps of Engineers and other institutions when their activities threaten to damage or destroy important natural ecosystems. By dealing with landscapes and waterscapes in the light of ecological principles, we believe it is possible to maintain our planet in a healthy state and thereby to make it a better place for human life.

We have become so convinced, indeed, that good environmental management is based on the scientific principles of ecology that we commonly use the phrase "ecological movement" to denote the modern environmental movement, as if the adjective "ecological" assured us of an environment satisfactory for human life. The truth is, however, that most aspects of human life imply a profound conflict with natural ecosystems, and therefore with the teachings of textbook ecology.

Consider, for example, the pride that the home owner takes in the lawn he maintains in front of his house, whether a bungalow or a mansion. Although his lawn appears to him as a tranquil and beautiful piece of "nature," it is in fact a monstrosity when considered from the point of view of scientific ecology. Almost everywhere, and especially in the temperate zone, the creation and maintenance of a lawn involves the expenditure of much energy and other resources to destroy and control the weeds, brush, and trees that would naturally grow on it and that indeed reestablish themselves as soon as the lawn is neglected.

A flower or vegetable garden is also a most unnatural environment. Few of the plants cultivated in it could long survive in unattended nature. After being planted in the garden, furthermore, they can prosper only if constantly protected against weeds, insects, voles, and countless other forms of life, as well as against natural forces that would destroy them or interfere with their growth.

Paradoxical as it may sound, the farmer's activities also imply struggle against nature. Practically all farmland had to be created out of the wilderness at great cost of energy—to cut down the forest, drain wetlands, irrigate deserts, and also to destroy many forms of wild animal and plant life in their native habitats. The success of crops and pastures and the maintenance of farmland quality require an endless fight against the native fauna and flora that would soon return in their wild forms if they were not controlled—often by violent means. Successful farming, like gardening, is thus usually incompatible with the ecological equilibrium that would exist under natural conditions. In fact, it implies destruction of natural ecosystems.

In the arctic and tropical zones, some forest areas and bodies of water have been less affected by the human presence than those of the temperate zone, but the effects of human activities now extend so far that all parts of the surface of the earth are undergoing changes that make them different from what they would have been in the original state of wilderness. Countless examples could be cited to illustrate that wherever human beings have settled, their activities have created situations that do not fit the laws of textbook ecology. It seems more useful, however, to review briefly how these situations can be traced to the origins of the human species.

The human presence has had such profound influences on practically all ecosystems that the continuation of human life implies, in fact, humanization of the earth. We have far to go before understanding all the subtleties of the relationships between humankind and earth, but we can at least begin to analyze them in the terms of several categories. I shall define these categories by five words arranged alphabetically but all beginning with the letter E—ecology, economics, energetics, esthetics, and ethics. This artificial arrangement will acknowledge the superficiality of our views (or at least of mine) concerning the place of man on earth, views that will inevitably remain superficial until we have a more profound understanding of the place of human life in the cosmic order of things. Instead of analyzing theoretically the rules of ecology, economics, energetics, esthetics, and ethics in the interplay between humankind and earth, I shall limit myself to a few illustrations for each of these categories in simple life situations.

Almost all human activities result in alterations of natural ecosystems, but these alterations need not be destructive, and many of them have been indeed highly creative. Some of the world's most productive and beautiful ecosystems are now very different, biologically as well as visually, from the areas of wilderness out of which they were created. This is illustrated, for example, by the famous agricultural landscapes and parks of Europe, Asia, and North America, most of which have been developed from different types of primeval forests.

It is an obvious advantage, on the other hand, that artificial ecosystems should be as compatible as possible with the prevailing ecological characteristics of the regions in which they are created. I have already cited one ecological monstrosity. A detailed study of lawns would reveal much concerning the usefulness of ecological science in environmental philosophy and practice. Someday botanists will cooperate with landscape architects to develop not only grasses but other kinds of ground cover suited to different types of rainfall, soil composition, and human use.

Since agriculture also implies a constant struggle against nature, it is most likely to be successful in the long run when it takes account of ecological constraints. All over the world many types of agricultural land that were initially created from the wilderness have remained productive for centuries and even for millennia because farmers have utilized them with ecological wisdom—in other words, they have used agricultural methods ecologically suited to natural local conditions. Certain contemporary practices, however, stand in sharp contrast with this ancient ecological wisdom. In several parts of Texas and of the American West, for example, very high yields have been achieved by irrigating semidesertic lands with underground water (in many places fossil water from the Ogallala aquifer) that must be pumped at great cost. Such reserves of underground water are being depleted, and since irrigation water contaminates the soil with various salts as it evaporates, this type of farming will eventually have to be abandoned, leaving behind a legacy of degraded land.

Ecological thinking is needed to deal intelligently with nature, but economic considerations usually intervene in ecological choices—

often with disastrous results. The only justification for the costly and destructive type of irrigation farming and aquifer mining I have just deplored is the possibility of achieving great financial rewards over the short period of time, regardless of future consequences.

Economics is still a dismal science, especially when it comes to evaluating the effects of human interventions into nature. Building very tall smokestacks may be an inexpensive way to disperse smogs and fumes and thus to decrease local pollution, but this method of pollution control results in the production of acid rains that are destructive of animal and plant life over vast areas, commonly far removed from the point of emission.

Many questions of value, furthermore, must be introduced into the economic aspects of pollution control and of environmental restoration. Limiting the control to the removal of 90 percent of the pollutants is usually an inexpensive operation resulting in marked environmental improvement. As environmental criteria become more exacting, however, pollution control becomes more and more difficult and costly while the increase in beneficial effects becomes less and less evident. Granted that the law of diminishing returns applies to all aspects of pollution control, there are types of benefits for which it is impossible to give a monetary value. Would it be an unreasonable criterion, for example, to require that Manhattan air quality make it once more possible for lichens to grow on the boulders and tree trunks of Central Park and for the Milky Way to become visible on cloudless nights?

All relationships of humankind to the earth are affected by the levels of energy consumption, and not only or even primarily by this cost. One single example will suffice to illustrate the wide range of influences that the level of energy consumption can have on human life and the environment.

An isolated, free-standing house, surrounded by as much open ground as possible, has long been one of the ideals of American life. This ideal used to be compatible with the social and economic conditions of the past, when there was much unoccupied, inexpensive land and when the family house was essentially self-sufficient—with its own water supply from a well or stream, its own fuel supply from the woodlot, its own food supply from the garden, domestic animals, and wildlife, and few problems about waste disposal. But conditions have changed. The free-standing house is now increasingly dependent on public services—for electricity, telephone, water, and sewage systems,

and dependent also on fuel for heating, transportation, road maintenance, snow removal, and practically all conveniences of modern life.

In the modern world, the way of life implied by the free-standing
house involves such high social costs, especially with regard to labor
and energy, that it will inevitably become an economic burden, too
heavy for the average person and perhaps socially unacceptable. Social
constraints are therefore likely to favor a trend toward some form of
cluster settlements.

The increase in energy cost may act as the catalyst for a restructur-
ing of human settlements and particularly for greater clustering of
habitations. This would make for economies in fuel consumption, in the
maintenance of roads, in access to utility lines, shops, and schools; it
would furthermore facilitate group activities and thereby foster community life.

Many architects and social planners are trying to design human
settlements that provide both the technological advantages of cluster
housing and the sense of privacy and space associated with the free-
standing house. If they are successful, the new types of planning will
provide opportunities for larger woodlands, meadowlands, play-
grounds, and other areas for community life. The village green and
public square will not be re-created in their traditional forms, but new
concepts of land use and of architectural design may favor the revival of
community spirit.

The first and last chapters of *Silent Spring*, the famous book by
which Rachel Carson made the general public aware of the dangers of
pesticides, begin with pictures of an imaginary town, the streets of
which lead toward a rolling landscape of meadows, grainfields, and hills
crowned with woodlands. These pictures were based on memories of
Rachel Carson's youth in western Pennsylvania early in this century.
She described in her book an enchanting environment in which every
form of life was

in harmony with its surroundings. . . . The town lay in the midst
of a checkerboard of prosperous farms, with fields of grain and
hillsides of orchards. . . . The countryside was famous for the
abundance of its birdlife. . . . The streams flowed clear and cold
out of the hills and contained shady pools where trout lay. So it
had been from the days many years ago when the first settlers
raised their houses, sank their wells, and built their barns.

Rachel Carson's make-believe countryside has widespread if not universal appeal. I have mentioned it not to discuss her condemnation of pesticides but to illustrate that most of us have an esthetic ideal of nature that is in reality a creation of the human mind. The sceneries Rachel Carson had known in her youth were not "natural" nature; they had been created out of the primeval wilderness two or three centuries ago. The settlers of Pennsylvania not only "raised their houses, sank their wells, and built their barns." In order to create open land for their farms and towns, they also cut down most of the forest that initially covered western Pennsylvania.

In fact, human beings have created artificial environments out of the wilderness over most of the earth, wherever they have made their homes. These humanized environments have become so familiar to us that we tend to forget their origin; we contemplate them in a mood of casual acceptance and reverie without giving thought to those parts of primeval nature that had to be profoundly transformed, or destroyed, to make them fit not only our biological needs but also our esthetic longings. Fortunately, a combination of woodland, open-space water-scape, and horizon is compatible with many different types of cultural expression. It can be satisfied by the classical French landscape style, by the more romantic English treatment of the land, by the complex and symbolic design of Oriental parks—and also by the tremendous creations of nature in the American national parks.

It may be worth mentioning at this point that we are only now beginning to acquire accurate information concerning what people really find attractive in scenery. Tests carried out with different social groups have revealed an almost universal preference for orderly sceneries, in which "nature" has been tamed, and even disciplined. Most of us probably long not for real wilderness but for a taste of the small-scale wildness that gives additional interest to the sceneries we admire.

In any case, except for several famous examples of real wilderness, some of the most esthetic manifestations of nature are found today in prosperous farming areas and on large private estates. Under present economic and social conditions, however, farming can hardly survive in the vicinity of urban areas, and large estates are also destined to disappear—the likely outcome of both of these changes being a visual degradation of the environment.

Long-term planning for the maintenance of esthetic quality of the countryside around large urban centers must consider not only the present condition and use of the land but also the potentialities inherent in the soil, topography, climate, relation to water, and so forth. Such knowledge might suggest new ways of managing the environment that would be compatible with both its welfare and that of humankind.

One can think of many possibilities of management for the areas of open land that still exist near urban centers—for example, allowing them to return progressively to a state approaching that of wilderness; establishing greenbelts; creating parklands designed for public use; developing human settlements combining high population density with large open public spaces; reintroducing agricultural production, especially of perishable crops such as vegetables and fruits. It is likely that we shall end up with a mix of these different types of management, but this cannot be achieved without generating controversial problems of zoning.

Zoning policies have generally aimed at achieving some form of socioeconomic and occupational segregation. They will probably increasingly incorporate in the future considerations of ecology and of environmental perception. Instead of being based on segregation, the new philosophy of environmental zoning should aim at creating areas where appropriate groups of uses can coexist in a suitable setting. This attitude has been entertainingly expressed by Nan Fairbrother in the following words: "Single land uses seldom create an environment any more than separate piles of butter and sugar and flour constitute a cake; for, like a cake, an environment is a complicated whole created by skillful blending and fusing of suitable raw materials." Ideally, zoning should be considered not as a restrictive but as a constructive process; its goal should be to integrate different types of land uses that would interplay interestingly in planned environments.

In the last chapter of A Sand County Almanac, Aldo Leopold formulated his view of a "land ethic" in statements that are probably the most famous and the most frequently quoted expression of ecological wisdom in all environmental literature. "We must quit thinking about decent land use as solely an economic problem. . . . A thing is right when it tends to preserve the integrity, stability, and beauty of the biotic community. It is wrong when it tends otherwise." These statements are often interpreted to mean that Leopold was opposed in principle to any transformation of the land by human activities, but I do not believe that this is a correct interpretation of his thoughts. He did not state anywhere in his writings that natural biotic communities are necessarily the most desirable ones. In fact, he described several ecosystems of which he obviously approved even though they are the products of accidental or intentional human intervention—for example, the man-made bluegrass country of Kentucky and the European farmlands.

Leopold properly stated that the land is healthy when it has "the capacity . . . for self-recovery. Conservation is our effort to understand and preserve this capacity."

It is as a contribution to this understanding that I have introduced the five "e" categories to evaluate the various aspects of human intervention into nature. My emphasis on "human" interventions acknowledges that human activities are now among the most powerful and most ubiquitous forces acting on natural as well as man-made ecosystems.

There is now widespread acceptance, in theory if not in practice, that the behavior of our societies toward the earth must be based on a new kind of ethics, embracing the land as well as animals and plants, and there are reasons to believe that this new kind of ethics has begun to result in environmental improvement. Unfortunately, there is much less agreement on aspects of environmental ethics that concern the rights of human beings with regard to the earth. In Sweden, for example, all people have free access at any time of the year to meadowlands and woodlands, and indeed to most nonbuilt areas. Similarly, in several European nations the general public can have access to most of the seashore. While I do not have the competence to express opinions about the relevance of these examples to property rights in the United States, I suspect that the people of all American ethnic groups will soon join the Swedes in believing that land not actually occupied and used should be available for public enjoyment.

The experience of the American national parks reveals, however, that public use may be devastating. The most difficult environmental problems, in my opinion, will not be those related to ecology, economics, energy, or even esthetics, but to those involving ethics: the rights and duties of people with regard to the earth. In principle, we all have the same rights, but in practice we can enjoy these rights only to the extent that the earth is maintained in a healthy state. This is, of course, an ecological problem but one in which the effects of natural forces must be evaluated in the light of human needs, activities, tastes, and aspirations.

# The Lichen Sermon

DEAN MORTON: With Professor Dubos we want to look at poverty and the lesson of today's Gospel in relation to science, particularly in relation to his disciplines of biology and ecology. In a sense, today's Gospel is the perfect takeoff place for an ecologist, for the Gospel story is the multiplication of the loaves and the fishes.

The multiplication of the loaves and the fishes is a gift to be shared. But look at the reverse of any gift! There is the temptation to say that it is not a gift. And the reverse of the gift, indeed, comes in the last sentence of the Gospel: the people said, "This is the prophet who is to come into the world." And our Lord, perceiving that they were coming to take him by force and make him a king, left them immediately.

This is precisely the lesson Dostoevsky taught in the story of the Grand Inquisitor. Turn the bread giver into a king—a spectacular machine for production. Just let the bread keep coming and we won't have to share. Sharing is a spiritual discipline, therefore, that can exist only in the context of scarcity or poverty.

For this Gospel of sharing as a spiritual discipline, we turn to science. Dr. Dubos, do you find a relation in your disciplines between sharing and poverty? Do you have any evidence that poverty is any-

From a Lenten sermon presented at the Cathedral of St. John the Divine, New York City, Mar. 9, 1975, with the Reverend James Morton, Dean of the Cathedral. Reprinted by permission of the Cathedral Church of St. John the Divine.

[ 409 ]

thing more than just deprivation? In nature, is poverty ever creative or positive?

DR. DUBOS: First, let me acknowledge that I have great difficulty in understanding deep in my heart the theological meaning that you give to the word "poverty." I had always assumed, and I suppose many of you believe, that poverty is deprivation, a deprivation of worldly goods, a deprivation of satisfying human contacts. And even though I began during the past two weeks—following my conversations with you, sensing that there was something more than that concept of poverty—it is only very recently, in fact the day before yesterday, that I came to realize that within my own scientific discipline, that of a biologist, there are many indications that scarcity is not only creative but is essential to the act of creation.

So what I am going to do now, if you allow me, is to behave according to that long conditioning of academic life and begin by presenting the topic in an abstract way. But fortunately, through the form of a parable! And then will I try to translate these abstract considerations into the terms of the problems of our society today.

Let me begin with the parable. It's a biological parable. I shall invite you to walk with me almost anywhere in the world. Wherever there are trees, where there are rocks, or the stone walls of old buildings, if you look at those rocks, at those trunks, at those old stone walls, at those old buildings, you will see that their surface is commonly covered with a kind of growth, exhibiting all sorts of colors, all sorts of different structures, often incredibly beautiful.

You all have seen them, and probably you have used the word "moss." What I am speaking about are not mosses: it is what biologists and many of you, probably, recognize as "lichens."

Now, you will say, well, lichens are just small plants, and that is what scientists used to believe. But one now knows that lichens in reality are an association of two very lowly kinds of microbes: a mold and a microscopic alga. And the remarkable thing, which will be the theme of my parable, is that, when these two lowly microbes become associated—in a single organism, so to speak—then they develop multiplicities of beautiful and complex forms, beautiful subtle colors, they create all sorts of new chemicals (many of them being used for the perfume industry), and they acquire all sorts of new properties that one could not have anticipated from just considering the mold or the microscopic alga all by itself.

We see, then, that each of these lowly microbes have the potential power of producing all sorts of wonderful forms, all sorts of wonderful qualities, but this potential becomes expressed only when the two become intimately associated. So the first lesson I derive from my parable is that associating and working together is essential throughout life for the creation of new values.

Now there is a second part of the lesson, one perhaps more directly and obviously relevant to the problem of poverty—namely, this: If there is too much food, then the microbes stop their association; they start growing on their own. They don't find the need to associate, to help each other. Separately, they continue growing as a mold or as a microscopic alga, but there is nothing interesting about them. Abundance, excessive abundance, makes them return to a dull, uninspiring kind of life. Thus, in a peculiar way, the lichens, their richness, is an expression of the poverty of the environment in which they develop.

What I have described here for lichens has been recognized for just about a hundred years. The word for this kind of association, invented at that time, is "symbiosis." This Greek word means "living together." In reality, it is more than just living together: it is working together, becoming integrated into one single organism.

Let us skip, for a moment, the word "symbiosis." Let us look about nature, and we shall see, wherever we look, at any level of development in living things, that there are countless such forms of association and cooperation. They have been expressed by all sorts of words. One very popular half a century ago was invented by the Russian naturalist and anarchist Kropotkin: he spoke of the "mutual aid" between different living things existing under difficult conditions. If you now transfer this concept to human life, you will see that, without any difficulty, you arrive at the word "communion." In fact, the word "communion" is the exact equivalent in Latin of the Greek word "symbiosis." I derive from my parable the conclusion that communion is more than just being associated. It is not only sharing, it's sharing in such a way that one engages in creative interplay. You can apply the word "communion" to all sorts of situations: you can think of communion with nature, you can think of communion with other human beings, and of course, you can think of communion with the cosmos as a whole and thereby arrive at the large theological sense, divine sense, of the word "communion."

DEAN MORTON: You would say, then, that communion is possible only if there is an openness, which I use as another word for "poverty." The human tendency, more often than not, is to build a wall—so that my goods will not be stolen—as opposed to being open and vulnerable. Vulnerability is another word for this openness, for poverty.

The rhetoric of our society says that the good life is posited upon more and more and more. This is, we are coming to recognize, a very high-energy society. Professor Dubos, must we be so extravagant with energy? Could you apply poverty, as you have shown it at work in nature, to our energy economy?

DR. DUBOS: As you all know, in public discussions about energy or about resources, the only consideration is how much of it we can get, how much it will cost, what the bad effects will be of any kind of shortage. Now, I am not unaware of the problems caused by shortage of resources and energy. But what is important is not how much we have, it is how we use it. Paradoxical as it may sound, we often do damage to the world and to our own lives by excessive use of resources and energy. In many cases, creativity demands that we limit our consumption of both.

Let me take three very concrete examples. I have selected them not for theoretical reasons but because they are problems from our life today. The three examples that I have selected deal with agriculture, with architecture, and with our physical and mental health.

Speaking about agriculture, I must become a bit pedantic, once more acting in my profession as an academician. I shall ask you to think of those many parts of the world where, more than 20,000 years ago, people created the land out of the wilderness. Ever since, they have used it extensively and have not only maintained its quality and its beauty but have even enhanced it by their management. During the past fifty years or so, we have decided that we can change all that, that we can increase enormously the productivity of agriculture by pumping energy into the system, whether in the form of high-power equipment, like tractors and whatnot, or in the form of synthetic fertilizers and pesticides. I know how beneficial this has been; I know how dependent we are on the intelligent use of these forms of energy for the production of food for the world as a whole. But I also know that if we are careless in our use of energy and resources in agriculture, we destroy that very system upon which we depend.

It is well known, scientifically—and the ancient farmers knew it empirically—that the soil, natural soil, has fundamental biological mechanisms that enable it to produce humus and accumulate numerous fertilizers. There exist in the soil certain kinds of microbes that capture the nitrogen from the air and feed it into plants. Well, we are learning that as soon as we pump too much energy into agricultural systems, we tend to inhibit the expression of those fundamental mechanisms. Humus gets destroyed and the bacteria that fix the nitrogen from the air can no longer function. So here we see a situation where too much energy prevents the expression of the recuperative and curative natural mechanisms of the soil.

Now the case of architecture: Until about fifty years ago, all over the world, builders and architects used to adapt their structures to local constraints. The shape of the roof, the thickness of the walls, the type of windows, the orientation of the building. All this was determined by the snow, the rainfall, the winds, the temperature, and so on. From their awareness of the fundamental constraints imposed by the environment, the architects of old—and for that matter, ordinary people—had developed everywhere local architecture that with respect to Dean Morton's question had an immense variety and charm that was very comfortable, that was inexpensive in its use of energy. Those of you who would be entertained by reading on this topic should look at *Architecture Without Architects*, a book that shows how people over the years had the sense to build to suit natural conditions. Well, during the past fifty years, as I said, we have been pumping energy into our buildings so as to avoid respecting those constraints. We have become so careless in our use of energy that we overheat our buildings during the winter and overcool them during the summer. All this results in the anonymous kind of architecture that disgraces all our cities all over the world.

I have no doubt that if we become more economical, more reasonable, in the use of energy we can give to architecture once more the kind of quality that depends on its being suited to local conditions.

DEAN MORTON: You could use just another word again: "communion." The New York glass skyscraper, with windows that can't open, precisely refuses communion with the environment. It refuses the symbiotic back-and-forth vulnerability. It is a sort of a shaking-the-fist-at-the-environment architecture. To hell with the environment in which it sits!

DR. DUBOS: The last example I want to give is about our physical and mental health. Without being professional biologists, you all know that we are born with a wide range of potentialities, physical and mental.

And you know that those potentialities become expressed only to the extent that we give them a chance to function.

Just think of muscle. Each one of us is born with the potentiality for vigorous muscles, but those muscles become vigorous only to the extent that we exercise them. This is just as true for all the other functions of our body. Children are born with the ability to learn to experience, and to love. These potential gifts, that we have at birth, become reality only to the extent we make the effort to learn to share with other people, to experience the loveliness of nature.

My personal feeling is that during the past hundred years or so there has been an increasing tendency in all Western societies, increasingly all over the world, to use energy only to avoid effort instead of using energy to experience the world with our bodies and with all the faculties of our minds.

So to be very dogmatic about it (for lack of time), our physical and mental health depends in large measure on the extent to which we use our potentialities and begin to express them as early as possible. If we could rearrange our society in such a manner that we do not spend energy to avoid effort but spend our energy to become involved—in things of humanity and nature—we would improve our physical health and our mental health.

DEAN MORTON: Could you in conclusion, Professor Dubos, say something about the place of humankind within the larger creative order, within this understanding of communion and poverty?

DR. DUBOS: This is the kind of question that I formulate for myself and, usually, only answer to myself. To answer such a question, I would have to go way beyond the field of knowledge that I have mastered and . . .

DEAN MORTON: . . . become a theologian!

DR. DUBOS: . . . and have to engage in interpretations of a very highly personal nature. So let me again speak from a parable—namely, the Biblical parable that Adam was created from the earth. For me, as a biologist, there is a very deep scientific meaning in this parable. It is a symbol of the fact that we were created as a species and that we create ourselves as individuals by functioning within the natural order of creation, by experiencing all of creation during our evolutionary development as a species and during our individual development as a person. So in this scientific kind of explanation, I have rediscovered or restated the words of the Greek theologian Origen, who said that man is the mirror of the cosmos.

From this I derive the conclusion, which I try to apply to my own life, that we are healthy—and the word "healthy" has etymological relationships to the word "whole"—only to the extent that we participate actively with our own energy, with the energy that is us, in the life of nature and in the life of other human beings.

DEAN MORTON: We could push the etymology just one step further: health, wholeness, holiness! Amen.

# L'Ecologie
# Civilisatrice

ON DECEMBER 9, 1980, I gave the opening address before a huge international conference on environmental problems, held in the UNESCO headquarters in Paris. The fact that the meetings were held at UNESCO indicates that they dealt not only with the scientific and technological aspects of the environment but also with the sociocultural aspects. The large number of participants—some six thousand from many countries both developed and developing—is evidence that environmental problems are very much in people's minds all over the world.

In his speech, President of the French Republic Giscard d'Estaing paid me the compliment of quoting from a book I wrote: "Man can improve on nature."

Actually, the original author of those words was Theodore Roosevelt, one of the pioneers of the environmental movement, at a White House Conference in 1908 dealing with the management of forests and waters. Lest this unorthodox ecological view be identified with the Republican party, I am happy to report that it was repeated on many occasions by Theodore Roosevelt's cousin Franklin Delano Roosevelt. That man can improve on nature had been my conviction for many years, but I had hesitated to say it so bluntly until I discovered it had such presidential authority.

Speech delivered at his eightieth birthday tribute dinner, January 1981, The New York Hilton.

[ 416 ]

The view that human interventions into nature can be creative has been criticized. Many people share this view but do not dare express it, because it does not fit the present orthodox doctrine of the environmental movement. Two people who early expressed sympathy for my attitude are Ruth and Bill Eblen. Some five years ago, we began discussing ways to disseminate this humanistic approach to environmental problems. The Eblens managed to obtain funds from individual people, from a few corporations, and from the National Endowment for the Humanities to help us do so. We could thus start a number of limited projects under the name of The René Dubos Forum. These projects were so successful that we have recently transformed the Forum into The René Dubos Center for Human Environments.

There have long been in this country admirable organizations dedicated to the protection of the wilderness and more recently others that deal more specifically with problems of pollution and other forms of environmental degradation. We have, of course, full sympathy for the purposes of these institutions. But instead of dealing with the defensive aspects of the environmental movement, our center will focus its activities on the creative aspects of human interventions into nature. For example:

1. Detailed case studies of the processes through which environments that had been grossly degraded have been brought back to good ecological condition. It was while studying the "renaissance" of the Willamette River, in Oregon, that we became acquainted with Governor McCall, who has now accepted our invitation to serve as chairman of our board's executive committee. We believe that widespread dissemination of ecological success stories and of the social and technical methods through which they were brought about would help to create an atmosphere of environmental optimism and to make practical information available to communities and corporate groups eager to undertake reclamation projects.

2. The establishment of facilities not only for storing documents and for making them readily available to interested people and groups but also for gathering corporate and governmental officials, technical people, and citizens to consider in advance the difficulties to be anticipated regarding the development of new industrial and commercial enterprises. A sad

example of the need for such anticipations is the case of the proposed and happily abandoned Con Edison pumped-storage plant at Storm King Mountain. Many other such examples could be cited.

While operating as The René Dubos Forum, we gained much experience in the organization and management of symposia focused on practical problems (the role of energy in modern life, the use of the biomass, the coexistence of rural and urban environments, problems of zoning), with participants representing governmental, corporate, technical, and humanistic interests.

We have also experimented, and continue to experiment, with techniques for the dissemination of information to interested groups—for example, to community colleges and their local constituencies.

In the course of his speech at UNESCO in Paris, President Giscard coined the French phrase *"L'ecologie civilisatrice."* It is unfortunate that this phrase does not translate well into English, because it integrates many of the attitudes that we would like to foster at The René Dubos Center for Human Environments. To be successful, creative human interventions into nature must naturally respect ecological constraints, but this leaves much room for original creativeness. Human intervention in the environment can contribute to the development of civilizations. I have used the word "civilizations" in the plural because each inevitably takes a different form, depending on local ecological conditions.

Successful human environments are the concrete manifestations of the human ability to improve on nature by giving expression to its varied potentialities, while keeping in mind the local ecological conditions that give to each particular place and human community its personality, what I like to call its ecological genius.

With our technological and ecological knowledge and with a sense of responsibility for the welfare of humankind and of the earth, we can and will create environments that are ecologically sound, esthetically satisfying, economically rewarding, and favorable to the continued growth of civilization.

This is the faith on which we shall base the activities of The René Dubos Center for Human Environments.